1866-1991

125th

ANNIVERSARY

MEXICAN VOICES

AMERICAN DREAMS

An Oral History of
Mexican Immigration to
the United States

MARILYN P. DAVIS

HENRY HOLT AND COMPANY
NEW YORK

Copyright © 1990 by Marilyn P. Davis
All rights reserved, including the right to reproduce
this book or portions thereof in any form.
Published by Henry Holt and Company, Inc.,
115 West 18th Street, New York, New York 10011.
Published in Canada by Fitzhenry & Whiteside Limited,
195 Allstate Parkway, Markham, Ontario L3R 4T8.

Library of Congress Cataloging-in-Publication Data
Davis, Marilyn P.
Mexican voices/American dreams : an oral history of Mexican
immigration to the United States / Marilyn P. Davis.
p.   cm.
1. Mexican Americans—History—20th century. 2. Mexicans—United
States—History—20th century. 3. United States—Emigration and
immigration—History—20th century. 4. Mexico—Emigration and
immigration—History—20th century. 5. Immigrants—United States—
History—20th century.   6. Oral history.   I. Title.
E184.M5D28 1990
973'.046872—dc20   90-31640
                                                    CIP

ISBN 0-8050-1216-8
ISBN 0-8050-1859-X (An Owl Book: pbk.)
Henry Holt books are available at special discounts for bulk purchases
for sales promotions, premiums, fund-raising, or educational use.
Special editions or book excerpts can also be created to specification.

For details contact:
Special Sales Director
Henry Holt and Company, Inc.
115 West 18th Street
New York, New York 10011

First published in hardcover by Henry Holt and Company, Inc., in 1990.

First Owl Book Edition—1991

Designed by Katy Riegel

Printed in the United States of America
Recognizing the importance of preserving
the written word, Henry Holt and Company, Inc.,
by policy, prints all of its first editions
on acid-free paper. ∞

1 3 5 7 9 10 8 6 4 2
1 3 5 7 9 10 8 6 4 2
pbk.

WITH LOVE TO MY GODCHILDREN . . .

Jaime Ortiz O.
Ana Villa O.
Sonia Ruiz A.
Claudia Enriquez C.
César Gomez V.
Jazmín Ortiz M.
Alfredo Villa O.
Martha Montes V.
Alfonso Barrera S.
Ana Rosa Torres M.
Cecilia Gavilan A.
Dámaso Rodriguez C.
Fanny Guapo M.
Flora Flores A.
Jaime Lopez L.
Jesús Barrera R.
Jesús Orozco U.
Joaquin Rojo V.
Jose Gonzalez T.
Juan Carlos Macias T.
Juan Pedro Santana H.
Leonardo Garcia P.
Maricruz Ramirez P.
Oscar Guapo M.
Salvador Ponce M.

WITH HOPE FOR OUR FUTURES,
WHICH, LIKE OUR COUNTRIES,
ARE INEXTRICABLY ENTWINED.

CONTENTS

Acknowledgments   ix
Preface   xi

Introduction   1

PART I: PUSH-PULL

1. Ballad of the Immigrant:
   The Long History of Mexican Migration   9

2. I Will Buy You the Moon:
   The Reasons for Going   35

3. Two Dollars an Hour:
   The Employers   67

PART II: PASSAGE

4. To Cross Is to Die a Little:
   Crossing the Border   99

CONTENTS

5. The White Man and the Chicken Keeper Win:
   El Coyote   127

6. How They Have Suffered for Me:
   Those They Left Behind   143

PART III: EL NORTE

7. Breathless:
   Dreams Versus Reality   171

8. Those Who Come to Immigrate:
   Life in the United States   199

9. Up with the Raza:
   The Best and the Brightest   247

PART IV: THE FUTURE

10. When You Sing There Are No Borders:
    The Artists   291

11. Those They Call Chicano:
    The Children—Part I   325
    The Children's Children—Part II   368

12. El Corrido Nuevo:
    A New Verse   405

Glossary   425

Index   435

ACKNOWLEDGMENTS

I would like to thank Claire Siegel, Jo Ann Kendall, Carol Detweiler, Margaret Cesa, Ophelia Basgal, and Audrey Berger, who read parts of my manuscript, lent their thoughtful criticism, and spurred me on.

Many wonderful friends were generous with their time, ideas, data, contacts, and moral support. My most heartfelt thanks to: Ann Cervantes, Judge Claude Davis, Guillermo Dellemary, Conchis Enriquez, Lic. Alba Enriquez, Teresa Enriquez, Paul Espinosa, David Hayes-Bautista, Lic. Alberto Hernandez, Judy Hopkins, Micheal Hutchison, Treacy Lau, Raymond Friday Locke, Lic. Alfonso Magaña, William Mueller, James O'Kane, Ron Scheibel, Ellwyn Stoddard, Wil Van Overbeek, Graciela de la Vega, Alfredo Villa, and Constance Zandstra.

As I traveled across the country, Michael and Susan Axelrod, Beverly and Robert Buehler, Helen Davis, Carol and Richard Detweiler, Joan and Jerry Maffei, Herb and Cheryle Potter, Ron Rodgers, Vada Shelley, Ronnie Shushan, and Donald Wright offered their warm hospitality and thoroughly indulged my compulsive quest.

My thanks too to Hector and "El Mexico," who brought me across the border and protected me as if I were their mother. They (or anyone else) would accept no remuneration.

I am truly grateful to my agent, Michael Hamilburg, for having confidence in me as well as for introducing me to Cynthia Vartan, my editor. It was a pleasure to work with her, and to the extent that the book is interesting and readable this is, in no small measure, due to Cynthia's skillful editing.

I cherish the stories and friendships of the hundreds of people who opened their hearts to me. Though all of their lives could not fit in one book, every story is a reflection of their spirit.

If my family, James and Johnna, Tobin and Tosha, and most of all my husband, Jim, had doubts about me chasing around the country or crossing the border with *coyotes,* they never let me know it. They believed in me. Thanks.

PREFACE

In November 1985 I returned to San Juan, a little village in western Mexico, fully intending to complete a fifteen-year project documenting the transition of a traditional people moving into the twentieth century. I think I had sensed it, but this time, talking pueblo economics, I recognized the truth. While I had been unraveling social structures, relationships, attitudes, and values, in the background there was a great coming and going.

In every family, at least one person was working in the United States. Over half of the people had been there. One in five of the husbands, fathers, and sons were in *el norte*. In Los Angeles there was a fully equipped soccer team made up entirely of San Juanes playing their counterparts from villages throughout Mexico. Virtually all improvements in the village were made with money earned in the United States: new construction, restoration of the four-hundred-year-old church, new businesses, and purchases of land, animals, televisions, and refrigerators. In surrounding communities, the story was the same. The Colegio de Jalisco had determined that at least 20 percent of the banks of that state would fold if not for deposits sent home from the United States.

As the villagers talked, I began to understand that something much deeper and more significant than money was at work, but everyone was overlooking it.

Hurrying back to the United States, I stopped at the Tijuana–San Diego border crossing and took a motel room that backed onto the international line. Standing on the rim of the bathtub, I could look through a gap along the top of the barely openable window, past security bars and over the no-man's-land buffering the two countries. For two nights I stayed at my bathtub post from dusk to dawn, leaving only for takeout coffee or tacos from Jack-in-the-Box next door. With heavily equipped Border Patrol officers in wait beneath my window and all along the line, Mexicans by the hundreds swarmed down those hills and disappeared into the southern California darkness. In the night skirmishes, relatively few were caught.

Back in Berkeley I spent the next week searching through twelve years' field notes, collected clippings, the university library, and electronic data bases. In Los Angeles, of course. But also in Chicago, Detroit, Denver, Atlanta, and even Alaska, throughout the country, the evidence was there. Schools, churches, and cities; television and radio; the language of official documents and public places; our politics; even our shopping patterns: all changing by their influence. There are estimates that by the year 2000, Spanish will be as common as English in the United States.*

Yet it was equally clear that even in the midst of this largest migration ever, its significance was not understood. Politicians, academics, and bureaucrats told whichever story fit their purpose. Even with all their studies and statistics they were far removed from the lives of the people immigrating. And the immigrants remained shrouded in myth, misinformation, or no information. I knew these people intimately and felt certain that they, and no one else, held the key to this phenomenon.

It was January 6, 1986, Three Kings' Day. Crossing the border that night with the *coyotes* (men and women who guide illegals across the U.S.-Mexican border), I was overwhelmed, not only by fear and adrenaline surges, but by the unbelievable numbers of people. Hector, my young guide, carried my camera and tape recorder in one hand and pulled me uphill and down with the other. My heart was pounding and

*Thomas Weyr, *Hispanic USA, Breaking the Melting Pot* (New York: Harper and Row, 1988).

I could hardly speak. The thought Who was I to question these people? would have taken hold except for Hector, who thrust the microphone into small groups, introduced me, and practically asked the questions. Of the hundreds and hundreds crossing that night—impossible to count—I interviewed fifty-three men and women in search of a new life, new opportunity.

As so often happens when you find yourself at great physical risk, something inside you changes and your life is never again the same. My ethnography of San Juan went on the shelf and I began the chronicle of this story, locked in memories and scattered across North America. To begin, I returned to its genesis, the pueblos of western Mexico.

At Central Camionera, Guadalajara's big bus station, loaded down with potatoes, oranges, and a glorious pineapple, I hurried to catch the late afternoon run to San Juan. In her corral, cooking over an open fire, María de Jesús was surprised to see me back so soon. She warmed a bowl of fresh beans and tortillas and we quickly fell into conversation as if I had never left.

Twelve years before, her husband was dying of cancer. My children and I moved in with her and her ten to help while she cared for him. Later I was godmother to one of her children, and over the intervening years we had grown to be like sisters.

"No, comadre, so many men go to the other side. In the spring it is like a village of widows and orphans. You know, the women don't talk about it often. The men come and go, but we're always waiting for word."

I fell into the flow of this movement in the corrals and patios of the pueblos of Mexico, met them resting to cross the border, searching for a missing husband through the barrios of North America, and stopping in kitchens, offices, and rectories along the way. They told me their stories. They let me browse through their family albums and letters. They introduced me to brothers, cousins, and compadres. Everywhere I went with tape recorder in hand, they put their memories, hopes, and feelings to voice and their saga unfolded.

Others, such as respected anthropologists Manuel Gamio, Julian Samora, and Ted Conover, have written of this history. But this is the first time the immigrants agreed to tell their own story directly on tape. Even more significant, no one—legal or illegal, on this side or the other—refused. Two safeguards protect their privacy and ensure the integrity of their words: they spoke under names of their own choice; and the project was conceived and completed without funding from, and fully independent of, any third party.

The lives and struggles of these ninety persons is just the beginning. Others will continue. They will pass this epic saga on to their children who will then know the stake they have in what went before them.

Heretofore hidden in hearts and obscured by layers of time, this is their story. Speaking, shouting, and singing, they give voice to this struggle, their heroic journey. In the telling, a link missing from our history is forged and put in place, and their story becomes a part of all of us.

Marilyn P. Davis
Berkeley, California

MEXICAN VOICES/AMERICAN DREAMS

INTRODUCTION

It was Houston, it was hot, it was a supermarket opening; an unusual and obviously successful opening to be sure. Shoppers and gawkers and hawkers, and probably a few pickpockets as well, jammed the aisleways through *puestos* selling every kind of food and clothing. Stalls of flowers, cookery, gifts, and *cositas,* and bright suspended piñatas created layers of color while the fragrance of Mexican kitchens added another. Over all floated the mixed song of birds on sale and mariachis. Emphasis was on the vivid, the hubbub, the Latin. The object of all this? Texas's big Hispanic population. This was the latest Fiesta market, a chain flourishing in an oil- and cattle-crippled economy where others floundered. Like the people at whom it was targeted, this idea had come from the other side of the border.

In a kind of crazy alignment of events, at the very moment that the great American marketplace was, in its own way, confirming Hispanic importance, in Washington, D.C., Congress and the president were establishing legislation to set limits on their numbers and influence. Known as Simpson-Rodino in the immigrant community, the immigration reform law of November 1986 was set on eliminating that which was just being ratified by business and commerce.

To deepen the irony of the opening, the concept of the new market

1

was modeled on the open-air markets of Mexico, called *tianguis,* Nahuatl for "people's market." The lingua franca of the Aztec empire, Nahuatl had melded into the tongue of the conquering Spaniards over four hundred years ago. Often thought dead and forgotten, its presence is evidence that the immigrant, a mixture of European and Aztec genes, cultures, and cosmologies, brings with him something more than expected. As the language spoken by Francisco Vasquez de Coronado's Mexican soldiers when he led them north in 1547, in search of the seven golden cities of Cibola, its presence is also a reminder of how long these people have been migrating and the significance of their journey.

They founded the first city in the United States, Santa Fe, in 1610— ten years before the Pilgrims landed at Plymouth Rock. In 1777, when the Spanish Empire embraced all of what is now Texas, New Mexico, Arizona, California, Nevada, Utah, and part of Colorado, Mexicans were recruited by Alta California's governor, Felipe de Neve, and came north to build and work haciendas that supplied the military presidios strung along the Pacific edge of his vast administrative territory. Some of those haciendas were the foundation of modern mega-cities such as Los Angeles and San Jose, California.

In those times, however, *el norte* held little attraction. Fortune was to be found in the mines of the Mexican highlands or the intrigues of the capital, not in cattle and crops beyond the edge of civilization. Settling the immense territory was slow; so slow that there were too few Mexicans to occupy or defend it from the rambunctious Americans expanding rapidly from the east. First Texas broke away in 1836. Then, in 1848, to end the Mexican-American war, the government in Washington grabbed off the rest for fifteen million dollars, cancellation of claims, and withdrawal of troops from what remained of Mexico. Even before the war ended, however, the United States used the first immigration law to establish its authority over California. On December 27, 1847, Colonel R. B. Mason issued a military proclamation: Mexicans from the state of Sonora would no longer have the right to enter California.

That prohibition lapsed with the end of hostilities. It wouldn't have mattered. Gold was discovered the next month, and people from everywhere, including Mexico, poured into the gold fields. In the 1860s Mexicans were recruited to build the new railroad lines, and by the

1870s there was another pull as American government and business pressed to open the West to agriculture and mining.

Throughout the decade beginning in 1910, the coincidence of violent revolution in their own country and a world war, provisioned largely by American farmers, created a doubly powerful pressure on Mexicans to move north. Chaos throughout Mexico and abundance of available work across the border pushed and pulled 220,000 into the United States.

Then, in 1921, disillusioned by the aftermath of the Great War, and bent on creating "Fortress America," Congress instituted immigrant quota laws and established the United States Border Patrol. Mexicans, however, were exempt from the quota laws and simply paid a head tax to cross the border.

In the years that followed, Mexicans were recruited by publicity promoting climate and the good life. But when boom times fizzled and the Great Depression set in, thousands were deported and another cycle of exclusion began.

Within ten years and the coming of another war, U.S. farmers and industrialists again went a-courtin' south of the border. This time word-of-mouth promotion and newspaper advertisements weren't enough. In this new war, strong backs were needed to feed, clothe, and supply Allied armies that were spread around the globe. An agreement was struck with the Mexican government in 1942, and for the next twenty-two years, 4.8 million braceros ("arms" in Spanish) came seasonally to work American farms and ranches.

When braceros returned home with money in their pockets and stories of even more where that came from, the numbers of job seekers heading north doubled. If they couldn't go legally, then illegally would do just fine. In this massive movement was born a tradition of great significance for families and pueblos throughout Mexico.

The bracero program ended in 1964, but the tradition continued. In the seventies and eighties more illegal immigration than ever prompted passage of the U.S. Immigration Reform and Control Act of 1986, after fifteen years of turbulent congressional debate. The new law, including the agricultural worker's provision, gave legal resident status to approximately 3 million illegal immigrants, with the possibility of American citizenship.

The consequences of the act's supporting provisions, such as those instituting stiff employer penalties, seem not so clear. Except for a brief period after the new policies took effect, illegal immigration levels have actually increased since 1986. A *Los Angeles Times* poll taken in 1989 showed that even with the stringent new laws, almost 5 million Mexican citizens planned to emigrate to the United States in the next year.

What began as a trickle over a century ago with a few people trekking north has, through the decades, ebbed and flowed as a shifting tide over our southern border, swelling to a great tsunami at times of stress such as the economic crisis Mexico now faces. From a quiet beginning has grown the greatest migration of people in the history of humanity.

NOTE: The preludes to each chapter are *corridos,* traditional epic ballads. Hundreds of these songs have themes of immigration. Broadcast over Spanish radio throughout the United States and Mexico, they attest to the significance of *el norte* in the lives of Mexicans.

I

PUSH-PULL

CORRIDO
DEL INMIGRANTE

México, mi patria,
Donde nací Mexicano,
Dame la bendición
De tu poderosa mano.

Voy a Estados Unidos
Para ganaré la vida;
Adios, mi tierra querida,
Te llevo en mi corazón.

No me condenen
Por dejar asi mi tierra;
La culpa es de la probreza
Y de la necesidad.

Adios, lindo Guanajuato
Estado en que yo nací,
Voy a Estados Unidos,
Lejos, muy lejos de ti.

BALLAD
OF THE IMMIGRANT

Mexico, my homeland,
Where I was born Mexican,
Give me the benediction
Of your powerful hand.

I'm going to the United States
To earn my living;
Good-bye, my beloved country,
I carry you in my heart.

Don't condemn me
For leaving my country,
Poverty and necessity
Are at fault.

Good-bye, pretty Guanajuato
The state in which I was born.
I'm going to the United States
Far away from you.

1

Ballad of the Immigrant

THE LONG HISTORY
OF MEXICAN MIGRATION

In Mexico in 1910, revolution, famine, and chaos reigned. The way out was north. On foot, on horseback, in wagons, and by train, mile after treacherous mile, they came by the thousands, streaming into San Diego, Tucson, El Paso, Brownsville—the frontier cities of the United States. By 1920, more than a million Mexicans had crossed the border in search of safety, freedom, food, and jobs. It was temporary and many went back, but 220,000 stayed to start a new life, including the family of María Márquez.

MARÍA MÁRQUEZ ZANDSTRA
Retired Secretary
Albuquerque, New Mexico

We were traveling on a train. I believe it was from Zacatecas to the north. It was night and very, very dark. We were supposed to be very quiet; they were trying to sneak the train through enemy lines. The seats lined the sides, unlike the way they are today. It was dark and my feet dangled. I remember looking down at my shoes, which had little buttons. I distinctly remember that, and being scared, then the lights, tiny lights in the distance. That is my first recollection.

The next thing I remember was sitting in a courtyard with the rooms all around, in the colonial style. It was almost dusk and all my relatives were there, and they were telling me what a brave girl I was. After that I don't recall anything until we came to El Paso.

They used to talk about old times, but when you're young, you don't listen.

María Márquez was born in Jerez, Zacatecas, in 1915, to a very religious, conservative family who held closely the traditional values. Her grandfather, the bookkeeper for a large hacienda, was not himself affluent, but his values and his connection to the landowners forced his family north during the revolution. The oldest of twelve children, María Márquez spent her early years in El Paso, until her father moved his growing family to New Mexico.

She was a very young child when she left Mexico, but Mrs. Zandstra has never lost her ties. Each year she visits relatives still living there.

After the Revolution of 1910, the Catholic church and the government viewed each other with hostility. The political leadership of Mexico confronted a Catholic hierarchy opposed to the goals of the revolution and the modernization of the country. The constitution of 1917 nationalized church property, established that only Mexican nationals could be priests, forbade religious processions, and banned the clergy from appearing in public in habit, voting, discussing politics, owning property, or being involved in education. These provisions were not observed, however, until Presidente Plutarco Elias Calles was elected in 1924 and immediately began a fierce campaign to enforce the constitution. In response, the bishops ordered the clergy to boycott the churches. Peasants in the western states of Mexico, whipped into a frenzy by antigovernment priests, launched a guerrilla war to the cry "Viva Cristo Rey!" ("Long live Christ the King!"). Nicknamed "Cristeros," they slashed a three-year swath of murder, rape, arson, and sabotage across the face of the country.

In that same year, 1927, with a rabble of Cristeros close behind, Don Heliodoro Barragan escaped to the United States.

DON HELIODORO BARRAGAN
Retired Farmer
Las Barrancas, Mexico

How did we go? We didn't know buses or trucks at that time. We didn't have any of those things. I went on foot to Catarina. It took about one and a quarter hours from my house. Because of these questions of the *Cristeros,* they were chasing me. They wanted money; it was very dangerous. They had already killed José Luis Chavez and raped two young women down by the bridge. When I heard they were looking for me I went into hiding. I slept in the fields, and when I arrived in Catarina I hid in a pile of manzanita and sent a young man off to buy my train ticket. But when I was about to get on the train, on the second-class cars, there came those who were following me, with all of their escorts. They were all very drunk. Well, I quickly ran between the cars. When I reached the first-class train I got on and paid the difference so that they wouldn't see me.

I left with five hundred pesos in gold. It was Easter Monday, April 11, 1927, and I was thirty-two years old.

Sitting on the footstone of a small bridge near his home, Don Heliodoro takes the morning sun. Now at ninety-two, his features have sharpened. His small frame and dark, shiny, darting eyes, which acknowledge everything that passes, have given him an almost birdlike quality. Don Heliodoro learned to read and write well as a child. Today he earns money writing letters for those in his village who can't. At a recent three-day fiesta in Las Barrancas, he was responsible for the program, festivities, and decorations of the church. On Tuesdays he doesn't receive visitors. That's the day he takes the bus to nearby Zacoalco to do his errands. But on any other day he can be engaged on virtually any topic. A long lifetime of experiences, from fighting in the Mexican Revolution as a young boy, to an old man's perspective of today's economic crisis, is recounted with sensational precision.

They had just finished the Pacific train line as far as Salsipuedes, just north of Tequila. I arrived in Guadalajara and went to the consulate to pay the fee: ten gold pesos.

That Sunday an excursion train arrived in Guadalajara from the border with 150 gringos. That was the first train to arrive from the *frontera*. It was one of those that burned coal, and it had fourteen cars and two engines. That's the train I went on. We arrived in Nogales on Tuesday. A ticket cost eight ten-peso coins.

Then the nurses came to vaccinate us. They didn't vaccinate me. I tightened my fist and showed them my arm, but they told me to go on, and on I went.

I stayed in a hotel. It cost $2.50, and a good meal, like Sunday dinner, cost sixty cents. It was Wednesday afternoon that I left for Pasadena, then to Los Angeles on a bus. They had streetcars there too. I went to Azusa and stayed with my niece, Rosario.

The next day I left for Stender. We passed Stockton and arrived at four in the afternoon. It was there I began to work at a lumberyard called Pickering. It was a big company; there were two thousand people working there. The payroll was $29,000, but the highest pay was $4.50 a day. I stayed there for part of 1927.

Then I went to Sacramento. There, a Japanese woman, a millionaire with her own train to ship her produce, was an asparagus farmer. So I worked in asparagus. Her husband was from the United States and they had a son who used to say, "For the growth of the country, that's why we work."

I went to Chicago too, but then I returned to Stender and worked there in 1928, '29, and '30. But then it was the big depression and they laid me off for two months from the twenty-seventh of April to the seventeenth of June. I had relatives who told me to stay with them. So, that's what I did. Then one day a muchacho asked me to cut his hair. I said, "With what? I'm not a barber." But he brought me a towel, scissors, and everything, and I sat on a big box and gave him a haircut. He gave me money for a soda. Then I gave haircuts to two more fellows and they began telling others. By the next Sunday there was a great line of people waiting for me to cut their hair.

I kept returning to the lumberyard, but they would always tell me, "No work. No work." I helped my relatives at their house, washing dishes and cutting hair to earn a little. But in the end, I decided that I didn't have a chance. I gave away all my belongings and got ready to leave. I thought, I'll make one more visit to the lumberyard. As I went in I was whittling a little stick with a knife. When the general foreman saw me his eyes opened wide; he turned red and started yelling, "No! No! No!" He thought I was lighting a match. When he saw I was just whittling, he was so relieved that he yelled over to a man moving some logs with a horse. His name was Severiano Jimenez. He told him, "Give this guy some work. Tell him to come to work this afternoon."

That's what he did. And this Severiano told me, "The only thing is, don't be absent. If you are always here, the foreman won't let you go." Well, I had already given away all my things, and I had to go out and buy everything all over again.

I worked in various positions in that company. Once I was stacking wood. The chain broke and a mountain of wood came down on top of me. They had to help me get out. Then they changed me over to the yard where I just boxed scrap. Anything that would roll around had to be put in big boxes. I had to straighten all the wood. I was working and the foreman came and said to me, "That's all right! Who taught you?"

I told him, "I learned by myself!"

I worked fourteen months there. We were sixteen men and we had to carry big sheets of wood, twenty feet wide and thirty-two feet long, to railroad cars. We had gloves. I would pass the sheet to the guy inside.

Then they put me where they make sawdust. They had a smokestack twenty meters high. I worked with a Greek, throwing sticks into the machine. He didn't like how I threw them, and grabbed one to hit me. When I saw this, I grabbed one too, but I didn't just threaten him, I hit him and opened up his shoulder. When the foreman saw what happened and saw that the Greek was responsible, he didn't fire me.

After that I worked with a man who was deaf. He had become deaf in the war, but he treated me well, very well. I worked four months with him making railroad ties. Once when a woman I was seeing came looking for me, I hid in the bathroom. When she left he made signs to tell me it was safe to come out.

He had married a woman named Margarita, a *mexicana* who was born in the United States. They had married through a catalog, one of these where they put announcements, "*mexicana* looking for a *gringo*, to marry . . ." One Saturday he, his name was Miguel, and his wife were going to a dance in Sonora, about eighty miles away. He had a very elegant car. Well, they went.

Then on Monday, the payroll clerk told me, "No more companion: dead, dead!" His wife had prepared some poison for him so she could collect his insurance. When he drank his morning coffee, she had put poison in it. By the time they arrived in Sonora he was having convulsions. She had on a purple dress and on this they found a few drops of coffee and poison, and they grabbed her. That's how my companion died. I went to court, because Miguel was my good friend. The day she poisoned him was the twenty-seventh of April. They sentenced her on the ninth of June—a lifetime sentence—ninety-nine years and one day.

Again they changed my work and that was when I had an accident. A board fell on my hand. They saved it, but I was in the hospital forty-two days with a swollen hand. They put compresses of hot water on it, and the whole time I felt nauseous. In the end, I knew a muchacho from Tepatitlán who was a masseur. He told me that my hand was out of place. I bought some cotton and alcohol and he began to massage my hand. Then he told me, "Look at the girls on that calendar!" And when I turned around to see them, he gave me a great jerk. ¡Aye Dios! I didn't sleep all night for the pain. But I bought some arnica and alcohol and by the next Sunday it was better. I was cured.

After that, they sent me to mark the wood. This was robbing the company. It wasn't work. The truck would come with seventy to eighty thousand feet of wood and I had to write up how many feet and what kind of wood, and the grade.

Then I went to pack wood in eight railroad cars that were going to Australia. Everyone except me went up on top of the cars to rest. When the foreman arrived he found me sweeping. He gave everyone fifteen days without pay and I was the only one left working.

Winter arrived. The big bosses of the company arrived and they greeted me. But in December I got very bad with the rheumatism. It was a very cold winter with lots of ice, and a German there, who spoke good Spanish, told me, "You aren't going to get better here. Ask for your time off and visit the coast."

That's what I did.

I began to sell shoes and shirts for catalogs. I would take the measurements for shirts with a tape measure the company sent to me from Madison, New Jersey. The shoe company was in New York. I won $300 in premiums for my sales. Aside from the money that I won, they gave me three shirts and a bottle of perfume—"Seven Flowers of New York." I would put a few drops in a gallon of alcohol and then sell it in little bottles. Whew, it was very strong perfume!

When I had come to the north the dollar was worth one peso, ninety centavos, and when I went home it was at two pesos, nine centavos. But I made money selling things, cutting hair, and working in the lumberyard. If I hadn't gotten sick I would have stayed for ten years. They couldn't have gotten rid of me. When I returned my daughters had grown a lot. The oldest was eleven years old and Rosaura was five. I saw to it that they went to school. If I hadn't returned, my daughters wouldn't have studied.

They never canceled my passport. I still have it, but I never really wanted to return.

DON EZEKIEL PEREZ
Son-in-law of Don Heliodoro Barragan
Rancher
Las Barrancas, Mexico

The first ones to go to the United States from here were Pancho Arenas of Santa Clara; he invited Santiago Toscano and Santiago Gonzales, who were from Las Barrancas. That was in 1914, and they went on foot, walking to San Blas. That's a little more than 300 kilometers. From there they took a boat to San Francisco, and then a train. They got off the train near Sacramento and went to work in the gold mines. They got off and stayed there.

Later, when they returned, this Santiago Gonzales came all dressed up, wearing a suit of pure cashmere. Well, they invited him to be the godfather to a young couple who were going to marry. He was a good dancer, and no,* he brought mariachis, the whole thing, the *ponche* that was mostly tequila, but the good tequila. And before the dance, he tipped the immense pot of *ponche* and washed the patio. Yes, he washed the patio with that good tequila. Well, you can imagine!

Well, from then on many of the men from Las Barrancas went.

---

*No is often used in Mexican Spanish as a softened positive emphasis or an affirmative bridge with the previous thought.

It's called Las Barrancas de Los Laureles, "Laurel Gorge," a community of sixty-eight ranchitos clustered and scattered, conforming to the terrain. Don Ezekiel Perez was born here, as were his parents and grandparents. This is where he married Rosa in 1941, and where they raised seven children. Now, all their children live in the city, but Don Ezekiel's brother lives next door and Rosa's father and sister live down the road.

Their house, like other houses in Las Barrancas, is adobe, but unlike other pueblos where the houses enclose the family activity, one long side is open under a wide, overhanging roof that slopes to a peak at the back wall. On this patio, open on three sides, overlooking the approach to the house and animals in the corral, most of the family's waking activities take place. Doors to two bedrooms open along the rear wall of the patio.

In his late sixties, Don Ezekiel still rides his horse, and though he doesn't work as much now that the children have left, he keeps a few cows, pigs, and goats. In the house, kittens, an occasional chicken or rooster, and the family dog play among feet and chairs.

In the cool shade of the big overhang there are four country-style chairs. Against the wall a table is pulled out for eating, and to one side a great mountain of corn rests, husked and dry. Rosa still grinds her own corn for tortillas, and everyone, including visitors, is drawn to shelling corn as they talk and pass the time with Don Ezekiel and his wife.

My father and brother went in '29. I went alone in '47 as a bracero. At that time I had three children, Joel, Angel, and Judith.

One day a young kid and I went to look for animals in the hills and then and there we decided to go as braceros. We took the train to Guadalajara, but there were many, many people waiting. Waiting and waiting and the army would push them back with their rifles. For four days we waited, then we gave up and returned to Las Barrancas.

We again talked about going. One morning we decided to throw our huaraches in the air and if they pointed to Guadalajara then we would go; if not, then no. Well, I threw mine, and they pointed to Guadalajara. Then he threw his and his pointed to Guadalajara too. *¡Vámonos!* And we again took the train, but this time we stayed in the Hotel Manzanillo. Someone told us that an attorney, a friend, would help us arrange things. We waited for him, where he said he would meet us, but no one came. While we were sitting there, I saw someone I knew.

It was Miguel Lopez, who was the *presidente* of Teocuitatlán, along with friends he was going to help get into the line. I told my friend, "There's a friend of mine, he's *el presidente* of Teocuitatlán. Maybe he can help us." Well, my friend said I was crazy. He didn't believe me, but I told him to wait for me a few minutes, and I went up to talk to this Miguel Lopez.

"*¿Qué hule?* What are you doing here?" And I told him the problem we had. He said, "Come with me, I'll get you in."

I said, "But I have a friend."

"No, well bring him along!" And off we went with Lopez and all his friends. He had two extra cards that he gave to us. So my name was "Jesús Mora Lopez." He told me, "When they call Jesús Mora Lopez, you go in." Well, I went in flying when they called. They gave us a green card, and with this we could go in.

Inside, there were American doctors. We had to take off our clothes and they looked us over. Well, my friend didn't come out well. I don't know what was wrong, they wouldn't let him go, but they accepted me. They gave me a red card and told us that with that card, in three days, we would go on the train to Irapuato.

There was the whole gang from Teocuitatlán. We couldn't sleep, and we were there early in the morning, ready to go. When we got to Irapuato, we all got a house together, and every morning for fifteen days we got up very early. Well, we hardly slept. No, they weighed us, they fixed our teeth, pulled our molars, vaccinated us, and finally they told us, "Tomorrow you'll have your contract."

The last card they gave us was blue, I think, and an immigration attorney from there told us, "Guard this card, because this is your train ticket for tomorrow. The train leaves tomorrow morning, and if you're late, you don't go." Well, we didn't sleep. There were nine hundred of us and the train was one of those cargo trains, very long. And you know how the people are, they all ran, climbing over each other to get in. Well I was in the last car. At six o'clock in the morning they brought our breakfast, a cup of *champurrado,* that's hot chocolate mixed with corn flour, then at twelve noon, a can of sardines with green beans. You had to pass your plate fast, because if you didn't, *zas!* You would miss your dinner. This is what we ate in Mexico.

When we arrived in Ciudad Juárez, they turned the train around and backed it in. There we changed to an American train with seats, and this time I was in the front car. The immigration officials with their pistols asked for our contracts. From there on, we were in the United States. They gave each of us sandwiches of ham, fruit, and juice. In Albuquerque, they began cutting off cars, then again in Denver. In Denver, we all got off to have a good dinner. They took us to a very big restaurant and out came the *negritos* with their trays filled with coffee and milk, and meat, and canned fruit. They served us all, very quickly too.

Then on the morning of the twenty-second of May, we arrived in Billings, Montana. We looked out the window, and everyone had on heavy jackets and red faces because it was icy cold.

When we got off the train, they told us to get ready, because now we were going to meet the little gringas, all very pretty, and they were coming to welcome us. Well, in came a mountain of nurses to vaccinate us. We rolled up our sleeves and *zas, zas!* When they were finished the ranchers arrived to find their men to work. After they picked us out, they took us to the ranch, and then to a store. They asked if we had blankets, but no, we didn't. So they gave each of us two blankets, a jacket, gloves, and a hat with flaps for the ears. Later, they took the money out of our checks, but it wasn't that much. The jacket only cost $9 and it was long, of sheepskin with fur inside, very warm. I had it for a long time.

The first day we didn't do hardly anything; we cleaned beets. But afterwards we really began. Little by little we learned and we worked in rows a mile long. Later we cleaned beans, then beets, then we threshed wheat and clover. We also put wheat and beans into the machine. They treated us like family, and we sat and ate with them. We worked ten months and then returned to Mexico.

The next time I went as an *alambrista,* over the fence, with some relatives. We arrived in Tijuana and they sent us with a *coyote.* At two in the morning we crossed. We were about to get on a bus when the immigration caught us. They hit us and put the *coyote* in jail. They told us, "You're going to your Mexico, and if you return we'll really give it to you."

Well, the next night a relative and I crossed again. We walked a little ways and they caught us again. "Where are you from?" they asked us.

"From Guadalajara," we replied.

"Then you must know the song 'Jalisco, Jalisco'?" Well, we were the only ones they had. They sent us back, but we came back singing.

We entered again. This time some mechanics, who had a garage on the border, let us pass over their fence. A man from Zacoalco, who had baths in Tijuana, told us to get a bus on the other side of the bridge. We did, but again they caught us as we were arriving in San Clemente. "How many times have you passed? What is your name? We've seen this shirt before." They put some in jail and others they sent back to Tijuana.

I worked eight days putting a fence around a house in Tijuana. Then three of us tried again. Again, they caught us. "Where are you going?"

"Well, I want to go to San Francisco or Sacramento."

"To Mexico! San Francisco and Sacramento are that way." He was American, but he spoke Spanish. I told him I would send a postcard from San Francisco or Sacramento in a week or two. We both laughed.

Then I met a *coyote* from Santa Catarina and I went with him. He was married to a relative of mine, and he invited me to his house. They received me very well, and invited me to stay there and sleep. I said, "Oh no, I don't want to bother you." But they insisted, as we were going to leave at one in the morning. There were eighteen of us this time, from Michoacán and other places. There was a door cut in the fence and as we passed through, it occurred to me to say, "I'm just an American citizen passing through." They all laughed. We went through orchards and fields of wheat, walking until eight in the morning, then we all went to sleep hidden in the tall grass. We followed the paths through the hills. There was a windmill and there we hid until seven in the evening, when we came out and began walking. Again the *migra* [immigration officers] arrived! We all ran; I hid in some bushes. We all ran, even the *coyote,* and we all escaped! I was still in the bushes after two or three hours when I heard a whistle. Then, again. Oh, I thought, it must be the *migra* trying to trick us. Then again, and finally we realized that it was our companions. They hadn't caught any of us.

Well, we went on. When we arrived in Del Mar we hid in an orange grove. We ate some of the oranges and then in the afternoon we started out again. This time the *migra* arrived on horses. "Hey, hombres!" We ran up the river and they followed us, then we ran back down the river, and we hid. When we had started running, we had taken our huaraches off and we were eating oranges. We had to leave them behind. We hid until night, and when we were sure the *migra* had left we came out and went down to find our shoes. We had escaped again!

We walked until we arrived at a government army base. Here the *coyote* told us that we were going to run. He said that we would see spotlights and there we would crawl on our stomachs. "We are going to pass very rapidly, but if they catch us, come out with your hands up." On we went, running. It was like from here [Las Barrancas] to Santa Ana Acatlán [about fourteen miles]. We ran fast, and we made it.

From there we arrived at Carlos Bell and we began to see fields of grapes. To me it looked very pretty. I wanted to stay, but we went on to Santa Ana, and then beyond there is Stanton. We left half of the men in Carlos Bell. The *coyote* told us he was going to bring two taxis to take us and the provisions. We were waiting for the taxis to arrive when a rancher with a rifle and two dogs was coming toward us. We quickly climbed up the orange trees. Who knows what he said to us; it was in pure English. But we told him, "May you go well!" We left running and hid until the taxis arrived. They took us to Stanton to work in the oranges.

We worked there for about two months, then we worked for some Japanese in celery near Los Angeles. They wanted us to move to Hollywood, but we went to have dinner with the others in Stanton and there we met a man who offered to get us work farther north. We said, "But we don't have the money to get there." And he loaned us $48 each and took us all the way to Visalia. He told us he had a friend who had a restaurant there. As it turned out, it was a friend of ours from here. He had a big jukebox and I made a bed in the back of it with some cardboard cartons. All night long, music!

After awhile I began to lose my fear and started helping my friend with his restaurant, meanwhile living behind the jukebox. Oh, how they liked to play "No Vale Nada la Vida," and I got so tired of it! Finally, some nephews and I went in together and rented a house.

There was a church of the Hallelujahs and a barbershop. Our boss was a Hallelujah, one of the deacons. Well, once some preachers were coming who were supposed to be famous and our boss wanted us to go. "No, no, not us," said the others. But I went with two others. Our boss picked us up and we arrived in the car. There were some Americans with guitars, and a piano, and they all had their sombreros on. Some were these famous preachers from New York. What could I understand? They spoke in pure English, and they gave us a mountain of books that were in English too. It was fine. Then three days later our boss fired everyone except the three of us who went.

I was happy working there with him, but everyone kept saying that if we went farther north we could make more money. Well, we went to Stockton to work for some Japanese in tomatoes. At first we stayed in the Hotel California, but then we rented a house. That time I was there for more than three years, from '48 to '52. I worked in many areas. I went to San Francisco, San Jose, Benicia, visiting, just to know these parts. I took a little boat in Martinez. That's what I liked most. Every week I would take that boat. I liked the sea gulls, they would follow us. I also went to Milpitas, Santa Cruz, Sacramento, and Concord.

Then one day I was with a friend in Suisun. He was a little drunk, and he went through a red light. The police stopped us. When they asked, I told them I was Mexican and to send me back to Mexico. First they put me in jail in the basement, then later, on the top floor. My window overlooked a girls' school, and I could see them playing in the yard every day. I thought of my own children. They kept me for eighteen days and then sent me to Sacramento. I was there one day and they put us on a bus to Mexico. If we had money we had to pay for it, and if we didn't they sent us free. I paid my way, but it was very cheap.

I came back with all the money I had saved, and we bought several parcels of land and animals—horses, cows, and pigs.

DOÑA ROSAURA BARRAGAN DE PEREZ
Wife of Don Ezekiel Perez
Las Barrancas, Mexico

Doña Rosa shells corn, occasionally getting up to refill glasses from the olla of agua de arroz (rice water). She is still a beautiful woman with a warm smile, large dark eyes, and hair in a single braid of jet down her back. Somehow she knew when her husband had finished. Without asking or being asked, she acknowledges the importance of his trips north, then quietly continues about the lives of the women who remain behind.

Yes, it was hard for me when he was gone, because I had three little children. I lived here with my mother-in-law, but every day my father would come and get me and take me home with my family. I ate with my family and stayed with them, but we slept here with my mother-in-law. My father came and got me because if I had walked to his house by myself, people would have talked. That's how things were in those days. It hasn't really changed that much. It's still very hard on the young women who have their husbands in the north.

Not very long ago, a young woman from here fell. I could see it was going to happen. Her husband went up there, but he never sent her money. She had little children to feed. Well, what could she do? She went to Zacoalco to work, and of course she met someone else, and now she's pregnant. You know how the people are. Well, I feel sorry for her.

No, it was hard, but my husband always sent me money. We always had money, and I had animals, chickens and pigs, so I never had to worry. It was good because when he came back we were able to buy the parcels of land and with that we've managed. We educated all our children. There are seven. Only the youngest isn't married; she is the one who teaches in Sayula. One is a doctor and another is a lawyer, two are teachers, and one has her own business with her husband, a store. So it was worth the sacrifice.

The Depression changed everything. The economic crisis brought "Okies," "Arkies," and Texans into California and the Southwest from the dust bowl. With jobs so few and takers so many, the pressure was on: get rid of the Mexicans! They became targets of unconstitutional raids and mass deportation. Many who were U.S. citizens were paid outright to leave the country. Until the Immigration and Naturalization Act of 1965, Mexicans were free to enter the United States if they paid the head tax and visa and medical examination fees. Yet the Deportation Act of 1929 and another law passed that same year also made them liable to deportation, and any illegal return a felony. The methods and tactics foreshadowed the treatment of Japanese-Americans in 1941.

During the decade of the thirties, emigration to Mexico, forced or otherwise, exceeded immigration five to one. But the flow dramatically reversed again with World War II and the coming of the braceros.

LEONORA RUIZ CARRILLA
Housewife
Sonora Desert

In this second-class bus, crossing the midsummer swelter of the Sonora Desert, Leonora Ruiz Carrilla's face shows not a trace of dampness. She is composed, her long gray hair braided and pinned up, wisps framing her face. Her eyes are striking even now in her sixties; though tired, they speak of warmth and friendliness.

I used to live in Mexicali for fifteen years. Five of my children were born there. Oh, it's grown since then. Where we lived was on the outskirts of town in housing for the braceros. Well, that's practically the center of town now.

My husband worked in the United States. He'd come back and forth, and sometimes they would send him to work in the lettuce or peaches, and he'd be gone for two or three months.

I had a passport too. But they took it away from me. Oh, I felt very bad. You see, I had a friend who lived in El Centro, that's just on the other side. She was from Guadalajara too. Well, she asked me to let her know when I was going back to visit my family because she wanted to send some things to her mother. I wrote her a note, but she never answered. So one day I just told my husband, "I think I'll go see her."

I crossed the border and got on the bus, but before I got to El Centro the *migra* stopped the bus and took me off. I think they took some others off too. I showed them my passport, and they grabbed it from me.

Then they kept asking and asking where I worked. I told them I didn't work, I was just going to visit a friend. I told them I didn't work there. I told them, but they didn't believe me. I told them where my friend lived, and where I lived, and that I had children and didn't work, but no.

"No, we know you work here, and if you tell us that you do, we will give you back your passport."

What could I do? I prayed to God for an answer, but I knew I couldn't lie and say I had a job. They would have found out.

Well, they kept me there for three days and then tossed me back. I cried and cried because it was so humiliating. It wasn't that I ever wanted to go back. No, I would never chance that again, but I wanted my passport. It had my photograph and I could use it at the bank for identification. For me it was like a memento of those years.

I've thought of writing to the American government to ask if they would return it. Who knows if they keep them? That was thirty years ago.

Although she hadn't realized it, Doña Ruiz had been swept up in "Operation Wetback," a 1954 military operation aimed at expelling Mexicans and securing the border against further invasion from the south. To accomplish his mission, President Eisenhower's commissioner of Immigration and Naturalization, General Joseph Swing, militarized the Border Patrol and gained the assistance of federal, state, county, and municipal forces including personnel from the railroad police, customs, FBI, army, and navy. They pressed their attack on land, sea, and in the air in what was called the country's largest peacetime offensive. Authorities also reverted, as Doña Ruiz experienced, to the intimidation tactics of the thirties. The Immigration and Naturalization Service reported impressive numbers of Mexicans apprehended—a daily average of 1,727 during the early weeks of the campaign—though they did not report on what happened to uncollected wages, personal possessions, and families of those caught in the sweep.

In spirit, Operation Wetback paralleled the Senate hearings held by Senator Joseph McCarthy that same year. That year was also a turning point in the country's attitudes. The United States Supreme Court unanimously ruled that racial segregation in public schools was unconstitutional. Never again would constitutional guarantees of human rights be so blatantly disregarded. Shortly thereafter the concentrated offensive of Operation Wetback was scaled back, with General Swing proclaiming, "Illegal immigration is no longer, as in the past, a problem of border control. The border has been secured."*

However, there were significant consequences from Operation Wetback.

*Mexicans were exempt from the quota system for immigrants adopted in 1924. In fact they were not "illegal" until 1965, when quotas were first established for countries of the Western hemisphere under the McCarran-Walter Act. They were apprehended and deported as undocumented aliens or undesirable aliens, i.e. prostitutes, criminals, or illiterates.

The expansion and militarization of the Border Patrol hardened the border. Illegals responded with more sophisticated strategies and techniques. The resulting escalation in the cost to cross simply meant a longer stay in the United States to recoup the expense. Increased costs and the likelihood of being caught made seasonal migration back and forth much less desirable. Immigrants began to stay longer and look for permanent, higher-paying jobs. A permanent job precluded visits to family in Mexico. So more and more families were brought along, or a new one, or even a second one, was started in the United States. A family in the United States entails responsibility and putting down even deeper roots.

With the border hardened, what had been a nomadic migration that moved with the seasons now more often became permanent underground immigration, with a large number of Mexicans virtually trapped in the United States by their circumstances.

Maclovio Medina worked nineteen consecutive years in the fields of California, migrating back and forth to support his family. His last season was in 1965. Four of his six children now work and raise their families in the United States. They have American children, permanent factory jobs, and make mortgage payments. They are illegal. Maclovio and his wife, Chuey, haven't seen their children in eight years and have never met their grandchildren.

MARÍA DE JESÚS MEDINA
Housewife
San Juan, Mexico

María de Jesús ("Chuey") moved into this house after she married Maclovio. Six months after their first child was born, Maclovio left for the first time to seek work in the United States. The house, which had once been a simple adobe room, has, through hard work, constant enterprise, and a regular check from her husband and now her children in the United States, evolved over the years. Two rooms have been added, the open-tiled roof has been replaced with a solid ceiling of brick, the packed dirt floors are now tile, and a decorative wrought iron gate marks the entrance. All of her children were born here. Her oldest son lives nearby with his ten children, the youngest daughter works in the city and comes home on weekends, and the other four children and seven grandsons live illegally in the United States.

Through the various enterprises that Chuey carries on from her kitchen door she earns enough for that day's food. Today she has decided to sell snow-cones, and there is a steady stream of children at the door to buy. She talks easily as she sits on a crude little wooden chair shaving the ice, topping it with jamaica *or* pineapple *syrup as the children choose.*

My husband worked many years in the United States when he was young. He's never said much to me, but I've overheard him tell his drinking companions stories about the *gringas* and *güeras* he's known. I've told him, if he's going to take me there, I won't tolerate his fooling around with *gringas*. He tells me not to worry, he says he's too old for that. Now he's mine alone.

Seven times he went to the United States. Each time he'd come home. Then when I was pregnant, he'd leave. I had all my children, except the last one, without him.

One thing I'll say is he never forgot to send money. The only times were when he didn't have work. But I would always manage. Once I got my basket and filled it with cheese and cream from the cow, and with my little ones I'd go out selling my cheese. Then I worked in a house with my daughter, cleaning and cooking. My husband never knew until I told him many years later. I think he always needed me more than I needed him. At least I never felt the same need he did, but perhaps that's how men are.

I have three sons and a daughter in the United States. They are just like my husband. They work very hard and always remember us. They send us dollars, and I have more than one hundred cards they have sent me for my birthday and Mother's Day.

They want us to come visit them and get to know our seven grandsons. All but one, little Freddy, were born there. I have mixed feelings about going, although my husband is ready to get our passports. I want very much to see my children and grandchildren, and I especially miss little Freddy. I hate to pass up the chance while we are in good health. Only *Dios* knows whether we will have another. But I worry about being robbed and having everything we've worked for taken; and my plants that I have cared for so much would probably die.

Children have stopped coming to the door, and Chuey has switched on the single light bulb that hangs from the center of the kitchen ceiling by the time her husband returns. He has been in the fields since early morning harvesting his garbanzo (chickpea) crop.

He goes directly into the patio and washes up at the lavadero. *Still in his sombrero he comes into the kitchen and, sitting down, spreads his hands on the table in front of him. The skin is cracked and raw from the fine prickly hairs in the garbanzo hulls.*

In his late sixties, his broad, pleasant face is boyishly smooth and still freckled. Don Maclovio Medina hangs his sombrero on his knee. In the simple pleasure he finds in a cold beer, he shows his enthusiasm for a life well lived.

DON MACLOVIO MEDINA
Husband of María de Jesús Medina
Farmer
San Juan

In '46? *Si,* '46. Well, those who had good luck went with contracts from Mexicali, the braceros. The only thing was, we weren't picked, but we were there too. That's where we crossed to the other side, but as illegals.

There were four of us, but we were separated at Santa Ana, Sonora. They had sorted us for different buses by numbers, two of us were picked for one bus and the other two went on another. The next day when we met up in, what was the name . . . Puerto Peñasco, there in Sonora, only one arrived. The other had returned to Guadalajara. He had lost his inspiration to go. So then there were just the three of us. There was Teodoro Hernandez and then Pili Diaz. Yes, we were the ones who went on. It was Lupe who returned. We continued on. We were there in Mexicali, wanting to pass to the other side. We stayed there and ran out of money, but eventually we found work in a lumber mill, named the Maderia Cabaña.

I had the job of drilling holes with an electric drill, following a pattern that sat on top of the wood. That was in Mexicali. And yes, from there we passed to the other side.

A brother of Teodoro's helped us. He sent a man named Silvano who was our guide and he took us to where they were. We passed in the night, without problems. But later there were problems, because the immigration came to where we were working and they threw us out.

They sent us to the other side, but just to Mexicali, and we came back. We came back through some hills called El Centinela and we crossed over a bridge that was there. We passed, and it wasn't far. We were working in a pueblo called Silas. That's where we were on a ranch. They caught us in the morning when we were working and sent us back because they didn't have very many jails. Well, we returned before noon. We arrived in time to work. But after awhile, it began to get more difficult and eventually we returned to Mexico. The first time we stayed about six months.

After, we returned again. Now we knew how to cross, so we passed by ourselves without a guide. We knew where to cross and where to find work too. We went back to our same boss. His name was Martin Dorman, and he gave us work again. He had a little ranch.

Then one time, on another trip, I made a mistake as to where I passed. I got on the road along a canal, but it was very wide. Very wide—and there were cliffs on either side. It was late when I realized that I had made a mistake on the road, and I wasn't going to get to where I was going. I had walked all night and from early morning; and now to go back? But only God knows how far. Then I saw a cliff with two cables, these steel cables like a swing crossing over the canal to the other side. I thought, *"Carajo,* can I do this? Well why not, they're made of steel. Well, *pobre Dios,* this is how I am going to pass!" I got up on top of the cables, and I went walking on the two of them, on top. *No'mbre,* it was farther away than the gate to the pueblo! From where I got up I couldn't see the water, but in the middle I looked down and there was a river running underneath. Sons of *carambas,* it gave me fear! And in the middle, the cables were hanging way down low. I thought, "I will just stay here." But thanks to God I passed. Passing over the cables, there was the *ranchito.*

When I got there I worked again. I worked about three times there. In that time they paid us fifty cents an hour. It doesn't seem like much, but it was okay at that time. If you were working here, the minimum was eight cents an hour. When we worked in the lumber mill they paid us twenty-five cents an hour, and for the same work in Guadalajara they paid six cents. It was good money. There we worked.

We lived on the ranch in some little houses that we made of boards. We made beds, and we left them for others who came after us. Each one had his little house. We built them for while we were there. But the immigration came in the night and woke us up. "Let's go, hombres!" And when we saw that they had arrived, we laid there like we were dead. No, well, "Do you have papers?" Well, what papers? No, they sent us back and again we returned. It's always been like that. This isn't something recent. For many years the Mexicans have made their own state in the United States. The people go, some return, and then others go. Then when they return, others go. That's how we go, back and forth.

Once when I entered, there was the immigration. I had been waiting all day; I was tired, hungry, and thirsty. There was nothing to eat, and I had been waiting for the immigration to leave, to move away from the gate. No, the minute they moved their car I took advantage of the chance. I went and arrived at a *ranchito*. There was a little canal with water. I bent over to get a drink; then the dogs started barking. The immigration must have been there because they immediately turned on some big, big lights. Good ones. I was on the upper road, and they were looking for me with their lights. They were looking for me, but I didn't want to jump into the canal, it was wide also. So on I went but they were in their car. No, in no time they caught up with me. But in front of me there was a little bridge. I crossed to the other side, and when I crossed, they passed me. When they saw they had missed me, they turned around, and when I saw they were going to turn around, I got on the road where they had been, and I was following them. I crouched down and hid. I thought I heard them put on their brakes, and I thought, "Now they see me." I think they were looking for me with their lights. What luck! If they had caught me, aye what a beating they would have given me. But I went on walking, hoping that the dogs wouldn't bark at the next *ranchito*.

I was alone this time, alone. Well no, now I was very hungry. I went to a field where they had a lot of melons. It was very dark, and I was walking among the melons, I couldn't tell which ones were ripe, I just sat down and ate melons in the night, whether they were green or ripe. I guess they were ripe because I never got a stomachache.

I arrived at the ranch late at night; there was nothing to do, because I had already eaten. Then they told us that we couldn't sleep there now because the immigration would come in the night. We had to go out and sleep in the fields. We went. I just took my blanket and we slept in our boss's field. Well, sure enough, the immigration came in the middle of the night and they took those who stayed in the little houses. "No," I said, "all the trouble it took to get here, and now that I've arrived, I'm not going to get caught again." It was a little cold, but not too bad.

Well, all these people in '51, you can't imagine how many there were, so many, working illegally, but now there were only two left. The owner now had contract labor. There were only two of us. Now they didn't want the illegals, because if they found any, they would take away their contract labor, the braceros. So now he told us, "Muchachos, now you have to look for work, because I can't give you work anymore."

We found another job close by. We worked for a Japanese. He had a field and needed help. They had taken away all of his people, so there were just illegals there. They wouldn't give the Japanese contract labor. It's certain that the government didn't like the Japanese. It was very bad at that time. It was the war and I don't know what else, but they wouldn't give them workers. This man had some good fields there, but they took away his people. He had melons and tomatoes, very good tomatoes. Well, we helped him, and he gave us work. He was very nice to us. We called him Jimmy. We said, "No, Jimmy, now we won't go where they have all the people they need, we're going to stay and help you." He paid us very well. Most likely he got good prices in this time, but he lost a lot because he couldn't plant all of his fields, he didn't have enough people. He paid us very well, very well, and the day we worked, that day he paid us. So if we got caught by the immigration we would have some money if we wanted to go home. No, he paid us well, and he gave us beer at dinnertime. We would go to his house and he would take out beer for all of us. He was grateful that we would help him. I was there with another young man from here, from Concepción de Valle, his name is Mario.

I had been there four years by then, I was twenty-nine years old. We had the three boys, Lupe, Juan, and Pedro, just the three. When I went the first time in '46, we just had Lupe. I went every year; this man always gave us work, and it was close to the border.

I worked in lettuce, melon, tomatoes, also the watermelon. Then I worked in cabbage and this—beets—sugar beets. The tractor would dig them up and we would gather them. Then also in the lettuce, we would have to go up the rows, you couldn't even see the end, and you would have to go bent over all day. It is very hard work, very hard. But this is hard work only the Mexicans do, because there are a lot of people here in Mexico who are very hard workers. And when one is young, you have your energy. I could see that the Mexican people there worked very hard, they're good workers. They want to demonstrate that they're good workers so that they will want them for work, so they won't fire them. No, if we worked here like we work there, Mexico would be very advanced. Here we don't want to work. They don't pay us here. No, they don't pay. There is contract work there that pays very well, the people make a lot of money, work where Mexicans make a lot of money.

After, in those years, I went farther up to Salinas, to Watsonville, to Santa Cruz. It's pretty there. I liked working up there better because they would let us rest from our work—a few minutes at each turn. Down near the border, no, it was very hard, no rest the whole day. But in the north, it was different, they had more consideration. They let us rest at the end of each row, about ten minutes. That was good. The people were good workers, good workers for this kind of work. That's why the agriculturalists there prefer these people, the Mexican people. They squeezed out the juice, they were happy with their work. They know how to work. This is what I liked, work in the fields. I don't like the city. No, I never like to work or live in the city. I worked in Los Angeles for a short time, but I didn't like it. I wasn't comfortable there. It was so tight, and so many cars, and, no, it was . . . *carambas;* I wasn't happy.

Then I went to work in Stockton. From there to Manteca and that area. I worked with someone who built houses. He would tear them down and build them again, new. I worked with him in Palo Alto. The climate is very pretty there in Palo Alto. It's not too hot or too cold, and the immigration isn't there. Oh, I tell you, I was very happy there.

Well, it wasn't much that I did with the money I made, because I had to spend there, as well as send money here, so much family I had to support here. I had to spend twice. I was happy there, but I don't think it was a good business deal. You can't do it. Chuey was here, she wanted to save money, but I told her, "No, spend it, eat whatever you want. I don't want you to suffer. I send you money to spend. Buy the children whatever they need." Well, and me, I never liked to go wanting for something. No, if I wanted something to wear or to eat,

I bought it. I would go to restaurants, I'd have my little beers when I wanted. No, I was very happy working there because I was able to maintain my family.

Then I would always leave my fields planted here. When I came back, I would harvest. We always had our little animals and our harvests, because I worked in both places. We also had a little boat, we would fish and get some little centavos from that. A little from here and a little from there, that's how we made it. When my sons were older, they would harvest for me. One year when I came home they had a surprise for me. They had harvested the corn and planted garbanzos. From that time on we had two plantings each year. They helped me. When I came back they had done such good work.

We've always made the fight. All my children are good workers. From the time they were little they liked to work. Of course when they're young, they like to have escapades and make mischief. We were young, too, but you can't give them much time for mischief.

I've always liked working in the fields, I never liked to be in the house. I awaken at four or five in the morning. Now I don't go to the fields until it's light out because I could fall on a cactus or something, but as soon as I can see, off I go. I used to go on horseback, but not long ago my horse threw me. I'll have to wait awhile until my back is better. Right now I'm cutting the garbanzos. What else would I do? One's life is working.

Two village men on their way home from the fields drop in to visit. Chuey has been roasting fresh garbanzos on the comal. *She seasons them with fresh-squeezed lime juice, salt, and chili and passes them to be eaten like popcorn. Maclovio takes more beer out of the well-stocked refrigerator, and the conversation drifts to the gossip and events of the day.*

But not quite finished with his story, Don Maclovio's words hang suspended in the air. In a pensive moment he runs his hand through his hair. When he finally speaks it is with a deeper voice, a sadness.

We will have to see about those who follow, the grandchildren. I wait for their parents to bring them here; to see if, perhaps, there are some who also love to work in the fields. I think they'll like the animals. I will take them to the fields on horseback.

AMOR ETERNO

No llores, prietita linda, no llores que pronto vuelvo,
Recuerda que nos juramos tenernos amor eterno;
Si me voy es porque quiero, quiero conseguir dinero,
Para volver y casarnos y hacernos un heredero.

Entonces te voy a hacer feliz
Y contigo siempre voy a vivir.
Veremos muchas estrellas,
Y juntos nos perdemos entre ellas.

Todos dicen que en el norte, se gana reteharta plata;
Dejame hacerle la lucha, dejame no seas ingrata.
Verás que cuando regrese y traiga mucho dinero,
Te voy a comprar la luna, te voy a comprar el cielo.

Rudy Fierro

ETERNAL LOVE

Don't cry, pretty little loved one, don't cry, because I will return soon.
Remember that we promised each other eternal love.
If I go it's because I want to, I want to earn some money,
To return so we can get married and make us an heir.

Then I will make you happy
And with you I'll always live.
We will look at the many stars,
And lose ourselves among them.

Everyone says that in the United States one can make a lot of money;
Let me give it a try, let me, don't be ungrateful.
You will see that when I return and bring a lot of money,
I will buy you the moon, I will buy you the heavens.

I Will Buy You the Moon

THE REASONS FOR GOING

Every day for weeks in the fall of 1986, U.S. newspapers were peppered with reports, items, columns, and editorials about illegal immigration from Mexico. PR machines, cranked to the maximum, aimed to either inflame or mollify public sensitivities: the Immigration and Naturalization Service budget hearings were coming up in Congress. Office seekers sought votes. Growers and others had their economic interests. There were threats: sightings of Middle Eastern terrorists, rampant drugs. Immigrants, no longer passive, were ambushing border patrol vehicles. There were counter-threats: without the illegals, crops would rot in the fields, prices would go through the roof, and civil liberties for U.S. Hispanics would be suspended.

But reality for four men on a Tijuana hillside this warm September evening was not recognizable in such hysteria.

Leonardo, in his late twenties, works in the manufacture of metal cabinets. Each year he takes his vacation in Mexico to visit his parents in Colima and each year he makes this illegal crossing. He's never been caught. Eight years working in the United States has given him a confidence that makes him unusually direct in his views.

Have you heard of this fanatic Ezell*? Why is he telling these lies? None of us are terrorists, we don't have time to be terrorists. All we are interested in is feeding our families. The truth is we don't take any jobs that Americans would want because they can collect more from welfare than the wages we work for. Look, if there were work in Mexico we wouldn't be here. We have to go where there's work.

Enrique, forty-five, is the quiet one. He has been in the United States two years and is just returning from a summer visit to his wife and six children in Chiapas.

Yes, that's true. I came to the United States because I couldn't support my family. In my own country I worked as a truck driver carrying sugarcane, but we couldn't live on the income I made. In the United States I work for minimum wage, but I have two jobs. On one I work from seven at night until seven in the morning. Then I sleep for a few hours and at ten in the morning I begin my other job and work until three in the afternoon. Altogether, I work about eighty hours a week. I don't get much sleep, but it doesn't matter. I am here to work.

I live inexpensively because I live with two other men. We each pay $120 a month for our apartment, and I am able to send $200 a month home to my wife. The rest I save in the bank. Both jobs are parking cars for an Arabic company in Beverly Hills. I'm a good driver and I don't have to speak English.

I'm very unhappy to have to leave my family again, especially now because I have two sons who are graduating from high school and they are going to enter the university. I would like to be with them on their graduation, but they need the money I can make here so that they can get a good education. They deserve it; they are good boys and have worked and studied very hard.

Roberto, the youngest at twenty, is self-assured, educated, and dressed surprisingly well for such an occasion.

Yes, of course I want to work and make some money, but the real reason is to know more about the world. For many years now I have studied

*Harold Ezell, former western regional commissioner, U.S. Immigration and Naturalization Service.

about the United States, and now I want to have the adventure and see for myself.

Jorge—the classic mexicano *with a round face that perfectly fits the big handlebar mustache and dark, flashing eyes—is about thirty-five years old.*

My parents have a business in Guadalajara and I was working with them. They have a woman who works for them as well, and I came to know her. We worked together.

But she is married. It is a situation that is sad, very sad, because this woman is very intelligent. I could see how skilled she is at handling money and business. But unfortunately, she is married to a man who is not her equal. It's not only that he is not intelligent, but he is lazy. She is the one who works and earns the living, and he foolishly spends what she earns—and even more.

I could see that even with all her talent and skill, with this husband she will never get ahead. I grew to care for her very much, and wished I could find an answer to the situation. I searched for a solution. I went to the Señor Cura [priest] and talked to him. I even went to a psychiatrist. They both told me that I didn't have a chance in this relationship. Well, what could I do? I couldn't stay there and work side by side knowing there is no hope.

So here I am, on my way to the United States. I have friends in Chicago who will help me find work. Perhaps there, I will be able to forget her and let God resolve this problem.

It is nearly 11:00 P.M. now. The team of coyotes *had moved them three times during the evening. Never far—the next hill, a little farther up, and a little farther down. There are others in the group, scattered in clusters nearby. They watch the* migra's *movements in the distance and wait, talking among themselves.*

It's an injustice. Look at how they have us, passing and catching us like animals. We're not bad; we don't want to take anything from anyone. All we want is work. Is that bad? No, truly this is an injustice.

In a country where a population of 85 million people is supported by a work force of only 20 million, most earning less than Mexico's minimum wage of

$3.45 a day, many are forced to seek alternatives to feed their families. If it is an issue of survival, then laws, sacrifices, the odds of success, and the possibility of being exploited are only additional risks.

But beyond survival other reasons motivate large numbers of Mexicans to take those risks: greater ability to be able to support a family, get married, educate children, pay off a debt, start a business, buy property, build a house, or simply make a better life.

El norte also offers opportunity of another kind—opportunity to cut the apron strings, to break off a relationship, for the dream of romance and adventure, to enhance one's status, or to save face, to leave the family or join them, to sow wild oats, and to see the world—not a possibility in the Mexican army.

But now there is a new, even more compelling reason, a reason that has grown into a tradition of deep significance. Suffering the risks, the injustices, and the loneliness of el norte has become the quest, the rite of passage to manhood for young men throughout the villages of Mexico.

AUGUSTIN PERÉZ
Auto Parts Shop Worker
Los Angeles

It's in the bag. With only a minute and a half to go, the team from San Juan, Jalisco, holds a two-point lead over their opponents from Villa de Reyes, Michoacán. In every detail, from their professional, matched uniforms to the referee in black and the fans scattered along the sidelines, this Sunday afternoon fútbol [soccer] match could be taking place in any number of towns throughout Mexico. This one, however, is being played in a public park in Los Angeles, California, by illegals representing their native pueblos.

San Juan has held its two points as the players come off the field, their arms draped around each other, catching cold Budweisers being thrown to them by their coach out of a big ice cooler. One member of the winning team is Augustin Peréz. A little less demonstrative than the rest, he is dark, clean-cut, and at five feet eleven a little taller than his teammates. As he sits on the grass, catching his breath, his eyes shed the intensity of the game and gain a kind of distance.

Look, in my pueblo of San Juan we need a lot. But when people become corrupt, it is difficult to work and it isn't easy to get rid of corruption.

There, the older people, not all of them but many of them, are the ones who have a clean spirit. But the youth have ideas and thoughts that are not good. I don't know what is going to happen or what is happening now, but I can imagine. I can also imagine what is happening with the drainage system, the new plaza, and the church. One year—my imagination goes around—I imagine . . . I imagine how the children are growing. And then something that someone who comes tells us, and letters arrive, and more or less I have an idea of what is happening; what is happening in the pueblo and in the country. This is what I have thought about since I came here.

In our pueblo there isn't any work; and although we are close to the city of Guadalajara where one can find work, they pay very little. In Mexico I have had various kinds of work. I worked for Coca-Cola, in construction, also as a plumber, and then in the fields. One comes here with dreams but the primary reason is economics. How can I say it? Well, it's very hard to live in my pueblo and in our country; and working here we are very comfortable even though the pay is low. There are jobs that pay better here, but I guess we don't know enough yet to get paid more.

I arrived here in January last year [1985]. It didn't take long before I found a job. By April I was working in the factory where I work now, along with my friends. I began at the bottom like everyone else, and I can't say I've risen a lot. Neither have my earnings, but the difference is that I'm not working where it's so dirty and greasy. Right now they pay me $3.50 an hour, a little above minimum. It's not much, but I live better here than in my own country. At least there is enough for me to buy clothes, more food—probably double the food—and I have time for diversions. I work forty hours a week here, and in my pueblo you work forty-eight. There's time to rest here. You can have your beer and diversions and you still have enough to save or help your family.

I have a lot of motivation even though I'm single, because I would like to buy a house or some land and return to get married. I had a girlfriend, but the first problem is I came here and she is there. She became angry, so now I don't have a girlfriend. My principal motive is to buy a house, then look for a woman to marry. In my mind I have a plan—if God approves—I would like to stay awhile longer until the month of May and then return for the World Cup in *fútbol*—Mexico '86. But first, it is one of my dreams to save a little money.

Little by little I am beginning to be accustomed to the activities, work, and people in this country, but I miss my family. From the first week I arrived I wanted to return, but I have stayed so that I could earn some money. One year isn't enough; perhaps three years. I am going to save as much as I can so that I won't have to come back.

I have the same responsibility that someone married does because I try to help my family, even though it's not much. When I write to them I send a little to help. They don't expect it; on the contrary, they want me to save money here.

The man we work for is very friendly and has a lot of esteem for us. We like him very much. He has told us that if we want to return to see our families he will give us work when we come back. If I return to Mexico and find a girlfriend or work that pays better than I had before, I would stay. But to come back to the United States I would have to think twice. We have everything here, the *fútbol* team and lots of friends from the pueblo, but I still feel very lonely. I think the others who don't have their wives and children here feel the same. Well, for them, it's even harder.

It's difficult here, there are many risks. In my pueblo and country, life is more tranquil. Here, even though your neighbors live very close you don't have confidence. You have to know them for a long time first. Not long ago one of our relatives' houses was robbed here.

The campesinos in our country, the people who live in the rural areas and make very little money—less than the minimum—talk with someone who has returned from the United States. They talk about the money, the life, and the customs, and of course one will mostly talk about the good, but never do they tell them of the battle and the difficulty of crossing the border, like coming in the trunk of a car. But with what is happening in our country many will run the risk. This country is very different than ours. When I return I am going to tell them the truth.

I will have been here a year and a half in May. It will be beautiful in Mexico then, with the new stadiums ready for the World Cup. I like to read and I know a little about literature. Mexico holds us like ancient Rome: with just bread and a circus the Mexican is happy. This is the life in Mexico. The World Cup games are going to benefit Mexico a lot, but from there on I think the same situation will just continue. The World Cup is only a period of one month. But this is how we are. If we don't have anything to eat, we begin talking, and then a friend will arrive and we forget that we are hungry.

The Mexican tries to let the little problems leave without noticing them. The grave problems attack him, but he always comes out ahead. I have seen in San Juan, in Guadalajara, in my family, and in general there are very few times that you see someone sad. Very few times. You see us here, serious. But if you saw us at the house, in the yard we're laughing and jumping around. Some watch television, some listen to music, and we forget our work and our problems.

In letters I try to convey to my parents and family that I am happy here. There, they imagine other things. Friends return and tell things in their manner, and one's parents become a bit worried about the little problems, whether their sons are working or not. And when they can't see, they think the worst. In the year I have been here there have been a few fights and punches but nothing grave.

When we had the earthquake in Mexico we didn't forget them. I was one of the first to communicate. The very afternoon of the earthquake, the nineteenth of September, I communicated with Guadalajara. The girl who was then still my girlfriend is the person I called. She told me in Guadalajara they didn't feel it but in Ciudad Guzman they did. But the good thing was that I communicated right away. The next day, the twentieth of September, we *mexicanos* here in Los Angeles filled the coliseum. We came to give anything we could: blood, money, clothes, everything. We stayed there listening to the reports, when there was another temblor. It was of a lower magnitude—the first had been much stronger—but that night in the coliseum, we didn't know. It was like the earth re-forming itself and for a time there were aftershocks of less force.

Then, the communication was cut off. I was here buried with the television and a Spanish newspaper that is circulated in Los Angeles, *La Opinión*. In truth we were very afraid because where my family lives the houses are made of another material, adobe or brick, and there is the risk that the roof can fall in. It would kill someone if they were asleep.

I entered into the work lines as soon as I heard the notices to organize for help. Very quickly. I don't remember what day the earthquake occurred, but by Saturday we went down to donate money, clothes, and medicine. We were ready to donate blood, but there wasn't a place ready to take it. I think our donations were among the first to arrive. The radio station and the Salvation Army were the first to send help. All of the countries of the world came to the rescue of Mexico, and this country helped the most and is still helping. The Mexicans who are here, the illegals, were the first to feel the pain. Even though our families weren't involved, it was our blood. It was our country and our people. We helped in the little that we could, all of us.

As we say in our country, it has rained hard on Mexico. Now we are losing one of our biggest helps, the petroleum. It's very bad, this affair. But what can one do for your government? With all the things we see in our pueblos, municipalities, or cities, you can imagine that we who come here are angry and tired of our government because of the system that has been in effect for many years now. It is a part of what makes us want to leave, because those who bleed the country are those who have the most: the governors, deputies, senators, and presidents; those who pay with broken silver. The majority of our people are poor. Of the 70 million people in our country I think only 100 to 500 are millionaires. If our country is a democracy, this isn't right—*ricos* with castles and mansions on the coasts, while in some pueblos the parents don't have food to put in their children's mouths.

To return . . . I want to help my pueblo. Economically I will never be able to, but morally, yes I can. There are the means, but they aren't channeled in the way they should be and the money stays with the same people. I think the situation is difficult and it's not going to get better. It's going to continue like this until what happens, happens. There is a lot the pueblo needs. But the way the young people think—it's clear we can't go back—but personally I don't like the mode of life in the pueblo with the alcohol and drugs. We need factories and places for jobs and instead they build a place to sell liquor.

This is what I am trying to say. Someone who comes to the pueblo, this is what they will find. And the children, when they go outdoors they don't hear a sane conversation. It's been like this for a while, but is this the progress of Mexico? Working six days a week only to find yourself in these conditions with drunks and comic books? This is the people. If they are happy this way, this is how it will continue. I have a brother and a brother-in-law, we all have alcoholics in our families who should be in Alcoholics Anonymous. I hope it's not too late.

When I came here these were the words of advice my family gave to me: not to let what is happening to those who come back happen to me. I saw what was happening and I have tried to use my energy in other things, in sports, and up to now I have influenced the others not to drink as well. I don't smoke, and since I've been here there have been two or three who have stopped smoking, and they don't drink as much either. Sometimes there are fights, but not very often, and what I have seen of those who come here from San Juan is that they come to work.

When I lived in Guadalajara I was one of the people who followed the rhythm of life in Mexico, working a little but not always steadily, and spending whatever I made on things that didn't add up—dances and beer. I didn't help my family. But I have changed. And others have changed too.

Here it is very, very different.

Augustin wasn't able to achieve his dream of returning for Mexico '86. He is still working in Los Angeles.

MARTHA VASQUEZ DE GOMEZ
Housewife
Guadalajara, Mexico

As the oldest daughter in a rural family of ten children, Martha Vasquez de Gomez has managed the workings of a household since the age of seven and pays scant attention to the soap opera novellas and gossip that occupy the time of her friends and relatives. She knows what she wants and learns what must be done to obtain it. She is lista, *prepared. Not grasping or an opportunist, she is a hard worker with the awareness and discipline to not waste her time on things that will not benefit her family.*

Though distinctly middle-class in dress, views, and ambitions, she, her husband, and their three young sons cannot yet afford to move from their small home in a working-class barrio of Guadalajara.

The house is typical: ten feet wide, with rooms lined up Indian-file for forty feet. It is built directly against others like it on three sides so that only windows at the front let in light. Midway back, between the living room and bedroom, is the dining room and kitchen. The sharp aroma of roasting chilies dances through the house as she prepares shrimp a la diabla *and chats through the curtain that separates her tiny kitchen from the dining room.*

I was sixteen when I passed the first time. That was in 1973. I had a passport, it was a contraband passport, so I passed easily. My aunt's friend had a job for me there. She explained to my father and asked if he would let me go. He was very ill, I knew he was dying, but he agreed because the money would help with his doctor bills. And I wanted to go. I was curious as to what it would be like, but I never was afraid.

My aunt's neighbor took me by bus to a friend of hers in San Antonio, Texas. But when the woman saw me she thought I was too young to be able to do the work. She said she would find other work for me. It was with a family with two children of six and eight years. It wasn't hard because they spoke both English and Spanish. The mother was pregnant, and I helped her clean house and take care of the children. Although I had Sundays off, I didn't have anywhere to go, so I usually worked that day too.

I didn't like to go out with them because all their friends were Chicano, you know, they were born there, but their parents are Mexican. They were nice enough, they never really talked to me. But you know even though they are the same as I am, I knew they thought they were better.

So when I had time off I would go out walking. I walked a lot. I went to stores and ate hamburgers for diversion. I wasn't sad; I really liked it. The only bad thing was that it was so hot. Oh, you can't believe how hot it was. Sometimes I had to bathe six times a day. But, I wasn't sad at all. I didn't miss anything, not even my friends, only my papa.

My pay was $13 a week plus room and board, and I sent all of it home to help my papa. I was worried that he would die and I wouldn't be there, so when my Tita [grandmother] called to tell me he was gravely ill, I returned. It was the twenty-third of December when I arrived home, and although I was happy to come back for my papa, I didn't have my fill of the United States.

Someday I will go again. We want to take the children and I save money, but then something always comes up.

Martha Vasquez married a city boy. Their house belongs to his parents, who live around the corner. Though her in-laws were unhappy that their son had married beneath his class, her mastery over the essentials of being an ideal mother, household manager, and wife to their son eventually won them over.

DON BENJAMIN REAL
Billiard Parlor Owner
San Juan, Mexico

Around ten o'clock each morning Don Benjamin Real swings back the double doors to the old adobe part of his three-room house, revealing four billiard tables in the large, dim space. He switches on the fluorescent tubes that hang over each table and the village vagos *begin to drift in. Soon each table is occupied; the players, all young, are laughing and chiding. A young boy sells beer, soft drinks, and snacks from behind the bar.*

Don Benjamin takes his place with the older men, watching, nursing beers, and talking with one another. At seventy-four, he wears two days of white beard with grace, and speaks with a formality and courtesy that is slipping away from pueblo life as television and work on the outside become the norm.

The last time I went was the day of the Fiesta of Independence, eleven years ago. I was drinking during the fiesta and discharged my pistol. I thought I was only shooting into the sky, but one of the bullets hit Don Justino in the leg. He was coming up the street a block away, down there by Simon's house. It was an accident, but the only honorable thing to do was to pay his hospital bill, and well, I didn't have the money. So, the next day I left for the United States.

Five months later when I returned to the pueblo I paid Don Justino's expenses and still had a little left. That's when I started the billiards. My son had bought a table when he returned from the United States. Since then we've added the other three.

I have been to the United States to work eight times. Five of my eleven children are there. My four sons have lived there a long time. They're established. I don't think they'll ever come back to live in the pueblo.

Two of Don Benjamin's grandsons returned from the United States this year. Both had been killed, one at the hand of another man, the other in an auto

45

accident. Don Benjamin buried them with their ancestors in the campo santo, *which goes back beyond written records to the time of the conquistadores.*

PATRICIA RUIZ CALDERON
Job Seeker
Tijuana, Mexico

This is Aeromexico's Guadalajara-Tijuana morning flight 182. The pilot informs the cabin that the Pacific coastline can be seen from the left side. A young woman in the middle seat stretches over her seatmate to look out the window. She is pretty, dressed in tight jeans, a sweater, and high heels. A modest gold cross on a chain and small pierced earrings are her only jewelry. With a comment of frustration at not being able to see anything, Patricia Ruiz Calderon and her seatmate strike up a conversation. She says she is on her way to visit friends in San Ysidro, but as the conversation warms, little by little the real story comes out.

Can you imagine, yesterday they played "Las Golindrinas" all day to make me sad about leaving? Of course I was sad, and I will never hear that song without thinking of yesterday, but I'm so happy to be going. It is something I had to do. It is the only way. I am the youngest child, and my mother and sister have treated me very unfairly.

When my father was living my life was fine. He always stood up for me. I was eight years old when he died, and after that everything changed. From then on my mother and sister, she's married, have treated me as though I am still eight years old. I'm twenty now, but they don't let me go out or do anything. It's either go to school, go to work, or come home and clean house. They constantly criticize me, but without reason. I always studied hard and truly I did well in school. Then I got a good job. I never disobeyed and was always trustworthy, but they would never give in.

I wasn't allowed to have friends, much less boyfriends. Forget that! I couldn't go anywhere except to work. I did make good friends at my job, and they were all very supportive of me when I told them I had to leave. They gave me the courage.

I tried to show my mother and sister that I was now a woman, not a little girl. Their response was to run me out of the house. They did that twice.

Well, I saved my money. They were very shocked and angry when they found out that I was going to the United States to work.

I feel very bad to leave my friends, and especially to leave my mother under these circumstances, but what else can I do? Of course I'm nervous about going to a strange place and a new job, but I think I'll do fine. Then when I return, in a couple of years, perhaps my family will see me as a different person.

ANA CHAVEZ DE SMITH
Mother/Research Assistant
Albuquerque, New Mexico

Ana grew up in a small pueblo in the state of Michoacán, where educational opportunity extended only to the ninth grade. She wanted desperately to study and learn more, but it seemed impossible. Her father, a sugar mill worker, had seven other children to support, and the one scholarship available to the family went to her older brother. She took a job in the state capital, where serendipitous circumstances brought her together with Michael—or Miguel, as he prefers —a young American scholar studying the Virgin of Guadalupe in Mexico.

A bright, articulate young woman, she is adapting well to a life she couldn't have imagined only a few years ago. Ana, Miguel, and their little girl live in a student apartment complex on the University of New Mexico campus. She has finally found her opportunity for further education and is taking courses in English and preparing for her high school equivalency. Each summer they return to Mexico, where she ably assists in Miguel's anthropological research.

I met Miguel in Morelia. This was September 29, 1984. My boss was hosting *una semana taurino,* an exhibition of bullfight paintings, sculpture, films, and conferences. He had been a novillero apprentice bullfighter when he was young.

Miguel came with *el Maestro Medina* and some other guests from Guadalajara. I had heard them speak of him: "It's likely that this young man will come. Truly he is very knowledgeable about Mexico, and he is a beautiful pianist." So when they arrived I had just returned from an errand and my boss introduced us.

Aside from work I had a very nice friendship with my boss, Ricardo, and his family. So that afternoon they invited me to join them and their guests for *comida* at their house. They had a delicious paella, but I sat out in the kitchen because there were so many people. And really, I felt a little out of place. They called me to come out, but by then I had already eaten, so I just had dessert with them. Miguel was talking about his research on the Virgin of Guadalupe.

After dinner we went to the exhibitions and a film. There was a piano in the theater and they invited Miguel to play. He played very beautifully, a piece called "Pelea de Gallos."

The next day, Sunday, was the bullfight. I had breakfast with them and then went to mass with the girls. All of the men went to the mass in the *plaza de toros* because at twelve noon they always have what they call the *sorteo* wherein the bulls are assigned to each bullfighter. When they returned, Ricardo's oldest son whispered, "Ana, Ana, how old are you?"

"Why do you want to know?"

"It's just that Miguel was asking my papa."

"*Aye*, storyteller!"

"No, it's true, ask him."

When I was in the kitchen rinsing the dishes Miguel came in and offered me a marzipan. Then Ricardo gave us our tickets, and Miguel and I sat with the children. Everyone else sat apart. We spent the time talking about the music, the *pases,* commenting on the *corrida.*

After, they dropped me off. I said good-bye and wished them a safe trip because they were leaving that night for Guadalajara. Miguel took out a Virgin of Guadalupe; he kissed it and gave it to me.

At home, I thought, "Ah, he's such an interesting person. I think he can help me do what I want." I was always wanting to know more, more about the history of Mexico, music, literature, whatever. But I never had much opportunity, or friends who could recommend books or with whom I could talk about these interests. I thought, if I don't call and ask for his help, I won't have his address to write him. So I waited a few minutes, calculating when they would arrive at my boss's house. But when I called, the line was busy. Again I tried. It was still busy. I thought, "Bad luck! This is the last time I will call, the third time." So I dialed.

This time they answered. I asked for Miguel and told him, "Please excuse me for calling. I would like to have your address so I might write to you. I am interested in your friendship." He sounded kind of surprised and he gave me his address. That was it.

Then I sent a short note telling him I hoped he enjoyed his visit and the fiesta and that I was happy to have met him. Really it was no more than a greeting.

Two days after writing, I received a letter saying that in his surprise and nervousness he had forgotten to ask me for my address. He had asked *el Maestro Medina*. I was happy, because in reality I didn't have any friends with whom I could talk or who had the interests that I did. In that I felt very lonely.

On the twelfth of October, yes Saturday, it was a three-day weekend for *Día de la Raza*. As always I arrived at work. But my boss's daughter phoned, "Anita, my mother wants you to please come right away." It was very early in the morning. I was worried; I thought she must be ill.

I opened the door, and: "Come in, come in," as they covered my eyes.

"What's going on?" I turned around and there in the dining room was Miguel. *"Aye!"* I never thought I would see him this soon.

I really didn't know why he had come to visit. He gave me a beautiful book and then asked if I hadn't received the telegram.

"No." It was a surprise.

He asked if he might wait for me until I got off work and then we could go for a walk. I told him, "Sure." But I didn't get off until two in the afternoon, and it was only eight thirty. While I was working, the *señora* came to the office and said, "What do you think, Ana? Miguel didn't just happen to come for a visit."

I said, *"Aye,* I think you're right."

She said, "What do you think?"

"Aye señora, he looks very tall."

At two o'clock he was there waiting for me. We walked for a long way—to the Sanctuary of Guadalupe, all over—and during the walk he proposed. He asked me to be his *novia* [girlfriend]. I told him it seemed very soon for a question like that; I wanted his friendship and that was all. Never had I imagined that he would be interested in me or that I would be interested in him other than as a friend, and a scholarly friend at that.

He plainly told me that he wasn't interested in a friendship. He had a lot of friends in Guadalajara, and he wanted more than just another friend. He wanted something more formal, with a future. I kept insisting that we remain friends. Well, we walked and walked, talking all the time. At the cathedral in the city center, we sat in the park and he asked me to tell him about myself. Again he asked the question. It was girlfriend or nothing. I thought, "Well it won't cost me anything. It may be an opportunity." So when we were almost to the house I said, "Okay."

I told him that the next weekend I would go visit my parents. I remember I was very emotional, I could hardly believe it. I told my mama, "You know the young man I was telling you about, well now he's my *novio.*"

She said, *"Aye,* you're teasing me."

"No, it's true." And then I told her everything and she was very happy.

She said, "Don't you feel odd?"

I told her, "No. I always have told him what I am. If I'm poor, I'm poor. If we live here, this is where we live. What else can we do?"

"But Ana, this young man is so educated, and it's sure he has another type of life."

"But Mama, I told him and he still wanted to be my *novio.* We're not getting married yet; I'm going to get to know him and he's going to get to know me. There's nothing to lose. That's all."

I told him to come every two weeks so that I could visit my parents, but no, he came every week from Guadalajara. We were *novios* for one year.

That February, Miguel asked me to marry him. We thought we knew each other well by then. When you are *novios* you cannot know each other any better in ten years than you can in one.

It's the custom that someone accompanies the *novio*—usually the *novio*'s father comes to ask—but Miguel asked *el Maestro Medina.* He knows Miguel well and was happy to come. It was the fourth of April. I had already told my mama we wanted to get married and when they would come to ask. My parents were in agreement, because my papa thought we were mature and our relationship wasn't capricious.

El Maestro Medina came in a suit to celebrate a special occasion, and when we arrived my father had just come home from his work at the mill. He had worked a double shift, starting at midnight the night before and getting off at four o'clock in the afternoon the next day. So when we arrived my father still had on his dirty work clothes with grease and dirt and was asleep in the hammock. I was hoping—they knew we were coming and that we were bringing *el Maestro Medina,* who had never been to my parents' house. And there was my father. My mother was dressed up and she had prepared a *mole* and *sopa,* but really, my father has always been very informal. I was a little embarrassed.

We set the date for the twelfth of October, a year exactly. It was a Saturday and a very significant date for us, especially for Miguel, because it was the anniversary of the coronation of the Virgin of Guadalupe as the Queen of Mexico.

Miguel's parents and three sisters came from Boise, Idaho. I met them the day before the wedding. We couldn't say anything because they didn't speak Spanish and I didn't speak English. Miguel had to translate, and he had to explain everything to his parents because they aren't Catholic. He was nervous. The priest who married us was a very good friend of Miguel's, actually his professor in the history of the Virgin of Guadalupe. Miguel had selected the music. We had godparents, and a friend of mine was the *madrina* [godmother] of the rice.

Afterwards, because we didn't have a fiesta, we all gathered to eat at a restaurant. We invited everyone. We ate enchiladas and flan. Miguel's sister went with one of my uncles and brought a mariachi band for a surprise. We danced—everyone—my father, Miguel's mother.

For our honeymoon, we took the *ruta de independencia* to Guanajuato, San Miguel Hidalgo, Dolores Hidalgo, and then on the return through León, a week's vacation. For those days I felt as if I was awake but like I was dreaming, walking on clouds. After, Miguel had to return to school because it wasn't vacation time, and I had to adjust to a new life.

We stayed in Guadalajara less than one year. We had always thought that we would live in Mexico. I never worried about whether we would leave or not. Perhaps underneath I had thought about it, but really it came as a shock. Little by little we began thinking about going to the United States so he could continue studying. Then I found out that I was pregnant. That settled it; we had to make plans rapidly. We went for a week in May to the United States to put in his application for graduate school at the University of New Mexico.

His parents offered for us to stay with them in Boise until the baby was born. So that's what we did. I didn't know them well, but they were very supportive.

The thing I missed most when I came here wasn't my parents—I had lived away from them for a long time—it was the way in which things are done. In Mexico you have more direct contact. In the street, the streets are full of people and the little stands where you can buy things. Here everything is so organized, so strict. I felt very strange.

Then the way people dress, the informality of the dress here. Oh! This was a surprise to me. The first time I came here in May to arrange the papers, I couldn't believe the young women in shorts, almost bikinis, pants all torn at the knees, and these shirts that are falling off the shoulder, the hair sticking straight up in the air. You never see this in Mexico. If you go to school in Mexico you go well dressed, maybe not elegant, but good pants, your shoes polished. You would never go in shorts! You wouldn't even go out on the street in shorts. Shorts are for the beach. Oh, this is what shocked me. I had the idea that it would be different. I thought it would be more relaxed, but I never thought it would be at that level.

When we arrived in Boise, Miguel's sister invited us for a couple of days to Seattle. She is a doctor. But when we went to her house she came out in pajamas and that's what she wore when we went to eat. I couldn't believe that she could go out to eat like that. *Aye!* I never imagined informality to that degree. We arrived and she was living with a young man she presented as her *novio*.

Miguel was always with me. If I was with him it didn't matter where we were, I was secure. He was my anchor. The baby was born in November, the third. She was two weeks late. He was with me in the room the whole time. His parents came with us and stayed the whole night. It took about twelve hours, but I completely lost track of the time. I could see everything in the mirror. Then I heard Miguel say, "It's a boy!"

The doctor said, "No, it's a girl!"

We don't know yet how we are going to educate her, because there are many factors to take into account. Here in the house we live more in a Mexican style. We usually eat *comida* as we would in Mexico. We aren't strict in this, but we listen to Mexican music. We often turn on the Spanish channel, but she likes "Sesame Street" in English.

She is too young to introduce to two ways of life. Right now we think it's important that she learn Spanish very well. She is learning the numbers, the alphabet, songs, and stories. Later she will have many opportunities to learn English. We plan to return to Mexico and really we want her to live in the Mexican experience, how they live there, how they do things. But she will have the opportunity of both sides.

LUIS RODOLFO DOMINGUEZ PEREZ
Semipro Soccer Player
Loveland, Colorado

If diplomatic skills are inherent, Luis is a born ambassador. He's one of those people who could make friends anywhere. Maybe because he was nurtured by so many sisters, or more likely, that he had to get along with them all, his friendliness and enthusiasm immediately captivate people's hearts. Luis has managed to combine the open, energetic, get-ahead style of young Americans with the formal, deeply emotional, muy caballero mexicano.

I have nine sisters, I'm the only boy. From the time I could remember I always helped my dad, working, since I was about seven years old. He told me it was part of my responsibilities since he happened to have too many women at the house.

We used to start school around seven-thirty in the morning and get out at two o'clock in the afternoon. From there I would take a bus to my dad's job. He had a shop that repairs clutch equipment and things like that. I would change clothes and work until eight o'clock at night. Then I would do my homework. As soon as I did my homework it was time for bed. I didn't really have much time playing like other kids did. I went through elementary school like that. I cleaned parts, swept the floor, mopped, sorted parts, things like that. We worked Saturdays too. It was always the same thing, working all the time.

By the time I was fourteen or fifteen, I was more mature. That's when I started to get the heat. He wanted to teach me how to be a man. You know how parents do with kids, man to man, harder, more responsibility. He let me do more things where I had to be responsible, and if I screwed up I was in big trouble. I didn't get paid, I didn't have a salary. He didn't say, "This is your paycheck" or nothin' like that. It was just, "What do you need?" So he would give me some for the movies, or give me some for shoes, but I never had any extra money, any money in my pocket.

Also, see, I always went from school to work. So I would eat just junk food—tacos or *tortas en un puesto* or *chicharrones*. He went home to have dinner with everybody but I wasn't part of that. He actually didn't trust the people working for him, so I was there to take care of the other guys and see they didn't steal money and tools—it's very common there.

Sundays, that's the only day I can recall having dinner with the family. Then it was nice. Sometimes on Saturday, he would give me a break. It was just sort of like a reward. He could see me working all these days real hard, and I could get off early on Saturday and spend time with my friends. I thought it was pretty good.

Everything was for my sisters. Like I say, he had always been hard, calling me down, just making sure. At that time I didn't understand why he was doing this. I always thought my dad was a jerk. "Man, he's a big jerk! This is not right."

I went only one year to *la prepa,* which is high school. I was a fairly smart kid when it came to grades. I was doing pretty good. But then I was put in a position where I had to make a big decision. It was my own decision, nobody pushed me.

My dad says, "How do you like school?"

"I like school, it's pretty good. I like it."

He says, "I'm starting to need a person full-time because things are doing much better, and you know I want you to be able to run my business."

So my dad did want me to go to school, but then again he felt it was not wrong for me to get out of school and help him. My dad used to tell me, "This is your business, if you make it work it's yours. I'll give it to you and you make whatever you want." So for me school was nice, but I could be my own boss. Still, I was not paid.

Even then I didn't know my future was going to end up in a foreign country away from home. Because my family is always . . . it's just a great family. Now that I see it as a grownup, I think it's the greatest. I know everybody will say that for their own family.

We were very close; then it happened that we had a major, major problem. One of my sisters got pregnant. It was an accident for her. She was older, she was eighteen. I was sixteen and a half. When this happened, when that happens in Mexico it is something that is really, really a disaster for a family, and that is what it was.

So my dad started acting like a big . . . you know how most males in Mexico are, macho types that just want to show that they're the boss. I guess that was the only way he could handle it. He was just doing what he thought was right. Nobody tells you how to handle those things, you just learn as you experience it. And the culture is different.

So the first thing he says is, "I don't want her in my house. She's just not going to stay here. It's a disgrace for the family. She can do whatever she wants, but I don't want her anymore."

All this time he was treating my family really rude with a lot of aggression, being very dirty-mouthed. I mean he was just pretty much bad. And I was just saying to myself, this is not right. I mean, here we're trying to set an example of not cussing in front of people, of not doing these things in front of people, not being mean like this with other people, and here all these things he was doing right in front of my little sisters. So I just thought it was wrong.

Well, then I told my dad. I felt sorta like I had some right because I had been working my butt off for him since I was a kid. I felt like I should say something. I said, "Dad, you know I think that's very wrong what we're doing here. I think you're just being too rough with my family."

Then all of a sudden he turns around and says, "Who do you think you are? Who do you think you are telling me that kind of stuff?"

I was really upset. I was about the same size as my dad at that time, and I was really upset because he didn't listen to what I said. He was calling my mom all kinds of names. I was sticking up for my sister and for my family that was going through all this hell, that's what it was, hell. He would not come home to eat, he would not talk to anybody. It was just like we didn't have a dad. Suddenly, we just had a mom and she was always crying.

That actually broke the ice between me and my dad. So he pushed me. I fell back on the chair, and the coffee spilled all over the table. Boy I was burned. You know, you never do this—I think I'm probably the only one in Mexican history, I don't know—but I got up and I started yelling at him with the same words that he was using on my family.

I started to say the same thing and then I said, "You think you're such a macho type, look at yourself, you try to say things loud so people hear you and they can think you're big macho. Why don'tcha come outside and let's have a round." Actually I challenged him. Well, he took it!

He said, "You little———," things like that and he comes out the front door. I had been going to karate and I was pretty good at it. He comes out in the front and there are the neighbors because there's this big commotion. They were just nosey. And I hit him in the face. Really hard with my fist. And I turn around and jump real high and kick him in the face. Boom, really hard. I'm not proud of it, but that's the way I felt. It's like somebody had to do something.

Now I was going to get killed if I ever got caught. If my dad would have grabbed me, I knew I was dead. But all my dad did was, he just looked at me straight in the eye, he didn't do anything, he didn't say anything. He just turned around. He didn't slam the door. He closed it, really slowly. From then on it was just like Whoa! what happened? Here I am standing there. Wait a second—this is wrong. What did I do? But I wasn't saying I'm going in to apologize, because I knew, as soon as I walked in, boy I was history!

At that time my dad had a second business. It's just over in the state of Jalisco. He had one business in León and this other in Lagos de Moreno, Jalisco, which is the one I was operating. "Now what can I do?" I had to go to work, I had the keys and everything, but I didn't have a lunch because I didn't take anything with me. I couldn't go home.

I was walking to take the bus and all of a sudden he comes up in his car and says, "Here, let's go, I'll give you a ride to the bus station." He didn't talk to me bad. He didn't say anything. I was still really upset, so you know I took advantage. I called him down more. Because he was being really nice I just called him down, as many names as I could. I mean, we're talking mouthing off. You don't do that. I don't care what country you're from, you don't do that, but especially in Mexico.

So here I find myself; "What am I going to do?" I went home and talked to my mom.

"I saw you, I opened the window and I was watching what you did. It was really bad. I don't know what your dad is going to do, but I know we're all going to pay for it, I know." She was afraid of him, you know the macho type. He was just a violent person, so everybody was afraid of him.

She says, "You got to go and open the store. Why don't you go and do what you have to do and think about it." So I opened the store. I thought about it and thought about it. Well, there's just no way I'm going home. This is it for me. That night I didn't go home.

At that time I had been going out with Lisa, who is now my wife. She used to come every summer to visit her relatives. It was summertime and she happened to be there. She knew everything that was happening and she was worried. She said, "Have you ever thought of the United States?" That was the first word of the United States that ever came to me. Me, the United States? What am I going to do over there? I don't know how to speak English. Well if that's the worst thing, I'll probably do pretty good. I was ready to go.

At that time all the values, all the responsibilities, all the things my dad taught me I took for granted.

I sold all the stuff that I had. I had $395 and my mom paid for my passport. I had decided, Okay, let's go to the United States. I was not thinking of staying, just going to see what it was like. My dad had worked in the United States. He always said, "The people in the United States are really nice people as long as you don't get into politics. If you do what they tell you, you can go anywhere you want to."

Lisa's dad came to pick her up, so I drove with them to the border. I had my passport and a four-month visa, but when I got to the border they say, "You can't cross because you need this certain paper." This is what the American immigration said. Here I am at the border, El Paso. I show them my passport and they say you can't come.

The guy says, "Just a minute, there'll be an officer to take Luis back through the tunnel to Mexico. You can cross when you come back with the paper." You know, like most Americans, being polite, not rude or anything, just polite.

So we waited. There was no policeman or immigration person to take me back. My father-in-law saw that. We didn't see anybody for five minutes or so. "Come on, let's go," he says. "Don't say anything, just get in the car." I was shaking already. I thought, whoa, we're breaking the law, and into the United States we went.

But in Alamogordo there's another crossing. Usually the Alamo-gordo office sees you have been approved with a stamp, then they can let you go wherever you want. But we didn't have that stamp. He didn't want to take the chance, so he says, "My brother is going to be coming into Denver in another three weeks, so this is what we're going to do. How much money do you have?" I only had $290 left. And all I had was just a pair of pants, a coat, my shirt, and my toothbrush, no suitcase or anything, just a little plastic bag. Then he said, "Let's go find a motel and leave you there. I'll make some phone calls and get somebody to come pick you up. Don't open the door unless it's somebody that calls your name."

There was a chicken place across from the motel. I was a good customer; for breakfast, lunch, and dinner, all I ate was chicken. So the second day somebody comes to the door and I looked in the little pokey hole and saw my father-in-law. But see it wasn't him, it was his brother. Oh, I'm telling you, even now they look so much alike, it's incredible. I say, "Hi, Roberto!" "No, I'm not Roberto, I'm Roberto's brother." "Wait a second!" But then he says, "I'm going to Loveland next week and I'm going to take you up there. I'm going to take the chance"—this is what he told me— "but it's going to cost you $250." It doesn't matter, $250. I only had $290, so I was going to be left with only forty bucks, which wasn't so bad. He actually paid the motel bill with his money.

So we went to his house, nice house, nice big house, and then he fed me. I was there for three days doing things with his boys. He would take me to town and I got to know a little of El Paso. For me that was exciting. It's just kind of nice to see these nice cars, big buildings, you know.

So he tells me, "My pickup has this seat, you're going to lie down in back of it. I'm going to crush you as much as I can, but I will make sure it doesn't hurt." I was pretty skinny, about 130 pounds. Well I was so skinny that the seat pushed so hard you could hardly see anything. There was only a little gap. I had to ride like that for about an hour and fifteen minutes before he could take me out. I didn't move. It was terrible. Oh man, when I got out everything was hurting.

So we came to Loveland. The first three days all I did was look around. They would take me out, vacationing. And then Lisa's father said, "Luis, there's this guy who wants some help in construction. They pay you $4 an hour." That's pretty good. All right! I worked with him for about two months. It went by in no time. I was making some money, so I got my cash built up again. There was no contact with my mom or my dad. My mom must have been going through really rough times.

In six months I had saved $850. I sent my mom $550. I decided to stay as long as I could, to make money to bring it back home. I was always thinking back home.

Then the job was done, they didn't have any more work until spring. I thought I could stay home and help Lisa's mom. I was living in her house. So the second day of being home my father-in-law says, "Luis, Luis, I got a good job for you. All you're going to do is shine shoes and stuff like that. It's a shoe place downtown, Quality Shoe Repair. They're Italians." I got hired and was making $3.50 an hour and working Saturdays. It was nice. I was making this money and all I was doing was shining shoes, cleaning up stuff, keeping things in order, and I was really good at that kind of stuff. And my boss thought I was really good. I worked there for about a year and a half.

The time flew and all of a sudden my father-in-law says, "You know, Luis, it's been over a year and you haven't talked to your dad. Let me tell you something." His dad was from Mexico too. "I had a fight with my dad too. We had a big argument. And I always wanted to go back and apologize, because he was my dad. And by the time I was going to, he died. I don't want that to happen to you. I'm going to Mexico for Christmas. Let's go back. If you want to stay you can, and if you want to come back I'll try to bring you back. It's up to you." So I decided to go. I spent a lot of money on things for my sisters and my mom and dad.

We got to Mexico and I talked to my mom. It was like, oh man, heaven. *"Mi hijo,"* and all that. It was, well, kind of sad. And then she says, "Your dad is upstairs. Why don't you go talk to him." He didn't know I was coming.

So I go up there. I say, "Hi, how are you doing?"

"Fine, how are you." You know, we were talking just like normal people.

"Sit down here." And we started talking and he says, "Man, you know I really missed you. You helped me so much. I have one of your sisters helping me out, but it's just not the same." And then he just started crying. Oh man, that was my dad. My dad, a macho-type person, I'd never seen him cry and all of a sudden he's bawling and I'm bawling. Oh man.

He says, "What do you think? Do you like it over there?"

"Yeh, I like it."

"Do you want to go back?"

"I don't know. I'm still thinking about it." But see, I kept thinking to myself, my dad always said that I was no good.

I stayed there for about two days. We talked to each other. Everything got solved with my sister. Once the baby was born it was all resolved. He didn't go to her wedding. Even now, every time we go to one of my sisters' weddings, that sister always cries. She says, "You know here I see my sisters going up to the altar with my dad. When I got married there was nobody with me." Oh boy, she always has a hard time with that.

My dad had one thing, he was always into English. He would get a book of English and try to read new words. He taught me how to conjugate verbs. Then he always said, "I'd like to see one of my kids be able to speak English." I still didn't know English then. I could understand a little, but I couldn't speak.

So I came back, the same way, illegally, hidden in a truck. I was willing to go through all that. I went back to work at Quality Shoe Repair. I thought, this is nothing. Here I am, all the values, all the things that my dad had taught me. My dad always knew I would succeed and I wanted to be like my dad. I wanted to be successful. I wanted to do something. I wasn't going to do it stuck in the shoe repair making $3.50 an hour. I never got a raise in a year and a half. So I quit. My father-in-law says, "There's another job. You want to take it?" It was working for a nursery. I worked with three other Mexicans and it was kind of nice, working with your own people.

But I felt different. We were a well-educated family. I understood them, I felt good for them, because here they are trying to do something for themselves. I thought, here these guys have a limit, they can only go so far. But I haven't found my limit. I know I can go farther. "I'm going to go to school. I'm going to try to do something."

My father-in-law went to the school district. And I appear using this passport. They don't have a clue whether this is a good passport. So he says, "He wants to go to school." So I got enlisted in Thompson Valley

High School. Lisa was in school too. She was a junior. It took me six months, English every day, special help from one teacher. He went through everything until he knew that I could do it. Then like any other kid, I took English classes, algebra, mechanical drawing. The people in the school were great. They knew where I came from, they knew my English wasn't very good, and man, they just helped me so much. I graduated with a 3.8 and felt really good. I felt like I had accomplished something.

After graduation I got a part-time job at a lumber company. It wasn't about three weeks and the boss said, "Luis, you got yourself a full-time job. I'm going to give you five bucks an hour." I had four guys from Mexico working there, friends of mine, they stocked sheetrock and delivered to houses. And I was sort of the translator. So here I find myself translating for my boss and my guys. I felt important. Then they said, "We're so busy we're going to make another crew and we want you to drive a truck and we want you to deliver stuff." So I worked, I was driving the truck and telling the guys what to do and things like that and we were getting paid really good money. That was the most money I could imagine. At that time construction around the area was pretty good and I was bringing home about $600 a week, that's a big amount of money.

So then I moved out from Lisa's house and got my own apartment. I was on my own. I was hoping that I would go home to Mexico with a big chunk of money. That was my idea.

I worked for another three or four months and then decided. See, I had always got along with Lisa. I said, "I'm going to marry her." My intentions were not to get my papers or anything like that.

I told my parents, "This is the date. Do you want to come? "Sure, we'll come." My dad bought Lisa's dress and my mom bought all the traditional things. They both came to the wedding. It was really neat. My dad saw all the things that I did: I was making $600 a week, I was speaking English, I had a nice little car, my apartment had really nice furniture, I had a nice TV, things that show whether somebody is doing good or not. And everything was paid for.

So my dad says, "Sit down. You know I'm really proud of you." Oh man, I cried. After all these years he didn't tell me until now.

So we got married. I think our baby was conceived that night. Exactly nine months later we had a little boy. So now I can't be thinking of going back. It's like, "Wait a second, now I have a little boy. I can't go back. I have to stay." I've experienced both cultures, both ways of living and there's no way I want my kids to go through that.

Now that we're talking about children, when a woman in Mexico is just about to have a baby, everything is really low profile. They say well the stork is coming, you know, the *cigüeña*. In Mexico when the woman is expecting a baby, the men, they're gone, they're as far as they can go. They just worry about it. Here, I went with Lisa to the Lamaze class and we had the baby together. Here we have modern ideas, going through that, to me it was really worth it. It brought tears to my eyes. Here I'm looking at Lisa and when I saw his little head come out, I'm telling you, it's a different feeling. You have a feeling for the baby. Oh man, you never lose it. I was there with both of my sons. It's the same feeling, even greater, because you experience it twice. To think that I went through this with my mom. All these things just go through your brain like a time machine.

Eventually I got a much better job in sales. I'm assistant sales manager for a drywall department in a lumber company. I've worked there for four years and it's really going well.

In high school I played soccer. It was a club. Rob Buirgy, my chemistry teacher, and I started the whole thing because he knew I could play soccer. When I was sixteen years old I was a recruit in Mexico for a professional team in León, Guanajuato. But then I moved up here.

So then I was asked if I would like to be assistant coach. I coached the JV team. They didn't know my story—not many people do—but because I was from Mexico when I would demonstrate a skill, they would go, "Wow!" You know how American kids get impressed so easily. I was assistant coach for two years, boys and girls.

So then I started relating to different people, teachers, administrators. They knew I had been a student and they seemed to be real proud, because they would say, "You've done very well."

When Rob Buirgy decided to quit, he says, "Okay, the position is going to be open and we're putting it out for interviews."

I had never been interviewed in my life. I see these big guys, ties, you know. "What is your soccer experience?" I tell them. They start looking at each other. I told them I was from Mexico, but I didn't tell them about how I got here or anything like that. "We're looking for a head coach and you're very qualified." I felt like I talked too fast, and everything. But then I got a call, "We're going to hire you as head coach for our program."

Me, head coach!

Right now I'm playing for a semiprofessional team called Denver Comets. They want to have a professional level before the 1994 World Cup that will be held in the United States. I started on the second team, but as of last week I moved to first team. So from now on my goal is to get to the professional level. Professional level here doesn't mean the same as in other sports. They aren't going to pay you a million dollars. But I'm not doing it for money. I want to play the sport.

These people that come here with no education and succeed, they should be really really proud. Because boy, I tell you, I'm proud, but I still know my dad sacrificed so that I could be prepared. That made it easier for me. Most of my advice to my kids came from my dad. I will set my dad as my example.

To finish the story with my dad, right now we're the best buddies. Our dad-and-son relationship is still there, but it's just great. I will remember this when little Luis is older. But see, my dad never experienced that. He just treated the situation in the way he knew how.

One of the things that was funny, but sad too, was when we went to Mexico at Christmas. I told my son Luis, "We're going to see your grandpa. When we get home, you get out and say 'How are you doing, Grandpa?' and give him a kiss and a hug." I told him in English.

So we get there and little Luis says, "Daddy, who is my grandpa?"

"See that guy sitting out there reading a book? That's your grandpa."

So he gets out of the car, goes up and says, "Hi, Grandpa," and then he gives him a big hug and a kiss. Oh, my dad just cried! "Oh, English! What I wanted you to learn and this guy has it already." My dad calls them and speaks to them in English, and all from a book. My dad has such willpower, and actually I got that from him. See, I always tell myself I can do anything I want to. And I can, I really can. And my dad is just like that. Learning English from a book. It's awesome.

A DOS DOLARES LA HORA

Recogido en Los Angeles en 1978

A dos dólares la hora,
Ahorita están pagando,
No será mucho, manito
Pero estamos trabajando.

"La migra" no nos molesta
Cuando estamos trabajando;
Con tarjeta o sin "la mica,"
Aquí mismo nos quedamos.

Cuando el trabajo termina
Entonces viene "la migra,"
De a uno nos van corriendo,
Ay, que suerte tan cochina!

En el verano, otra vez,
Regresamos por trabajo
California nos espera
A dos dólares pagando.

TWO DOLLARS AN HOUR

Collected in Los Angeles in 1978

Right now they're paying
Two dollars an hour;
It isn't much, buddy,
But at least we're working.

When we're working,
The Border Patrol doesn't bother us.
With a green card or without,
Here we will stay.

When the work ends
Is when the Border Patrol comes;
They'll run off everyone,
Oh, what terrible luck!

Then in the summer again,
We'll return to work;
California awaits us
Paying two dollars an hour.

Two Dollars an Hour

THE EMPLOYERS

Czar of the U.S. Food Administration and chairman of major relief bureaus in Europe, Herbert Hoover saved millions of civilians and Allied soldiers from starvation during and after World War I. He cleared distribution bottlenecks and cut through any barrier to boost American agricultural production. With nearly five million young men in uniform by 1918, labor shortages were snarling farmers' attempts to increase output. As Hoover emphasized in a letter to Labor Secretary Felix Frankfurter, he intended to overcome the shortage by bringing even more workers from Mexico. After listing a number of specific restrictions strangling the movement of labor north across the border, he ended by urging, "All these restrictions should be removed, if possible, in the immediate future. We need every bit of this labor that we can get and we need it badly . . . for years to come."

Ten years later, at the onset of the Great Depression and with jobs that had pulled Mexicans north rapidly disappearing, Hoover, by then thirty-first president, judiciously looked the other way as state and local governments deported thousands back across the border.

That one episode is the perfect, even elegant, distillation of the Mexican laborers' affair with los Estados Unidos. *When U.S. industry or agriculture, in peace or war, needs labor they open a door to the south. Be it wide or slightly ajar, even at the side, back, or cellar, secretly or with flags and whistles, Americans always make sure an opening is there when needed.*

American and Mexican analysts cite Mexico's weak economy, and the great difference in living standards between the two countries, as the reason that Mexicans leave their country to work in the United States. Then Americans, unaware of the Mexicans' deep love of their own family, community, and way of living, believe they come only to be American. This is absolutely not the reason a Mexican leaves Mexico. Without exception, they are fiercely Mexican, in the deepest sense that the word culture *can imply, in a sense that doesn't exist among Americans. A Mexican might want many things in* el norte, *but to be anything other than Mexican is not one of them.*

Both economic and cultural explanations for immigration ignore the fact that there is as much a demand for Mexican labor in the United States as there is a supply of it. The jobs are here, open and waiting.

Congress officially recognized this in the Immigration Reform and Control Act of 1986 by severely penalizing employers who knowingly hire illegals. Congress seeks to eliminate the reason to come, eliminate the pull.

But the jobs still exist. The risk is greater for both employer and illegal worker, but the work to be done has not disappeared. So, despite the barriers, most illegals still find jobs. If they can ferret out fraudulent identity papers or an employer who won't look too closely, they simply burrow their way deeper into the underground economy, where no one asks questions or keeps records.

The Immigration and Naturalization Service itself admits to at least tacit complicity. Addressing the fact that as many as 600,000 laborers had dishonestly obtained papers to do farm work in the United States under the 1986 act, Duke Austin, a spokesman for the agency, told the Austin-American Statesman, *"We suspect that there was widespread, huge amounts of fraud." The seasonal agricultural worker program had been given, he said, "very liberal eligibility criteria to ensure that agribusiness had a sufficient pool of available workers." Farmers, especially in the western states, had lobbied Congress hard for those standards.*

U.S.-Mexican relations specialist Wayne A. Cornelius noted that "Like the undocumented workers already here who didn't qualify for amnesty, the new arrivals have not become unemployable in this country because of employer sanctions. . . . It's just that their job options may have been reduced somewhat." Or, as one of the undocumented young men said, "Is it possible to be an illegal illegal?"

There's no surprise then in recent estimates that at any given time, half *of all field hands on California's 82,000 farms, and as much as 20 percent of manufacturing, restaurant, and construction workers are illegal immigrants. Sure, they work for a lot less than other groups, but is that reason enough for employers to risk fines and jail? Perhaps not, but coupled with the other strengths Mexicans bring to a job, the risks for employers seem worth taking. As a Rand Corporation study reports, "They take jobs other groups do not want."* But an even more important report is that of their employers: "Loyal," "hard workers," "fast learners," "enthusiastic," "dependable."*

Given the Mexican workers' performance, the intensity of international competition bearing down on American business, the pressure to keep costs low and productivity high, and continued growth in the U.S. economy, American businessmen and farmers will have a job waiting for any mexicano *ready to work in* el norte.

ROBERT BASCOM
Seed Grower
Sacramento, California

Handsome, impeccably buttoned down in tan chinos and chambray shirt fresh from the laundry, and with a pretty girlfriend on his arm, Robert is the image of a successful young college graduate. Shiny loafers, smooth manicured fingers, and the smell of Brut—he might work in the financial district or Silicon Valley. Instead, he leaves his girlfriend and family for six months of each year to work in the hot dusty fields of the San Joaquin Valley. With the intensity and bravado of youth he holds fast to his views, but beneath the self-assured assertiveness is a young man uneasy with talking about his work. He won't say what seed crop he grows or where he grows it, and Robert Bascom is not his real name.

You're kind of pinning me down, aren't you? Okay, I'll tell you. I grew up on a farm, and then through people I knew in high school I got a job in a seed-growing firm, vegetable seeds. While I was going to college I worked growing seeds in the summer, and when I graduated I was hired full-time doing pretty much the same thing, managing the

*Kevin F. McCarthy and R. Burciaga Valdes, "Current and Future Effects of Mexican Immigration in California," November 1985.

seed crop. So, I was an agriculture major. It's been my career and probably will be part of what I do in the future.

I was sixteen when I began with the vegetable-growing firm and that's when I first worked with Mexicans. I speak Spanish. I learned in school and working.

Now my main job is growing vegetable seed for six months of the year. To my company, what you do the rest of the year is inconsequential because they derive almost all their revenue from what they make in six months. We employ a lot of people because we harvest by hand. We can have up to a hundred people working at one time. Most of the time it's maybe five or six people.

I'm in charge of everything from the beginning to the end. I have to contract the ground, I have to get the services to work on the field, and hire the thinning crews, and the weeding crews, and the harvesting crews, and line up the machinery that I need, make the budget, make the payroll.

I go into an area where I'm the only one there. Nobody is supervising me. They come to look once a week or so. We have to go to an area that has the right climate. That's like in the south [of California] where it's really hot. I live there for six months too. It's like my second home. A lot of people in agriculture do this. They follow the seasons. Take lettuce for instance; it has a season. You start in Huron, then you go to Imperial, then you go to Yuma, then to Santa Maria, and on to Salinas, then back to Huron. It moves in the same cycle every year, every year. People move with the lettuce.

In farm labor in general you need a lot of hard work done, and the Mexicans are the only ones who are going to do it. Like with the Chicano-type people, they can get public assistance and stuff. So the Mexicans seem to be the best source of labor. They're hard workers and willing to work cheap. They don't need as much to live as a white person does, so that amount of money is a lot to them. It will fulfill a lot of needs for them, whereas a white person requires a job with more money and they will always want to go up, go up, you know. The Mexican will stay on the same job for many years, not trying to climb the ladder.

People used to make a lot of money and go home [to Mexico] and buy ranches and things like that. But I don't know, now the trend is to stay here all the time, 'cause things are getting bad in Mexico.

It's difficult to get other people to do this work. In my particular operation, physically, it's very hard. It's very hot, about 100 degrees plus every day. You sweat a lot, you're bent over a lot, it's boring, monotonous, doing the same process over and over and over for hours and hours. It takes a certain mentality. You'll get some white people out there and they just won't come back the next day. They'll call it quits. But once you start working with a group, there are cousins and uncles and brothers you can draw on when you need people.

Money is the motive you've got there. I've done all the jobs that I require these people to do. But for me, I could always say I only had to do it for a little while. Maybe they know that too. Maybe they think that when they get enough money they won't come back. But you know, greed, that's why they do it.

A lot of my workers go back, but it's their vacation. When I was in Mexico, the guys I knew from California weren't doing anything. They didn't want to work for my friend who was growing there because they were only going to make three dollars a day. Well, why should they when they can go back to California and make that in an hour? Why work at all when you go home? So they were lazy.

I live separately by preference. They don't usually live in very good standards. They're trying to save money, so they live a lot of people together. And sometimes there's one place they live, it's called the *gallinero,* "chicken coop" in Spanish. The lady charges them $75 a month. Basically it's just a slum, but she lets them have credit for a while and they have a place to live. The health department would probably close them down in a minute if they could find them. They're in the back of a house.

Do you want to hear about corruption? Some of the illegals are very good and try to do everything correctly. Then others try to totally take advantage of the system. They'll work under several names and collect unemployment under several names or collect from somebody who has gone back to Mexico. Like the guy who was arrested and went to jail under his brother's name. Then he was arrested under his own name, but they never made the connection.

A lot of them totally take advantage of the system. They're not very educated, but don't think their level of intelligence is any lower or any different than anybody else's. It's just that they're not educated. No, I find them very clever. They're enterprising and they can find ways to use physics and stuff, like the fulcrum. They know how to get a lot done with very little [sic] tools. They figure it out. No, I admire them, very clever, fun to work with.

I try to build a good relationship with the people that I want to work for me over and over again. They're illiterate and I try to do as much as I can for them, write letters, read for them, or help them get their license, this and that. I have to babysit all these guys. It's kind of like protecting my investment. I try and help them get legalized; it will be an advantage for me.

But these Mexicans, when they get papers, they're gonna want to move too. They're gonna be the upwardly mobile type. They're gonna go into industry. They're gonna want to make more money, not $3.35 an hour in agriculture. They're gonna want a better job than breaking their back doing this. This is the only thing they can do when they're illegal. It's probably moving up the ladder when they learn English. What's the price? Twenty-one dollars an hour? That's a lot of incentive!

Most of 'em don't collect their taxes, but just recently I heard the Mexicans talking about this tax thing, about getting their taxes back. And now they're all into getting their W2s and getting their taxes back. The group moves as a whole. You know what I mean?

I'm talking about the financial end of it. They buy the new car, they get the insurance and all that because now you have to have insurance to get the car registered. But then they let it lapse because they don't feel like paying the money. They'd rather have a color TV. I'm talking about the illegals. They go for the gadgets. They go for the cars, they go for the house. One guy bought a microwave. Then we have to pay the uninsured motorist premium each month because these people aren't paying their part; they're breaking the law. It doesn't make sense to the Mexican mind to buy insurance. Except my foreman, he insures everything. He's got something to lose. These other guys, they don't have property, they have nothing to lose. But what if they get in an accident? In their system of money—in Mexico—they can buy their innocence. Doesn't that piss you off? That's what pisses me off most about Mexico.

I've been lucky, I've never had a raid. But if I did have a raid at a crucial period it would be devastating. Especially with the new fine. It's a different story now. Everybody's going to hire only documented workers, or apparently documented workers. Just the documents may get better. It's a little more difficult now, but you can get a license or state ID, like, no problem. So it's not going to be that hard to get around the new law. It's just that I can't knowingly hire illegal aliens.

CATHY SOMMER
Restaurant Manager
West Los Angeles, California

Glitzy, bright, colorful, and loud. Waiters in tight-fitting black pants, vests, and starched white shirts with red charro bows at the neck carry trays of icy margaritas. From a booth in the raised section it appears almost choreographed, with waiters and busboys dancing in and about the tables, tubs and trays dramatically poised on one hand, missing one another by inches, all in rhythm to the mariachi music. At the entrance a pretty young woman conducts this ballet, greeting customers, signaling a waiter, conferring with the bartender, totaling tabs, all the while gliding between booths to check on her diners.

The upbeat, flashy atmosphere is a reflection of this young woman with long dark hair and flashing eyes, Cathy Sommer. She took this position after graduating from the University of Colorado with a major in hotel and restaurant management, but she has worked in the food industry since her first job at a local Sizzler.

Here at this restaurant I have forty people in my employ. This is a Mexican restaurant, but I don't think it makes a difference. In some Mexican restaurants they hire Mexicans for the atmosphere, but I would hire them even if I were managing a steakhouse. My head cook has been with us for more than ten years, and 80 percent of the people who work here are his relatives. Whenever I need someone he says, "Oh, well I have a cousin who does this." And that's how I've hired. They don't have to speak English. The only time I get in trouble is if I am hiring a busboy who doesn't speak much English. I run into that sometimes, but I don't have a large turnover, so it doesn't happen frequently. I have a few waitresses who are American and can speak Spanish. But most of my employees are Mexican, and 90 percent of them are undocumented.

They like the job and I am happy with them. That's part of it; the other part is that even if they were unhappy with the job or unhappy with me, they owe a certain loyalty to the family. So if they have to leave and say, go back to Mexico, or if they want to get another job, it takes them a little longer than someone else.

This is a college town and we've had college kids work for us, but our experience has been, especially in the kitchen where we've had whites, blacks, and Mexicans, that the Mexicans are the ones who work hardest and stay with the company longer. Our Hollywood restaurant is all Mexican in the kitchen, and that would never change as far as our owner is concerned because he feels a loyalty from these people. I have never had a white person or a black person ask for a dishwasher, busboy, or cook's position, and I have been with the company for three years. I've just never been approached. I have been approached by people from other countries, Iranians. They were also undocumented. But other than that, nothing.

We pay everyone minimum wage, $3.25 in California for restaurant workers. The other day we had a dishwasher who is not from this family and we started him at $3.50 because he's been out of work for three months and we felt sorry for him. He has a wife and child here, so he's grateful to have work, because he was fired. I don't remember the name of the other restaurant, but there was a communication problem or something where he had a toothache and couldn't come to work. They fired him for that. But that's neither here nor there. I didn't have a reference on him, I didn't call the restaurant to find out, and he's done an incredible job for us, just incredible.

Busboys get tips from the waiters, who get tips from the customers. There is a chance for advancement, but they don't stay for that so much as for the family situation. It used to be a very, very popular restaurant. We've been in business for about eleven years and the owners made good money. They used to do $100,000 a month. Now we're doing $60,000, which is a big difference. It's the competition here. It's ridiculous right now. And people don't want to wait anymore, especially in Los Angeles, everything is so quick. You tell people they have a ten-minute wait and they can't handle it. They'll go someplace else. But we have regular customers too; people who know the waiters. They come in and ask for a certain waiter. Five of my best waiters have been working from seven to ten years and have their own clientele.

One of my waiters spoke English when he came here. He was born in Mexico and raised both here and there. He went to high school here and then got this job. The others did not start out speaking English, but they worked their way up from busboys to waiters. I have one man that I just transferred to a waiter position. He's worked for the company for eight years as a busboy, but he's excellent. Excellent! If someone doesn't have an aptitude for languages say, or if he is not real bright and can't pick up English, then he won't advance. But if they're good at what they're doing they'll stay at a place and they'll make good money because the waiters know them. Then too, at this restaurant, because everybody knows everybody and everyone is Mexican, they're treated better as far as sharing tips. Even if the waiter hasn't made any money he'll give the busboy something because he once was a busboy and he knows, "This person is working as hard as I am."

Everyone makes minimum wage except the cooks. Depending on how long they've been with the restaurant, they make more. I have one cook on salary making $1,300 a month. His brother makes $6.75 an hour, but he's paid for eight hours every time he works regardless how long he's at the restaurant. So he's paid $54 a shift. Besides the tips, some of the busboys have other jobs. It used to be in this restaurant you didn't need to have another job, but it's been getting so difficult. The busboys are the ones who are single. It's the waiters, bartenders, and cooks who have families.

I'm not comfortable with the fact that most of my employees are illegal, but after working with them for so many years that's all I've ever encountered. I don't even look.

You could do something else. You could make an effort to go, say, into Watts, into black areas and say, "I'm hiring." You'd have terrible headaches, I'm afraid. Or you could go to high schools. What's the law now? They can work at age fifteen and a half with a certain amount of hours, I believe. But, you need people day and night. What about lunchtime, what about late at night? Then, they can't serve liquor. You would really have to make an effort.

We would definitely have to change our wage scale, because the labor force in the United States is getting older and you're not going to get a reentry woman leaving home to work for minimum wage. But then who knows what it would cost to eat here? As the labor force gets older they will demand benefits. Our salaried employees, full-time cooks, get insurance benefits, but to get them is like pulling teeth. At one point the owner wanted to take all that away. He did cancel the dental insurance.

It's outrageous what my employees put up with. One of my cooks is making $6.75 an hour and had been offered a job someplace else. There have been no raises in a long, long time. At this particular time his wife was pregnant. He said, "Cathy, I don't want to leave, but I don't have insurance here, and rent. . . ." I think he's paying about $500 a month. "If you ask your boss if she could get me insurance I would rather have that than a raise right now." But they wouldn't do it, they wouldn't give him insurance. There's another cook at the other restaurant who's making $6.25 an hour. He's worked the same amount of time.

These two cooks are line cooks; they're right below the head chef. They don't do any ordering or anything, but they are very necessary when you want to turn your tables and you are very busy. You have to have good line cooks. When this cook approached me I called over to the other restaurant to see what the other cook was making. When they told me $6.25, I couldn't believe it. I would never have guessed that. They just won't complain.

A raid. It has never happened to me, but it did happen at a restaurant where I worked about five years ago. I don't know if the owner didn't get along with certain officers or what. I've never been able to get the story. It also happened in Denver once to a friend. He had a fight with a fellow worker. There were bad feelings and the next day there was a raid. Later they found out that the other person had called Immigration.

Someone asked me today if I had ever had a raid. I told him, "Well, this area brings in a lot of money. To start bothering this area wouldn't be very smart." No, I'm really not very worried.

You know, a lot of the Mexicans would immediately go back to Mexico if things were better there. People do not feel comfortable here. They are Mexican, they know they are not American. Many people would love to be married to a U.S. citizen, which would give them a resident alien card and enable them to move back and forth across the border with ease. That would be a goal for about most of the people here. If there were jobs in Mexico, if the economy was good, they would not be here. Home is there.

TOM AND TERRY BELL
Farm Family
Lone Tree, Iowa

Tires sizzle on the summer sun-cooked country road. For miles the white line seems to float as far as the horizon. On either side cornfields, a torpid, heavy green, escort the lethargic wavering line. Asleep. Stop to listen. Even a breath can barely be heard. That's summer in Johnson County, Iowa.

As if the pause button had been released, when we head up the driveway the world comes to life and the story begins. A basketball game is being played out amidst a shifting cast of children and dogs. Everyone uses the back door. The simple single-story ranch-style house is a reflection of Tom and Terry Bell's modesty and spirit.

Handsome, pretty, lean, athletic, and charged with energy, Tom and Terry are the all-American couple. Their values: family, hard work, and fair play. But in the summer of 1989, when they decided to be their brother's keeper, they awoke Johnson County with a start.

TOM: I was born into farming. My father farmed and there's four of us kids. We've stuck together; we all four farm together. We farm about 5,000 acres.

Dad, see, he was not actually a farmer, he worked out to farmers. He was a hired man, for years. Then my grandparents helped him buy the first eighty acres up here. He built it all up from that. Then we came into it and he started all four of us farming. Then the eighties hit.

About 1982, Northrup King built a plant in Lone Tree and they come and wanted to know if I was interested in trying to make a little money detasseling corn.

Most farmers grow commercial corn. Like what you get for your cornflakes and your cornmeal, that's commercial corn. We feed the livestock commercial corn. At one time the corn yield was twenty to thirty bushels per acre, now it's up in the two hundred bushels per acre. To do that they developed hybrids, crossbred the corn to get the better genes.

See, a corn plant pollinates itself. You start with one hybrid male and one hybrid female. They leave the tassels on the male but they take all the tassels off the female. One row of male does the job on all the female, so when they're done, then the next generation is your commercial corn. That's what all the farmers in Iowa and the Midwest plant the next year.

But you need hand labor to pull the tassels off. There are machines to do it, but they can't get 100 percent, and some companies think the machines damage the plant too much. They've got to have the labor. Companies like Northrup King have been looking for ways to get away from detasseling. So far they haven't been able to, because their attempts have produced odd diseases.

So, we're farmers and we grow the corn for Northrup King or other hybrid seed growers. They contract a lot of farmers in the area to grow the corn. But in the contract it says the Northrup King Company will detassel the corn. So I'm not only growing it for them, but I'm contracting to detassel for them, not necessarily on my field, but wherever they put me as a separate entity.

My first experience with it was in 1983. We hired mainly high school kids. Well, the high school kids, you know the telephone was ringing all the time. This guy's mother calling, "You aren't giving my kid enough hours." "My kid's working too many hours." "My kid needs to get off for a ball game." It was just, well . . . when you have a machine out there, if one guy gets off the machine you're up a creek. We got through the year, and for a couple of years we had quite a few high school kids. But it got to where we were advertising more and more and there was less and less interest. You know, McDonald's pays the same and you work in air conditioning.

Then a lady in Muscatine, Margarita, called me. She asked if she could come to work. She came out and man, they did good. I mean, that was my first experience. They weren't really migrants because they were from Muscatine, but they were really good workers.

When we started we really didn't know any of this stuff. I had never been around migrants. We were really not very smart about it because we just sort of assumed that anybody that would be living there in Muscatine would be legal, see. It was only after we got into the season quite a ways that we realized they weren't. One whole crew—like one day I had fifty and the next day I had ten. I said, "Well my gosh, where is everybody?"

"They're in Mexico."

They rounded them up in Muscatine and they shipped them to Mexico. Heck, I didn't know. It come out in the paper, all these people got shipped away and it was my crew!

That's about the time the farming crisis hit, in '85 and '86. We were big and everything come to a screeching halt. Like Dad said, old Reagan he tried to help us but, "When you got a speeding freight train and make it stop immediately, somebody's got to get hurt." Really that's what it amounted to. He just stopped her. He brought the inflation to a halt and man, somebody's gonna get weeded out.

I'll tell you, in 1982 we bought enough seed corn that they sent us all on a cruise, a seven-day cruise. We all went. We're sittin' on this ship and it was our tenth anniversary and Dad made the toast. How did he say that? "It'll be a long time before we'd ever see this again." In the eighties anybody big just got hurt. You could see it coming, but there wasn't much you could do at that point and you just had to wait. See, in 1950 when Dad started farming, corn was two bucks a bushel and you can see, right now it's still two bucks. But that little tractor was $800 and now it's $80,000. You know it's just crazy. We're growing more bushels per acre and growing more acres.

TERRY: We were having financial trouble. I had started working and we had four kids. That was the year I asked Tom if somebody could come out and keep house.

TOM: So along about Christmas Margarita come back out and said she had somebody that needed a place to live. I called my wife at work. I said, "Terry, there's a lady here that's going to live with us and take care of the house."

TERRY: I didn't know if I liked the idea of a stranger moving into the house. Tom was a little apprehensive too. But she came to live with us and we had a great time. She was great. After about six months I was going to file her social security, and she says, "I'm really not legal. I got in a car and came across with some people who were legal and they just never asked." You know, at that point, you're close, you're attached to someone. What do you do? Do you say, "You're out the door"? You just don't do that. She ended up getting married to this older gentleman who is a real good friend.

TOM: I walked her down the aisle.

TERRY: Tom gave her away and I stood up with her. Now she's legal. They come out to see us every week.

TOM: My father, I didn't think I'd ever live to see it. He took her to Omaha to help her get her papers. Of course he's very—well, he don't take too much crap off too many people, but he said before he left Omaha he was wondering if he was a citizen or not. No, he didn't think they treated them very good at all. There was nothing he could do about it. She had entered illegally and somebody was going to make her pay.

TERRY: But since that time we've learned a lot and we realize you have to be really careful. Tom asked the Department of Labor people that very question.

TOM: They were here for about three days altogether and I said, "What concerns me is, in the past I didn't know that people had these falsified documents, just because I'd never dealt in that area I just assumed. They looked great, you know. How could you tell?" He told me that you're not expected to tell, but you're expected to have the paperwork on all of them.

TERRY: Another lady called Tom that same year. That was Lydia. She was a crew leader, and she wanted to talk about working for him the following year. So she and her husband came out. They were such nice people. Tom said, "Well, we'll give it a try and see how it works out." So they came the following year and brought about thirty people. That worked out for them and for us. It was so dependable because they want long hours, whereas the high school kids want to work three, maybe four hours, and that's it.

TOM: Actually detasseling is seven days a week, twenty-four hours a day. We'd be out there at four o'clock in the morning and at midnight we'd still be up. Out of the fields, but we'd be lining up work and schedules for the next day. The corn keeps growing, and when they say, "Go in and detassel this field," they expect you to have it done within a day or two. That's not just a little piece; up here the rows are a mile long. That's really when we began getting people from the south, from Texas. Before we always got people out of Muscatine. But then more and more people from the South began calling us.

TERRY: That was in '87. Since then we've mainly worked with migrants. Like I say, we had plenty of people wanting to work and Tom always enjoyed working with them. So last year we said, Well, they're going to come here to work. Let's try to do this right. We guaranteed

Push-Pull

to house them and $4.00 an hour. We didn't know how we would come out on it.

TOM: But then the seed corn companies had planted double the acres. They made a big push because of the drought in the past years. Also another seed corn company came into the area, Garst. That's why the area was concentrated for this kind of labor this year.

TERRY: I felt like these people should not be expected to come in here and have no place to live. You know, even if we don't pay the best, if we supplied them a place to stay while they were here, that would help. They wouldn't have to worry about electricity, deposits, any of that stuff.

TOM: Actually, we sent them all money. Lydia said a lot of the people didn't have gas money. Some needed an advance, so we sent it to them. I'd say a third of the ones we sent money to, we lost. But that's the risk you take. That's the migrant people. They might change halfway, they might decide to go to Oklahoma. I knew that when I sent it. But there were seed corn companies down there in Texas all year, recruiting in a big way, and we were just trying to get the number of people that we were going to use.

TERRY: So we decided we would house them here. Tom contacted the Department of Health, the Department of Labor, and he talked to the county zoning commissioner. We thought we were set up. Tom told them, "I'm hauling in five trailers here," because we have a big lot back here.

TOM: There were two other places I was going to park trailers, but like Dad said, "You have to have two separate services, you have to have two separate water systems." So I went ahead and put all of them out here at our house.

TERRY: We discussed where we were going to put it too because we have four children. I didn't know the people coming. I'm kind of timid that way and I was a little nervous about having so many people we didn't know live so close. We didn't know. They could have marijuana or whatever.

Still, Lydia brings neighbors she knows back in South Texas. So that put us at ease a little bit. We weren't just getting people that nobody knew.

So the housing—Tom contacted the zoning commissioner again and

81

he said, "There's nothing worse about having ten trailers than there is about having five trailers. The number of trailers isn't going to be any problem. The problem is going to be if people complain, saying you're a nuisance or that type of thing." He just said people might complain. We were thinking that maybe someone out this way might give him a hard time, but we never thought we had any problem with the county. Tom called the state fire marshal and he said, "Make sure they're placed fifteen feet apart."

And Tom says, "I'll put them twenty-five feet apart and we'll have plenty of leeway." Really, we had contacted so many people about it that we thought everything was in order.

Then I was at work one day and the zoning commissioner called me and said, "You need to come in and file for a variance on those trailers."

I told him, "Okay."

He said, "There's a lot of people calling and complaining about it."

Which I mean—look, we don't have close neighbors, it's just us. So, "Well, fine." And I stopped and got the paperwork. It was over the weekend, we were going to get all that in order, and get it back in the following Monday.

TOM: Sunday night he called and said, "Tom, the board of supervisors will be out tomorrow morning."

I said, "Well, what do they want?"

"All I can tell you is that all the arrows are pointing your way."

Then that Monday morning here come the supervisors.

TERRY: This was right when Tom and his brothers were planting corn. At that point these guys are out working almost twenty hours a day.

TOM: We put the 5,000 acres of crops in, my two brothers and I, while this camp was going in. I would be on the tractor planting and on the radio telling Terry to get the anchors for the trailer, and get the anchor drill, and so on.

But anyway, the supervisors come out and I made it a point to be here. Man, they were walking THAT HIGH when they jumped out of the van. They were madder than hell. I mean immediately. I don't know why, they were just red, totally, just furious. That guy jumped up and yelled, "They're here! These trailers are here, just like they sprung up!"

Come to find out the zoning commissioner hadn't told them that he knew anything about it. And it's his job on the line here.

So I didn't say anything that day, Dad nor I either one. We could tell that he had not even told them, because they were screaming, "You had not been in contact with the county, you had not been in contact with anybody!" Screaming. "Put the Goddamn Mexicans in the timber. You're not putting them here. You put them in tents in the timber." They were screaming at the top of their lungs. And all these people running around out here. All my workers, and they were just running. They were hiding, they were so scared they were hiding behind the trees. Why, you would not have believed it.

Here was the zoning commissioner standing there like he knew nothing about it.

They didn't care where these people were going to stay. The man said he didn't give a damn where they stayed, but it was not going to be in Johnson County.

"We have zoning in this county! You can't just put in a trailer court." But for us, this was seasonal. It was never a trailer court. See, the zoning laws also say that they don't have jurisdiction over agricultural pursuits. We didn't think we had to contact the county. Even the zoning commissioner didn't think we had to contact them. That's why he said, "What's the difference, you got five there, you got ten?" A trailer court is commercial, you take income off of it and it would be year-round. This is not set up for year-round. There's no furnaces. The water's all aboveground. It would be impossible to be used for anything other than temporary summer housing. As long as we were following all the state guidelines and that the county knows it, we didn't think we had a problem. But boy, the board of Supervisors they just started jumping up and down screaming.

So we had to meet with the county. Well, first they said they were closing it down. There was no way. They were going to get an injunction. Nobody was going to live here this summer.

We had people on the road. They were on their way from Texas, arriving in that next two weeks. And once those people got wind of the fact that we weren't going to have housing, you know what they did? They jumped in their cars and came up earlier, because they thought we weren't going to hire them at all. They thought if they were here, we would be forced to hire them, we would be obligated. It was just a nightmare.

TERRY: Tom met with the county. How many times did you meet with them?

TOM: With the county? About five or six times. Yes, and finally, oh yes, before the board of supervisors. You bet, and the county attorney. The funny part about it, the zoning commissioner recommended a lawyer to us, privately, quietly. He was the lawyer that wrote the zoning laws. So we went to him and he said, "We're going to have to take it to court. I helped write that law and I know what it said and it doesn't cover agricultural pursuits of this type."

TERRY: Finally Tom's dad told him, "You know, this zoning commissioner has been given plenty of opportunity. He could have told the supervisors privately, not in public, but privately and said, 'Listen, they did contact me. This is what I said, maybe I made a mistake, but this is what I did.'" I told Tom, if I had any respect for anybody it would be somebody that would do that, but to sit by and not say anything . . .

TOM: We went to two meetings and we didn't say anything. I mean we sat there and took all the crap they were throwing at us. Because we kept thinking they would calm down and then we could reason with them, but no. Finally, by the third meeting my dad got personally involved. We took our lawyer too.

That last time I took a lot of migrants and we took the news cameras in there. You know it was crazy. I don't know how it got so crazy. But anyway, Dad stood up and put his hand on old Ben, the commissioner's shoulder. He said, "Now Ben and I have been friends for a long time, but Ben, you were told long before this went in what was going on." He stood up in front of the board and said this, and Ben couldn't deny it. Then the whole thing changed.

TERRY: But by the next week I went to work because I thought things had calmed down. That was a mistake. They started saying, "We're not going to allow this because you're exploiting people." See, they just kept coming up with something every week. Something different. We told them that we had sent disclosure statements to the people in Texas, that they knew how much they were going to make an hour, that they knew how they would be housed, what the conditions would be. But still, they didn't like it that we weren't paying enough per hour. We were paying four dollars.

TOM: I know that four dollars isn't great. But to set up the camp and pay rents, that type of thing, and not know how we were going to come out. We didn't want to guarantee more in Texas than we knew we could do once they got here. Many people ended up making five dollars. You always end up doing that, but you can't guarantee more than that beforehand. Everyone doesn't work the same.

Every week the supervisors come up with some other reason. And it's printed in the paper too: "Tom Bell was exploiting people." How can you say that? I know one of those guys that sits on that Board of Supervisors has a restaurant there in town. What do you think he pays those waitresses an hour? I'm sure it's less than minimum wage, and he doesn't house them.

TERRY: You know what it was. You know what the problem was and so does everyone else. This county does not want migrant workers living in it! That was the problem! Yes.

TOM: Now wait a minute—This was the final straw. See, we did not buy the house and immediate property until last year. Okay, it was cut out, right? It had been surveyed and everything. You know what the county hit us with when we went to the next meeting? "Your little acreage that you bought is illegal."

TERRY: It was recorded in the deeds book in Johnson County. How it was not legal I don't know. Next day they came out in the newspaper and said we have a history of illegal activity. That was after the exploitation charges. The county was aggressively, yes, aggressively trying to make it sound like we were really crooks sitting here. Like Tom said, if we had said, "We're not going to house anybody, we'll just hire them—they can live in their cars or whatever they want when they come," you know we wouldn't have had a problem with the county.

TOM: Over in Donnelson they have the migrants housed in a communal area, no privacy, no family unit.

TERRY: That's why we wanted the trailers.

TOM: I could have bought schoolhouses. I thought about it. There was two here I could have bought. But what do you do with a classroom? With the trailers I figured each family would have a kitchen and shower.

Like the one lady came up here the other night. They were leaving and she thanked us and she said how she enjoyed it. She hoped we could keep the camp because last year they had been in a camp where everybody had one shower, I mean men, women, everybody. Who wants to go take a shower with somebody you don't know? I had that in the army.

TERRY: Now some of these trailers are older. But we went through and painted, put new linoleum, fixed the plumbing and whatever they needed. They were clean, they had their shower and their bath. They had a stove and refrigerator, each family unit. They had tables and chairs and they had beds. They were not beautiful. Tom always did say, yes they are older trailers, but we had them up to state codes. They had to pass the inspections.

TOM: You take Lone Tree, the local town up here. A lady from PROTEUS went with me to one of the supervisors' meetings. PROTEUS is the government agency that helps migrants. Normally workers don't start working the day they come, so they have to have something to get them through that period. PROTEUS offers vouchers of $100 for people who come and don't have anything. I rode back with her and at the grocery store she says, "Let's just stop here and I'll go in." So she says, "Would you be willing to give these people groceries on government vouchers?" Well boy, he got to adding that up, you know that's $10,000 or $15,000 that they were going to guarantee, and that's just the start of it. Our wages here per week were running into the $80,000 to $100,000 range. You know where that money went. I mean those people didn't have time to go anywhere else to get groceries or gas. One day I stopped in at the local gas station and asked them, "Well how you guys doing?"

"Well," he says, "my business has doubled this summer over last year."

And besides which, townspeople are surprised. They expected lots of bad things to happen in the community, but they haven't had one complaint. We had a drunk driver in Iowa City, but we haven't had one complaint to the board. When you figure the percentage, 320 people, in comparison to the general population. That was just the working number, but when you count kids, I bet there must have been 500. A lot of them lived in Muscatine, but we had about a hundred people living right here. We didn't want that many people, but once they were on our doorstep we just found work for them.

They've never had anyone actually apply for a migrant camp in Johnson County. They say they have jurisdiction over it from a mobile home park status. Well hell, they can say whatever they want. They're sitting there, five people and they got the county attorney. The county pays the county attorney. The three days that I hired that lawyer cost me $6,000. They got me right where they want me. So I got to take it to court.

The best thing to do is to try to work something out with the county, and we're willing. But you know it gets to a point. They're wanting only trailers after 1978, trailers of that vintage or newer.

I walked into the Farm Fleet in Iowa City, it's a store where farmers buy scoop shovels and that sort of thing. Of course when all that was at its height you never knew. If someone walked up to me on the street I didn't know if they were going to knock me on my ass or what. You just never knew. So I walked up to the counter and the woman waiting on me said, "Aren't you Tom Bell?"

I said, "Yeh, I'm Tom Bell."

"Well, I think it's wonderful what you've done. That county! My trailer is twenty-seven years old. I'm paying rent on it. I'm living in a trailer park, I'm paying my monthly park fees, and I'm working two jobs and they're both minimum wage." She's telling me all this.

It's like where's the county come off saying you can't have a trailer of a certain age?

TERRY: You can't imagine the problems. My gosh, we had two babies born! Then we had one guy, he was in the field a mile from the road. They had to carry him out. We've got these two-way radios, and they were screaming, "Get the ambulance!" and I thought, my God he's having a heart attack. He was an older man.

I heard Frank on the radio, and he's saying to Lydia, "Trujillo has pain."

I was in another field but I went running over. His pain wasn't up that high, so I knew he wasn't having heart problems, but that man was sweating blood.

He didn't want to go anywhere until his son, who was at the other end of a mile-long field, came back.

We finally get the son, and I'm explaining to the man, "We want these guys to look at you, just try to relax, they'll be here soon." He was scared.

"No, don't call the ambulance."

I tell him, "Well, it's not exactly the ambulance."

But you know what? He had a kidney stone. He passed it on the way to the hospital. Oh, that poor man.

Then one lady passed out, out in the field. Her husband brought her back in and I just happened to see him riding back out on the bus. He yelled out the window, "My wife isn't feeling very well, would you mind checking on her?"

So I checked on her right away. She said she was taking a bath and she felt better. I told her I would be back in a half hour. When I went back I didn't like the way she looked. She could not breathe very well. I said, "Let's just go to the hospital." By the time we got to the hospital, I kept saying, "You tell me, Juanita, if you feel like you're going to pass out." I wanted to know because I had the radio and Tom was going to call First Responders and meet me. We got to the hospital and as we walked through the doors I could feel her go. She just passed out, right there. I did the best I could, but I'm not a medical expert or anything.

She had come here with a bronchial problem. Then she got a sinus infection. See, she had passed out in the field, and that really scares me. You know what those cornfields are like? You could never find anyone. She said she was standing there hanging onto two stalks of corn hoping her husband would come through quickly. That's why we're real careful to make sure there's water on each end and somebody's there counting, making sure that the right number of people are coming through.

There are things that you need that you can't necessarily provide. One lady had mentioned to us that there was going to be daycare over here in Muscatine. So we talked to them early and they were equipped to handle us. Being Johnson County, it's not really in their territory, but they were willing to take it. Tom supplied the bus and they had a driver from Columbus Junction School District that would pick up the kids and take them into Muscatine. Then they brought the kids back at four thirty. But their parents didn't get home till seven o'clock at night.

Then Salvation Army from Johnson County called and said that they would be glad to set up something for Saturday and Sunday and for those hours from four thirty to seven in the evening. It was a big help to the parents. They could stay in the field that much longer and make that much more money. Well, who would pay for that, and Tom said, "Hey, you know for what that would cost, we'd pick that up." That really was going to help everyone.

TOM: Like a little city, that's what it amounts to. I had volleyball set up for them out here, then I had TV and VCR set up for them. I see the TV set's gone.

TERRY: No, Catalina Vasquez put it in her trailer because she was afraid it was going to get broke.

TOM: But anything I put out there I figured if I got it back, I got it back.

We had five automatic washers in the shed there, and clotheslines. They really appreciated that because otherwise they had to go to the laundromat.

TERRY: The thing is, if we set up the camp somewhere else it would be somebody else's problem, the neighbor's or someone. We thought if we set it up here it would be our problem first. We would know what the problems were. The farther away you are the less likely you are going to know you are having problems. Here we know who is pulling in and out. Someplace three miles away we just wouldn't know.

TOM: Then you don't think about paying them, but they want their money. If you give them a check they want to cash it. The bank told us, knowing that we were going to run between $80,000 and $100,000 payroll a week, they didn't want that many people filing through the bank Friday night.

And I needed them in the field. The next day, Saturday, I'd be short a lot of workers, not so much spending it as cashing it. And they would be out a day's work.

TERRY: So Tom tells me we're going to cash their checks for them.

I said, "Oh my gosh. Do you mean we're going to bring between $80,000 and $100,000 into this house and cash checks?" See, everything he suggested at the beginning, I'm going, "Oh no!"

TOM: It worked really well though. My sisters-in-law took care of the payroll. It was on a computer, it just printed the checks out. They had their receipt, just like a business, and they had their check. But we didn't do it here. I did it over about a mile away. Then with each check we put the coordinating amount of cash in an envelope and the workers would sign the check back and we'd stamp it PAID and count the money out right there. They loved it.

TERRY: Last night when we were talking about it, I was telling Tom, for all that has happened, at least I feel good about the kids. They had a great time.

TOM: That's something we didn't look at either. Terry was worried about the people, not knowing the people.

TERRY: I'll tell you what I was worried about. I have a fifteen-year-old daughter, and that's not a good age to have a lot of people you don't know around. I work at the university and I took my three weeks' vacation during the detasselment, but there was a month before that when people started coming in. And I have a nine-year-old daughter. How did I know who we were bringing in here? You know, I was a little bit intimidated until they came. Then I started meeting these people and I could talk amenably with them, I mean enough to get a feel. I tell you what, it wasn't but two days and I wasn't nervous about going to work.

TOM: And all the kids, they went out together. My son was, well, not dating, but he was going to the movies with this very nice girl. She was pretty good looking too, and he's not too happy that she's going back to Texas.

TERRY: But for the kids, for those kids and for our kids I think it was good. The migrant kids when they came in they'd say, "Where are your kids?" I'd say, "They're out detasseling in field number four."

"You mean they're working?" They couldn't believe it.

My kids got to be very good friends with these kids. Just last week Darla says, "Erica's mom's going back to Texas to pick up her little sister. Erica really doesn't want to go, so I thought maybe she would stay with us." So we've inherited a kid for a while. She's going to go to school in Lone Tree and that's going to liven the place up.

On a personal level we had a very good experience, and I think everything will work out financially, too. Tom and his brothers expect to make money detasseling corn, but the risks are still there.

TOM: We put everything that we had into this year. But if the good Lord don't have rain, or we couldn't get our workers, the expense I put out, if I couldn't talk the bank into holding it off for another year, then I would have to take bankruptcy. There would have been no other way.

It's not just our operation. We could go and there'd have to be someone else replace us, because this hybrid seed corn is what every farmer who grows corn will plant next year. Every farmer. To get it requires these workers. So Johnson County may not want them here or someone in Washington may not want them, but the fact of the matter is that these workers are helping farmers like us to put food on the tables in America. And I can assure you this, no one else has come around to offer a hand in their place.

LYDIA CASAREZ
Crew Leader
Lone Tree, Iowa

Lydia sits down at the big kitchen table to talk. There is strength in her quiet voice.

This year everything really changed for our people. When we had to be over there in tomatoes we used to have to stand in line to get a shower after we came in from work. And over here every trailer had its own facilities. So they were real happy about the housing. In other years when we'd come in from work, it would be seven o'clock and we would still be in the shower line at ten thirty or eleven at night. This year nobody had that problem. Everybody was in their own house with their own showers.

The kitchens were better too. Before, we would have to cook two families in one place. There's even been times that we didn't have any place to live. You know, years back we used to have families that would live in their own cars and work out there until somebody would find out and report them. But see, it comes to that point where people want to work and they'll go to work any way they can.

The mothers especially were real happy about the way it worked out. The Salvation [Army] came out here after hours. After the migrant school left the children off, we had someone to take care of them here also. That really helped because we would come in at six thirty or seven at night. They'd still be here till about eight with them. The children were happy. Well, even when we finished work, the Salvation still came for about a week because they were happy with the work and the children liked them so much. It really helped.

Everybody wants to bring more people back next year. Even before going they told us they wanted to bring more of their families up. If they didn't like it they wouldn't even talk about coming back. All of them have made plans to come back next year, so I think they were happy.

The people who thought the workers here were exploited didn't know what they were talking about. They really don't. Because, I mean who's going to spend money before they know you? There's no way. They talked about Tom exploiting migrants, but they wouldn't spend a dollar on anybody they didn't know.

I've been doing this since 1968. My family didn't used to migrate before I got married, and when I got married, you know I was always wondering. When people would say they had been to Nebraska I thought it was the other end of the world. And then when I started migrating with my husband, I liked it. I won't stay back in Texas, regardless. If there's not jobs here, then we'll go somewhere else. And it's the same with my kids. I have a married daughter and she's on the same route. On the *pizca* you will probably have two or three out of a family that will stay back. But most of them get into the habit. You earn the money quick and it's there. Most of us get used to that. It's quick. You come and work hard, but you get the money. If you stay back in Texas it will be just an hourly thing and you'll never progress. There you're always at a certain level all the time. You never can advance.

Out of a family you will have two or three that will actually go for an education and settle down in one place. Like in Texas, anyone who has a job, they won't let go of it. But at my age and education, I will never get a job down there. When they ask what you have done, "Well, this and that. . . ." They will never call you. It's pretty hard. I've been in factories, but I always would rather be out in the field. I don't know, maybe there's others that would like to get out of the migrant stream but I know a lot of them and the moms stay back, but the sons and daughters keep coming up.

Well, I don't know, some people just take that heading, "migrant," and they just think you are the worst person. But to me it's a great thing. You know, you're a migrant, you're free, you're going to live anywhere.

But you're not going to live anywhere if there's not any housing. And I can tell you I've lived in the worst houses.

My husband, Frank's, family were always migrants. He has three brothers who stay in Texas, but he won't stay there. See, his dad used to be a migrant worker. Frank was the oldest, and when his dad died he took over and saw to it that those kids got their schooling, and now his brothers work in Texas. All the children are educated. He put our youngest daughter through college. She's in Muscatine and she works for the government now.

On December 7, 1989, the Board of Supervisors voted not to allow any migrant housing in Johnson County. Tom and Terry Bell vow to fight their decision in Federal Court.

II

PASSAGE

VAMOS A CRUZAR, JULIAN

Allá me están esperando,
Esperando, así dicen;
Si es verdad que allá me esperan
Será verdad lo que dicen.

Dicen que están deportando
A mil braceros por hora;
Aunque tengo mucho miedo
Yo me meteré en la bola.

Cruzar es morir un poco
Dijo el sabio en la frontera;
El sabio tenia razón:
Ellos quieren que me muera.

Vente conmigo Julian,
Iremos al otro lado;
No hay nada peor, Julian,
Que un "mojadito" espantado.

Julian, ya estamos llegando,
Ahorita estamos cruzando.
Será verdad lo que dicen,
Que allá me están esperando?

Juana Valdéz Patino
1978

LET'S CROSS, JULIAN

They are waiting for me there,
Waiting, that's what they say;
If it's true that they are waiting
Then what they say must be true.

They say they are deporting
A thousand braceros an hour;
Even though I'm very fearful,
I'm going with the gang.

To cross is to die a little
Says a sage at the border.
The wise man is right,
They want me to die.

Come with me, Julian,
We'll go to the other side.
There is nothing worse, Julian,
Than a scared wetback.

Julian, we are arriving.
Soon we will cross.
Will it be true what they say,
That they are waiting for me there?

4

To Cross Is to Die a Little

CROSSING THE BORDER

They come from all over Mexico carrying every centavo their families could save or borrow. Hundreds amass at the border every evening, waiting, hoping that tonight will bring them a chance for opportunity and a new life.

January 13, 1986

"Patrol cars will be thicker than flies in a Tijuana meat market," says one of the young men on the church steps. The church is as far from the border as it can be and still be in the city. Only soft light remains from the day when a car pulls up. Two women get out and sit a short distance from the men; quiet conversation continues. Warmth lingers for now; the January air is almost balmy. Moments before dark, another car stops at the curb. The two men walk over and climb into the backseat.

In front, their coyote turns to greet them, then glances back. The women, still sitting, are barely visible through the dim light and dust-caked window as the car pulls away. The coyote is Hector Olivares, nineteen. He humors the driver, who grumbles about something that has accursed his radio. Finally, he tells him, "Just worry about not attracting attention, and follow last night's route."

They cross the sprawl of Tijuana entirely on side streets. Rutted and pocked, these are not the first choice of the police. The big 1968 LTD shudders and lurches, rolling as the driver pilots around vicious potholes, jolting into each miss. Other cars are occasional but menacing as they swerve and dodge past in rumbling, roiling clouds of dust. The car body and frame snap and grate, up and around a switchback, snaking along the crest of a hill. As the car eases to a stop, the two in the backseat are instructed to get out and walk—". . . as if you live here"—to the end of the street, where Hector will meet them.

Far down the hillside, parallel to the street, twelve-foot-high chain-link topped by three strands of barbed wire marks the border. Below the street, houses scatter over the hillside in a jumble, tumbling down to the fence.

At the end of the street the coyote gets out, says a few words to the driver, and puts on a light beige Burberry trench coat. The two on foot arrive just as the car moves away, and they all walk on to Stevie Wonder's "Superstition," booming from the boom box swinging at Hector's side.

Over one block, through a backyard, down the side of a hill, over a fence, down through a culvert, up and across a residential street, to a hillside path where they enter tierra-de-nadie, no-man's-land. Broken into plateaus, it is an easy climb, but it's dark and only Hector, accustomed to this night walk, moves with ease in his red high-top Converses. The last stretch rises steeply for 300 yards.

There, at the crest of the hill, ilegales bunch, silhouetted against the lights of "the other side." Peaceful. A breeze, music playing softly, the hillside and valley behind them carpeted in lights: Tijuana, its jumbled shabbiness masked by night, is quaint, even beautiful.

Ten minutes, and they're up and walking again. Hector leads his pollos [chicks], the illegals, down gullies then up, sometimes straight up, sometimes traversing switchbacks that stitch the steepness. They keep moving until they meet two others of the team. A few words are exchanged, Hector leaves his boom box and coat, and they advance to the next crest. He stops, concentrates on listening, face feeling for the wind. He whistles low. Nothing. He shrugs slightly and tells the others, "We'll wait here for a while."

As the minutes pass, people seep in around them, milling over the hillside. The quiet turns to a low murmur of conversation. Other members of the team bring along their pollos in twos and threes. The women from the church steps arrive; the pollos are now eleven. Tonight they are mostly young to middle-

aged men, from Michoacán and Jalisco. But two are from Guatemala, and two are women. The mood is alegre, *optimistic, and determined.*

One of the women, middle-aged, nicely dressed and coiffed, could be stepping out her door for work. She is a teacher joining her family in New York. Before, she has always been able to get a visa, but this time the U.S. consulate refused. Rather than insist and call attention to herself, she is crossing with a coyote. Though insulted to be crossing in this manner, she maintains her dignity and lends support to the others.

Anger tempers optimism in another knot of people. Two Mexican police officers have robbed a young man of the savings and hope of his family— 30,000 pesos ($75). He acts subdued, but his compañeros *are enraged.*

Starlit picnics, campfires, music, and masses of people scatter over this area called "the soccer field." The migra—*U.S. Border Patrol—have yet to appear. "There they are!" A powerful light switches on in the distance, reaching in great arcs across the nightscape. No one pays much attention, and within a short time its rhythmic sweep becomes part of the festive scene.*

Hector whistles again. This time there is an answer from the hillside below. The team moves its pollos *down, linking up with others. They seat the women 100 feet below, to keep themselves between them and trouble. Chinese food, roast chicken, and soft drinks arrive with one young* coyote, *a handsome Guatemaltecan. Blankets are spread out and the food is shared. Out of pure energy and high jinks, the* coyotes *entertain themselves and the others singing, joking, laughing, wrestling, and yelling.*

"See the lights? That's the airport." Hector points off into the distance. "That's where the rateros *[rats], those who exploit illegals, work. There is an agreement. They don't work here in the 'legitimate' area. If they come here, we put ourselves between them and our* pollos. *We run them off, because bringing people across is our business. Our clients come by recommendation, and we don't get paid until they reach their destination."*

With their plans finalized, Hector can't sit still. He wants to be there when the action begins, so he takes his charges back up the hillside. There are no markers on the mountainside, but they are now in the United States, only a ten-minute walk from San Ysidro. Tonight it will take five hours to get there, but on the plateau between Tijuana and San Ysidro time has no measure.

At nine-fifteen there is a brief flicker on the horizon, then another. The migra *are stirring. Three silhouetted vans file slowly across the night skyline. Disappearing off to the north, they are replaced by a helicopter hovering in continuous concentric circles. The circles enlarge imperceptibly until they cover an adjoining area.*

Little attention is paid to el mosco *["the fly"]. Conversations carry on. Hector and his companions join a group around a fire; they joke about getting their papers and the perfect solution, marrying a* gringa. *By ten-thirty the chain of circles has slipped closer. Not until its lights stare from directly overhead does the helicopter have an effect. Then people slowly fall back before the cacophonous gale of* el mosco's *whipping rotor.*

Suddenly a chorused alarm surges across the hillside. While the crowd has been mesmerized by the racket and powerful light, migra *on horseback have moved up and closed in on a group of sixty or so clustered on a plateau to the southwest. In moments they are caught. Mounted officers herd them toward empty vans. Hector and his charges join the throng scattering toward lower ground, stopping only to whistle; the signal is returned. The rest of the team comes down too. Together, they watch the vans drive away. The helicopter leaves and a very quiet dark remains.*

Campfires, music, and conversations slowly rekindle. The blanket is spread once more and Hector, after giving his coat to one of the women, stretches out for a nap. Two others of the team crowd on. It is twelve-thirty; the excitement has consumed a large chunk of the night.

Peering out into the darkness, the pollos *stir. Another light has appeared, a small one, working its way up the hillside. A* coyote *glances but doesn't acknowledge the erratic point jiggling, zagging, stopping, then moving up again. Only when the light reaches the group's edge does it reveal two boys, maybe eight and eleven years old. With big smiles, they don't say a word. Hector orders: "Eleven," and fishes money out of his pocket. The older boy begins pouring* canela—cinnamon tea—*out of a plastic thermos into styrofoam cups. With or without? The younger carries a bottle of straight alcohol.*

Another half-hour and two coyotes *head out alone. Within minutes comes the signal, low but clear. Everyone is gathered, a few words are exchanged, and the* coyotes *separate with their* pollitos *exuberantly heading back to the big plateau. The whistle. Up and ahead it is returned. Hector holds back. Then the whistle again, and they move quickly across the plateau. Strategy takes them to the western edge running, crouching in the scrub, then running again. Hector leads, his followers spaced behind. At the crest, the big light sweeps back and forth. Below, the illuminated signs of San Ysidro read clearly: Jack-in-the-Box, Immigration Consultant, Travelodge.*

Again the signal. They traverse the hillside, angling down to the north.

As the slope flattens, they dive on their bellies, each behind a clump of scrub. The evening-damp earth smells good; gulping air, they catch their breaths. Unseen movement rustles all around.

An alert from the darkness ahead and they're up and running; low, down the final slope, across the flat, toward a siding of railroad cars blocked out against the lights of San Ysidro.

Now they huddle behind the trucks of a boxcar. The final push has taken less than five minutes. Behind, movement and voices scatter down the hill. When their breathing has quieted and the way ahead is clear, they cross the tracks and a vacant lot at a dead run, slowing abruptly to a self-conscious walk at the street. They stop for a signal change, cross, separate, and walk north three blocks. Hector steps into a small all-night market, buys sodas, and catches up to the others just as they reach the corner. There, the three turn on to a residential street. In the middle of the block, through a wooden gate, they arrive at the safe house.

Some guess that 1,500 illegals pass here, at Tijuana, on any given night. Some guess that 90 percent of all illegal crossings occur here. Some guess there are four to twelve million illegals in the United States, but no one is certain. Educated guesses are based on other guesses. The quest for certainty turns guesses into estimates presented by "experts" in articles, books, and congressional hearings, which turn them into facts. But each expert has a different view, a different interpretation, a different set of calculations depending on the position taken or defended.

There are no reliable bases for any of these numbers. The Border Patrol can give numbers of illegals they catch, but some are caught and released two or three times in a matter of hours. Others, who cross frequently, are illegal, but not immigrants. They live and work in the border towns of Mexico. But by the frequency of their presence at the border, they are often detained and counted in illegal immigrant tallies. Those who return to Mexico are never counted.

One thing is agreed: there are many. It is difficult to find a family in the pueblos of central Mexico that doesn't have members who are, have been, or are soon going to be in the United States. The Mexican film industry provides an interesting indicator. In recent years, 35 percent of all production has been devoted to movies with an illegal immigrant theme. These are made for distribution in border states.

Beneath the illusion created by numbers, two facts about the border have real significance. The first: bringing people across is a major service industry with juicy profits for both countries. The second: the simple fact is that everyone who wants to cross, does. They may be caught, but if they persist they will succeed.

Of those who cross the border, most will stay for a short time to see what it is all about, make a little money, and return to their pueblos. Some will return cyclically, generally timed to the harvest season. A few, particularly those successful in large cities, may remain for many years, perhaps permanently.

MARÍA MEDINA DE LOPEZ
Daughter of María de Jesús and Maclovio Medina*
Housewife
Compton, California

Southern California's suburban slums have always been deceptively palmy. Here on a sunbaked street in Compton, small indistinguishable houses are set in identical lawns, dried to the same golden brown, and enclosed in chain-link right at the sidewalk. The inhabitants are mostly black and mostly on welfare, though a scattering of immigrant Asians and Latinos have recently moved in. Only a few elderly of the previous Hispanic community remain.

Behind one exceptionally maintained home, centered in the backyard, sits a vintage house trailer. What had been sleek streamlining in the fifties now gives the unmistakable impression of an inverted bathtub. Inside, through an almost aircraft styled door, the interior is cozy and immaculate. The seating, table, counters, cabinets, all in their allotted spaces, are fitted out in varnished wood. The feeling is nautical except for the small potted plants that crowd each sill and ledge. This is the home of María, age twenty-six. She lives here with her husband and small son, Freddie.

María brings out soft drinks and begins cutting fruit, preparing food, just as she would for guests in her adobe home in the pueblo. Roundedness describes her. She has a true moon face, a full rounded smile, and a rounded melodious voice. She is very pretty, very Mexican. María finishes the fruit, dries her hands, and brings the platter to the table.

Where should I begin? My husband, Frederico, called me in Guadalajara from Los Angeles. He asked if I wanted to come. See, I wanted to, but

*See chapter 1.

104

he didn't want me to because it's very dangerous to cross the border. But, I missed him so much, and well, we agreed that I would come.

So, I went to Tijuana. I went with my papa and mama and Freddie, my baby. We took a hotel, and the woman who was going to take us across came to where we were. First she took Freddie. If I knew then, I would have kept him. I told the woman that she was to take Freddie to his father; if not, I wouldn't have her take him. The woman said yes, but she lied to me. She told me that she would cross in a little while.

That day I called Frederico on the phone from Tijuana and he said no, they hadn't brought the baby and the woman who took him hadn't called.

The woman was a friend of Frederico's friend. Well, his friend had confidence in her. I thought the woman would be more responsible but she lied to me. I was mortified from the beginning because the baby was crying and crying when she took him from me. My mother and father also began to cry. No, now I was very worried.

The next day I called Frederico again. "No," he said, "the woman hasn't brought him." I cried and cried. I wanted to cross however I could, by whatever means. I didn't care about anything but finding my baby. They didn't tell us where they would have him and I didn't know. Aye, yes, I was very afraid because I heard talk about women who cross children and then sell them. They sell them to people who can't have children.

The next day I talked to Frederico again on the telephone. I told him to call the woman and ask her where she had the baby. I told him to go there himself because I was very worried. He said he would.

Then, another *coyote* came for me. He came to the hotel where we were staying. There were two other women and a young girl. They had been there eight days and couldn't cross. They had been caught and returned, who knows how many times. I felt that by comparison I was in heaven, because here I was and I had my mama and papa and other relatives. If for one reason or another I couldn't pass, they could bring me back my baby and we could return to my pueblo. These poor women didn't have even five pesos. They had thrown them down the telephone calling their husbands who were over there. And now, they didn't have any money, not even to call again, nothing.

We were told to leave all the things we had brought with us. I said,

"Well, I don't have anything of value." And the money, except for a little, I had left with my mother. So I left my bag, a small one.

Then from seven o'clock in the morning, for four hours, we walked. They brought us walking, just walking and walking and walking all through and around Tijuana, around and around. It was pure dust and dirt. We were scratched by scrub and sticks, and we waded through water and mud. The *coyote* wasn't the woman who had taken Freddie. This was a man. I think the woman was supposed to be waiting for us on the other side and he was to bring us across. So the man told us, "We are going to pass now." Well, I don't know. Surely the man thought he was going to pass us, but he said, "If something happens, remember we are all going together, I'm not taking you across." When we were almost to San Ysidro, they caught us. The immigration arrived. Well, who knows, the *coyote* had to stay. I think they must have caught him at other times. The man became very nervous.

When they caught us they spoke Spanish and asked where we were coming from and our names. That's all. I told them the truth, what my name was and all. Aye, we passed and now they were going to throw us out! So, they locked us up for an hour and a half, then they threw us back into Tijuana, at the border.

I wasn't afraid or anything. My cousin Nico is on the border; he has a booth there. And then I had a little money so if they threw us back I could get a taxi. I could go to his house. But since we were on the border I found his booth. My cousin just stood there looking at me. Then he asked, "Well, what happened? Didn't you cross?"

I told him, "Well, they caught us."

My father was at Nico's house, so I asked him to take us there. We all went, the two women and the little girl too. They were hungry, and by now they were very thirsty. My cousin gave them water. I told them to come with me and I gave them some money. The two women and the poor little girl. She was about ten years old. The poor thing, I felt so sorry for her—she was so thin—and the women too. Eight days, and they were just eating whatever they could find. They came with us, and we went to get my bag from the hotel. That was the last I saw of the women and the little girl. I never knew what happened to them.

I told my cousin that I was going to call Frederico and tell him that if they are going to have me cross like that, then it's just as well I don't pass. No! Walking that much for nothing, and the woman was supposed to come for me. I thought she was going to pass me in a vehicle. I didn't think I was going like that. Then my cousin told me that he knew a woman. She is a woman who passes people. She is a widow in whom he had confidence. He knows her well. He said, "Let's pass by her house."

Well, by now my father and mother were very afraid. They thought it was very bad, right? But I told them that no, nothing happened, they just caught us, locked us up for a little while and then sent us back again. The only thing was walking for four hours for nothing. Well, then my father calmed down a little.

It was Friday. It wasn't until Friday that I knew—Wednesday, Thursday, Friday—yes. I called Frederico and he said, "Look, I have the baby." The baby was crying and he put the telephone up so I could hear. I could hear him crying and I too began to cry. When he went to get Freddie, he said the baby was—like, drugged—like he was stupid. He was never anything like that. I don't know if he was tired from crying or if they gave him something to make him sleep. I don't know. But when the baby saw Frederico, he put his little hands out as if he knew him. But the baby couldn't have known him; he was only a month old when Frederico left us to come here. It had been three days. It was Wednesday at two in the afternoon when they took him, and it wasn't until Friday that Frederico went to get him. I was so angry at Frederico. I told him that it was his fault. I said, "Look, they probably gave him something because the baby isn't like that. He is always very lively. Probably he was crying the whole time and they gave him something."

I told Frederico that I wouldn't go with that *ratera,* now that she wouldn't even show her face. One doesn't know. Me, I didn't trust her. I told him that my cousin was going to get me a *coyote,* and now he didn't have to do anything. My father told him that this was someone we could trust. I said, "You don't have to do anything, the only thing you have to have is the money. For certain, I will be there tonight."

About 7:30 in the evening, it was the same day, I was bathing because I was covered with mud. Nico arrived from the border. He said, "Get ready, because at 9:00 P.M. you are going to cross." Now I was happy, I felt sure I was going to pass. He told me not to wear high heels because I would be walking for a while. For a minute I thought, "Oh no, not again!"

Another *coyote,* a man, took me. We went up above on a little hill.

I just had to jump over the fence, about two meters high, then down through a ditch along the fence. The man took me. He took me by the hand pulling me, uphill, then down. Awful. I almost fell, more than once; you can believe it. I wore my mother's shoes, they were flat. My high heels were in my bag, and later another man brought it to me in Los Angeles.

Very quickly we arrived on the other side of the border at a café. The man left me there and told me just to ask for a coffee or a soda. He told me not to be nervous. I was going to go in there and buy something. So, I asked for a soda, they gave it to me, and there I was drinking it in the United States. It's right on the border. The *coyote* had told me that a young man would come shortly with a truck. It would be yellow, he said; "You just go out and he will take you." That's how it was. I didn't even finish the soda. When the truck came I quickly got in. It was very fast, fast. Only five minutes to walk across. It was nothing.

I sat in front just as in any car. The driver began talking to me. Who knows what the man told me; San Juan something . . . yes, San Juan Capistrano. This is where we stopped for gasoline and to call Frederico. He told him, in so much time we would be there. He told me we might have to stop someplace overnight. I was very nervous, being alone, and the man was very young. Oh, I was so afraid. He was from Tijuana. I tried not to be nervous. I talked to him, asking him if he was married, and who knows whatnot. So I talked to him and he talked to me, but nevertheless, I got very nervous when he told me that it was possible we would have to stay someplace. I was praying that nothing would happen to me.

But we didn't have to stop at any point. We arrived at twelve or twelve-thirty at night in the center of Los Angeles. Frederico and my brothers were waiting for me.

When I didn't know about Freddie, I thought, "For what am I doing this?" I also sent the birth certificates for him, Frederico, and my brother, and not one of the birth certificates did the woman give us. She said, no, she didn't bring them, that it was another man. Who knows, we went twice to the woman's house, but we couldn't get anything. When I talked with Frederico, he told me that it wasn't how they had told him it would be. It was very different.

It's very dangerous, not only for women, for men too. They charged

$300 for me and $200 for Freddie, and this *ratera* gave him back naked. I sent him with pants, boots, socks, a shirt, and a cute little jacket that I had just bought him because he was going to see his father. And she gave him back naked with just one sock. Look here, I still have it. That was it. He was also very sick. I think he had been perspiring and they took him out with nothing on. For a long time he sounded as if he had asthma. The next day we took him to the doctor, but he didn't get better. It was just awful.

No, my mother and father didn't leave Tijuana until they knew that we were safely here. My mama said, "No, daughter, we are going to wait until we know that you are with Frederico, because if we go and then you get thrown back again, oh no."

They stayed another week in Tijuana. At the end they called and talked to Frederico. My father told him, "Now we have brought your wife. We are giving you the responsibility, because we are returning."

They had planned to go to La Paz, but instead they returned directly because my papa was very nervous. He had been drinking from the time we left, all along the way. It was because he was so sad. Not so much for me, but for the baby. The baby lived with them since he was born, and my father took him with him everywhere.

Yes, little one, I am going to save this sock so that when you're big you can say, "This is what I wore when I came to the United States."

JUAN DE COMPOSTELA
Jewelry Store Owner
Los Angeles, California

The girl could easily be the ingenue of a television sitcom but instead she has been arrested by the U.S. Immigration and Naturalization Service. A little blond six-year-old in a pink jogging suit, she says, with her front teeth missing, "I put my hands on my head just like the rest. They weren't mean to me or anything, but they didn't give us anything to eat and I'm very hungry." She holds her uncle Juan's hand as they trail her parents and another young man. They're at the tail end of a block-long line of ilegales *being herded back through an inconspicuous gate in the fence separating Mexico and the United States.*

On their side of the fence, a building sculpted of flying concrete contrasts with a solid, ponderous one on the other. Each bridges the thirty lanes of auto and foot traffic and a vast parking area for officials. One houses U.S. Border Patrol operations, the other, its Mexican counterparts. Each is imposing, symbolizing a nation trying to out-declare the other. If a statement must be made, this is the place to make it; more people pass here than any other place along this 2,000-mile border. This is the Tijuana–San Ysidro portal.

In a stream of cars and pedestrians, the apprehended shuffle back toward Tijuana. Her uncle, the obvious leader of this family group, keeps the little girl's spirits up with an animated discussion of where they should eat, ignoring the coyotes *and* rateros *that line their way, barking out their services. "I'll take you across safely." "My services are very cheap, very secure." "With me you'll make it."*

He is her Tio Juan; Juan de Compostela, age twenty-seven.

This is the third time we've tried. So far, we've gone on our own without the services of a *coyote*. We've decided to try seven times, and from there we'll make new plans. We're from Compostela, a little town in the state of Jalisco. In our village there is no work for my brother or sister-in-law, and over there they can both work, and my niece will get a better education.

Now Miguel here, he would like to try his luck too. What he wants is a start, right Miguel? Before you settle down and have a family? The problem is he doesn't have a girlfriend. Maybe he will find a *gringa*.

Myself, I live in Los Angeles. I own a jewelry store downtown on Broadway. I've made this crossing many times; I'm more or less used to it now. You have to learn what to expect. The first time was pure fear. I flew from San Diego to Los Angeles. I had never been on a plane before, but I went like a tourist with my suitcase and sunglasses. I buckled my seat belt like I knew what I was doing, but I was more scared than anything. Then in the Los Angeles airport I got lost. I was supposed to meet my friend at the PSA terminal, but I couldn't find it. Instead I fell in with a group that was departing. Once I realized, I turned around and found the front of the terminal. I bought a pack of cigarettes and a magazine in pure English. I decided it would be best to wait in front and hope my friend would find me. I smoked the entire pack of cigarettes and read for forty-five minutes, but I didn't understand a word. I don't smoke anymore, but if I'm going by myself, I always fly; I guess that's how the United States has changed me.

We crossed over early this morning, but we were picked up at 8:00 A.M. in San Ysidro trying to find a way to Los Angeles. They only held us five and a half hours, but we haven't eaten since yesterday, and we're too hungry to cook. Would you like to join us? We're going to eat at the market.

See that area? Never go into that part of Tijuana. Its six blocks of cantinas and clubs is not safe for a woman. When you want a good, inexpensive meal, go to the *mercado*. You can find one in almost any Mexican town. When you see people here with parched lips and dark circles under their eyes, you know they haven't eaten in at least three days. There are a lot of hungry people in Tijuana.

I go back and forth. For us over there, to go home to our family is food for our spirit and soul. It's very hard over there. One is at the mercy of his employer. Nevertheless, I have had good luck and people have been very good to me. I would work for a North American any day, but never a Chicano. Those are the people you have to look out for. They hate Mexicans and reject their heritage.

Of course, any Mexican would rather be on his own soil, but with our government it's not possible. The presidents come in, you know they are mostly foreigners, that is, they may have been born in Mexico but their parents weren't. Mexico is not in their roots or their hearts. They come into office and see what is left in the pot. Then they borrow, increasing the debt, and leave with at least half the money. They send it to foreign bank accounts. Everyone knows that. All Mexican presidents leave office wealthy; then we are left with a huge foreign debt. The corruption goes down the line, and you can't get a job unless you're related to someone. It's not like the United States. There you're hired because of your skills.

The worst robbers are the Mexican police. For a Mexican the border is worse when you're returning. If you've been in the United States without papers, the Mexican border police will take everything you have to let you back in. They know you can't turn around, and if they won't let you go forward, well, where can you go? No, the only way we'll ever end our problems is with a revolution.

Personally, I can't complain. Like I say, I have my business in Los

Angeles and I go back and forth when I want. Well, we'll rest up now so we can try our luck again tonight.

JULIA GARCIA DE MORALES
Housewife
San Juan

Julia wrote these letters on behalf of her husband, Faustino, who was caught crossing the border and put in jail. She wouldn't see him again until 1980.

12 August 1974

Dear María,

My desire is to find you well and in the company of your family. We are all fine here in Mexico. I hope you will pardon me for sending these lines, but Faustino and the son of Don Alonzo, along with several others, are in jail in San Diego. They have been there for two weeks. Can you tell the officials that you are a relative so they will release them? Write to me. Greetings from Pedro, Felicia, and Rosa. Sonia is going to be the queen at the fiesta.

Your friend who never forgets you,
Julia Garcia

Less than a month later Julia wrote again:

9 September 1974

My esteemed friend, María,

I hope to find you well, in company of your family as are my desires. I am very grateful that you called the jail. Faustino used the name of his brother. He and the others got out of jail on the thirtieth of August and are now in Chicago. Greetings from Pedro and Felicia. She is now a mother-in-law and soon will be a grandmother. Salvador and Rosa also send their greetings.

With the affection of your friend,
Julia Garcia

Julia and two of their children eventually joined her husband in Chicago. (See chapter 8.)

LUPE MACÍAS
Babysitter
Lynwood, California

In a working-class neighborhood of Lynwood, California, along a street of single-family homes, someone has inserted six stucco rental units. They occupy a single lot in a familiar southern California plan, the court: across a narrow central walk, two rows face one another. Each has a token postage-stamp lawn. Sun glares off the gray and beige of concrete and dried grass. Sullen quiet prevails along the walk; eyes peer out from behind screened doors and windows. At the last house on the right the atmosphere suddenly changes. Waves of noise and laughter roll through the door.

Hospitality and warmth are evident from the first beer offered. Continual TV flickers over the children playing on the floor. Several young men watch while they carry on an animated discussion of the previous evening's televised boxing from Mexico City. The peppery smell of chilies, cilantro, onion, and garlic from the kitchen lets everyone know there's fresh salsa with today's tortillas and frijoles. The five rooms are home to Lupe Macías, twenty-eight, her husband, another couple and their two young daughters, eight young men, and a young woman, all cousins from the same pueblo. Carrying the beer and a Coke for herself, Lupe threads her way through the living room full of activity into one of the bedrooms. The walls of the room are hung with bags of sewing, knitting, crocheting, and embroidery projects. The noise is abruptly muted as she closes the door and sits on the bed.

I come in here to do my needlework in the evening while everyone else watches television. They like the lights off and I can't see what I'm doing. Yes, there are a lot of us—all cousins of my husband—but we are all family and there are no problems. I am the only one without a job so I do the cooking, keep things clean, and take care of the little girls. I'm glad that we can be together, I wouldn't like it as much if it were just Benito and I alone. We have this bed and Marta has that one, then Beto, Amalia, and the two girls have the other bedroom. All the men sleep in the living room. They work different times, so there is always someone coming or going out there. No, like I say, we're all relatives so it's almost as if we're in our pueblo.

I have been here almost one year; it will be one year the twenty-first of March. My husband and I left Zacatecas on the sixth of January. When we arrived in Mexicali we stayed with his aunt. Then he went on to Los Angeles and left me there. He wanted me to come up, but I was afraid to go by myself. Then he called again. Again, I was afraid, but oh well, I decided to take the risk.

From Mexicali I went to Tijuana. I had to go alone and you can't imagine how afraid I was. In the bus it was okay. A *señora* sat next to me and we talked. She said Tijuana is different now, now there's no reason to be fearful. She said you just have to watch out that the immigration doesn't grab you at the bus terminal. No, no, I told her, don't frighten me any more than I am.

Well, what could I do? I had already told my husband that I would come, and he had arranged that a friend would come for me. This friend of his had a sister in Tijuana who was waiting for me. I just got off the bus and there she was. She took me to her house and I called my husband to tell him that I had arrived.

I stayed there for about four days waiting. Then a *señora* named Rosa, she's a relative, said, "Come on, let's go! I have a friend who is a *coyota*. She has passed a lot of people. Come on, don't be afraid." I was so nervous. *Aye, Dios mio!* I couldn't have imagined all this.

Finally this *coyota* came. She gave me identification and said, "Look, this identification is yours. You are going to pass through the border, but you can't be at all nervous. No shaking! No dancing! You have to pass as if it were nothing. Just in case they ask you, you will tell them you are going for an errand in San Ysidro." Aye, no!

"Listen, you have two daughters. One's name is Monica, she is thirteen, and your other daughter is six."

I said, "Do you think I am going to remember this?"

"Yes. Now tell me, what is your name?" I was supposed to tell her in English. Well, I forgot. She said, "No, no, don't be nervous."

Aye Dios, I said, "This isn't going to be possible."

"Come on, let's see. What is your name? How many children do you have?" I had to learn this in English. *Dios mio,* I was perspiring with fear. "Listen," she said, "you are going to be carrying a bag because you have an errand. You and your husband work in San Ysidro."

Well, I learned everything and just as soon as I did she said, "Okay, you're ready, let's go." We went right to the line, you know where the people walk across. It was a long line with every sort of person carrying all kinds of things. Many were gringos carrying bags and bags of souvenirs and things they had bought in Mexico. There were a lot of Mexicans too. Well the *señora* told me, "You get in line here and I will go ahead. In the case that you pass, I will be waiting and give you a sign. Then follow me, but a little behind." I wasn't going to talk to her or even look like I knew her.

The line was very slow. After awhile, I could see where they were checking everyone. Oh, no! There was a very fat woman—like this—with her *pistolas. Aye madre mia!* And she was sending back so many people. I went asking the benediction of the little saints. Aye, please don't let her turn out the lights! Well, I just kept in the line and as I came up to where they were checking people there was some kind of disagreement or something. A man was in front of them with his bag open and they had everything out, they were speaking pure English, all of them, and well the fat woman was talking to the man next to her and would you believe, she didn't ask me anything. She just glanced at my card and went back to talking with the other *migra* and off I went. Aye little *Dios,* I passed, I passed!

I went to a store across the street. There were four others who had passed too, and the woman who was going to bring me up. She just said, "Are you the girl I'm supposed to pick up? Well come on." She had to pick up her daughters at school and she had errands, but wherever she went she took me. She even bought me a hamburger, and I came to know San Diego.

Well, there we were at her house. I helped her wash dishes and just waited. I didn't even think about why we were waiting until a young man arrived and said, "Good, you're here. Now you passed once, but you have to pass again."

I screamed, "Aye, no! Don't tell me I have to pass again!" No, what could I do? Just let God do what he wants. The young man's name was Alexander. He could speak pure English. They told me he would leave me in a car near the airport while he went to buy the tickets. Well, we didn't wait. He drove to the airport right then and he parked the car. I could hear planes but I couldn't actually see any except in the air. Well, he told me that we had to be careful because the *migra* is always around there. *Dios mio,* I was very nervous all alone in the car. It was a beautiful car. Well, just a little time passed and he came back. From then on everything happened very quickly.

He left his car and we went in. They told me in English to pass my purse onto this machine. Well I didn't understand what they were saying, but I saw the lady in front of me do it, so I put mine on too. When I saw my purse come out at the other end, I grabbed it. We ran to the plane because they were waiting for us. This Alexander went with me and we were the last ones on.

My husband met us at the airport. This Alexander had to return that same afternoon because he had left his car at the airport in San Diego. He was a North American from San Diego. He pronounced everything perfect.

That was it. I believe my husband paid $500 and the plane fare was included, but now that I was here, I didn't care how much he had to pay. He was the one who wanted me to come, and when he would call on the telephone he would say, "What I want is for you to pass, without problems. I don't want you to pass over the mountains." Later a cousin of my husband's and his wife came. They arrived so dirty because they had to cross in the mountains. It was very difficult for them. No, it's so much fear. You have to take the risk and suffer to get to this side. No, I never imagined how it could be. For me, believe me it was luck. I thanked God that I was able to pass at the line.

JOSÉ VASQUEZ ORDAZ
*Brother of Martha Vasquez de Gomez**
Fisherman
Guadalajara, Mexico

Adolescent males gang one corner of this working-class barrio in Guadalajara, strutting and agitating among themselves. On the next corner is a small

*See chapter 2.

116

two-story structure, inconsequential even in turquoise. Its entry is marked less by the steel door than by a 1958 Hillman Minx at the curb. There are few cars in this neighborhood, but a Hillman is a rare sight anywhere. This one is even more eye catching because over its long life it has lost almost anything that could be removed—bumpers, grille, side glass; a detailed list would be very long. A jalapeño chili can replaces the long-gone gas cap.

Seen through the steel door, the stairway is narrow and, like everything else, painted turquoise and worn. At the top it opens into a small eating area. Here, everything is lighter and freshly painted—a pastel turquoise. Straight ahead in the outdoor kitchen a young woman cooks on two simple burners. A variety of cups hang in an arc over a narrow work surface. The kitchen is open to a cramped service patio cluttered with a tank of cooking gas, plants, a pigeon coop, assorted tools, odd bits of hose, rope, and wire, and a clothesline with a few baby clothes. Across the patio is a single low-ceilinged bedroom for a mother, father, and baby. Two dogs are on the roof. This is the home of José Vasquez Ordaz, thirty-three, his wife Angeles, thirty-two, and their five children.

José is sitting at a table in the large room, teasing the two-year-old with a toy. Shirtless on this hot summer evening, José is stocky with powerful shoulders. He has a wide smile and talks with animated gestures about how he and Angeles completed the new paint job in less than two evenings, and how the Hillman really has a Datsun engine and can only be made to stop running by some combination of brakes and an immovable object while the transmission is in gear. Everyone hoots when he reveals he has named it "El Challenger."

Children come and go, usually touching or hugging their father. He always acknowledges them, even in midsentence. All the while the aroma of Mexican cooking seeps through the room until its promises materialize in a heaping platter of tacos. Reaching between the children, José turns down the volume on "El Chapulín Colorado."

Three times in my life I've tried to cross. The first time was the hardest, I didn't make it. Perhaps I was too young. The second and third times I made it. But the second time, you know, was the best, the most successful.

Hijo de la chinga . . . no, the first time, that was a disaster. My father had been there and I too wanted to have the adventure, and no, I wanted to work. I was not yet eighteen years old. My papa didn't want me to go, he said I was very young. I told him, "If you won't let me go, I'll go anyway." The result was that he said, "Well, then go."

He gave me money, I don't remember how much, but very little at that time. We were seven from the pueblo. There was Luis, Ruben, Cardenas, Chavelo, Juan, Jorge, and myself. The case was, I had just enough for the ticket, but not enough to eat. Oh, the other who went with us was my cousin Pedro; and as we always went around together, we sat together on the bus. The others took money, but he and I didn't have enough; someone had to pay the difference. In the bus all we did was look. At the stops for breakfast or dinner, we didn't even get off.

Well, we arrived in Tijuana and looked for a *coyote* with the intention of not paying him when we got to the other side. We agreed that once we were inside we would run, and if the *coyote* caught us we would say to him, "Do you know what? It would be better if you let us go, because we will tell the *migra* that you brought us across." Can you imagine? We were risking our lives.

In the meantime we were working, making clay figures with a cousin living there. He didn't pay us, he just gave us our meals.

Well, after three days we found a *coyote*. *Hijo,* not even in my dreams did I think it would be like it really was. We were to pass from the *fútbol* stadium. At ten in the evening we were all together waiting. The *coyote* never arrived, but a friend of his came. We asked, "What happened with your friend who was going to take us across?"

He answered, "I don't know, but right now you have a chance to pass."

So I said, "Come on, let's go. *Vámonos muchachos!*"

But no, we were trying to cross and the *migra* were on all sides. They tried to separate us, and they pushed us around. I remember it was in September, the fifteenth of September, when they put us in jail. You know, the day before Mexican Independence. At twelve midnight, we were about 200 Mexicans, we asked the immigration permission to yell the *grito* of independence. They told us, "Well, even though you're not in Mexico, go ahead." They elected Ruben to lead the *grito,* I think because he always dresses well. But when they heard his high voice they said, "No man, no way! With that voice you sound like an old woman." We all yelled the *grito,* "Viva Mexico!"

They kept us in jail until the next day. Then they put us back in

Tijuana. Since this was the first time I had tried and we were treated a little bit bad, I felt morally defeated. We returned to the house of my cousin and worked. But I was thinking of returning home. I thought, "I don't have any reason to stay here. If I go home, I can work on the ranch, and I have my parents there. Here I have no one." The only companion I had was Pedro, because the others weren't really close friends. They had money and went out to eat daily. We had to stay with my cousin. His wife fed us, but with bad feelings. So I returned, hitchhiking. I returned to San Juan thin, dirty, with a beard, no shoes, and no money.

Later, I went again. The second time, that was when my father died. He died of cancer but it was caused by anger. A man in our village let his goats into my father's field and they ate all our garbanzos. My father became very angry, very hot with anger. He came home from the fields that day and with the heat of anger, he drank cold water. That's what caused the cancer. It was only a few months, I don't remember exactly, but a very, very short time until the doctors discovered that he had cancer of the stomach. He lived for Christmas but then died on January 17, 1975.

I was very angry with the *cabrón* who caused his death, and I was afraid I would kill him. At this time, I can truly say that I was crazy. But I had friends, Americans, friends of my family; and when my papa was ill they offered their hospitality if I was ever in the United States.

So, on the seventh of March I left. We went without papers, without money, without anything except the luck to take the food we'd eat on the way. This time we decided to try to cross in Mexicali. So, we went, a companion named Miguel and myself. He was a person who was ignorant about these things. He didn't know anything about cities—nothing. I could tell when we arrived at the bus station that perhaps I had made a mistake in bringing him, but everything went well on the trip.

Once we arrived in Mexicali we walked the streets looking, not knowing what we were going to do or how we were going to cross. Then near the principal market we met a man who knew us. We didn't see him—he just started following us. I knew someone was following and at first I ignored him. But after about three blocks I turned around. "What is it? What's going on?" Then we recognized him. We were so happy. You can imagine, we didn't know anyone. No one. The result was, this man was from San Juan and he was working in Mexicali with his sister, whose name is Luisa. She married someone from Mexicali and they had a fruit stand. He told us to come with him, at least we would have a place to sleep. We were hungry and he let us have some oranges.

The only thing I had was the telephone number of my friend in Los Angeles. I called and told her we had come to visit. I don't think she knew that we were going to pass as "wets," because the next day when she arrived she asked about our papers. I told her we didn't have anything. All of us, including her young son and Luisa and her husband, were sitting in the back of the fruit stand talking about it. All she said was, "Okay, we have to see what we can do."

My friend had a paper that she presented to the *migra;* I don't know what it said. In this moment, when we were there, it was, "Well yes, and well no." She was almost crying with sadness, or maybe it was embarrassment. But the result was, they wouldn't let us pass. The *migra* told us to go to Tijuana to talk to the American consulate there.

Well, we weren't sure where we were going and the officials were busy investigating a car behind us. So we drove off looking for the turn to Tijuana. When we looked up we were in the United States. We said, "We're inside, we're inside!" I don't remember who, but one of us had the idea to stop for a cup of coffee. We had to think of what to do. We stopped at a café right on the edge of the border, near the immigration. You could hear the cup rattling against my teeth. No, it was awful the way we felt, very emotional. When we had our coffee and saw that no one was after us, we looked at each other and that was it. "Let's go, let's go!" And we got on the freeway.

By then it was late. My friend and her son were tired, so we stopped at a hotel for the night. We didn't sleep much for the excitement and the fear that the *migra* would break in at any moment. But the result was, nothing happened.

The next day was beautiful and sunny. Driving along, it seemed like we were meant to be there. The road was long and straight, nothing to either side, just a little up and down. Then, I still remember exactly, coming up over a little hill, ahead on the highway, we saw it. A checkpoint—the *migra* again! Well, we were very far away, but they could clearly see us. There was nothing we could do, so we just kept on. They asked for papers for me and Miguel. Thinking they were going to give us a good one now, I was very quiet. I don't think any of us were breathing. My friend presented the same papers she had the day before. At the border they weren't worth anything, but here they were, because they let us go. I think they thought, "Well, if they let them pass there, then we might as well let them pass too." We drove away, and for about five minutes none of us said a word. My hands were sweating. Then we all screamed—the *grito* of independence. After Indio, I had this feeling that from then on there was nothing to fear.

At first I felt like a young child because I didn't know how to look for work, how to ask, or where to go. Finally, my friend found me a job as a busboy in an Italian restaurant. I worked two days a week for four hours each. They paid me the minimum, something like $2.25 an hour, and I began to work hard because I wanted to earn more. My dream was to make some money, come back, and start a business. Little by little I got more hours and finally a complete shift. Then I got a job there for my friend, Miguel. After being a busboy I became a dishwasher.

Then I made the daughter of my boss my girlfriend. Her name was Linda. I think that my boss thought, "I'm not going to want a dishwasher for a son-in-law," because one day he came to me and said, "Joker." That's what they called me; he was telling me in English. I didn't understand, but a friend who worked there was Chicano and he interpreted. He told me to learn a little English so that I could go into the kitchen and learn to be a cook. *Hijole,* I was so happy. I arrived at the house like a kid with a toy and told my friend to start teaching me English, because I was going into the kitchen.

I learned the simple things so that when people ordered something, I understood. I learned to cook. Within a short time, days really, I became responsible for the kitchen—even with the right to invite a friend to have pizza without paying. This was with the permission of my boss.

We had a lot of fun there, too. I played soccer in a league of foreign students at the university. There was every kind of person on those teams—Africans, Turks—but I always played with the Latin Americans. We saw crazy things too. You know North Americans are very funny about their dogs. Once we saw a woman who had her hair cut and dyed to match her dog, or maybe it was the other way around.

I remember one time—this was the craziest, but it's true—we took a trip to San Francisco. We were waiting for a cable car at Fisherman's

Wharf and a woman ran by completely nude. Can you imagine? She didn't have a stitch on. Miguel and I couldn't believe our eyes. She was a "streaker." "No," I thought, "if my grandmother knew this, she would die."

I cannot remember why we left the United States, but I wanted to see my family and take my place as the oldest, now that my father had died. So it was, after being there exactly one year, on the seventh of March we arrived back in San Juan. We returned exactly as we had left, walking the ten kilometers from the highway. It was a grand adventure, that year.

When I returned I did the things that one does. I drank a little, enjoyed the fiestas, and mostly looked for girls. That's what I did, and that was how I met my wife. After two or three months we were married. I was still a little crazy. I was twenty-one, but I think I still had the spirit of a juvenile.

Then when I was twenty-four, through my sister's husband I entered the secret police. I was still in training when we were caught with some contraband. Well, it was used clothing we had confiscated from some people smuggling it in from the United States to sell. Instead of taking it in, you know, giving our superiors their bite, we divided it among ourselves. From there we had a problem. They found out about it and were looking for us, to put us in jail. They caught my brother-in-law.

My wife was expecting her first baby when the problem occurred, and well, what was there but to go? This time I got the money together and had the address of relatives in Tijuana. The result was that I got work in Tijuana with an old man named Don Beto, making huaraches. I have a lot of respect for this man. He's a poet, and he treated me like a son. He didn't pay me, but we ate well every day.

While I was there I met a lot of men associated with the Mexican mafia. One muchacho named Rafael was in the "League of the Twenty-third of September." He told me, "Gordo, I want to speak with you seriously." My cousins told me not to get involved with him because he was a drug dealer. Well, he bought some wine, and in three glasses he drank a bottle by himself. He ended up drinking three bottles of wine to my one, and I was drunker than he was. He said he had some hard work for me, that it required bravery. He said, "I want you to help me rob a bank. Just tell me yes or no."

I said, "Let me tell you the reason. I am waiting for my woman. If she doesn't arrive on Sunday, then on Monday I'll help you."

He told me, "Fine, but if you ever say anything, I will kill you." Well, of course I didn't say anything, and the result was that my wife arrived on Sunday. He robbed the bank alone and they never caught him. This same person offered to help me cross the border.

My sister and my two-month-old son had come with my wife. So I had all of them. My American friends met us in Tijuana. They took the baby across as if he were their own, then waited for us to come that night.

With Rafael, the crossing was not really difficult. We had to wait about a half hour in the Tijuana stadium, watching for the Mexican police because, well they're worse than the *migra*. We waited and when there was no one, we passed through a hole in the fence. We went holding on to each other so that when the *migra* would see us in their infrared lights, we would appear to be one person and they wouldn't pay much attention. We ran and entered a marshy area, but there wasn't a lot of water in it. Then we crawled a long, long way through bushes and brush. We saw three *migra* jeeps but hid from them. When we were across there was an old truck to hide in. I think they moved it around all the time to trick the *migra*. The windows had black cardboard inside so that the helicopters couldn't see in. This Rafael knew all the places to go. We were supposed to find our friends, but there were helicopters flying all over, right over our heads. *Hijole,* it was just like a war movie. Several times the sound and light was so strong that I was sure they had found us.

While we were hidden in the truck, Rafael called our friends and told them to meet him at the White Horse Motel. They couldn't find it. It was about two o'clock in the morning and they drove all over San Ysidro looking at every motel. Nothing. Finally they stopped and looked in a telephone directory. Nothing. At this point they had no idea what to do. Then they looked up and a block away, on top of a motel called El Rancho was a huge white horse going around. I guess Rafael couldn't read English.

Finally Rafael was back. "Keep low," he told us. We didn't have to run far. I could see the *migra* patrols all over. We ran through someone's yard, and then there was our friend's car sitting in a driveway. It was a little pickup truck with a camper, and the camper door was wide open.

We started to run but had to dive back into the bushes because here came a helicopter with his spotlight right down the street we had to cross. When it passed we ran as fast as we could and dived all at once into the camper, so fast that we all landed in a pile on top of one another.

Our friends had the baby and a room for all of us in San Ysidro. We were all muddy and our clothes were torn, but we were so happy.

Anyway, we did get to sleep part of the night even though the baby cried. The next morning we were going to fly from San Diego to a town called Burbank. Before we left, we all dressed up and my wife put on her baby carrier. I was scared, not for myself but for my wife, my sister, and my son. We flew to Burbank and waited for our friends to pick us up. When one is traveling alone, what fear there is, but when you are with people you care about, and my first son, well you can imagine.

This time we stayed six months. My sister had a job with a family that had a new baby, but I couldn't find steady work. I did construction, gardening, and clearing land, that kind of thing. On one job, remodeling a house, my boss wanted all the bricks from the chimney cleaned. I asked if I could bring my wife to help me and he thought, "If he brings his wife, he probably won't get much done." So instead of paying us by the hour, he paid us ten cents a brick. When he came back that night he couldn't believe it. We had cleaned almost eighteen hundred bricks, and he owed us $175. If he had paid us by the hour, we would have earned only $50. That is the most money I have ever made in one day.

Well, my wife was homesick. She was worried that she would never see her grandmother, who had raised her. The result is that ten years later her grandmother is still living, but we came back to Mexico. Now, with five children, it's not possible to go back. Maybe when they are grown, we'll go on vacation.

It has been twelve years since José returned from the United States. But it has been difficult. A victim of Mexico's economic crisis, he recently lost his job as a diesel mechanic. With his severance pay for the trip, he decided to try his luck in el norte *a fourth time. But the anxiety of leaving his wife and five children alone with no income, magnified by the threat of the* migra *catching him several times, led him to turn back at the border. With the profit from selling "El Challenger" he is building an adobe house in his pueblo and moving his family from Guadalajara. His hope is to support them by working with his uncle as a village fisherman.*

GANA EL GÜERO
Y EL POLLERO

Cruzan y cruzan braceros
En verano y primavera;
En verano y primavera
Cruzan y cruzan braceros.

Gana el güero y el pollero
Y a mi no me queda nada;
Y a mi no me queda nada,
Gana el güero y el pollero.

Pero yo sigo cruzando
Porque allá tengo trabajo
Porque allá tengo trabajo
Por eso sigo cruzando.

Voy y vengo, vengo y voy
Buscando pan pa' mis hijos;
Buscando pan pa' mis hijos
Voy y vengo, vengo y voy.

Magdaleno Rosales

THE WHITE MAN AND
THE CHICKEN KEEPER WIN

Braceros cross and cross
During summer and spring;
During summer and spring
Braceros cross and cross.

The Anglo and smuggler make money
And there's nothing left for me;
And there's nothing left for me,
The Anglo and smuggler make money.

But I continue crossing
Because there I have work;
Because there I have work
That's why I continue crossing.

I go and come, come and go
Looking for bread for my children;
Looking for bread for my children
I go and come, come and go.

The White Man and
the Chicken Keeper Win

EL COYOTE

From all over Mexico, los pollos *flock to this 2,000-mile line. Waiting for their chance to cross, they confront a world light years from pueblo life. Sandwiched there between* la policia *and* la migra, *they see exotic schemes, money, hunger, violence, hope, treachery, ludicrous tales, physical hardship, and unimagined sin swirling about them. In confusion and fear,* el pollo *turns to* el coyote.

Though he is just a varmint to the Anglo, for the Mexican el coyote *carries the significance of the mythic past:* Canis latrans, *cunning four-legged scavenger, loyal parent and mate of the western prairies; in other incarnations a trickster-hero of shamanistic powers, who passes in the night without a trace and can carry mere mortals to another reality. At the border it's the same. There he passes immigrants illegally but safely to the other side.*

Once, only a little more than sixty years ago, there was no border. It was somewhere, but not exactly marked, and there were no guards. Mexicans and Americans simply passed back and forth without much notice. But checks that were first instituted as simple formalities have become, for most Mexican citizens, impossible. The jobs they need are on the other side. Yet unless they have the right collection of permits and approvals, the U.S. Border Patrol faces them with a powerful array of men, women, equipment, and barriers to keep them out.

El coyote *is a specialist in eluding, avoiding, skirting around, fading away from and passing over, the trials of the border. The more difficult the border becomes, the more in demand are his services. And, despite the high cost of being taken across, people keep migrating.*

This huge service industry is pegged by immigration experts as the fourth largest business sector along the border after tourism, commerce, and the maquiladora *assembly plants. As the border has been hardened, the immigration industry has grown until it now generates an estimated $350 million a year in underground and regular economic activity.*

But ballooning demand and big money bring out el coyote's *counterpart,* el ratero *[the robber].* El ratero *always passes himself off as* el coyote. *El* ratero *is as easy to find as* el coyote *is difficult. Journalists and anchorpersons from north of the border are his favorites. The perfect photo-op, he prances, he gesticulates, he boasts, and all in perfect Spanglish. Revelations pour forth about his cleverness, his latest tricks on* la migra, *the high fees he pockets, his connections with* la policia *and perhaps even* los mafiosos. *All made known in the spirit of neighborly relations, no?*

Most of the time, however, he has more serious quarry to stalk. Barking his pitch at the bus station as people disembark from the interior provinces, or speaking in sotto voce along border approaches to catch those just turned back, he promises, "With me it's secure." If they believe him, they will surely lose their money and maybe their lives. He may be small-time, operating alone, or part of a mafia-type crime family trafficking in drugs or prostitution and backed by paid-off police. Anything is possible at the border and becomes increasingly probable as people bring more and more money to buy their way across.

Only the naive or the ignorant would travel to the border without already having made arrangements for a coyote. *The risk is too great. That is why* el coyote *is not found on the street or in the bus station or in a bar. He doesn't risk a setup and so works only by referral. His references come through informal networks that reach from the Mexican interior to destinations as far as Alaska, Chicago, or Montreal. These networks are integral to a particular pueblo or family, and it is difficult for an outsider to know of their connections. Money does change hands along the network, but, except right at the border, it is not the primary motivator. Rather, the network is integrated into the cultural system of favors. These networks are Mexican for Mexicans. They are not part of the big international rings smuggling Cen-*

tral *Americans, Asians, and Africans. They are simply one compadre helping another.*

At Tijuana–San Diego el coyote *receives $50 to $100 to pop someone
just over the line to San Ysidro or Chula Vista; it's $300 to take them to Los
Angeles by car trunk, or $500 by plane. Chicago will cost $1,000. The money
involved looks impressive to the casual observer, but these fees cover all
transportation, housing, and food.* El coyote *is paid only when his "chicks"
reach their destination. Then the fee will be split between a number of players
such as drivers and safe-house operators, as well as spent on telephone charges
and airline tickets, all north of the border. If the* pollo *isn't apprehended
somewhere along the line,* el coyote's *take will be a modest $30 to $50 per
person delivered to the other side.*

Like most Mexican business owners, el coyote *will probably pass his
livelihood on to his children when he is ready to retire. Because, as long as
there is little opportunity at home and work in the north, his countrymen will
want to go there. And as long as there are* la migra y los rateros y las policias
in their way, they'll need el coyote's *guidance across the borderlands.*

KEVIN THOMAS
*College Student
San Diego, California*

*Kevin is the first American many people meet when they arrive in their new
country. The all-American kid, charming, forthright, serious but not without
humor, he is almost solely responsible for forming their first and most lasting
impressions of Americans and the United States. He would be a credit to the
diplomatic corps. New immigrants often recall their friend "Kayben
Tómas"—what a good person he is, how well he can speak Spanish and how
fast he can speak English, how he taught them their first words, and how
he took them to the families they hadn't seen in years.*

When I meet my clients they are really happy. They have just crossed
the border and they're in the United States. Sometimes they don't even
know they're not home free yet. A lot of times they are still trembling
with fear. I have to sit down and talk to them in Spanish. We discuss
the plan. Usually I just have to make the reservations, take them to the

airport, pick up the tickets, and wait with them until I see that they are on board.

I've never had any trouble, but that's because I know the airport and I know the Immigration there. I can speak Spanish, but I have a policy of never speaking Spanish in the airport. At the airport I always speak English to my clients. They don't understand, they just kind of have to respond.

See most people are going to be real nervous, and that's what Immigration looks for, plus they're looking for campesinos dressed in clothes like they just passed. I try to help them out, like I coach them. I tell them exactly what is going to happen, how they have to act, about the X-ray machines and seat belts, and we don't go to the airport until they look like they're flying to the big city. Sometimes I even have to go out and buy shoes and clothes for them, but my job is to get them to where they are going, so I do what I have to. If they get picked up you know, I don't get paid.

It's a good job for me. My classes start at nine in the morning and I'm out by noon. So other than studying, I kind of have my days free. I really only handle airport detail, and sometimes they need me early in the morning, if someone has to take an early morning flight. But if I have to fly to L.A. with someone, it's usually in the afternoon or evening. So the money's good, at least it's better than working as a waiter or something like that. I'm my own boss, so I can afford to be flexible.

Of course it depends on the job, but say reservations and trip to the airport—I charge $50. If I have to fly to Los Angeles it's usually $100 plus my airfare. That's standard, but if someone can't afford it I will go down. On the other hand, if it's a businessman I might charge more. It's not like a salary with benefits, but I'm booked every day, so there's a steady income. Sure there's a risk, but it's an adventure too and I'm very cautious.

If the client is an older woman or a woman with children I prefer to fly with them. They are in a foreign country for the first time. It's just safer. It costs them more money for me to fly there and back. But I get to know these people, I admire their determination, and I really want to see them get there. And then when they see their families there to meet them, God, you know it's worth it.

JESÚS MANUEL HERNÁNDEZ TOVAR
Pasador
Ciudad Juárez, Mexico

To the casual observer this could pass for a low-scale water park. People are playing in the water, swimming, going down the river in rubber rafts and inner tubes. On closer look, you notice a conspicuous absence of children, and a young woman in a bright pink dress and high heels is being carried across by a man in a bathing suit. Farther down the river a young man is taking off his clothes. He takes them all off, folds them carefully into a little bundle and holds it on his head as he steps in, stark naked, and wades across. The water is above his waist. On the other side he unfolds his bundle, puts on his underwear first, then pants, shirt, and shoes. He takes a comb out of his pocket, combs his hair, and walks up the sloped concrete embankment of the canal. At the top he walks through a doorway cut into the barbed-wire-topped chain-link fence and disappears in a labyrinth of boxcars.

This is the El Paso/Ciudad Juárez border crossing. Above, groups of people can be seen crossing the bridge and forming lines that reach the customs agents on each side. This is the legal lifeline between the United States and Mexico.

But one hundred yards to the east, lounging in the shade of the overpass, are others employed in the border drama. They are the pasadores, *the guides, about a dozen young men sitting on the concrete wall or on the hoods of parked cars bantering back and forth.*

There is an easy camaraderie, even with the competition that is obvious when a car comes into the large parking lot situated for the convenience of people crossing to the United States legally or illegally. They can tell if a client will want their services by the way he is dressed. A man dressed in a business suit, or the traditional white shirt, tight pants, and sombrero, won't want to get wet. They all run to the hustle, because this means business, whereas a young man in Levi's and a T-shirt will merit only a few bored offers in passing.

Jesús Hernández is friendly and enthusiastic. He's neatly dressed in a white shirt and tan chino pants, and sprightly-topped in symbolic irony with a McDonald's visor cap.

I have been to five border crossings between the United States and Mexico, and I can tell you that this is the most reputable. The others are very dangerous.

When we pass people, we pass them across the river and then take them up there to the train tracks. We take them wherever they want to go, to the house of relatives, to a hotel, or sometimes they want to go to other places, like Los Angeles, so we take them to the airport. We take them ourselves because we also know El Paso.

This is the easiest place to cross. Over there, farther west, it is easier because there is no fence and the river isn't as high, but it is very dangerous. There are dangerous people there, *narcotraficantes, drug adictos, y rateros.* So it is easier to cross here. We pass people on rubber rafts or inner tubes because sometimes there are people who don't know how to swim. Sometimes we have to pass babies and pregnant women and elderly women. The river isn't very high now, but at times it is very high and fast. It can be very dangerous.

It is also dangerous when people don't know the trains, because they don't give a signal when they are going to move. Not very long ago a man lost his foot right over there. The train rolled backward before it went forward, and went over his foot. That's why we signal for our customers, and when we pass families we wait until they are safe before we return.

Here we see people coming from all over Mexico, from the south, and even from Central America. We also take across entire families, but most of the people who cross are from Juarez and they work or have family in El Paso, so they cross back and forth every day. We have customers that cross with us every day because they know us and have confidence. They are our steady customers. They cross with us in the morning and come back over the bridge at night.

I don't know, I think in California they say *coyotes* because they have to cross over the mountains at night. It is very dangerous and they know the terrain. They know exactly where to go. Here it is different. We pass people during the day, mostly at eight o'clock in the morning, because that's when people have to go to work. Then, here and there people want to cross during the day. But we don't work at night because it is too dangerous. Here, we call ourselves guides or *pasadores.*

For many people we have a bad name. But they don't know us. These are usually people who don't live near the border or who don't have to cross every day. But to the people who live here and work over there, we are just like the taxi driver. In fact, we have taxis that pick people up on the other side. They pay us the same as a taxi driver. The amount depends on where they want to go. If they just want to cross the river it is two dollars and fifty cents. If they want us to get them to the other side of the tracks it is five dollars. If they want us to take them farther, say like to the airport or to New Mexico, it would be twenty dollars to twenty-five dollars. Mario and I work together and then we split the fee. They don't pay us until we arrive at the destination.

We don't make that much money, but we have obligations. I have a wife and three children to support. The oldest is eight years old. Mario is married too, and has a little girl. We make enough to feed them, buy clothes, take care of them, and bring toys to the children once in a while. But it is very difficult in Mexico. I was born in Juárez and have all my family here.

See, this is the problem. Mexico must raise the salaries and there has to be less corruption. The police here are very corrupt. That's why we have work, because the people have to go to work over there. The people can cross here and earn more in one day than they can working a week in Mexico.

Working here, passing people, I too earn more in one day than I can working for a week in a factory. At times we have worked in El Paso, but here there is opportunity for us, and over there we get picked up by the *migra*. Nothing happens. They just hold you for an hour or so and then send you back. They will only get mad if you run, but if you behave well, they will treat you fine.

Our biggest fear is that we would be put in jail either on this side or the other. So far it has never happened, but I think about it because we work so much. But the ugliest thing is when a customer comes and says, "Can you take me to Fort Worth?" Then we make all the arrangements, provide the transportation, and when we get to Fort Worth they show us their badge. They are the *migra*. To me this is very ugly and underhanded. I don't think it is even legal in the United States. They think they can come to Mexico and break the law, and we go to prison.

EL MÉXICO
Coyote
Tijuana, Mexico

He is young, clean-cut, with short hair, shiny cheeks, and a shyness about his manner that makes El México an unlikely candidate for a coyote. *He, his wife, and their six-year-old son live in a converted garage in the hills of Tijuana. The small space is crowded with beds, a couch, and other assorted furniture so that one has to step over and around. The even smaller kitchen has an apartment-sized stove and refrigerator and a table covered with a bright, cheery oilcloth. The walls are lined with full-color posters of Mexican singers and fantastic race cars—Lotuses and Ferraris. In the United States we would say the family who lives here is poor, but there is always a festive atmosphere. Outside in the courtyard an aviary of singing birds competes with the radio. There is constant activity—playing children, nervous people reassuring each other and trying to rest before the night's crossing, and the comings and goings of the men organizing the evening's work. All visitors are offered* refrescos *or beer.*

I first started bringing people across when I was about twelve or thirteen. At that time I lived on the other side, in San Ysidro with a woman who is like a mother to me. My parents are in Mexico City, and they sent me to live with her when I was young so I could go to school. Our house was right on the border, across from the schoolyard there, and I knew the area with my eyes closed. That's where we played when we were kids. So when I would see people crossing and know that they needed help or they would get caught, I would bring them across. I never charged anything. I guess people got to know me, other guides, and they would ask me to signal for them. That's more or less how it was.

People want to cross with us because they know we are secure and we're serious. They know we are not like those who look for people off the street, or are looking for people to take their money, or those that take people across so they'll have money to drink. We are fathers, we have families to maintain, and our interest is to cross people. When we take someone across and a friend asks them if they know someone, they recommend us. They say, "Oh yes, I know someone secure and responsible."

With those in the street it's no more than an adventure to see if they can make it, and often they're caught or they leave the people with nothing to eat for two or three days. Oh, and there are those who take the people to one side of the fields and leave them when the Immigration isn't around. They tell their clients a vehicle will be by to pick them up, but it never comes.

It's like any other business, if you are a mechanic or an engineer, it takes time to build your clientele. When people see you do good work they will look for you. I am very familiar with the terrain and the techniques. It's like a game of chess. Each one of us takes one or two, and then we reunite, or if it's tranquil we can all go together. Some nights we will have up to twelve people to cross.

Oh, we've been caught. I would say one or two times every six months or maybe four times a year. Each time we give a different name. They want to know your name, where you were born, your father and mother, how old you are, how you entered, and where you entered. You give whatever answer. They put it in a computer, but you answer differently each time.

When I was little in San Ysidro, I was dedicated to passing people, to helping them hide. One time the Immigration saw me and picked me up. The lady who is like my mother didn't know where I was. She thought I was in school, but it was about three or four in the afternoon and they put me in jail in Chula Vista. They gave me some slaps and told me that if I would get caught a second time they would put me in juvenile. I was there a week and then they sent me to the center of California. They were crazy, I was underage, I was maybe fifteen then. They left me without any money. I was going to hitchhike back to San Ysidro. The only thing I was afraid of was Torrance, California. I had heard it was horrible there, and I was afraid they would be going to Torrance. So when I would get a ride I would say, "You aren't going to Torrance, are you?" At one point the police picked me up. I told them I was a Mexican and to send me back to Tijuana. They did, and from there I crossed back over to San Ysidro. My second mother was frantic; she had been looking for me all that time.

My wife is from Tijuana. I was living in San Diego and I would cross to come visit her. When we got married, she didn't want to leave her family. That was when I moved, and I have been here ever since. Now, I'm accustomed to living here and I like it better than the United States. It has a different ambiance, much friendlier, not so uptight.

This is how it is. Tonight we will have these two men to take across and there will be three of us. They will pay $50 each, so we'll make about thirty dollars. That's not much, is it? It's what anyone would make in a day, well, not here in Mexico, but on the other side, even more. A professional or skilled person will make about $50 a day, and this is what someone who is unskilled would make, the minimum. There are times when there are more people and we make more money, but then you have to save some of it for when there is no work. This month we had two weeks with no work. The bad months are from September through Christmas. Then it picks up again. In January we have all the people who went to Mexico for the fiestas, then in the spring farm workers come over, in the summer we have students, and at the end of summer we have parents crossing to take their kids back to school. The people from several little pueblos in Michoacán and Jalisco come to us; the whole pueblo knows us. But we also get people from El Salvador, Guatemala, and Peru.

It's $50 to cross to San Ysidro and $300 to go to Los Angeles. But to go to Los Angeles, you first have to arrive at a house. There is a *señora,* she doesn't like to do this, but she has a son who has an infirmity where he can't walk. The *señora* doesn't have a husband. She has other children, and she gets welfare, but it isn't enough to cover the child who is sick. So the *señora* helps us, taking care of the people. The people she takes in are better off than others, because she does care for them. When we get there, she makes them breakfast, lets them bathe and wash their clothes, for the little bit of money she gets.

Then we have to pay an American with a car. He gets a little more, about one hundred dollars per person. Then arriving in Los Angeles, we have another person we pay to take the people to their houses. Sometimes, when we want to, we go to Los Angeles too, but usually we don't. The person who takes them collects the money when they arrive in Los Angeles. He pays the person who takes them to their houses, and when he returns that night, he pays the *señora* and us. When someone brings us a client we pay them $5 for making the connection. The person who drives has to get paid well because he has to drive a nice car. If it was one of the little old cars we drive, no, they'd stop us for sure.

Those who make good money are the ones who sell drugs. They make money coming and going. Besides all this, the little that one makes, and then the Mexican police want $100 if they catch you with one or two! We play the game on this side to avoid the police, because when you're caught you have to pay $100 or $200 just so they will leave you alone. And think of it, there are the municipal police, the state police, the *federales*, the governors, and beyond that, those that pass for police. And they all have an interest. What can you do? You have no choice. Sometimes you have to pay them.

LIDIA SANCHEZ
Safe House Owner
Chula Vista, California

It's an insignificant little stucco house, beige with white trim, in the middle of an older neighborhood. A well-maintained square patch of green lawn, roses lining the driveway, and a bicycle and scooter on the front porch; an "average American family" must live here. Inside it's the same. The living room–dining room combination is neat and orderly, furnished with the standard couch, easy chair, rocking chair, TV, coffee table, dining table, and six chairs, all in an early American style. From the books and games on the shelf and pictures on the wall children obviously live here, but at ten in the morning they are in school and Lidia's day is well underway. She has already been to the grocery store and has a load of wash in the machine.

So where are all the illegal aliens? Four who stayed last night left with rides early this morning. A pretty young woman in an old-fashioned print dress with pink roses and a white collar is washing dishes. The conversation is about children: getting them to eat, high fevers and ear infections. Obviously comfortable in Lidia's kitchen, she must be a friend or relative, certainly not the skulking fugitive from the Border Patrol—but she is. Her husband, who has resident papers, and her baby boy, who was born in the United States, passed yesterday. But with only four years here, she always has to pass with a coyote. *Her sister-in-law will pick her up this afternoon. She is one of Lidia's clients.*

Lidia has coffee and is putting groceries away. Her warm and easygoing manner makes people comfortable.

When I graduated from high school I got a job in food service at Mercy Hospital. I was thinking I'd like to be a nurse, but I met my husband there and we got married. When my son was born I left my job, and before you know I had three children. I really never had time to go back to school. At that time I was busy with the children, and my husband supported us, so I didn't think about working.

Then in 1979 he left us. He left me with a five-year-old, a two-year-old, and the baby was just six months. That's when I moved here with my mom. This was her house. At first I thought my husband would come back, but I'm sure he's got another family in Mexico by now. I get aid for dependent children, and for the first few years I babysat my neighbor's children. She has three too, so I was taking care of six little kids.

But the thing is, my oldest son, from the time he was a baby he was sick. He learned to walk and all, but by the time he was eight he couldn't walk anymore, and I had to spend every day going to the hospital, or to the doctor, or therapy, so I couldn't babysit anymore. But by that time all the kids were in school, except my daughter.

Of course I would like to go out and work, but what would I do with my son? He's in eighth grade and goes to a special school. The bus picks him up at nine o'clock, but they bring him home at one and I have to help him do everything. That's why I can't just go out and get a job. They pay his medical bills and that, but to feed and clothe three kids, it isn't enough. We can't get by on what I get from welfare.

My mom, she died in 1985, but she always helped people coming across. So she always had someone here. Then when I wasn't babysitting, I would help her. Around that time more people started coming, so I've just kept it up.

It's quiet today, but it gets hectic around here sometimes. I don't mind. Really, it's the only thing I can do and stay home with my son. My other boy is in sixth grade and my daughter is in fourth grade, so they still need me too. I think of it as a job, but it's not bad. Most of the people are real nice, and it's good for my son. There's always different people to talk to. He likes that. He's in a wheelchair now.

The men begin bringing people from ten o'clock at night on. Oh, sometimes we have someone come during the day, but most people cross at night. But they have the key, so I don't have to get up for them. I have couches and cots set up back there in the garage so they can sleep. As it is, most of them leave early in the morning between five and six, so I get coffee for them. Some people have to stay. They have other arrangements, or they have to fly to other places, or relatives have to come pick them up. But they can stay here and I let them bathe or wash their clothes. They eat their meals with us. They can sit here and watch TV, whatever they want.

I get to know the people who stay over. I've had people stay for a week or more. Sometimes they're waiting for their money to arrive. They mostly come from Mexico. I've never been there myself, except to Tijuana. But we always spoke Spanish at home, so I can speak with them. Some of them are from other places in South America. When you talk to them it makes you realize how much we have here, because they come from areas that are very poor. I'll often have to show them how to use the shower or washing machine because they have never seen one. Some of them don't even have toilets and indoor plumbing where they come from.

When they get to where they are going they will call and thank us, or they'll recommend us to a relative. You'd be surprised, we often hear from them again. You get some that go back and forth so you see them. One lady, who went to Chicago a couple of weeks ago, sent a postcard to my son. They come here with hardly anything, but they always want to leave us something.

They pay me $10 for each person. If they stay and eat meals and all, it's $20 a day. It's not like a fancy hotel, but I always have a pot of beans and tortillas. They can have eggs, fruit, bread, milk, whatever they want. For dinner I make some meat or fish. Whatever we eat is what I serve. When I have women here they always help me. I don't ask them to, but they're nervous and always want to clean, wash, or do dishes.

I've had up to forty people here in one night. But that doesn't happen very often. Usually there are three or four, and I almost always have someone eating with us. Every once in a while I'll get a day off with no one here.

I always try to treat the people who come here fair. I think about the hard times they're going through and all. I always think, we're the first family they meet in the United States. I feel sorry for those poor people. Sometimes they're left off at a motel. You know they don't come here with that kind of money. Then the *coyote* tells them someone will pick them up and no one comes. There are *coyotes* that leave people in the back of trucks, for days, without food. You wouldn't believe the stories. I feel sorry for them. I only deal with a couple of people I know. They were friends of my mother's, so I know them pretty well.

You know these people just went to a lot of trouble to get here, so they're not going to do something stupid now. No, really they never cause me any problems: drugs, fights, nothing. Oh, sometimes you have someone who is very nervous, or upset, maybe crying and like that, but I just talk to them.

Really, I never think about this being illegal. I know it is, but I don't have time to stop and think about that. In my mind, this is my house, and I'm not endangering anyone. I think I'm helping people and doing what I have to, to make a life for my kids. At the same time, I am careful. I have rules. They always bring people around the back alley, and they are picked up out in back. The people have to be quiet. My neighbors know what I do, they understand, but I don't have a lot of noise and people back there bothering them. I know they would never report me. I grew up in this house and I've known them since I was a little girl.

LEJOS DE MI TIERRA

Ahora que me encuentro lejos de la tierra en que nací.
Ay de mis padres queridos, como han sufrido por mi!
Pobrecita de mi madre, varios consejos me dió,
Con lágrimas en sus ojos, sus bendiciones me echó.

Ya no llores, madrecita, ya sé que debo sufrir;
Déjame rifar mi suerte, voy buscando porvenir.

También dejé a mi amorcito que le prometí volver,
Pues yo sé que ella me espera, que Dios me ha de conceder.
Quisiera ser como los aves y de un solo vuelo cruzar
Estos valles y montañas y a mis querencias llegar.

Virgencita Milagrosa, quien sabes mi padecer
De rodillas iré a verte si me concedes volver.

FAR FROM MY COUNTRY

Now I find myself far from the country where I was born.
Oh, the parents I love, how they have suffered for me!
My poor little mother, she gave me advice
And with tears in her eyes, she gave me her blessings.

Now don't cry anymore, little mother, I know I will suffer;
Let me take my chances, I'm going in search of my future.

I also left my little love, to whom I promised to return,
Well, I know she will wait for me, God has granted me this.
I would like to be like the birds and in only one flight
Cross these valleys and mountains and arrive to my loved ones.

Miraculous little virgin, who knows my suffering,
On my knees I will come to see you if you grant my return.

How They Have Suffered
for Me

THOSE THEY LEFT BEHIND

The personal costs of Mexican migration are not found in the statistics. They are never mentioned. Can the loss of a husband, father, or son be accounted for? Not in Mexico, where the family is the center of the society and life itself. The costs are carefully hidden in the myth of family unity and strength. Yet for every Mexican immigrant in the United States there is a family whose unity is broken; individuals, wives, mothers, fathers, and children whose lives are in limbo. But the loss doesn't end there. There are millions of families in Mexico suffering financial, emotional, and spiritual loss, many more individuals whose lives are spent in desperate waiting, and entire pueblos of just the old and infirm, and the women and children. It is in these terms a wartime population, in a war without battle lines or the possibility of truce. Such costs to a developing country cannot be measured.

But it isn't only Mexico's cost. In Distant Neighbors, *Alan Riding says the family is crucial to maintaining Mexico's political stability, a stability in turn crucial to our own. In Octavio Paz's words, "We are condemned to live together."*

Our own government not only ignores this fact but unwittingly contributes to it. The Immigration Reform and Control Act of 1986 made it possible for all illegal immigrants who had been in the country unlawfully before January 1, 1982, to receive legal resident status; approximately three million applied.

But the new law made no provision for the families of these immigrants. They were liable for deportation if they didn't meet the requirements. In July of 1989 the Senate took a significant step in rewriting that section of the law, granting a stay of deportation to those family members in the United States on November 6, 1986, the day the new immigration reform came into effect. At this writing it still remains for the House of Representatives and the president to pass and sign this bill, and there are still questions unanswered. Do these family members have the same freedom to travel back and forth as those who qualified for amnesty, or are they prisoners in this country? What of those who have qualified for amnesty and who didn't bring their families illegally to the United States? Are they condemned to a lifetime of separation?

The U.S. government has taken a strong position against the Soviet Union's human rights record, going so far as to deny Most Favored Nation Trade Status until the USSR agrees to cancel all restrictions for Russian Jews seeking to join their families in Israel. Clearly there is a parallel for as many as three million Mexican families in our own country. Infidelity and bigamy have been institutionalized under our law. Millions of young immigrants will be husbands and fathers in both countries, and their American wives and children face a risk of abandonment equal to their counterparts in Mexico.

LETTER FROM OSCAR VASQUEZ CARILLA, AGE TWELVE,
To His Father, José Vasquez Ordaz*
Guadalajara, Mexico

When he was two months old, Oscar crossed the border with a coyota and his parents picked him up on the other side. This story has been told to him many times, and he is proud to say he has been to the United States. His father was going again, and Oscar wanted very much to go with him rather than stay home with his mother and siblings. But this time he had the responsibility of being the man of the house.

18 June 1988

Papa, I hope you are okay. I know it was a long trip. My mother asked my teacher how I am doing in school, and he told her that I am doing

*See chapter 4.

very well and will not have to go to summer school. I also want to tell you that my brother and sisters send you many greetings. They want you to bring them a present because they are very sad that you left. I hope you won't be gone a long time. Papa, I would like you to buy me a bicycle, and I want to tell you that I am taking very good care of the animals. The chickens now have twelve eggs and two chicks have hatched. The rabbit now has her little bunnies. I hope you will return very soon because we feel very bad without you. I know you will have a lot of work, but I hope it doesn't tire you too much. I would like you to bring back a truck because it's something we could really use here. I also want you to send us letters so that we will know how you are doing, but even if you don't write to us we will continue to send you letters so that you won't be sad. But I hope you won't forget to write to us.

Papa, I am sending this letter for Father's Day and I am waiting for you with my arms open. I send greeting in the company of my mother, and my brother and sisters.

Your son,
Oscar

SOCORRO ESTRADA DE MENDOZA
Housewife
Cajititlán de los Reyes, Mexico

Socorro Estrada de Mendoza, pregnant with their third child, writes a letter to her husband.

3 February 1980

Pepe, I hope I find you well. I send this letter, Pepe, I don't know what you will be thinking of me, but I have sent letter after letter and I believe that not one has reached you. It is only now that I learned that the address is not correct. Pepe, I want to tell you, I don't know if you have any money, but I need some because I think they are going to operate, and I am desperate because I have no money and I'm scared. I am taking the opportunity to send this with Juan. If the other letters arrive, I hope you understand and if you have the money you will send help. Well, Pepe, this is all that I have to tell you. I hope you don't believe that I didn't want to answer you. I wanted to, but because they never returned my letters I didn't know. With this last one I have sent five letters, and it seems strange that they haven't returned them. Well, Pepe, I hope you aren't mad. Receive greetings from your sons, who don't forget you and ask every day when you are returning.

Greetings from your wife,
Socorro

On February 8, 1980, Socorro's baby was born by Cesarean section. Her letter was delivered by Juan, but because of slow communication between Mexico and the United States she did not receive money from her husband until February 27. Pepe returned home in November to meet his new daughter and see his family for the first time in a year and a half.

SUSANA RIVERA DE PEREZ
Housewife
Tlaquepaque, Mexico

Afternoon sunlight streaming in the open window fills the small room. This brightness and the gay colors in the pictures of the Virgin and the flower-embroidered pillowcases contrast with the pale young girl with dark circles under her eyes. Susana Rivera, age twenty, has returned to this room of her childhood to recover from childbirth.

My mama says I should try to recuperate for the sake of my little girl. She is only three years old and doesn't understand, but it's very hard. My sister has been like a father and mother to me during these last few days. She has held me and talked to me, and I'm very grateful to have my family. But it isn't the same as having your husband.

You see, the doctor said I had to have the baby Cesarean. Well, I agreed. Even though I was fearful, I wanted whatever would be best for the baby. Then when she was born I was awake, because they only put me to sleep from the waist down. I heard her cry and I was so happy.

Later, when I asked to see my baby, they told me she was born dead. That's what they told me, yet I know it wasn't true. And when my mother came to take her home she said her face was badly bruised with a deep cut on her cheek.

But what can I do? I must leave it in God's hands.

My husband called his sister from Los Angeles. He had been waiting to hear. She had to tell him his baby daughter died. He cried. He wanted to come home, but what good would it do?

He's been there four months, and if he can only stay a while longer we can build our house. We have the lot. Before he left he and I together made the adobe bricks with our own hands. When I am filled with pain and longing I think of how hard we worked and what it will be like to have a house of our own. It consoles me, but it's not the same as having him here.

EVA CECILIA RIOS DE VASQUEZ
*Sister-in-law of José Vasquez Ordaz**
Housewife
Guadalajara, Mexico

January 29, 1987

Her house isn't easily reached: three bus rides through numerous barrios on the outskirts of Guadalajara, to the end of the line; from there a ten-block walk through fine dust and hot sun. In this most recent subdivision for families migrating from the countryside, the houses are new, mostly of brick, but also of sheet metal and cardboard, none of them finished. There are children and dogs and an occasional chicken, all the gray-brown color of the insidious dust. The house can be spotted from two blocks away because of the slicker-yellow 1950 Chevy parked out front.

Eva is sweeping and life is going on as normal. Cecilia, her seven-year-old, in her uniform of navy pleated skirt and sweater with a white blouse, is ready for school. Eva has cut her daughter's long curls to within an inch of her scalp, but she still is a beautiful little girl with luminescent bronze complexion and the dark almond eyes of her mother. Her little brother, Tonito, is playing on the floor. It has been two days since Eva's husband, Antonio, left for the United States with her sister's husband, Carlos.

*See chapter 4.

I just can't believe it. Here I am alone. No warning, nothing. Oh, he had talked about going to the United States, and when we were mad he would say he was going, but the next day it would be over. I guess he just wanted to go. He didn't have any reason; we didn't have a fight. No, we went to bed, everything was fine. Then Carlos knocked on the door and Antonio got up. He said, "Well, I'm going."

I told him, "May you go well!" But when he wanted to give me his good-byes, I told him, "No, just leave." He wanted to say good-bye to the children, but I told him, "No, don't wake them for me." In the morning when I told Ceci, she cried.

He said, "When I get a job I will send money." I told him not to bother. I was very angry. Can you believe he left me, pregnant as I am? What am I going to do? He didn't have any money with him, and I don't know if he had anything other than the clothes on his back. I'm sure Carlos will have to pay for everything. No, he just left without saying anything to anyone, not even to his mother, but he must have had plans.

It's all the worse because he had no reason. He had a good job, and he was getting paid well. I suppose he has lost it now. I have to say he has always been responsible. Even though we were so young when we got married—we were only eighteen—we always had money. If I wanted something, he never told me no. That's why I can't believe this. His brother José tells me that Antonio needed a chance to grow up.

I don't know what to believe, but since he left I have found out all kinds of things. He never told me, but now . . . well, I have to believe them, and the more I think about it, the more I do. You see, he didn't tell me, but he told my brother-in-law that he had another woman and he has a baby by her. My brother-in-law told his brother, who told my sister. I don't see how it is possible. When I think of it, he was with me all the time. We are accustomed to going out every Saturday and Sunday. There were three, maybe four, times that he didn't come home at night. Once for two nights. I was so worried that I went to his brother. That was a Sunday, and the next morning he called his work and Antonio was there. He had been drunk. Well, I don't know. I wish I could talk to him and ask him to tell me yes or no. That's what hurts, thinking all along you have been faithful and then to find your husband was unfaithful.

Well, he stopped drinking and I was so happy. I thought, "Now our life will be happy, I won't have to worry." But it's ended up worse. And me pregnant! I didn't even want to get pregnant, but he has been wanting another baby for so long that I finally gave in. And now he's left.

The house is very small—a kitchen, living room, bedroom, and corridor in between that serves as the children's bedroom. The three-piece red velvet couch on a matching rug dominates the small room, the rest of which is filled by a long dining room table and buffet. Everything is uncommonly neat and organized, almost like a house without children. The one firm rule is that they are not allowed on the furniture.

Ceci, hurry, get your book bag—you'll be late, they'll leave without you. Hurry so I can bless you.

Cecilia puts a new pencil in her book bag and Eva puts twenty pesos in a little coin purse for her. She blesses her, making the sign of the cross on her forehead, and asks God to watch over her, then sends her out the door to join her two cousins.

"May God go with you." I used to walk them to school, but now that I'm pregnant I get very dizzy walking that far in the hot sun. We walk down in the afternoon to pick them up.

Tonito keeps asking for his papa. When it's time for him to come home from work he says, "Is he coming soon?" I tell him yes, but Ceci tells me I shouldn't lie, even to him.

He promised to be back before the baby is born, but now I don't know what to believe. I think of my poor little creature without a father. I know that there are lots of uncles, and one way or another he will have a father. And we have our family. That's the case. I have the house, the car, my children and family, and Antonio is there with nothing. Do you think he has arrived by now?

Eva's two sisters arrive. One is Chela, whose husband, Carlos, took Antonio. Four sisters and two brothers have all built houses on this block, on land purchased by their father. With their olive complexions, flashing eyes, engag-

ing smiles, and straight, white teeth outlined in gold, they are all pretty. But Eva is the prettiest, a classic beauty, even with eyes swollen from crying and no makeup.

Eva can't remember where the men are going. Chela thinks it is Anaheim, California, where Carlos was living before he returned to Mexico for Christmas.

Carlos and Chela have never lived together any length of time. He left twelve years ago, shortly after they were married and Chela was newly pregnant with their first child. At that time he went to Chicago and neither wrote nor sent money for three years. Eventually he returned, then left again. He comes home every few years for no longer than a month. She now has a second child, a little girl three years old. He has sent Chela money every month since he came back the first time, and she has managed to have a small house built on the lot her parents gave all of their children. This last Christmas was the first time Carlos had been home in three and a half years. He stayed for a month.

Eva speaks up for her sister.

We want to know if Carlos is living with another woman. That must be the reason he doesn't want to stay here with Chela and his children. He writes and sends her money, about $100 every three weeks. Sometimes he sends more, like $500, but it doesn't seem like much. He is working as a carpenter, and he said he could get Antonio a job. But I'm not like you, Chela, I won't put up with it. I'm not interested in the money, I want a husband.

I don't know how Antonio will do. He has never had physical work like a carpenter, and I know he would never wash dishes. He's always worked in a factory. He was talking about how he wanted to buy a machine that cut out shoes so he could work at home and have his own business. That would be fine; no boss, he could work for himself. Maybe that's why he went.

We'll see. How long do you think it will be before I hear from him? My main worry is having the baby. I have to try not to get upset, because it could affect the baby. I lost one before, and if I have the same problem and have to have a Cesarean . . . and now without insurance and no money. How much does a Cesarean cost? Oh, I know it will be a lot of money.

Well, if he had left me when I wasn't pregnant it wouldn't be a problem; I could get a job. But what can I do now? I have wanted to have my beauty salon, but now without money, and you know the government wants everything perfect before they give you the permit. I want to put it upstairs on top of the kitchen. I could start here and just move this table into the other room. I don't think they would know, just working in the barrio. At least I would have the money to eat.

Antonio's so jealous, I'm sure that's why he left me with a big belly. Do you think he actually had that planned?

ANTONIO VASQUEZ ORDAZ AND CARLOS FLORES
The Husbands
Santa Ana, California

May 4, 1987

Antonio isn't living at the address he gave Eva, but the young men there know him and know where he can be found, about six blocks away. In this neighborhood Spanish is the language of choice, and the ambience is pure mexicano: throngs of people on the streets and sidewalks talking and greeting the cars passing by, children playing in the yards even though it's past ten in the evening, and ranchero and salsa music bombarding from all directions. Strangers might think they had stumbled onto a fiesta, but it's an ordinary weeknight in this immigrant enclave.

Antonio and Carlos are waiting out in front, a little nervous about their circumstances but eager to hear news from home.

ANTONIO: I guess Eva is pretty mad? I called her at my sister's house, but she doesn't try to understand. Oh, I know I shouldn't have left like I did, but if I had told her there would have been a fight. No, it was better this way.

Three families including seven children and numerous young men—between fifteen and twenty people—share this small, very neat two-bedroom triplex. Chela's husband, Carlos, lives here with the mother of his two American daughters. They serve sodas and beer; in true Mexican hospitality the glasses are never empty.

ANTONIO: How are my children? Ceci cried when I talked to her on the phone. When you see her, I want you to tell her that I will bring her her Barbies [Barbie dolls].

No, to tell you the truth, I don't like it here. I don't want to offend you, your country is very pretty, and I've gone to the beach and everything, but I'm only going to stay long enough to pay the *coyote.* I've been out of work for two weeks. You see, I hurt my back. I work for a brick factory, and I can't go back until I can carry bricks again. No, it's hard work! Dirty, too. Imagine working like a dog all day and then coming home and not having anyone to wash or cook for you. No, I owe the *coyote* $400, but then I'm going home. I'm not going to stay around to save money. It's too hard here. I have to cooperate with the rent and the food, and by the time I pay for the bus, there's nothing left. At home I don't have to pay rent, you know.

What did she say about the other woman? My sister told me, but who told Eva? Well, nevertheless, they were lying, I don't have any other children. She'll have to believe me. But she's no saint either. Once I came home and she wasn't there. I went to her sister's house, but they had all gone to that club, you know, the Las Vegas Club. Her brothers didn't say a thing; they took her with them. She didn't have any business in a place like that without her husband. They made a fool of me. Think of how I felt. I was mortified. No, I can't forgive her for that. And her family, they're always there. You can't do a thing without them knowing about it. No, that's why I came up here, not because I had another woman. That's just what they're telling her.

They can't say anything. I give her all my money. Every Saturday I come home and give her all my money. What would I use to entertain other women? No, when I go back I'll just have to straighten it out.

CARLOS: Well, Tonio, your problem is you never let Eva know what you're really like. I remember when you were *novios;* you didn't drink, you didn't smoke, you were never late, you always bought presents for her. Man, she thought she was getting the prize of the barrio. It's clear why she doesn't understand you now. You should have been like me. I didn't even drink because I was playing in the band, but just to get Chela used to it I sprinkled myself with a little tequila. I smoked, and I even told her I ran around with women. No, she knew what she got.

When I went home after three years I had to tell her I had a daughter here. She didn't like it, but I let her decide. She knows I'm married to her. Sure I felt bad about it. It was a terrible thing to do, but that's life. I feel it was better to tell the truth. You know there are some men who have a kid here and another kid there, and they don't even acknowledge them. They abandon them. It wouldn't matter how many kids I have; I'll always support them. Now my youngest one here, Chela doesn't know about. I'll have to tell her, but I want to wait until I go back for good.

It's hard to leave my kids here, but I want to go back. My kids there need me too, and I have never lived with them. When I went back at Christmas I bought property in my pueblo for my daughters here; so they'll have something. Even though they're Americans, I want them to have something in Mexico.

I have never cared about my papers. There'll probably be a long line tomorrow signing up for their permits, but I'm not interested. [This was the evening before the amnesty registration began under the new immigration reform law.] No, I'm going back with Antonio in June.

It's midnight and Carlos cooks pork chops with beans, tortillas, and spicy salsa.

ANTONIO: I would send Eva money, but you can see the situation. Not working for two weeks . . . but she has money, there was money in the bank. I'm going back to work next week, so I'll be home in June. I called my boss in Guadalajara and he told me he will give me a job again.

CARLOS: Tell our wives we'll see them next month. But may I ask a great favor of you? Please don't tell Chela about my family here. You understand, it's something I have to tell her myself.

Every Saturday through June, Eva and Chela bathed and dressed their children and themselves so they would be ready for the expected return of Antonio and Carlos. But June passed. There was no money left. Eva sold the yellow Chevy. At the beginning of July she sent a telegram to Antonio asking him to come back; the doctor had said she might need a blood transfusion during the birth of their baby. No answer. On July 10 a healthy baby girl was born by Cesarean section. She was six weeks old by the time she met her father.

Antonio went north with just the shirt on his back. Seven months later, on August 29, 1987, he returned carrying: a dress and sweatshirt for his wife; a dress, two sweaters, two jogging suits, and two Barbie dolls for his daughter; a T-shirt, a toy Mercedes-Benz police car, a Fantasycar, a construction set, and nine metal race cars for his son; nine stuffed toys for the new baby; four pairs of pants and six shirts for himself; a flashlight, three batteries, three Bic cigarette lighters, three umbrellas, thirty cassette tapes of Mexican music, five yo-yos that light up, a Walkman-type tape recorder, a color TV antenna (although their television is black-and-white), a video recorder, and two hundred sticks of incense.

Carlos has never returned.

TERESA OLMOS
Housewife
Guadalajara, Mexico

The historic barrio of Guadalajara where Señora Olmos lives is now bleak with the gray residue of small industry that has overtaken it. Inside her modest door, just off the street, one is immediately in a living room of startling contrast. The bright yellow walls are lined with bookcases, dressers, a couch, chairs, a double bed, and sewing machine and adorned with saints and photographed portraits of the family either marrying or graduating. Bright pink plastic flowers snake their way out of colorful planters intertwining in an arch over the doorway. Vases of plastic or paper flowers, more saints, porcelain figurines, stuffed animals, bottles, and decorations of every sort, all carefully dusted, cover every horizontal surface. Any potential bare spot finds modesty under a freshly starched doily: five on the couch, three on each chair, more on all the shelves, the sewing machine, and the television, and one on top of the telephone, which Señora Olmos removes to answer the phone and replaces when she hangs up. The dresser is completely covered with all manner of perfumes, lotions, lipsticks, and makeup in a pleasing arrangement. Under it all the tile floor shines, and the effect of the whole is an ornately decorated cake turned inside-out to create a fantasy room.

Señora Olmos is a thin, worn woman in her fifties who wears her light brown hair pulled back tightly in a roll. Dressed in a cheerful, if stiff, yellow polyester dress with short cuffed sleeves, she apologizes for her cold hands; she has just been washing clothes.

At the dresser a young woman is getting ready to go out. She gives lavish care and concern to putting on makeup, lotion, and perfume, trying numerous pairs of shoes, then earrings, in front of the mirror. She doesn't acknowledge the conversation, which is about her.

This is my youngest daughter. She's twenty-five and is studying business administration. Can you believe she is worried that she is too old to get married? I tell her you can always get married. The woman across the street just got married last year and she's in her fifties. So you see, it's never too late to get married, but she won't have another chance to have an education.

Well, I raised seven children by myself. It's been hard, but they're good and they help me. I have had problems with one of my sons, the second to the youngest. I thought he was fine. He was studying in high school and he went every day, so I really didn't know that he was going around with hoodlums. Every day he would leave with his backpack and books, but I didn't know he wasn't going to school. It was only later that I found out. Then he got a job working in a warehouse, but he had bad friends there too. He lost that. Then he got another, but he lost it too. That's been a couple of years ago. At that time I called my husband, but it didn't do any good. It's a little better now. The boy is twenty-two and he has a job with his sister at the *mercado de abastos* packing cabbage. But who knows how long that will last?

Her youngest son knocks on the door. She can see him through the textured window, but they have a certain ritual.

"Who is it?"
"It's me!"
She opens the door with a great smile and obvious affection. "Look at how funny he is. He always knocks even though he has his own key."

A handsome, enthusiastic young man comes in wheeling his bicycle. He greets everyone, politely shaking hands.

My youngest son is nineteen. I don't worry about him; he's a good worker, he gets ahead, and when he goes out, it's to watch soccer or baseball with his friends. He likes sports and he has good friends.

Right now I have three children left in the house. My oldest daughter is married and lives in Chicago. She first studied in secretarial school, then she went back in—what is that?—to be a social worker. She was going to graduate in April, but she got married in December and didn't finish. Of course she got pregnant right away. I told her, but she didn't listen. Then she comes to me with the baby and asks me to keep her while she finished school. I told her, "You should have listened to me. This once I will keep the baby, but this is your only chance." She graduated, but then she went to Chicago. Now she has another baby. I hope she doesn't come back and want me to keep both of them. I have four grandchildren here every day. Two of them I have had since they were born, but I'm getting too old to start all over again. I now have seven grandchildren.

I was never able to go to school. I started primary school, but my father would find things for me to do every day. "You have to stay and take care of the babies, you have to help your stepmother with the washing or the tortillas." Well, I missed too much, so I never learned to read or write. I feel very bad, because whenever you go anywhere they want you to fill out papers, and I have to get someone to help me. I can barely sign my name. Oh, I know I could have gone to school to learn to read when we moved here, but when the twins came, with five little ones there just wasn't any time. That's why I have wanted all my children to go to school. They have all been to high school.

With my husband, well I don't have contact anymore. He used to go over there [to the United States] to work for three months or six months and then he would come back, but it's been, well, my youngest son was seven years old the last time he was here. That was twelve years ago.

It's been hard. I don't go anywhere. I never go out at night, and I don't go visiting like other people. I don't visit with the neighbors. I say good morning and good afternoon, but I have so much to do with what has to be done in the house. On Sunday I go to church and come home.

I'm from Zacatecas, from a small pueblo. That's where I met my husband. We lived there when we were first married. My husband had gone to the United States once before we were married, and then things were hard, so he started going again. We had some land, so he would plant it and come back for the harvest, but I got tired of living alone in the pueblo. It's very difficult there to be responsible for everything, the money, food, family, and animals, and then the crops too, so eventually we moved to Guadalajara. My sister is here. By then we had three children and I was expecting my twins. My husband would go back and forth, but after a while he stayed longer. The last time he had stayed two years. I asked him to take us with him. It would have been easy when we had just the three children. I don't know how to do anything, but I would have been willing to work. I have gone up there twice with my brother, but I can't stay—I miss my children too much. The longest I stayed was three months and twenty days. I called my children every fifteen days, and I knew they were fine, but I just couldn't leave them.

At first my husband would send us money, but after a while he stopped. My children have had to help me. It's hard because I don't know how to do anything except raise animals, make tortillas, and sweep. I always try to keep a couple of pigs, and when my children have needed supplies for school or their tuition I would sell a pig.

If a man loved his family he would be concerned about them; he would communicate with them. But then I don't think a father ever has the love for his family that a mother has. He never worries about them or wonders if they are okay.

No, he has never cared for them the same as I do. He didn't come to the weddings or graduations. The only one who hears from him is my youngest son; sometimes he receives a letter. I guess he has another family over there and doesn't have time for us. I used to call my husband every year, but not anymore. What for, just to have a bill for feeling bad?

His ideas are very different. He always made me wear black dresses up to my chin with sleeves down to here [her wrist]. Well, if one day he comes back, he'll just have to take me as I am. I would never dress like that again for him.

ROSA MARÍA MUÑIZ DE NAVARRO
Housewife
Buena Vista, Mexico

This story begins in a little village rising out of sugarcane fields in central Jalisco. To get there you take a muddy dirt road up from the highway past the sugar mill, which employs the majority of the men in the town. The road winds through the village, where houses line each side. Just beyond the tortilla factory, distinguished by the colorful line of women and children outside, is a small unfinished redbrick house with a black metal door. Rosa Muñiz and her two sons live here.

Inside, the two rooms are dark and cool. The only light comes from an open door that leads to the corral she shares with her in-laws. Along the walls of the one room are brightly painted chairs with rush seats, an open cabinet of clay dishes and pots, and a small stove. A small wooden table covered with an elegant hand-crocheted tablecloth topped with clear plastic is in the center of the room. Children's toys are stacked neatly in a cardboard box in one corner. In the other room are two double beds, each with a bright pink chenille bedspread. On one wall there is a wardrobe topped with a small black-and-white television. On the opposite wall, a little altar holds glasses of flowers and candles, which illuminate a picture of the Virgin with letters from the United States tucked into the frame. Even with unfinished brick and dirt floors this is a very orderly and pleasant little house.

Rosa is pretty and looks closer to sixteen than twenty-four. She has shiny cheeks and bright eyes, a well-scrubbed look that needs no makeup. More traditional than her contemporaries, she almost always wears a dress and keeps her long, dark hair in a single braid. Her figure is small and lithe, giving no hint that she has borne two children.

Eight years ago she was married, and four years later her husband, Nicolas, left for the United States. For the first three and a half years he sent money home on a fairly regular basis and Rosa managed to put both the children in school. Then in July 1987, she received a check for $2,000 from her husband with the welcome news that he would be home for Christmas. Christmas has come and gone and she hasn't heard from him.

He went to be able to build this house, make it larger, or rather to fix it—everything—a living room, rooms to sleep in for the children and for us, and a kitchen with running water. That was his dream and mine too. But in the beginning he suffered a lot. When he passed the border they beat him up. He didn't tell me this, but I found out from my brother-in-law.

I told him he shouldn't go, but he said, "No, I'm going. I don't want anyone to say anything about me, and in a year, more or less, I will return." But he suffered a lot. He didn't have work; finally he had work, but it was really hard because he tried even harder to send me something when he wasn't working.

But now, no. He should be telling me why. He sent the last the 27th of July, and with this we are subsisting. That is why I am very upset. He said he is making this sacrifice for his home, but it has been three years. When he left the youngest child was a year and six months and the other three years, not yet in school. And he . . . yes, he tells me he wants very much to see his sons, but I can't believe it.

He tells me that the life is very expensive there. I talked with him by telephone and he wanted us to come. Then some time passed. He said he had everything ready so we could come. He had a *coyote* with passports because we were going to pass through the line. This was in June of '85. So I was going to go with my brother, but then Nicolas sent me a letter and told me not to move, to stay here. I asked why, what motive he had. He said, "Look, the *coyote* got caught and is in jail." Well I stayed here. Just my brother went. Oh, I wanted very much to go, but . . . I have an aunt in Tijuana, so that wouldn't have been a problem.

Only God knows when he will return. My mama tells me, "Go with him, daughter. Leave your sons with me." But how can I leave my sons?

He used to live on a ranch there, but now I don't know. He told me he was going to leave the ranch because they were going to tear it down. I don't know if it was true or not, but that's what he told me. I have the telephone number, but if they've torn it down what good is it? I don't know where he works. My *compadre* does, but I couldn't ask him. I feel so humiliated I just can't talk to him now, but I can ask my brother to get that information.

I know Nicolas and he has all my confidence. I've thought about it, and that's what I think, because the only thing he thinks of is his children. Nothing but his children. He says he's suffering only for them.

I've asked God for a reason. No, now . . . now clearly it has been too long.

If he doesn't return, who knows? I don't want to obligate him. I want to know if he is okay, or if something happened. That's what I've been thinking—that most likely something happened.

His parents write to him, but he doesn't answer them either. They don't know if he will come home or not.

Yes, one person or another tells me, "Well probably he has another woman, or probably he has children there." But they don't know. He can have twenty children! I'm not interested! It doesn't interest me. Put yourself in my place.

I feel very bad. When I'm washing clothes or whatever, I begin to think. At times I leave and go down the street to visit my sister just so I don't have to think. Then my mother-in-law will tell me, "You are always going out enjoying yourself." *Aye* no! One time she told me I was influencing my children so that now they don't love their father. I didn't answer her. The truth is, I try to tell them about the best of him. What good would it serve for me to say bad things about him when one day he'll come home? No, I make the best of their father, but on their own they think bad things in their little heads.

One day I was crying and my son said, "Mama, don't cry about my papa, I will be the papa." Can you imagine, six years old! Then he told his brother, "Now you have a father. I'm your papa."

I told him, "No, son, I'm not crying for your papa, I just have something in my eye. See if you can get it out."

You can see I'm very preoccupied. I feel very anxious or something. I have to suffer alone, what else? Yes, I'm fearful and think about what could happen tomorrow. I feel something, but I'm not sure what. They tell me the only thing I have to do is go to the American consulate in Guadalajara and they will send him back. What do you think? I want to know about him, but I'm not sure this would solve anything.

If I just had his address and phone number I would go and find him. I want to go see Nicolas, but the only thing I'm worried about is if I don't find him there. I have a cousin in Los Angeles. If I could only know what is happening. If he would just say, "Look, I couldn't write to you." If he doesn't have work and he's embarrassed to write, then he should just tell me. That isn't a problem. But to write nothing. What else can I do? Like I say, I just don't know. He works planting, and my *compadre* says that they can take his work away.

What I want is for him to say whether he thinks or doesn't think he will come back—to tell me once and for all. It's bad for the children. I tell them, "Your papa is coming home for Christmas," and "Soon your papa will be home," and then he doesn't come.

Aye! I know my family thinks the worst, and I think about it too, but they don't know and they can't communicate from here. Nevertheless, I know they talk. But I ask, why are they burning at the mouth? They have told me many things about him, and I don't believe them. Never! Even though my mama says I am a *pendeja*. "You are a very foolish daughter!"

I tell her, "No, Mama, only I know. Only *I* know, and I have confidence in him, and I hope you will too." I tell them, "I don't want to talk about these things."

But really, I don't know. Only God knows. Nicolas isn't a saint, but he isn't that bad either.

Judy Curtis, an American friend of Rosa and Nicolas's, wrote to him in the United States telling him of the plight of his wife and his family's disappointment that he hadn't returned at Christmas.

Mrs. Curtis didn't hear from Nicolas, but a month later she sent a message to Buena Vista asking Rosa to come to Guadalajara. She had received a letter postmarked Stayton, Oregon, from a woman asking her for help, on behalf of Nicolas, in getting him a divorce. She was very anxious for Nicolas to be divorced as soon as possible, she wrote, because she and he were "planning to get married and start a family."

Rosa later recalled that at that moment she had wanted to die. Yet she realized that the letter really told her only that he had another woman. It wasn't clear that these were his feelings. Rosa suffered the torment alone, thinking of nothing except her husband, powerless to do anything.

A month later, Rosa received a letter. This one, though written in Spanish and signed by Nicolas, was in the same hand as the letter to Judy Curtis. In it Nicolas said he wanted to start a new life, he would take the boys if she didn't want them, and he hoped she would pardon him for having ruined her life.

Rosa had never said anything to her parents or Nicolas's parents about the first letter, but when she received the second she showed it to her mother-in-law. In their hearts they didn't believe that he knew about the letter. But they agreed that they must find him in Oregon.

So it was that Rosa and her mother-in-law, Doña Lupe, two women who had never been farther than the twenty-five-mile bus ride to Guadalajara, began a 2,650-mile trip to Stayton, Oregon. They had said good-bye to their families. Their friend, Judy Curtis, took them to the sprawling Guadalajara bus depot and stayed to see them off. Their spirits were high. They had suffered alone, but together they would bring Nicolas back.

Thirty-six hours later in Tijuana they had located Doña Lupe's cousin, a coyote. He happily received them and was willing to take them across.

In the pocket of her only pair of pants Rosa carried all the money they had between them, about $75. At seven o'clock they joined the group with *whom they would cross—all men. The border patrol was out in full force, but the little band skirted and dodged up mountains and down, through culverts and mud-clogged drainage ditches, and over fences, one of which was more than eight feet tall.*

Rosa recalls that journey:

At one point my mother-in-law's heart was beating so hard, she thought she couldn't endure it. She wanted to turn back, but I told her to come on. I myself was huffing and puffing, so you can imagine how worried I was. One of the men grabbed her by the hand and pulled her up and down. It seemed endless, as if we would never get there, but it had been only two hours and we were in a little apartment in the city of San Ysidro. There were fifteen others also waiting, and Doña Lupe's cousin was worried about leaving us with all those men. He made a telephone call and almost immediately a car came for us. Oh, but what a ride. We had to lay down on the floor under the backseat, three of us because there was a young man who also went. Now this wasn't a big car, it was new, but it was little. The *coyote* had the backseat made to take out. Last year he had seventeen cars. He has only three left, the rest were confiscated when he was caught. It was lucky the young man was skinny, because he was in the middle. I still have the bruises from metal ridges pushing into my bones. By the time we arrived there was no feeling left, we were numb and could hardly uncurl to get out.

It was frightening too, because they had to make a stop. The driver had told us about the check, and we could hear it. Believe me, we didn't breathe. I just said my Hail Marys all the way.

He took us to my cousin María's house in Los Angeles. You can imagine her surprise. We hadn't seen each other in eleven years; we were just girls at the time. I think I was about thirteen. And now we both are married and have two sons. Her sons are almost the same ages as mine, and they are very sweet, but they speak only English.

María took us shopping and bought my mother-in-law and me shoes; ours were completely ruined with the water and mud. And she bought me a dress to wear for when I would get to see Nicolas. María's husband received us very well too. One night he took us all out to dinner and for a drive to the beach. I liked Los Angeles. Sometimes I think maybe I should go back there.

We called my sister-in-law in Oakland. At first she didn't believe that her mother and I were in the United States, even when we told her to meet us at the San Francisco airport the next day. Well, she wasn't going to leave us stranded, but I don't think she believed we were really coming.

María and her husband paid our plane fare and took us to the airport. Just before we left he gave us $150. I don't know how I can ever repay them. You know, I had never even met him, but he told me he wanted me to have it. He teased us, telling us there were lots of *migra* at the airport. As if we weren't scared enough. I thought we would be grabbed at any moment, but María said we looked almost like *gringas*. I wore some pants and these big earrings that she had given me, and she combed my hair out. Of course we didn't understand a word of what they were saying on the loudspeaker, but we just watched and did what everyone else was doing. We put our bag in that machine and buckled the belts and everything. We closed the window shade so we didn't have to look out and the time passed very rapidly. Really, I couldn't even tell that we were on the ground again.

Conchita, Doña Lupe's twenty-one-year-old daughter, was at the airport to meet them. It was a tearful reunion. Conchita hadn't seen anyone in her family since she had come north more than a year before to help finance her younger brother's studies to be a doctor.

It had been arranged that someone would drive them the final leg of their journey. They left early the next morning for the twelve-hour trip. Stayton is a small, almost rural town, and without much difficulty they found the address on the envelope.

As Rosa and Doña Lupe approached the house, Nicolas and a woman came out of the door. For a moment he didn't recognize them. Then, when they stepped on to the front porch, he reacted violently, bolting past them and running into the street, screaming incoherently. Rosa followed him and when she tried to put her arms around him, he pushed her away roughly.

In just minutes their plans and the months of hope disintegrated in a barrage of anger and hate.

DOÑA GUADALUPE (LUPE) CHAVEZ DE NAVARRO
Buena Vista, Mexico

Three months later, sitting on the covered porch that overlooks the corral she shares with her daughter-in-law Rosa, Doña Lupe talks about her son. The herb tea she is drinking is reputed to cure the chronic pain in her neck and shoulders, which she attributes to the stress and worry over her son.

I've tried not to think about him so much, but I can't help myself. There seems to be no answer, but in my heart I know he needs help. He was never like that. I don't know if he's sick, you know, mentally, or if he's on drugs. He used to drink and those were the times he would fight with his father, but he never took drugs. But now, I could see he had enough money—a nice house with furniture, a television, music, a bicycle, and a new car. I can see that he could have the money to buy drugs too.

It hurts me, you know, for his wife and sons. They don't deserve to suffer like this. When we got back to Oakland my daughter got Rosa a job. She started that very night. I wanted to work too, but my daughter wouldn't let me. She said it was too hard. They had to work from midnight until nine in the morning, cutting fruit and vegetables, kilos and kilos, for restaurants. Rosa was so tired that she was afraid she'd fall asleep and cut her finger off. They gave them very sharp knives. The worst was when they had to cut onions, sometimes twelve boxes of them, but it was mostly fruit. The girls would bring me home some fruit salad each morning, fresh fruit, very good too, but they couldn't bear to eat it. They couldn't even stand the smell. It was fine though because they paid her $100 a week (approximately $1.85 an hour). If it weren't for her job we would still be there, because Nicolas never sent the money for us to come home. We called him, but when Rosa tried to talk he hung up. Then I called him from the airport as we were leaving and he hung up on me too. I cried and cried. I still can't believe my son would reject his own mother.

My husband and I have talked about it. He agrees that something must be wrong. That's why I am so worried. My husband says we should go to the American consulate and see if they will send him back so that we can cure him. I think we should too, but then I wonder about bringing that grief on Rosa and her little boys. They have already suffered so much. And if he came back I would worry that her brothers might kill him. I pray to God and the little virgin for a solution, because in my heart I don't have the answer.

Because of Nicolas's uncharacteristic attitude toward his family and especially his mother, and the fact that his physical appearance had changed greatly, Doña Lupe and her husband felt he must be either mentally ill or on drugs. After several months of worrying they decided they must try to get him returned to Mexico.

They sent the following letters to the American Consulate in Guadalajara, the U.S. Immigration and Naturalization Service in Los Angeles, Anaheim, and Portland, Oregon, and Senator Mark Hatfield in Oregon.

November 25, 1987

To Whom It May Concern:

I, the father of Nicolas Navarro Chavez and my wife, the mother of Nicolas, have found that our son, who is currently residing illegally in the United States, is ill of his mental faculties. For this reason it is my desire to report this. I, as his father, promise to undertake charge of him and to provide the medical care necessary as soon as he is returned to his family.

Carlos Navarro
Guadalupe Chavez de Navarro

November 25, 1987

Dear Immigration Office,

I, the wife of Mr. Nicolas Navarro Chavez, am writing you this letter with the purpose of calling your attention to the situation concerning my husband. In March of 1983, he went illegally to the State of Oregon seeking a better life for his family, his two children and I. In the beginning everything was fine, but after some time we no longer heard from him. As we didn't know what was happening to him, his mother and I went to look for him. We found him in Oregon this past April. It made us very sad and a little afraid to find that he was obviously mentally ill. We don't know if drugs are producing this situation or simply mental problems. He was very violent and he was never like that before. Since that time we have been worried about him because from here there is nothing we can do to help him or cure him.

I, for my part, as Nicolas's wife, cannot support our two children alone, and they also need the support of their father. I beg you to return him to his own country and his family where he can get help. My in-laws have promised to take responsibility for him as soon as he is returned. They will hospitalize him if it is necessary.

I include photostatic copies of our marriage license and the birth certificates of our two sons. He is working in the city of Stayton, Oregon, at this address: . . .

His home address is: . . .

I thank you in advance for any help that you may be able to give us.

Sincerely,
Sra. Rosa María Muñiz de Navarro

This is the answer Rosa received:

December 14, 1987

Dear Mrs. Navarro,

Thank you for sending me a copy of your recent letter to the Immigration and Naturalization Service regarding your husband.

While I appreciate your concern for your husband's health and well being and your need to support yourself and your children, I regret I cannot be of assistance to you in this matter.

I suggest you contact your husband directly or through his employer to express your concern and desire for him to return home to Mexico.

Kind regards.

Sincerely,
Mark O. Hatfield
United States Senator

Neither the American Consulate nor the U. S. Immigration and Naturalization Service replied.

III

EL NORTE

DESDE MORELIA

Desde Morelia vine enganchado,
Ganar los dólares fue mi ilusión;
Compré zapatos, compré sombrero
Y hasta me puse pantalón.

Y ahora me encuentro
Ya sin resuello,
Soy zapatero de profesión
Pero aquí dicen que soy camello
Y a puro palo y a puro azadón.

FROM MORELIA

From Morelia I came as a bracero,
To earn dollars was my illusion.
I bought shoes, I bought a sombrero,
And even put on new pants.

And now I find myself
Breathless,
I'm a shoemaker by profession
But here they say I'm a camel
And I work just with a shovel and a hoe.

Breathless

DREAMS VERSUS REALITY

Streets of gold: that is the vision they carry setting out from their villages heading to el norte. *There are wonderful tales about the other side: the good jobs, the beauty, the* gringas, *how someone got their papers. And the treasures! People bring back televisions, VCRs, and these new microwaves that cook dinner in less than a minute! Many an afternoon has been spent with com-pañeros and tequila going over and over those stories, stories the younger generation are raised on.*

No one ever has a realistic view of the United States before arriving, and it can never live up to their expectations, either as a place or in the possibility of fulfilling their dreams. After a short while, many immigrants see past their fantasies, adjust their expectations, and stay on to make the most of what the opportunity offers.

Some, like Pancho Barrera, are coldly objective: "Everyone told me how beautiful it was on the other side. Working bent over all day long in 110 degrees? No, it was an inferno! I stayed fifteen days and I'd never go back!" Pancho returned to his village, joined with his neighbors to form a cooperative, and over the years became a successful farmer.

Most, like Miguel Jiménez, will return home before the year is out with glowing reports that perpetuate the myth: "No, it was great! I got a job right away. Working in a restaurant I made more in a day than you do in a week.

And you should have seen the girls. I had at least five girlfriends. Before I could even offer them a beer they would buy me one, they would teach me English, and then they would leave me a tip."

Bringing gifts, new clothes and money, they will be welcomed as returning heroes. Now that they have experienced the otro lado *(the other side), the pueblo seems too confining. After all, they're used to "life in the big city." This is exactly Miguel's experience. He returned, and by virtue of his new aura attracted a wife. He left his pueblo for Mexico City, where he has a good job in a paint factory and is the father of two daughters.*

Others never adjust their dreams and expectations of el norte *with its reality. They hang on, imagining their fantasies are true, or they return to Mexico believing it all really happened.*

JUAN MONTOYA
Classical Guitarist
Guanajuato, Mexico

In Guanajuato, music envelops la plaza principal. *Two little boys singing ranchero songs, the mariachi playing behind them, the staccato of an exuberant violin leaping from a balcony window, and in the distance indistinguishable musical notes, all form concentric circles of sound. In this city of music, sitting under a blue-and-white umbrella at an outdoor café, Juan is examining a manuscript of the sonata he is working on. He orders a* café de la olla *and talks about going to the United States.*

The people in your pueblo talk; they say they earn a lot of money over there. That's why I thought of going. I wanted to earn the money so I could continue my studies, but also to learn more about the United States, to see if what they told me was true.

The first time I went was the twelfth of May, in 1985. I remember, because it was two days after Mother's Day. I took 10,000 pesos, a bundle of clothes, and that was it. My mama was very sad. They don't want to let their sons go, even when they're grown. I'm the second son, there are eleven of us. Most of my brothers have gone too. My youngest brother is seventeen years old and he just left last week. He escaped! He left secondary school and off he went. I imagine he's in Tijuana by now. Of course they wouldn't let my sisters go.

When I went, there were six of us from the pueblo, all friends. One was an older man, about fifty. He had been many times before and acted as our guide. He had been going back and forth for fifteen years. He used to be a campesino, but now he has money in the bank. He works there for six months and comes back here to live until it's time to go back. The first time he went he had to look for work, but from then on his boss would write him a letter telling him when he would need him. But he wasn't the one who convinced me to go. I had already decided, and when he was going it was an opportunity to go with him.

We took a train from a pueblo near here to Nuevo Laredo. There we crossed the river in a boat. When we got there the river was very full, so we walked along the river and found some people with a boat who offered to take us across. At first they wanted to charge us 10,000 pesos apiece, but then they agreed on 2,500 for all of us. Those who are passing people across the river are all Mexican. They just take you to the other side. We crossed at two o'clock in the afternoon and we hid under a tree until nine at night. After that we walked until five in the morning. Then we rested for a while and began to walk again. We walked for nine days, hiding. At times we stayed in cabins; there are a lot of cabins. Sometimes people have left food to eat and you can sleep there. It would have taken us less time but one day we got lost. That's why it was nine days. We were running out of food. We had only one can of tuna for six of us. After that we killed an armadillo with a slingshot. With a knife we cut away his shell and cleaned out the innards. Then we made a fire, and when the coals were hot we cooked it. It doesn't taste bad really, sort of like pork, or between pork and fish.

After nine days we arrived just outside San Antonio where there is a man, a Chicano, who helps us. He loaned us a truck where we slept for two weeks. We bathed in the river and ate potatoes and beans. In the meantime we had a little work cutting beans. We would start at six in the morning and finish at twelve noon and he would pay us $7. It wasn't much, but we could buy a little food and beer.

See, if you bring him a number he will call the boss collect. If the boss pays, he will take you; if not, then you have to stay there. The boss wasn't expecting me so he wouldn't pay my transportation, but this man, the *coyote,* paid for me. It was $350. He took us to North Carolina. There were about fifteen of us in the truck; we made two stops. I paid him in payments. Every time he would arrive with more people I would make a payment.

We arrived on Saturday. Sunday we slept all day and on Monday we went to work. We cultivated tobacco. It isn't that bad. The first week of cutting, the muscles in your back and waist are sore. It's a big plant and you have to cut from the bottom leaves, so you are bent over all day.

We would get up at five in the morning and everyone would make their own breakfast. Then at six or seven we would get off and that's when we would have our big dinner, because at noon we only had an hour.

We got $3.50 an hour. They had told us $3.50, but when we got our checks we saw that they had paid us only $3.35. We had to ask them to pay us the fifteen cents they owed us. They took money out for the taxes, but we didn't know how to get the money back.

I was there from June to October. We also cut cabbage and cucumber. While the tobacco was growing there wasn't any work, but our boss got other work for us because he didn't want us to leave.

We bought a car when we were coming back from North Carolina, but before we got to Miami the police stopped us and confiscated it. But it was an old car—it only cost $260, and we split it four ways. A stereo and speakers cost more. They put us in jail. That was a Sunday morning. We got out on Wednesday and they took us to Brownsville. It wasn't the *migra*. They treat you well in jail, it's not like being in jail here. But at the same time they charged us. I had to give them the $500 I had and my clothes. And they gave me a receipt for $250, so they charged me $250. They told us we didn't have any rights because we were here illegally. They told us we had to give them the money for our food and transportation.

I knew the risks, about *la migra,* even about the Mexicans on this side. I knew we could get lost. And the snakes—there are lots of snakes in May, because it's hot then. And there are parts where you actually have to crawl. I wore high-top tennis shoes. You just have to be careful. I had a pocketknife; it isn't worth bringing a big knife or a gun. You'll just lose it; then if you're caught you would be in even more trouble. The other thing, when a lot of people go together like that there can be a fight, for hardly any reason. People are tired and hungry, and they can get upset over anything, even though they're friends. One guy had a box of crackers; he got mad because another one took some. They worked it out, but it's better not to bring any arms.

Some people bring medallions of saints and things, they go to Mass and confession. I personally didn't do any of these things. I guess I had the faith that my mother would pray and intervene for me. In reality the benediction of your *madre* is what gives you the most hope and spirit.

So I arrived home with $250. I had also sent back $350 in money orders. With this money I started a ceramic business. I bought the equipment, a tank of gas, and an oven. So I had that and with the money I made from it I was able to continue studying. But I lost almost a year at the university when I went to the United States.

I like all kinds of music. I had wanted to study music since I was in secondary school. But my parents wanted me to go to high school first. So I went to a technical school in Mexico City and studied mechanical engineering. When I came to the university here I already knew how to play the guitar, and in secondary school we had a teacher who played classical music. Then in Dolores, where I lived, there were concerts frequently. It's a small pueblo, but it has a big auditorium.

I like classical music, but what I find myself listening to now is contemporary music. If I had to choose music to listen to, I would take rock—progressive rock—or something classical, perhaps by Tchaikovsky or Mozart. In rock, I would take something by Pink Floyd. I'm working on a tango I found by Francisco Tarrega, a Brazilian rhythm, then a suite by Manuel Maria Ponce, a *mexicano,* and a sonata by Ferdinando Carulli. That's what I'm doing now.

I would like to be a concert guitarist, but I don't think there will be work in that. There is work, but you have to be the best, or you have to have influence. Sometimes even when you are good, really the best, it doesn't matter. If you don't have friends with influence, you don't play.

I'm going back to the United States in June, and if I get permission from the university I will stay until October. I'm hoping to go back to North Carolina, but it costs a lot of money to get there. I didn't really like North Carolina. There are very few Mexicans, and when you go into a supermarket they follow you with their eyes and treat you with bad humor. Not everyone, but many people. So I'll have to see. Hopefully, with the dollars I bring back this time, I can finish my studies.

PEDRO MEDINA GAVINO
Son of María de Jesús and Maclovio Medina*
Unemployed Concrete Worker
Tucson, Arizona

The dried-out vegetation and sunbaked houses form a monochromatic gray landscape. Other than the sound of barking dogs, there is no life on the narrow streets. The rear unit of a duplex on the outskirts of Tucson is home to Pedro, Rayann, and their three little boys. The entrance leads into the small kitchen, where a table, the stove, sink, and refrigerator line three walls. Already the modest interior is made much more cheerful by the sounds of music, colorful drawings pinned on the walls, and the banter of children. But times are hard and Pedro's job undependable. They never seem to have enough money for more than the two mattresses, bookshelf, four chairs, and table that furnish their house.

Pedro realized the dream of many young Mexicans: to marry a gringa. *But the freedom, legal status, and economic security that are said to be part of it have eluded him.*

When I came to the United States in 1976, I went to Oxnard, California, and worked in the fields cutting celery. I came with my uncle; we came together. From there a young Chicano guy told me, "Get together some workers and we'll go to Chicago, Illinois, two or three, and we won't charge you."

I got some guys and told him, "I have three guys, then with myself and my uncle there are five and with you there's six." So off we went. They took us to Colorado and from there we went to Chicago. Oh, it's a long ways away. But Chicago is beautiful and very big—the buildings are so tall. I didn't have any fear, but then I didn't have a wife and children and I was only sixteen years old. I got on the train, the El. I wasn't afraid, I just got on. When they opened the door of the train it was like looking at a movie, everything very elegant, passing by the doorway.

*See chapter 1.

I spoke only a little English. There were Hispanics who spoke Spanish, but a lot of words were in English, most of the streets and everything was in English. I had the address of where I was going, a hotel where I was going to work. They were beginning to build it. I worked cleaning, clearing the garbage and all. When it was time to eat, they would call us from the kitchen. "Eat whatever you want." We were paid well too, almost $5 an hour. In construction they pay you well. We worked from early in the morning until six at night. We would leave with our legs numb. I would give my uncle a pat on the shoulder and he'd say, "No, no, I'm too sore." It was great.

I was also in jail once. That was fourteen or fifteen years ago. I was drunk and I hit the policeman. That was in Los Angeles, and I was supposed to stay there for thirty days, but I talked to the judge and explained to him that I was drunk and I was very sorry it had happened. So he let me out. I didn't have to pay the fine either—I think it was $750. But they sent me back to Tijuana.

That same night I came back. There were about fifteen of us. We went through the tube where the black water comes out. It's like a big canal, it doesn't smell that bad, but we covered our noses and ran. It's about fifteen blocks, but once you go in there's no way out. There was a van waiting for us and we went to the *coyote*'s house. They gave us dinner: "Come eat, whatever you like, there's meat, eggs, coffee, milk." They were really nice. They asked me, "Who is going to pay for you guys?" I told them I had to go to some friends' to borrow the money. They thought I wasn't going to pay, but I said, "No, I'm going to pay, come with me." We went to my friends' house, but none of them had any money.

"See what I told you?"

But his wife said, "Wait, maybe he can come up with it." She was the *coyota*. It was $400 that I owed them.

"Look, I am going to work tomorrow. I get paid in two weeks. Believe me I will pay you then."

The man wanted to take me back to Tijuana, but his wife, *la coyota,* said, "We'll be back in two weeks. If you don't pay then it will be very bad for you." So of course I paid them.

I met Rayann in Los Angeles, but she is from Montana. It was at a dance, and she smoked and everything, I even bought cigarettes for her. My brothers couldn't believe that she smoked. But then when we got together I told her, "I'm going to stop smoking. You have to stop too." So now she doesn't smoke. It's really not good for you.

Everyone says they want to marry a *gringa,* but I never really said that. I never really thought there was a chance. But she spoke to me first. And I spoke only Spanish, so I couldn't even answer her. I don't know how we managed to communicate; it's something like magic. But we decided to get married. I said, "We should think about it a couple of days." I told her she should ask her parents, because I couldn't ask them. But she said she had already asked them. I said, "And what did they say?"

"Well, they said it was okay."

She was very young, I think she was eighteen years old. I was twenty-five. We didn't really think; we were kind of ignorant. But that's the way life is.

We got married at the courthouse. Actually we got married two times—the first time in Los Angeles, but then when we went to stay with Rayann's parents she wanted to get married again. So we got married again in Portland. I said, "I do," in English. Of course here they get married in English. I would listen to the judge. He would talk, "Bla, bla, bla." And when he stopped talking and looked at me with his chin down, I would say, "I do."

I'm still here illegally. Once I got picked up at work, but I told them that I was married and had two children and one on the way. He said, "Do you have a marriage license?" I told him I did, but that it was at home. He said, "If you have a marriage license I won't send you to Mexico." He brought me home and I showed it to him and he let me go.

I could get my papers, but they tell me I have to return to Mexico. How can I leave my wife and children for six months? I've thought about it, but you know when you get married you become like one. It's like magnetism, you live together, and you think alike and say the same words, it's like you become one person, you and your wife. I don't think I could leave them.

We stayed one year in Independence, Oregon. I worked in the lumber there. It smells so good, the wood, and it's very pretty with the snow and everything, but aye how cold it is! But the economy there has many problems and a lot of times there was no work. So five years ago we moved here.

I like it here, but right now I don't have work. I'm waiting for my boss to call me. That's how it is in concrete. Some weeks there's work and some weeks there isn't. Rayann works nights at Circle K and I work days.

Here my children live as if they were in heaven. Imagine how it was when I was young. I was born in my own house. My mother didn't go to a hospital or anything. My children were born in a fine hospital, with every luxury. And now look, they go to the bathroom, they have hot water and can take a bath every night. They don't know the comparison, but in San Juan we didn't have a toilet, we didn't have a bath, and we didn't have hot water. Here they get up in the morning and it's warm. We have nice warm floors. I remember when I was their age we slept on *petates* [woven mats] and oh, I hated to get out of bed and stand on the cold dirt floors. Here it is much cleaner. We have garbage cans and the garbage men come. Some people here don't appreciate it. The people in front just throw their garbage around. But I pick it up, because I know what it's like if everybody throws their garbage out the door. To me cleanliness is beautiful, principally because it prevents many illnesses that people can die from, right? No, my children don't know that they are growing up in pure luxury. Someday I would like to take them to San Juan so they will know the luck they have.

Of course I would like to become rich. I would like to have $4,000 in the bank and furniture and all. But I think the most important thing is for my children to go to school, get their education. I want to see them graduate and be whatever they want. This is possible here, because it doesn't cost money. And oh how happy I would be if they could speak two languages.

JUAN MEDINA GAVINO
Brother of Pedro Medina Gavino
Son of María de Jesús and Maclovio Medina*
Factory Worker
Los Angeles, California

Saturday morning finds Juan outside painting the wrought iron security bars on the doors and windows of the little wood frame house. His brother Amado

*See chapter 1.

is working one step ahead, sanding them. The house, squeezed in between apartment buildings, is one of the nicest on the street, with a white picket fence and flowers blooming in the yard. Surrounded by some of L.A.'s most dangerous neighborhoods, their block seems safe and quiet except for the train that passes by every half hour: the windows rattle, the floors rumble, and all conversation stops. Amazingly enough the babies don't awaken.

Juan and Amado came to Los Angeles with their brother, Pedro, but their luck was better. In a cooperative effort, they were able to attain the American dream, their own home. They are both married and have two sons. But the price is high. They are still undocumented, and with a house and families to maintain, the risk of returning to see their parents is too great. They have been gone eight years.

When we were little we lived in San Juan, but when we got a little older we went to work in Guadalajara. At first I wanted to study, but there was no money, so I had to leave school. That was in 1970. My father was working here in the United States. When he went I took advantage because he wasn't there and left school. But it was because we didn't have the money. So I went to work for *la Coca* [Coca-Cola]. I worked there for about eight years. I really wasn't thinking of coming here. I was happy there and more or less I earned enough money. Well, we didn't really get paid for the work we did, but that's normal there. See, I was single and I would give some to my papa, and I would have enough for myself. But then my brother Pedro came back and he said, "Come on, let's go." He was going. So I said, "Sure."

I was planning to stay for about six months; I wanted to earn enough money to go to high school. I found work right away, but like everyone else who has recently arrived without experience, they paid me the minimum and I could hardly get by. I have friends with families who earn the minimum and they manage, and I was a bachelor and still had a hard time making ends meet. I got $118 a week, and at the end of the week I would have to borrow money for the *marketa*, groceries. There were six of us living together in one apartment. That was ten years ago and I have only returned once, in 1982, when the factory gave me a month off.

Now it's different. Before, you would say, "Well, I don't think I'll go to work today. The thing is there'll always be work tomorrow." But now, if you say you're not going to work you begin to think of the children, or a payment you have to make, and you decide you'll be better off going to work. The work here is very strict. If you miss work and don't have a justification they count it against you, and without very much provocation they will fire you. I was working at Western and Second, packing plastic things such as cups and glasses into sets. But I had just arrived and I was accustomed to making more money, so I wasn't happy with the pay. I only worked there nine months and they were laying off people, people who had worked much longer than I had. Finally there were only three of us left and they let me go. That was on a Wednesday and they called me back on Saturday, but by Friday I had already found work in a furniture factory, and they were paying me more. The thing is, we came here to work. I worked there two years, but they wouldn't give me a raise so I left. I thought I would rest for a while and I had this car that didn't have papers, so I thought, "I'll get the papers while I'm on vacation." I was going over to the Motor Vehicles and I saw a factory on the corner. I thought, I'll just stop in here and see if they need help. I asked the secretary if I could fill out an application, but usually when you fill out an application they never call. So as I was about to leave, she told me to go around the block to the other side and have an interview. See, at that time I didn't speak much English, but I went and they talked to me. They wanted to know what experience I had had. Then they wanted to test me to see if I could use the cutting equipment. See, I had cut wood before, but this was foam rubber. Oh well, it was easy, I cut it real fast. This was at two o'clock in the afternoon, and they asked me if I could come in at three thirty. I said, "Why don't I wait until tomorrow?" But no, they wanted me right away. "Okay." I didn't even have time to get the papers for the car.

Where I'm working now, in the Chinese noodle company, my *padrino de matrimonio* works there too. A friend had told us they were accepting applications. They called us this time too. The owner called, his name is George. He said, "We have openings if you want to come to work."

I told him, "No, what I want is more information. I want to know how much you pay." He was paying $4.70. So I said, "Well see, that isn't enough. Where I am now I'm making $6.10. Do you have any other work where I can make more?" I told him I could drive a truck or a forklift.

He says, "Do you know how or did you just put it on your application to get work?"

I told him, "No, you can test me if you like." It still paid only $5.50, so I told him I had to think about it. He told me that was just the starting pay and that they give raises every three months. So I thought about it and decided to take my vacation and try it out over there. That was in 1984, and I have been at the Chinese noodle factory ever since. Within a year I was up to $7.00 an hour. Then each Christmas they give us a bonus of $150. I'm real happy there and I get along with the boss.

At that time we were saving money, my brother Amado and I, to go back to Mexico. We were going back to work with my papa. How much did we have? I think it was about $3,000. Then a *comadre* came to live with us in the apartment where we were living. She brought her children and all, and there were too many people living there. I told my *compadres* that they should stay there and we would move. So we were looking for an apartment to rent and we had this telephone number. We called and the man invited us to come talk, but it was a real estate and they had houses to sell. Well, we found this house. It was $77,000 and they wanted 10 percent. We saved and borrowed from friends, whatever we could. We had one month to pay the down payment. Somehow we managed to raise the money. It's much better because there are two little houses, and we have three bathrooms here. And they say that soon the Metro going downtown will pass by here.

We weren't married yet, but once we bought the house we decided to get married. I had met Josefina at a dance at the Convention Center in June. "Los Bukies" from Mexico were playing. We got married a year later in August. Then Amado married Martha in February. They had been *novios* for four years.

At first we all lived together in this house and rented out the back. But now that we both have two children it was too crowded. If one baby cried he would wake up the others. Also Josefina couldn't sew with all the children right here. So a few months ago Amado and Martha moved to the house in back. There are two bedrooms back there too.

The problem we have now is we have to pay a second [mortgage]. We have to pay $12,200 in 1990. At the time it seemed like it would be easy to save that much in five years. But now with a family it's very different. We only have one year left and we have to save $10,000.

Young, naive, and infatuated with American life, families like Juan's and Amado's are prey to rateros *in disguise, in their case, disguised as a water purification company. The "company" tested their Metropolitan Water District of Southern California water and found it to have high levels of toxins. Pleading to the Mexicans' deep concern for their children's health and their coming from a country where pure water is not only an issue but a national, almost religious quest, they persuaded them to sign a contract to install a $5,000 purification system.*

And now the looming $12,000 balloon payment threatens to turn their dream into an illusion.

MARÍA DE JESÚS ORDAZ VIUDA DE VASQUEZ
Mother of Martha Vasquez de Gomez
*and José Vasquez**
Widow
San Juan, Mexico

María de Jesús was only thirty-four years old when her husband died of cancer. She was left with ten children, ranging in age from nineteen years to eight months. Through the years, as they became old enough to work, the children helped support the family. There are no jobs in her small village, but she did what she could too. Raising chickens and pigs, and selling Avon cosmetics, she managed to put three of her youngest sons through secondary school, but there was never enough money to finance a business enterprise. It was always her dream to go to the United States.

In 1988, her opportunity came along. A friend in a nearby village had a compadre *in Oakland who owned a restaurant and needed help. It took almost a year to make the arrangements: finding a new school in the city for the two youngest children, who would stay with one of her daughters, gaining the approval of her brothers and sons, and raising the money.*

As she cooks comida *over the open fire outside the two-room adobe house she shares with her son, daughter-in-law, their five children, and two of her own, she talks about her trip to* el norte.

*See chapters 2 and 4.

How should I begin? I wanted to go to work. I had been offered work and I had the desire to go to the United States. It was very difficult, because the Immigration caught me two times, the first time before arriving at San Ysidro and the other in San Clemente.

They wanted to put me in the trunk of a car, but I didn't fit. The man was very mad and bawled me out because I didn't have makeup on and wasn't dressed nice. Well, I was all dirty. What do you think, without water, without clothes, without anything? The driver really bawled me out. He was really angry. This was the *coyote* that was going to pass us when they caught us in San Clemente. And seeing that the Immigration was there, you know how they shine their flashlights, he said he was going to see what happened. And those who were in the trunk, they didn't have air, they were gasping for air. So when they caught them they were thinking it was better to shout *gracias a Dios* that they caught them, because they were suffocating. From there they put us in a big corral. We stayed there until they had enough to fill the bus and send us back again to Tijuana. Then we were without money. We called my son-in-law in Guadalajara, and he told us he would send some. But then we called my *compadre* and he came with the money we had given him to guard while we were passing.

By then we had gone two days without eating, and my son wanted to return to San Juan. He didn't want to try again. But I intended to make the fight and get myself in. I found someone who would cross me at the line, but he charged a lot. It cost me $600 to cross at the line, but this time I made it.

I had to stay in San Diego for several days until someone could take me to the house of my patrons in Oakland. I stayed with the Señora Lidia. She has a house where people who are crossing can stay. She was very nice to everyone, and gave us food and everything. The only thing is, we were hidden and couldn't make noise of any kind.

It was about eight thirty in the morning when I arrived at my patron's house, and by nine o'clock the same day I was working. I didn't know my boss before, not until that day. He took me to the restaurant to meet everyone. They were all very good people, very friendly because they're all Mexican, right. They treated me very well. In the end the *señora,* my patron's wife, said I shouldn't go back, that I could stay with them.

In the restaurant I worked part of June, July, August, September, and part of October. They were paying me $300 every two weeks. The others who worked there got $300 [a week], but I didn't pay any rent, I didn't pay anything. My patron gave me a room and everything.

My work was in the kitchen. The first thing in the morning when I arrived I would heat all of the different dishes. Then I would clean tables, wash windows, make up the place settings, put ice out for the glasses. I would clean the refrigerators. In the kitchen I would cut the meat, debone the pork, cut the beefsteaks, and then cut up the *menudo* [tripe] and all the vegetables. When people arrived for lunch I served plates and cleared tables and even attended the customers. I liked the work a lot. I worked all week and they gave me one day off. It wasn't always Sunday.

When I got Sundays off my patron would take me with his family to the *lienzo charro*, the rodeo ring, where he was in the association of *charros*. If it was another day I would go visiting or take the bus or the BART [rapid transit]. That's how I got lost one day. I also went to San Jose, to Reno, to Lake Tahoe. I played the little machines there. Then I went to Sacramento to a wedding. Where else? Oh, also San Francisco. I liked everywhere I went. When my boss's wife went to the flea market in San Jose she would take me. It's a market like the *tianguis* here. It's very pretty there.

I worked until the middle of October, when there was a report to the Immigration. The only thing is we don't know on whose account they received the report. So the day that the Immigration arrived, because the boss has two restaurants, he had sent me to the other one, the smaller one. So when the Immigration arrived I wasn't there. They caught five of my companions. So from then on I worked only a few days and then my boss told me it would be better if I stayed in the house so I wouldn't risk being caught and returned. That's why I didn't work there anymore.

Later my boss told me about a lady in San Jose who was obtaining papers for immigrants. He asked if I wanted to get my papers. I told him yes, but then she was charging $600 for the card to work on a ranch. So my boss told me I should wait to see what happened, to see what the results were, because some had already given her the money. If they were able to get their papers then we would try to get mine too. My boss's nephew had paid $600. So I told my boss yes. I was anxious to give my money too so I could get my papers, but then he didn't pay me for two weeks. So I only paid part of it, $400. He went and took it to the lady. So one day we went to see the lady, to see when they were going to investigate and interview us. She was going to put everything in order for the Immigration and we were going to have to say just a few words and that would be it. But when we went to see the lady she was no longer there. She had left, with the money of five people. What could we do?

So after that I just did housework in my boss's house, but now they weren't paying me. So I told myself, I'll just stay here. My boss told me I could stay until I was settled in another job or for the time that I wanted to stay. Once in a while they would give me something to spend, my *domingo,* my allowance. But I did all the housework there.

I wanted to stay, because it had been so little time. I looked for work a lot, but wherever you went they wanted your social security number. Then I bought a social security number that they sold me, a nun's. But this card wasn't any good, because it was old and it was a different color and now they have a new color. So I couldn't work using that. I looked for work cleaning apartments, but it was so very far away I needed someone to accompany me, and they were going to pay very little. It didn't work out. My boss said, "If they are only going to pay $50 a week, it would be better if we paid you that here." So I cleaned house and some weeks they would pay me and some weeks they wouldn't. But I couldn't say anything because they would leave me a key. They left me everything, and they always gave me my food, the whole time.

Finally I found work with another woman in her house. I had been there for three days when my family called to tell me that one of my daughters was going to have an operation. And at that time my legs were very bad from the cold and ice so I decided to return.

I came back fine, but it was a very long trip. You can't believe how long it took. So long that road. There is a place called Fresno, and the bus was stopped there for a long, long time. *Muchísimo tiempo.* Waiting, I don't know what for, but a long time, and all the people desperate, they wanted to go on. Oh, that was a long, long trip.

To me it was very hard, very hard. When I left here I took 2,300,000 pesos [$1,000]. This is money that I had borrowed from friends and relatives and that my children gave me. When José decided to return I gave him part of the money. I kept 250,000 pesos [about $109]. I changed the money and I arrived in Los Angeles with $60. That was it, nothing else.

I started back with four big suitcases and six small bags. Money—I had just a little, $290, that was what I had. I think the ticket from Oakland to Tijuana was $63. And from Tijuana, they charged me $80 for my suitcases. Then in the Old Bus Station, that was the first check, they took $20. And in Sonorita they took, how much was it, 150,000 pesos [$65]—now it was pesos—they charged me for the weight of the suitcases. That's what I paid. I say it's bad, because it was too much what they were charging when one is bringing back just used clothing for their family. Right? That's what I told the Immigration, "I'm bringing all used clothing and it's for my family."

Then they told me, "A lot of people say they are bringing clothes back for their family, but they are really bringing it back for a business."

I told them no. I promised them that it was for my family because I have a lot of children. So one *aduana* told me if I didn't pay what they were asking they were going to let me take only two suitcases and I could leave the others until I had the money to return for them. Can you believe that? Well no, I paid it and they let me come.

But then in the night I got cold and when we stopped I asked the driver to let me get my suitcase, the black one. We looked and looked, but it wasn't there. I made him take everything out, but now it wasn't on the bus. I had bought these warm jackets for my sons, three of them. No, it was four, one for my grandson too, and I thought I could cover myself to keep warm. But the suitcase wasn't there. They kept it in Sonorita. I had opened all the suitcases to show them and they made me pay for it. But they didn't let the passengers put their things back on the bus. After we paid, we had to wait for them to load the bus. They just kept it, the Immigration, or maybe the driver, I don't know. It had the jackets and a little television with a radio, and then I bought a video recorder and some calculators for the boys. All these things were gone. What could I do? I cried and cried all the way home. If I had known, I wouldn't have bought anything. Nothing.

I knew how the work was going to be more or less. It had been explained to me, so I went knowing how it would be. And I really liked it. If my legs get better I am going to go back. I will go back, but I won't buy anything to bring home. I think if God gives me license, I will go again, but this time just to Los Angeles. My sister-in-law's first cousin, Choli, has a business and she has promised me work in Los Angeles. What do you think? No, she says, "What are you doing there? Here you have work and a house with me."

If my legs get better then I'll go. If not, then I'll stay here and keep quiet. Oh, but I'll still have the *ganas*.

CUAUHTÉMOC MENENDEZ
Construction Worker
Guadalajara, Mexico

All the while he's on the ladder painting the intense terra-cotta-colored wall, he's thinking. He never stops. His formal education ended in the ninth grade, but when he goes home at night, muscles tired from a long day of hard work, he finds pleasure in reading. Reading, so that he'll have something to think about on the ladder tomorrow, politics and government, ideology and philosophy, but what interests him most is history. On Saturday afternoons he takes a class in Nahuatl, the ancient Aztec language of Mexico, and whenever he sees an American in the street or on the bus he practices his English.

Cuauhtémoc's nine years in el norte *was in response to a nightmare rather than in search of a dream. Now, behind the gentle, thoughtful manner, is a man radicalized by his experiences.*

In 1973 I went to the United States. I believe I went like everyone else, with the illusion that when we return we will get out of the hole we find ourselves in. I didn't have work. Before I left I hadn't worked in five months. So, I went with the motive to find an alternative, to improve the family economy. I had my mother and son to support.

The mother of my son had died in childbirth. I have never married; I consider it nothing more than a social compromise. What is better is the affection that two people have, not a social compromise on paper. But yes, the mother of my son died eight days after he was born. Then it was necessary for me to have work, and I couldn't find any here in Mexico. So I left my son of fifteen days with my mother.

My mother is a widow. She had also worked in the United States. That is to say, it's a tradition to go to the United States when one is young, to contribute to the economy of the home.

Bueno, there is always the question, yes there was work in the city, there was work in industry, but I think the industry in 1973 wasn't advanced yet. It was difficult because they asked for certificates for grammar school, letters of recommendation, letters from the police department; they ask for a mountain of papers. Bureaucratically useless. What one needs is work, to be able to work. After asking for work, if you have relatives who stand well in the company, they might give you a job. Even then it was difficult, because they had a mountain of applications from young people looking for work, and there wasn't any. They took people that had family in the company, or a relative in government. You could get a job with a good recommendation, from the right person, but if you didn't have this, you didn't have the possibility. So, it was difficult. It's still difficult. You can go around and around with the industries here. Now it's a little easier, but the older you are the harder it is.

I went to the United States alone, like a tramp, in the trains. I passed in Tijuana, you might say I passed with borrowed money; with $400 relatives there had loaned me. I had a legal passport, my own. After I arrived I sent it back because I had a tourist visa—so that later I could go back to the United States again.

When I entered the United States and saw the huge highways, no, everything looked very different. It seemed as though I was in another world, another very different world. That was my first impression. Crossing the border, it's something else. Another country, another world. So close and yet so far for someone who is accustomed to living in Mexico. This was my first impression.

I thought I would have more help from my family there, but no, because of envy or of my work, they didn't help me. Instead, they gave me notice on my first days of work there that I had to find my own manner of existence. I had relatives and friends, but it was my friends who gave me a recommendation, first sweeping a factory where they make parts for airplanes, the machine shops.

My family knew I was coming, but they behaved very differently. Although they accepted me, you know the family economy just makes it. So when one arrives, he has to go to work and cooperate with his family there. So, they told me, "You have two weeks here to find work. If you have come for a vacation, you have two weeks. If you're not here for vacation, you have two weeks to begin contributing to the house." No, I only stayed with them three days. But the good thing was I had work.

I lived with some other *mojados* in a house where there were about ten of us. Some of them were working nights and others evenings, and others days. Sometimes we slept in a mountain on the floor. It wasn't easy to sleep. I was there for a time, and then when I changed work, I got my own apartment, in a garage behind a house. There were only two of us there, so we could live better, more tranquil. When I lived with the others, the *cucaracha* [cooperation] was about $180. It was a little house, so it was $180 for the rent, the lights, and the bills. Then aside from that we cooperated for the food. But usually, by the middle of the week there was no food left, just beer. Then we would see who would put up for the food, because since there were different shifts, some would eat more than their share. The first days we would all eat, but the last few days before our checks, there would be no food. Two or three days of beer, Budweiser or Coors, but no one would buy food. They would just get drunk. But it worked out okay economically, because we were able to have enough money to send back to our families.

I learned English fast. I bought some books and studied so I could speak complete sentences. I wanted another environment, because I saw that where there were just Mexicans working, the pay was very bad in comparison to places where the citizens of the United States worked. Then I went with a friend to an electronics company where I knew they paid well. We put in our applications to see if they would accept us. They gave us a test in mathematics, and I passed it. I think the foreman liked me; he hired me. There were Americans, Chicanos, and Negroes working there, but very few Mexicans, so I had to learn to speak English to be accepted. I had to write notes in English. With this job I entered an environment that was better. I liked it.

No, I liked it and I liked the young women who were working there. This is how I learned English. I had an American girlfriend who corrected the words for me. Yes, I think a woman is the best way to learn a language. This way I spoke more English than Spanish. Even though there were some Mexican-Americans who could speak both English and Spanish, the majority spoke English. This was about forty miles from Los Angeles, in San Fernando, California. I lived in Pacoima, Burbank, and Simi.

I worked for three years in electronics and then returned to Mexico. I wanted to see my family. When I asked for permission to leave, my boss said no. But I left anyway; I was anxious to see my family. When I was in the United States, the whole time, I think all the *mojados* feel the same way, they are in the United States but they are crying to go to Mexico. They are saving their money just to return. I think this is a sentiment that ties us all. Even though many earn some money and begin to have roots in the United States, nevertheless, they always think of returning. Even though eternally they think of returning, sometimes they can't. They have a family there. Their family changes them and they aren't the same Mexicans who left.

When I returned my son was bigger. Of course he didn't know me and there wasn't the trust. But the affection one has keeps you tied to your family. I stayed for twenty days.

Then I went back to the United States, but I didn't have work in the electronic company because I had left. I began to work in foundries. First in the foundry that makes locks, the name was Price-Pfister. Then a foundry to make rings for cars, work where one sweats. After that, I liked working in hard work. I adapted to it. The heavy work paid better than assembly. In the foundry there wasn't much contact because of the noise, so I didn't use my English as much. It was a different environment, but I still spoke English. I think it's necessary for any person who wants to go to another country to learn the language.

I usually went out only on weekends. During the week I didn't have time for anything else, to go to the movies or anything. I didn't have a car, and to go to the market in the United States takes time. I had to buy dinner that was already cooked, or dinner that was easy to fix. Really, I didn't have any time during the week for diversions. My day for fun was usually Sunday, because I always worked on Saturday. Sundays, I would go with friends to places where they had Mexican dances. After a while I changed and began going to places where they had cowboy and country music, to get to know different environments. I really like country music. At Hanson Dam and Pacoima is where I liked to go. This was my entertainment, to go out dancing and drinking, to keep from drowning in the problems of that week.

Later, there was an opportunity. Some friends invited me to work with them in construction. I was interested because it's an industry where you can make quite a bit of money. You always have to continue looking out after your own interests to get ahead. So I entered construction because there was more money. The work was harder, very hard, but it's well paid in the United States. You can say it's the industry with the highest pay. On the contrary, here in Mexico, the construction worker is spoken poorly of, abused. In the United States he's an esteemed worker in all senses. I worked five years in construction.

The problem was, when you work in a job that is very hard, you need someone to help you. Well, I met a woman at a dance. Her background was Spanish, her parents were from Spain, but she was born in the United States. So I began living with her. The truth is, in work such as this you need a woman to help you.

I had told my mother, *"Madre,* it's time you come and help me so I can save some money." She came up with my son, but she didn't like the United States. What's more, after one week she wanted to return to Mexico.

Well, I felt very lonely, and I knew this woman. She had seven children. Yes, seven children. She needed help too. So really, all the money that I earned stayed in the United States. I had bills to pay, I had to pay for the house, and then after six months, I had a compromise. She was pregnant with my little girl. Now I have two children there. I had eleven mouths to feed. But I managed. At $21 an hour, I had enough to feed eleven, but I spent all my money there and what I brought back was very little.

I never forgot to send money home, because my mother and son here depend on me. So I always sent them money, but it was only a small part of what I earned. I knew it was enough for them to live here, and my mother saved some of the money. It was with the money she saved that we bought the house.

I was returned four times to Mexico. After I had been there for a while and had learned English, I didn't have any fear that they would send me back. Then it was easy for me to come in. If they caught me and sent me back, the next day I would be back again. The first time they caught me I was working in construction. That was great, because I went home for two weeks, and when I returned I had work waiting for me.

Only once I didn't come home to visit, and that was because of pride. An American who was working there was the person who reported us, put the *migra* on to us. So, it was no more than the time from Los Angeles to El Centro, then from El Centro to Tijuana. That same night I came back, and I was back at work the next morning, to show him that it didn't work to call the Immigration. I could have gone home, but because of pride I went back the next day.

Once they came checking papers. The Immigration officer asked me for my papers. I answered in English, "Why do you want papers, I don't need papers!" I told him if he wanted I would show him my driver's license. I showed it to him and he left me because I told him I was an American citizen.

When I finally came home for good, I flew. I didn't have anything to bring back with me. I had to sell everything. I had been unemployed for nine months.

Really, what happened was, when I ran out of money, she ran out of love. You have to look at things as they are. The North American woman has the man like a little machine, and when he stops running, her love stops. That's what I've seen. When there was no work and no money, there were fights over money at home, and I had to leave. With what I got from unemployment I rented a little apartment with another young man. Half I spent on the apartment, because it is very expensive there, the other half I spent on food. So there was nothing left. I have never been able to adjust to the feeling of doing nothing. I could have worked at something that paid the minimum, but the truth is that with the minimum you can't live, it's the same as I was earning on unemployment. It was better to wait and see if the economy would get better and there would be work again. But after nine months they were going to give me an extension of another three months, but I felt like I was lazy, and then I was eating pure beans and doing nothing. I thought, it would be better to go back to Mexico where I can eat pure beans and do nothing, cheaper. Sure you feel bad to eat only beans in Mexico too, but you're not so lonely, you're in your own country with your family.

What was sad for me was after ten years to come back and live life at a much lower level. There was enough money to buy the house, so I only have to worry about the food. But it's still difficult to have enough to buy food here. There is a very high rate of unemployment. The people here are underemployed as well as underpaid, especially the construction workers. So with these wages and the disparate prices, you have only enough to buy beans. The employment isn't secure either; you may work one week, but who knows about the next. It's very difficult. I've adapted though. I'm accustomed to "tying the tripe." Yes, but I have the hope. They say that hope is the last thing to die, but I have hope that things here will change.

I won't return to the United States. I think that all of us who come back have to fight to make the song better here. I think we can do it here too. Mexico is big like the United States. It's sad to see Mexicans in the misery they are in, with so many natural resources and human resources, without making good use of them. There is over 50 percent unemployment in Mexico. We need to change. I think that a crisis, wherever in the world, makes the people open their eyes to the problems they face, to their own reality, to how they are being personally affected. When you have work, and your work is secure, your social services are secure, really you don't need anything else. To be human is to have rights. It is your right to work. I don't think I'm the only one. I have been awakened, but not just because I have worked there.

When I was a young man, I joined the Mexican army. I was proud of wearing a uniform, and I worked very hard to be a good soldier. But a terrible event took place, and I was suddenly a changed person—my pride in my country, my beliefs, everything changed. I was on duty in the Plaza de Tlateloco in Mexico City in 1968. There was a big demonstration. We had orders to control the people and to fire on our own compatriots. The memory of that slaughter haunted me for many years; it still comes back to me sometimes. I left the army soon after, and my thought was to leave Mexico for good. Now I know that there is the possibility for change. Those of us who have been to the United States and have seen a different world have the responsibility to come back and work here to change Mexico.

My son is now thirteen. If in a couple of years he wants to go, I will tell him to go, so he can feel the heat, so he can have his own experiences, right? Do you know why? Because how can I say to my son, this is bad or this is good? I can give him direction. I can tell him this is what happened to me, these are my experiences, but often they don't believe you. So, if he wants to go, I will tell him that's fine. It's as if I told you that someone slapped me and I felt this sensation of pain. And you would say, that's interesting, isn't it? But if it happened to you, it would be your own experience. So, if he wants to go or if he wants to stay, I can only tell him my experiences. That's all I can do.

Nothing more, except a warm greeting to the *pueblo* [people] of the United States with wishes that this crisis of immigration, in which they too are a part, will soon find a remedy where there will be work and opportunity for everyone.

VIVAN LOS MOJADOS

Porque somos los mojados
siempre nos busca la ley;
porque estamos ilegales
y no hablamos el inglés,
el gringo terco a sacarnos
y nosotros a volver.

Si uno sacan por Laredo,
por Mexicali entran diez.
Si otro sacan por Tijuana,
por Nogales entran diez.
a'i nomás saquen la cuenta
cuántos entramos al mes.

El problema de nosotros
fácil se puede arreglar.
Que nos den una gringuita
para podernos casar,
y ya que nos den "la mica"
volvernos a divorciar.

Cuando el mojado haga huelga
de no volver otra vez,
¿quién va a tapiar la cebolla,
lechuga y el betabel?
El limón y la toronja
se echará todo a perder.

Esos salones de baile
todos los van a cerrar,
porque si se va el mojado,
quiénes van a ir a bailar,
y a más de cuatro el gringo
no las podrán consolar.

¡Vivan todos los mojados!
Los que van a emigrar,
los que van de vacaciones,
los que vienen a pasar
y los que van a casarse
para poder "arreglar".

Luis Armenta

LONG LIVE THE WETBACKS

Because we're wetbacks
The law is always looking for us;
Because we're illegal
And don't speak English,
The gringo fights to throw us out
And we fight to return.

If they throw us out at Laredo,
Ten come in at Mexicali.
If they throw others out at Tijuana,
Ten come in at Nogales.
Just add it up
To find how many enter per month.

It would be easy
To solve the problem.
Just give us a gringuita
To marry.
Then when we have the green card
We would divorce.

When the wetback goes on strike
And doesn't return,
Who will cut the onion,
Lettuce, and beets?
The lemons and grapefruit
Will all spoil.

The dance halls
Will all close,
Because if the wetback leaves,
Who will go to the dance,
There will be at least four women
For each gringo to console.

Long live the wetbacks!
Those who come to immigrate,
Those who come on vacation,
Those who come to cross the border,
And those who come to marry
So they can get their legal papers.

Those Who Come to Immigrate

LIFE IN THE UNITED STATES

"We find these people in the damnedest places," offered the fellow filling up at the self-service in Libertyville, Iowa. He had transferred to the U.S. Immigration and Naturalization Service (INS) three years before. "You're going to see them in every state, even Alaska."

Though the INS officially disputes it, the Colegio de la Frontera Norte in Baja, California, estimates that in addition to almost five million legal Mexicans, there are another two million more living and working illegally in the United States. As numerous as they are, they are treated as invisible by the general population, who prefer to assume they don't assimilate, don't learn English, and are unwilling to fit in.

Statistics, even though extrapolated from the gray world of the undocumented, show differently. Mexicans integrate into North American society at rates and in patterns similar to those of other immigrant groups of the past. Still, the impression of separateness lingers; it doesn't fit the heroic Ellis Island melting-pot image so central to America's view of itself.

This difference, the contradiction between what happens and what most Americans feel happens, reflects the contrast that characterizes the immigrants' expectations when they come and their actions once they are here. They never come to be Americans. They don't intend to stay. But when they do, even after years, they always believe that they will eventually return to Mexico.

And too, home is so close. A short visit is always a promise, and friends and relatives regularly come and go bringing news, food, and presents. Under such circumstances, ambivalent feelings are not blurred by time and distance but are, instead, constantly renewed. Ambiguous sentiments were not unusual for previous immigrant groups either, but those blemishes on the face of the national myth have faded over the years, and our belief in the melting pot carries on. Perhaps it is simply that these immigrants are brown, and descendants of European immigrants feel a need to find something with which to separate themselves.

Still, the root cause of the misperception of these immigrants by the larger society seems to be something more basic: simple lack of understanding. Unlike Europeans before them, these people think and act out of a tradition that is very different from that of most Americans. They spring from a culture that, as Carlos Fuentes describes it, is "far more intricate and challenging to the North American mind than anything in Europe; a country at times more foreign than anything in Asia."

The Mexican people are of an alloy forged from the Aztec empire, the viceroyalty of New Spain, and the modern nation of Mexico. They are a mixture—viscerally, psychically, and spiritually—of each. The silent presence of the previous Indian world still pervades religious customs, family structures, political practice, economic views, the visual arts, legends, and beliefs. New Spain, in turn, brought not only the religion, language, and politics of old Spain, but also, through the conquistadores, the influence of Islam. Those soldiers came directly from battle with the Moors to conquer the New World. Though they had finally pushed them from the Iberian Peninsula after seven hundred years of continuous rule, the Spaniards could not eradicate North African ways from their own, so brought them along to New Spain. In time New Spain was supplanted, yet prolonged too, by the Republic of Mexico. Each transformation has retained the veiled presence of the others. These three traditions are carried in the very core of all Mexicans. Genes, cultures, and cosmologies all mixed to create a new race, the mestizo.

Mestizo, a mix of Indian and Spanish blood. Mestizo, a pigeonhole in the complex pecking order of racial categories devised during the Spanish conquest. Mestizo, an epithet of shame, rejected by both Indian mother and Spanish father and denied social, economic, and legal standing in the world of either. Yet, as Octavio Paz notes in Sor Juana, *"It was the mestizos who authentically embodied that society, they were its true children." From their lowly, outcast beginning, armed only with elemental audacity, skill, strength, tenacity, resourcefulness, and fortitude, these "true children" were able to overcome their cruel lot and rise above their parents to create modern Mexico.*

The Mexican immigrant is a communicant in this heritage and at its very heart it allows him to give, to take, to survive, to prevail, and finally to assimilate the culture of the new society to his own strengths.

GLORIA T. MUÑOZ
Housekeeper
Oceanside, California

A very pretty and determined young woman, Gloria has a confidence unusual for a new immigrant. Her enthusiastic use of English creates the impression of someone who has lived in the United States for a long time, but it was less than two years ago that she made the decision to marry her American husband and make a new life for herself and her two daughters in el norte.

I knew just a little bit of English from Ramón and listening to people, but I couldn't take classes until we moved here. I would look in the dictionary because I wanted to learn.

First we went to Adelanto in the California desert. But the house didn't have electricity or water, there were no jobs or transportation, and the schools were far away. So we went to Los Angeles, then to San Francisco. In San Francisco, we lived in a big apartment building, but I didn't like it. I was afraid for my daughters because there were lots of scary people there. There were homosexuals who dressed up like women. No, I was afraid to go out of the house. So from there we went to San Jose, to stay with Ramón's mother while he went to find a job and a place for us to live. Then on January 15 we came to Oceanside. The girls started school the next day, and I started English classes then too. In May I got a job. I've been working six months.

I found that job. Ramón had gone to San Francisco; my daughters and I were here. I really didn't feel confident with my English, but that Sunday I read the newspaper, I saw somebody, "Needs babysitter full-time, eight hours a day, five days, good pay, in Oceanside."

In Oceanside—that's for me. But I was afraid. Maybe she won't understand me because I don't speak good English. But I had to call; Gloria you have to call! I called her, looking for my first job. She says, "Well, I want to interview you."

"But I don't have transportation, because my husband won't be back until next Sunday."

"No, but I need you tomorrow."

She needed someone right away. "I'm sorry." I was afraid of taking the bus, and Ramón wasn't here.

I wanted to go, but I didn't have any friends. So I called her back and said, "Give me your address and I will try to come."

She said, "I will come to your house and interview you."

"That's great." I gave her the address and she came here in fifteen minutes.

She interviewed me, but she said, "I have another girl to interview and I have to ask you for references."

"Yes, I have references, another lady, you can call her. The lady where I work on Saturdays, cleaning house."

"Well, I will call this lady and then I will call you back." But she didn't call me.

I thought, oh no. I was sad, because I wanted to find a job. But I decided, I'm going to call her again. I called, "Sharon, it's me, Gloria. Did you find someone else?"

She said, "No, no. I want to give you a job, but I want you to start next week. Are you sure you have transportation?"

"Oh yes." So when Ramón came back I said, "Ramón, I got a job."

"Nah, I can't believe you."

"Yes, it's true. Call the lady."

Ramón drives me at seven o'clock in the morning. He used to pick me up but now I'm not afraid. I catch the bus. I learned to take the bus. I want to learn everything here in the United States, everything. I bought a car. I wanted a little car. I'm afraid too, to start driving, because I never, never in my life have tried to drive. I've read the book already. But I am going to practice.

See, I didn't work after I got married. It's tradition that the wife doesn't work. But then my husband came to the United States and he didn't send me any money. I had two daughters and I had to feed them. My father-in-law said, "Well, you'll have to work to support your daughters. If you want to go to Mexico City to work, your daughters can stay with us."

I thought it was a good idea. My older daughter stayed with my husband's parents and my younger daughter stayed with my parents. It had been six years since I had worked and I didn't know anything. Finally I found a job with the owners of a restaurant. I worked for them for two years. They were nice, but they looked at the workers as slaves. It didn't matter, I had to support my children.

It broke my heart because my daughters didn't want to be without me. I thought, I have to work. But after one year I told my boss, "I can't work for you anymore because I just can't leave my daughters any longer."

They said, "You can bring your daughters with you."

So I brought my daughters to Mexico City, but it was really hard. I had to bathe them between midnight and one o'clock in the morning, because there was so much work to do. That was the only time I had free. My daughters couldn't go anywhere, they had to stay in the room because the people didn't want them walking anywhere in the house. It was heartbreaking. I wanted them with me, but it wasn't a good life for them. I worked there until my daughters were seven and eight years old. By then I couldn't take that situation.

I had divorced my husband two years before because he never sent me money to support my children and he never stayed with us. When he would come back he was always drunk. One day he got into an accident and almost killed someone. I wanted to live with him because he was my daughters' father, but it didn't work out. My daughters didn't want me to marry another man. But my husband had been gone seven years.

There were times that he told me that I could come with him to the United States. I wanted to come, but it didn't seem like a good idea. It's funny, because the last time he wanted to bring us here was when I met Ramón. Yes, I met Ramón at a restaurant in Mexico City.

I said, "Oh my God, now I have two opportunities." I felt better with Ramón because he doesn't drink. But I didn't know him. We had just met three weeks before. My first husband was my daughters' father, so I had to decide which of the two ways to go.

I decided to start over and forget about the past. So I am here with Ramón.

When we came here Ramón didn't want to give me any money. He said, "It's not a good idea for me to give you money. You'll buy expensive things. It's better if I buy for you." But I didn't want it that way. I wanted to spend my own money. I wanted to show Ramón I knew how to shop. My first time in the market the cashier asked me, "What do you want, paper or plastic?"

"What? What, paper? I don't understand."

Ramón says, "See, that's what I told you, you don't know. *Mensa.*" I was so frustrated. Plastic bag or paper bag! Then when they said $10.65, I didn't know what they meant. I didn't know anything about dollars.

But now that I work, I've got my money and I spend my money. Yes. I give to Ramón sometimes for the telephone bill, but I don't want to pay telephone bills, and gas and electricity. I hate paying bills. I hate it, but we have to do it. That's the bad thing about the United States, bills! But I have my own money. Sometimes I take my daughters shopping on the bus.

Now I feel better than when I was in Mexico, because in Mexico I didn't have a lot of money. I feel more freedom now.

I have my house in Toluca, and one in my little town, and another house that I own half of with my ex-husband. Ramón and I want to work for five years. Then we will decide what we want to do. We could live here and go to Mexico on vacations, or we can move back to Mexico.

But I want to live here, with Ramón or without Ramón. You know men, sometimes they change their mind. Here in the United States especially, the men like a lot of divorce. Probably Ramón will say to me, "Well, I want a divorce." We never know. It's different now because we're older. When you're young you say, "I don't care." I want to spend the rest of my life with him. But you know men, sometimes they change their mind and you have to be prepared. With Ramón it's better, but we don't know these men, they always change their mind. *¡Son muy complicatos!* I will never understand them. He's a very nice person and he doesn't drink and he doesn't smoke. But nobody's perfect. It's always a struggle.

When I started school I was in the beginning English class for three weeks. Then I told the teacher, "I'm bored. I know all this, so maybe I should go to another class."

She said, "Great," and sent me to the intermediate class. I was there for three months, and now I have been in the advanced class for one week. As soon as I finish English I am going to take classes to pass my GED. Then maybe I can go to college.

There is still so much I don't know. I don't know anything about banks or about business. I don't know how to open an account, but I want to learn. I want to deposit my money every week, even if it's just a little bit. I have to learn a lot of things.

I know most people don't think like me. All of my companions from school now have ten and twelve children. They look old already. They don't have time to keep themselves up. Since I was ten years old, I thought that's not for me. I'm always thinking of the future. Now I'm thinking about when I am old. I want to live in my own house, I don't want to rent a house. I want to take my grandchildren shopping and buy them ice cream.

When I fought with my family, when I married my first husband, and when I had to leave my daughters to work, were the saddest times in my life. I thought, I have to overcome them and go forward. I have to go forward for my daughters, they are my life. But even more, they see me, I have to show them how to live.

MADELIN TELLEZ
Daughter of Gloria T. Muñoz
Junior High School Student
Oceanside, California

With her long, thick, wavy hair, and wearing the latest bicycle stretch shorts with a big T-shirt, Madelin looks like any thirteen-year-old American— except for the yellow rubber gloves. It's Saturday morning, and with a big smile and not the least hint of gloom, she's scouring the bathroom and kitchen.

When my mama told me we were coming here I was a little sad, and a little afraid about how it would be. I went to sixth grade in Mexico and now I am in seventh here. I didn't know any English, but I found some friends who told me which rooms I had to go to. There are other kids here from Mexico, so I don't feel lonely and it's easy to make friends. All of my teachers are very nice too. It's a little bit different

205

here. There are classes in English and Spanish. In Mexico everyone spoke Spanish. Also, we never had P.E. In Mexico the girls don't run or play basketball or volleyball, only the boys. I like it.

The thing I miss most about Mexico is to be able to pick fruit off the trees. There are lots of fruit trees there. I really miss eating mangoes. But my mama cooks almost the same food here as there.

One of my friends has been here longer and already speaks English. She's in eighth grade. When she comes over we speak in both languages. We like to go bicycle riding or skating, and sometimes we listen to music. If I had a friend who was coming to the United States, I would tell them to put a lot of effort into learning English, because some words are very difficult.

When I grow up I want to stay here and work in a career until I earn enough money, then I want to go back to Mexico.

VIDAL OLIVARES
Truck Driver
Los Angeles, California

This is Vidal's house. The focus of life here is in the living room. Unending discussion, meals eaten day and night, children, laughter, and in the background, always the television. With his wife, Estela, their two young daughters, his cousin and his cousin's wife, his wife's sister, and seven young men from his pueblo, Vidal heads a household that is certainly not typically American and certainly won't be approved under the zoning laws.

But working for low wages in one of the most expensive areas of the country, and accustomed to large extended families, Vidal and his household have adapted a feature of Mexican society to survive in the United States. Each man contributes $160 a month to cover rent, utilities, and maintenance. The three women share in the cooking and cleaning. And rather than the chaos we would envision from the perspective of a family of four, the house is very neat and orderly. The joyful ambience, cooperative spirit, and sense of belonging make this home especially suited to children. For the little girls, there is always someone to play a game with, read a story, or sing a song, and a free lap to sit in.

My origins are in a *ranchito* in the state of Jalisco, but I came to the United States in 1976. I have gone back three times. I had no trouble passing the first time, because I had a friend's green card. We look very much alike and he loaned me his papers, so I passed for him. At this time I was a bachelor. I stayed for two years, and when I returned to Mexico I met my wife and we married. But again, for economic reasons—I didn't have a job—I returned to work here.

My brother always wants me to come home. He can tell me that because he has work. He's a truck driver for a big company there and makes good money. That's why he doesn't have any interest in coming here.

It's very hard, the life in Mexico. We hardly had the money to eat. I had to leave my wife. We were newlyweds, we had been together only about ten months, and when I left she was pregnant. I wanted to get together the money for her and for my baby that was to be born.

When I first came here I met this man who had just begun his business and began to work with him. When I came back he gave me work again. There was never any problem; I have always had the same job.

One comes here thinking he is going to see only Americans, but then you find that there are a lot of people who speak Spanish and understand you. Not long ago, I had an experience in Texas. I was thinking that I was going to a city of Americans, El Paso. I was wondering how I would ask for the street. When I stopped, I tried to ask in English and they said, "No, we don't speak English here."

The second time I came, I had no knowledge of the kid who loaned me his card before, so I had to pass with a *coyote*. It was a big problem. At the border there are these *cholos* or *rateros* that rob people. We managed to get by them because we were all men, thanks be to God, but they made us run. Aside from this we had to walk from seven o'clock at night until five in the morning. We arrived at where the *coyotes* had their car. Some of us had to get in the trunk and others inside. They took us to a house. It was a Wednesday, and they kept us there until Sunday—waiting! They gave us hardly anything to eat. This was the hardest time.

When my daughter was born my wife called me, but I couldn't return. I wanted to save the money. I stayed until my baby was a year old, trying to save money to build a house in my pueblo. I came back for her first birthday. I had been gone a year and nine months.

Well, I met my daughter and again returned to the United States. Passing the third time was really easy. When I arrived a man asked if

I wanted to go to Los Angeles. I said, "Yes, but first I want to eat breakfast."

He said, "No, right now it is easy. Come now, I will give you breakfast." And yes, he gave me breakfast in his house in Tijuana. From there we jumped over the fence, then we waited for a few minutes because there was a patrol. As soon as the patrol passed we quickly ran, it was only about 100 meters, and we jumped in the car. There were about five of us. Quickly they took us to a house very close by. I think it was Chula Vista or somewhere near there. In this house there were something like forty people. From there they put us in a big truck with wooden boxes closed with chains, the kind they put heavy machines in. It was easy; we arrived in Los Angeles at about three in the afternoon. At times one has good luck.

Later I wrote and asked my wife if she would come. I had a friend, a woman who said she would help me. I paid her; it wasn't free. She picked my wife and the baby up in Tijuana in a pickup. It was very easy. The only thing was, she charged me quite a bit, $500 for both of them.

But there is the risk. The first time I passed, I gave the kid $30 for gasoline and a little bag of marijuana, about $10 worth. The second time they charged $225. As I remember, the third time they charged $275, but it seemed cheap because it was so fast.

Now I have about five years here. When my mother died in December I returned again, but I stayed only a week. Now I have my family here, and then I can't leave my work. But it was easy to pass this time. Four times I have passed, and not once have I landed in jail. I know the *migra,* but only from a distance.

Not long ago, my boss suggested that I try to get my papers because I travel, driving a big truck all over California and Arizona. So I went to an attorney, and when he asked me about my daughter and my work he told me not to try to get my papers. In this class of work they don't give green cards. There really isn't any problem, except the fear one has at times. I have seen the patrols. I am very careful, but because it's a big truck, they have never stopped me. But yes, I am a bit fearful that one day they will.

For those of us who are raised in a pueblo in Mexico, here we find a life that is really nice, beautiful. One becomes accustomed to the life and doesn't want to return. Now that I have my family, I am planning to stay, if they let us. If someday they send me and my family back, we will return, because I like living here very much.

I think it is good that my children will speak both languages. My oldest daughter is four years old and goes to preschool. She can speak various words, count to thirty, and say the days of the week, all in English. At times she surprises me. I get home from work and she says, "Poppy, you have a happy face." She can sing in English too. My youngest daughter was born here. She is from the United States.

Bueno, when one is married and has his family here, he hardly has time to think of his family there; rather, he thinks of his children, his wife, and his responsibilities. He tries to learn how to live. My father and sisters and brothers are still there. When I go there I never tell them about how it is here. Here we live better than we do there, yet if you earn dollars, you spend dollars. I tell my sisters and brothers that it isn't like they think. Sure we live better, there are more conveniences, but we aren't rich. I write to my father and tell him not to believe that just because someone lives here they have a lot of money. With working we hardly have enough to pay at the market, the rent, and clothes, because it is very expensive. But one becomes accustomed to living here.

Well, to my way of thinking, I don't know if it's good or bad, but what I want now is that my daughters grow up here and learn English. That is, if they don't throw us out. When they are older we'll take them to know Mexico. If one day we can get our papers, then it's all the better. That's how I think. The life is better here, that's why I want to raise them here.

Thanks be to God, I have never had any bad experiences here. The American people have treated me well. Never have they treated me badly, that's why I'm happy here.

ESTELA PARILLA MORALES DE OLIVARES
Wife of Vidal Olivares
Auto Parts Factory Worker
Los Angeles, California

I wanted to come. My husband would often ask me to join him. I always thought it was impossible, but I wanted to come. I was living with my parents. They told me to think about it because it was very far away, but they thought we knew best. My husband always sent me money, for a long time, and I would save it in the bank. Then he sent word for me to come, but I never felt ready. Finally when I told him I would come, he sent money for the trip, so I would have what I needed for the little girl, because the trip is very long.

When I arrived, everything seemed so strange to me. They were going to take me to buy some clothes, because I didn't have any, and when we arrived at the store I didn't want to get out of the car. I imagined the *migra* was going to grab me. They told me, "No, get out. The Immigration isn't around here."

"No," I said, "with all I went through, I'm not going to get out so they can catch me now." Finally I got out, but I had to look all around; I just felt they would jump out and get me.

Well, I thought my husband had his own house. So when I arrived and found that we were living with other people I yelled at him, "Do you mean to tell me this is why you brought me here?" But this is the way it is, the way one has to live here.

I had imagined that it would be beautiful; well, it is pretty, but I had thought it would be beautiful to live here, everything easier, but no, it's very difficult. It would be very hard for my husband and me to rent a house by ourselves. To live like this with everyone together, no, it's difficult. I miss my parents too, but what can I do? It's so far away. We want to save money then return, because to stay here, no. I want to be here a little more time so my children can learn a little English, then we'll return to Mexico.

In the beginning, I didn't know anything here. My friends told me that to have a baby here would be very expensive. I wanted to return to Mexico for that reason. The way it is, with the little money that my husband makes, and with what they would charge me, I said it would be better if I went to Mexico. There, with $100 I would have the baby fine. But my husband said no. He said that I would have to stay here, that he knew it would work out, but that I would stay here whatever it cost. So I said, okay.

Then after, I talked with some women who told me I should go to a government clinic. I went, but I didn't know what to say. I was all alone, keeping my eyes peeled. They spoke pure English. I almost cried. I got there at seven o'clock in the morning. I just sat until eleven, trying to see what to do, but I didn't have the nerve to speak. Well, I decided.

I stood up and asked a checker if she spoke English and if she would interpret for me. Well, yes she did, and they gave me an appointment to return. Then I returned and they took care of me. But who would do it for me? I had to do it myself. I lost my embarrassment and did it. My husband had said he would take me, and he would take me. That's how it was for five months, but I was almost due and he still hadn't taken me yet. I said, "Fine, I'll just go myself!"

He told me, "I will ask a lady to go with you," because I didn't know how to go.

But I told him, "No. Do you think I can just go bothering people?" And then if he had to lose time at work? No, I said, "I'll go by myself." And that's how it was. When I went for my checkup, they did it in English, but someone translated for me. Then in the hospital, it was all English, but since my husband understands a little, he helped me.

My first daughter was born in a hospital in Guadalajara. It was much uglier, and the delivery was uglier too. But the people were friendly in both places. Here, my husband took me, practically carrying me, because I could hardly make it on my own, and he was with me until the time to deliver. It cost $750. Well, there was a nurse who told me if I signed these papers they wouldn't charge me, and yes, I filled them out and signed them, but by then I had already paid. Then later these little cards arrived, but it was too late. I had already paid. I was told that if I went to a private doctor they would charge me $3,000.

I told my husband, "The pain is the same."

I was fearful because with the first baby I was in labor three days. I had told my mother, "Just let me die." You can imagine—three days without eating or sleeping. I thought it would be the same, but it was different, only one day, and the little creature came.

Here at the house we cooperate and pay the rent among all of us. They buy their groceries, and I buy what I need for my children, my husband, and my sister. Before the other *señora* arrived I would cook for everyone. Now I am working with my husband and she cooks for everyone. We cooperate.

I just began working. It's very dirty, but it's work. It's dirty, dirty, pure steel parts that I have to clean on the machine. I put the parts in the machine and move them until they are clean, but to take them out and put them in gets you so dirty. I wear the same thing every day. My husband's cousin is watching the children, and I pay her each week. I feel good that she is taking care of them for me; they are her nieces.

I think we saved more when I wasn't working. I don't know how, but we spend more. I can't save like before. My husband would give me the money, not all of it, but most of it. We'd go out to eat or to a movie. The life here is the same as in Mexico. You can't save money. The only way you can save is if you are living in the pueblo and your husband is working here, sending you money. Living here together, and we like to go places, we can't save money.

There are people here who are very self-centered. Like some of the black women. They see that someone doesn't understand and they won't pay attention to them. If you can't talk, they shove you to one side. At least it makes me feel bad. *Ay Dios mío,* it's sad. You need to know how to speak to defend yourself, because they curse you and you don't know what they are saying. Where I had my checkups, there were some black women, you should see how friendly they were. Nevertheless, there are others that laugh at you.

I have been here three years. It's very hard. When you don't know, you think everything is nice; but now that I know, it's very different. If someone had told me how it is, I wouldn't have come. Everyone tells you about it, how pretty, and one thing and another, but they never tell you how they suffer. Well, it is beautiful here, I won't say it's not, but with money. When you are there you always have that temptation of *el norte, el norte.*

Under the 1986 immigration reform, Estela and Vidal received their permanent residents' permits, and for the first time in seven years they are returning to Mexico to spend Christmas with her family.

VENTURA GOMEZ
Housewife
Muscatine, Iowa

The little three-room cottage on a busy artery, just two blocks from the Mississippi River, is where Ventura, her husband, and four children live. She is in demand on all sides. Dinner is cooking on the stove, clothes to be folded wait on the couch, her mother wants a ride home, her baby niece needs a diaper change, her eight-year-old son wants to know how to spell a word, and the four-year-old wants her to play a game. She is sending the thirteen-year-old to the grocery store and paying the auto mechanic who has just delivered her car; meanwhile, the phone is ringing. Methodically, as if moving pieces across a checkerboard, she advances through the day's tasks.

Attractive, almost chic, with a fashionable asymmetrical hairstyle, she shows neither the stress nor her forty-one years. Ventura is upbeat and optimistic.

At four years old my parents brought me to Matamoros so we would be closer to the border. Our family tradition, and the way we were able to make ends meet, was for my brothers, my father, and my mother to go to the United States to earn the money we lived on. In all there were fourteen of us, but eight brothers and sisters died and then there were six left, *tres* brothers and *tres* sisters.

Actually we are all here now except two of my brothers, who are still trying to arrange their papers. They always came as braceros, and when the work was finished they would return to their houses and wives. When they needed to work again they would come back to the United States. But the law changed. They need papers to work now, so they're unable to come.

The rest of us got our papers years ago. At first one brother came and then the rest of us followed. My oldest brother lives on both sides. He has a house in Brownsville and one in Matamoros. He never lost the custom to go back and forth, so he lives two lives. Really, that's what we would all like to do. You always want to go to Mexico; you're always wanting to see your family. And just because we live here doesn't mean we've been able to give up our customs.

We mostly picked cotton, in Brownsville and Matamoros, but in Matamoros they only paid twenty centavos a pound and on this side they paid twenty cents a pound. It was much more. When we were sent back by Immigration we had to work in Matamoros, but whenever we had another opportunity we would come back.

Yes, the Immigration sent us back many times. I remember once when I was very little, it was my sister, my mother, and me. We were trained by then, trained to not speak. The Immigration didn't talk to individuals, they asked everyone: "Who doesn't have papers?" The thing was to hide and not to talk. So the Immigration came up to my sister and asked if she had papers. She didn't, so they took her, and neither my mama nor I said anything.

We got to our work, and when we were working the Immigration came again. My mama started to run, and the Immigration said, "It would be better not to run."

I understood English; my mama didn't. So I told my mama in Spanish, *"Mamá no corra, por favor."* So they took us.

It was a Friday, I remember; we had worked the whole week. She was really mad. I think because my mama was older she didn't have the fear that the Immigration was going to break her. She said, "I haven't come to rob, I've come to work. It cost me a lot of work for what I earn. My daughter and I haven't eaten anything, and with all of this we are working however we can. And you come and catch us when it's Friday. Why? So that the boss won't have to pay us, right? You send us to Mexico and end up with the money we worked for."

So the Immigration said, "No, you are going to get your money. Yes, we are sending you back to Mexico, but we will send you your money. You leave your address and you will receive your money."

My mama was still very mad. She said, "My daughter is very hungry. You don't have to give me anything to eat if you don't want to, but give my daughter something." And yes, the Immigration passed by a little store and bought me one of these little cartons of milk and a roll.

Then they sent us back to Mexico. They charge to pass, so the man gave us the peso, because we didn't have anything. My mama was still angry, and she yelled, "We'll be coming back." But the money eventually came. It took two months or so, but they sent it.

When I was little, picking cotton, I didn't have a sack. I would go in front of my mama and leave little piles for her. When I was older I had my own sack and they paid me. It made me very happy, because I was very little and the money that I earned was mine. I always looked forward to working in the fields because it was like a fiesta. You come to like it, right? You like the fields, you like the work, and you like the money. Whatever I earned my mama and papa let me keep, and from that I learned to save my money, to use it for the things I needed. Mainly my money went for school expenses.

So for me to study I had to come to the United States and work during the summers to earn enough for my expenses. As a result one of the tragedies of my life occurred. With all the money I had earned picking cotton, I went to buy my books and pay my tuition. I had with me all of my money. I was always looking for the best price and would go from one bookstore to another. Well, I don't know when or where but I lost my money. It was a tragedy, because I knew my parents couldn't give me the money to buy my books or for my expenses for the whole year. I didn't want to return home. I knew that this would be, for my mama, something tremendous. It was about twelve noon when I lost my money, and I didn't return home until seven at night.

I explained what happened. But my mama thought I had been robbed. "Look at you, your clothes are all torn." That's when I noticed. I must have unconsciously torn my dress pulling on it. I looked and looked. I went to every bookstore with the hope of finding my money. But I hadn't noticed my dress. I don't know how, I have no idea how it happened, but I returned with my dress all torn. It was my nerves, no? For me it was the loss of one year in school.

My mother knew how important it was to me to be able to study. She was the one who was always pushing me. Every year she would say, "If you don't bring me the highest grades, then why are you going to school? Go to work, we need you to go to work. If you have a boyfriend, then school can't be that important to you." So I knew that if I had a boyfriend they would take me out of school. I didn't have a boyfriend, I did everything that my mama told me, and I tried to earn the highest grades out of necessity. I always was first or second in all of my classes. I'm not that intelligent, I know that, but I was very dedicated to my studies.

In 1970, when I was ready for the *escuela superior,* because there aren't any *superiores* in Matamoros I went to study in Mexico City. That's when I met my husband. I studied up to vocational school, but then my husband asked me to marry him. So I got married. When I returned home, they didn't like him at all in my house. My family hadn't wanted me to marry. But I thought it would be better to bring my husband to live with my family rather than stay in Mexico City with his. I thought, if I stay in Mexico the tendency of the man is to be the one in total control. He's going to tell me I have to stay in Mexico, and I won't be able to return to see my family. Unfortunately, that is the tradition in Mexico. This was my fear. I knew it would be my luck because he was from the capital. I thought, now is the time. We are newlyweds and there is more opportunity now. So I told him, "Let's spend our honeymoon with my sister." So, we went to Houston.

We stayed in Houston. My husband was working there and we saved a little money. But after my daughter was born he began to get very nervous, always in a bad mood because he hadn't seen his family. He said, "We're going back to Mexico." So we returned to Mexico. We lived on the money that we had saved.

At that time, in 1975, you could get your papers if your child was American. Before, I hadn't wanted to get my papers, because I wanted to have a career. If I had my papers to be in the United States I could see that I would end up like my brothers and sisters, just working and without the opportunity to continue studying. But now that I was married, I thought it would be better to have them so I could be close to my family. Otherwise I would end up in Mexico, which would be worse.

When we returned to Mexico City after living in Houston, my husband could see that he couldn't find work and what he made wasn't enough to even live. So he had to accept the idea that it was better to come to the United States. Even if the life was difficult, it was the only way he could earn enough. That's how I won.

When we came to Muscatine we participated in a program where we went to school to learn English. Well, I have always been interested in school, and I passed these classes and advanced a little. I went for two years and earned my credits. Because of the language, I didn't advance as someone from the United States would. In secondary school in Mexico you learn the English from England, which doesn't really help you when you come to the United States. And no, no, no, what you learn in school isn't sufficient for what you need to speak, to have a job, or to go to school here.

The program here helped us a lot, but I wanted to run. Fortunately there was a teacher who is a very good person. She was good with all of us. She encouraged me and said what I needed was college classes, and for this I needed a high school diploma. When I found out about that, I took all the exams. At first I was afraid. I thought they would be very difficult, but since they were in Spanish it was very easy. I got my high school diploma and began to take classes at the college. In the meantime my husband took classes in welding, carpentry, and things like that. He got his certificate for welding.

I worked at Heinz for five years. I have always liked to save money; I like to be able to stretch it, and I'm not one to spend a lot. So we were able to save money. We paid for this house in two years. After we had paid for the house, when my children were very young, an accident happened right here in front. A man ran into a post out here in front and came flying into the house. He died right here. This was very upsetting and made me very nervous. I didn't want to live here thinking that another car could miss the turn, run into the house, and kill everyone. So I kept telling my husband that we should move.

Finally we found another house, put up the down payment, and moved there. My mama stayed here in this house. So we began paying off that house as well. Then we decided to put in a little market here. But to be near the children and to be able to get their meals, we put a down payment on the house on the corner as well. By law we couldn't live in the same house where we had the little market, but really it amounted to much more than we earned. It was beyond our possibilities. We began paying for it, but it didn't go well.

It went fine in the market, it was a little Mexican market. Every week I would go to Chicago and buy food, books, magazines, and all kinds of things from Mexico. It went well in the market, but after five years I was very tired because we had to work Saturdays and Sundays and open early and close late. My husband, my daughter, and I ran it. My daughter was very little yet, but she helped as much as she could. But it was very difficult because my children were so little. My youngest son was born while I had the market. Perhaps if they had been a little older, but my husband had his own work, you know. Most of the work at the market was mine, then I had the children, and the cooking, the house. We decided it would be better to sell it.

That's where we went wrong. We had a contract signed in front of an attorney and all, but the people who bought it didn't sign anything about the manner in which they would pay us. They would sell things and then spend the money rather than restock the store. Soon there was nothing left. When we lost the market, we were without money. We couldn't make the payments, my husband and I began to have problems, and in the end we lost the house. This wasn't the only problem, there were others, but that's how it ended up.

Within one week my oldest daughter will be entering the university. She has been accepted, she has her room, and she'll be going to the

University of Iowa. She was thinking of California, or Texas, places where she would have more independence from her family. But perhaps someone convinced her that she would have more opportunities because she is a resident of Iowa. She is happy with her decision. She wants to study law. Fortunately she has had many opportunities and we are very proud of her.

My greatest hope is with my daughter, that she will finish the university. I also hope she is able to help us with the others. From the time she was little, Cindy was very smart and always got high grades. I hope that my other children, when they are a little older, will work hard in school and achieve what Cindy has. That's what I want for them. I want them to have careers.

For myself, maybe someday in the future I will again have another business. For now I am recuperating. It was so much that I lost. I lost the house, the store, it was very hard. It took years to save for all of this and we lost it all so quickly. It was as if a tornado came through. But you have to have the hope and the dream that you will do something. The hope is the last thing to die. We have to get up again. *¿Adelante otra vez, no?*

JULIA GARCIA DE MORALES
Factory Worker
Chicago, Illinois

In 1975, Julia wrote a letter* on behalf of her husband, Faustino, who was in jail at the border. Within a month he had been released and made his way to Chicago. Years passed and their five children grew up and finished school, and the older ones married. Faustino was never there for the graduations or weddings. Although he sent Julia money and they corresponded, there was no sign of his return. For three days in March of 1979, Julia walked on a pilgrimage to the little village of Talpa to plead with the Virgin, who is renowned for her miracles, for her husband's return. Another Christmas passed; it seemed as though her prayers went unanswered. Then during Easter week she received a message that he wanted her to join him. It had been almost six years since she had seen her husband.

*See chapter 4.

I thought about coming, I wanted to, but he never said anything to me, right? And the day that he told me I could come, well yes, of course, I would go. I came with two of his nephews, and a niece. I brought only one daughter, Betty. I left Mari with the others. We took the bus from Guadalajara to Tijuana and from there some people passed us to Los Angeles. We were in Los Angeles one day and the next day we flew in an airplane. It was easy, nothing happened. I came in May, thinking I would return in December. That was in 1980, and it wasn't until December 1988 that I returned. But no, we didn't have any problems.

It was very pretty, the city, and I was happy to be here. I was a little afraid, because I wasn't accustomed. Mostly I was afraid that I would be picked up. At first I stayed at home. We lived with his nephews. Then everyone would go to work and I would stay home until Saturday or Sunday, and then my husband would take us to the parks.

Then in 1982 we left his nephews and moved here to this neighborhood. Betty was working in a restaurant. But I stayed here and took care of the children, cooked the meals. I was happy, and once I lost my fear I would go shopping. When Betty got off work we would go to the stores.

It's always difficult here; it's not the same as Guadalajara. But I have friends who speak Spanish, and then I like to go out and talk to people. Everyone talks to me. My daughter is always saying, "You go out and everyone in the street talks to you." But yes, because I always greet everyone.

I worked at the laundromat for a year, only on Saturdays. I also took care of the doctor's children from the time they were babies. The oldest one is now nine years old. They call me mama because I have raised them since they were little. They always call me on the phone, or they want to come over. They will bring them over to spend the day. But last year the mother of these children decided to stay home.

So I went out and found another job. I began working in McCormick. I worked there six hours daily. It was like a cafeteria. It was a big building, with many floors. Many people come to present their work from all over the United States. There are many kitchens and many rooms. I would just sweep and collect garbage, mop the floor when people would spill sodas or coffee. I didn't have to wash dishes because everything was disposable. But then in December I had to tell them I was going to Mexico. I told them I would be available again when I returned, but no, they hired another *señora*. They called me again, but I told them no, because I didn't want to take work away from the *señora*. She has needs too. We're all here trying to live.

I found this other little job in February. I can't explain my work to my friends in San Juan. We make collars for dogs and cats, all kinds of things for animals. No one would understand it. In San Juan you can't catch the cats to put a collar on. It's not something people there would buy.

Right now we're filling orders for Christmas. We fill these socks with things for dogs, little bones, squeaky toys, and things. I know it's kind of crazy, but you can't believe how many orders we have. It's easy, we have chairs and everything. If we get tired of sitting we can stand and we talk. The tables are huge and there is room on both sides. There isn't any pressure except you have to be very careful that the boss doesn't see you talking, because he will always bawl you out, or if you're not working. I work Monday through Friday, and on Saturday they give us only five hours. We get out at twelve noon. I'm happy there; it's not hard work.

I don't think I would want to go back to San Juan to live. Well I can't say never, because I have my children and my friends there. But I would rather live in Guadalajara. I have my house there. We have a house in San Juan too, but my son is living in it. The thing is I have three children there and two here.

Well, we've been thinking: this time when we went to San Juan we thought the pews in *el templo* were in bad shape. We would like to have them painted. That's why we would like to go back. I promised that I would buy new robes for *el padre*. Then I want to buy little strings of lights for each pillar in the church. They have some here that are very pretty and they blink on and off. This is what we're thinking: to bring new robes for *el padre,* and then lights for the pillars, and a crown of lights for in between the first pillars, just in front of the altar. I would also like to find a smaller crown of lights for outside above the arch of the doorway. That's what I've been thinking.

After eight years in Chicago Julia decided to return to her pueblo for Christmas. Even her children didn't recognize her. Always tall and thin, she was now a little rounded with an extra twenty pounds, and rather than the long dark braid she had worn since she was a child, short gray curls frame her face.

And pants—no woman of her age had ever worn pants in San Juan. People are still talking about it.

But it doesn't bother Julia. Without looking back, she has traded her life in a small, closed society for the inner city. Julia and Faustino live with their daughter and son-in-law in an upstairs flat in the middle of Chicago's Back of the Yards district. Originally the back—the place where the stench blew—of Chicago's famed stockyards, this area has been home to the United States' most recent immigrants for over a century. Only a generation ago it was the Polish neighborhood; most recently it has become Chicago's Hispanic barrio.

Like the other houses on the block, this one looks as if it's seen too many hard winters. The stairway up is dark and gloomy, but inside the cheerful yellow kitchen the mood suddenly changes. It would have been considered modern by our grandmother's standards, but the appliances aren't built in; there isn't the double-door refrigerator, the built-in dishwasher or trash compactor. But to Julia, coming from her one-room adobe house with an open hearth outside that served as the kitchen, the linoleum floors, kitchen curtains, chrome dinette, toaster oven, and food processor are about as much as one can expect in one lifetime.

The kitchen is a practical room. But the fantasy living room! That's where her hopes and aspirations literally shine. The color is red—wallpaper, velvet curtains, and hanging beaded macramé sculptures that serve as tables, planters, and chandeliers. A plaid sofa and matching armchair are set in the middle, facing the room's central feature, a wall covered in floor-to-ceiling shelves. These are overwhelmed with Julia's prize collection: glass and china figurines representing at least one version of every animal and bird in the Lincoln Park Zoo, along with clowns, saints, and Virgins set among the family photos. For Julia, this wall is her life in the United States.

FAUSTINO MORALES
Husband of Julia Garcia de Morales
Busboy
Chicago, Illinois

He could be seen every morning riding his horse through the village to his fields. On the way back, in the afternoon, it was his custom to stop at the corner tienda for a beer with his compadres. He'd sit on his horse or the big flat rock out in front and talk to everyone passing by. During harvest time Faustino and Julia would spend the evenings with their compadres *roasting ears of fresh corn with chili, lime, and salt, drinking beer, singing the old ranchero songs and telling stories from years past. From birth they had lived their lives in the pueblo.*

When Faustino left San Juan he was thirty-seven years old. Sixteen years in Chicago have changed him. He too has gained weight; as Julia says, they look well fed. With his hair now graying at the temples, he has a close shave and a full mustache. He is serious and dignified, the carefree spirit of his youth left behind.

I remember it was in July; there were five of us. I came with the thought to look for work. My friend lived here and he came back to Mexico. He's from Chicago, so we thought we would come here because he could help us. We came with him. But they caught us after we crossed the border, in San Clemente where the Immigration is. They kept us for thirty-five days. We were treated fine, but they wanted to investigate who was bringing us. They discovered that some *coyotes* had brought us across, so they kept us in jail. Every three days we had to make a declaration. But in the meantime they paid us a dollar a day. I thought, "Well now I have dollars." This was in 1974. Three days after they let us out we crossed over again, all five of us. We flew from Los Angeles to Chicago.

When we arrived we rented an apartment, all of us together. My companions all had work, and they got work for me in the same restaurant where I still work. It was very different, I had never worked in a restaurant before. I never even thought of this kind of work. I had never washed dishes. You pick up a plate and swish, it slips from your hands. At first I was a dishwasher, for six months. Afterward they raised me to busboy. It's a Greek restaurant; there are lots of Greeks. I don't like the food that much. It's not that good. I don't like the work, but I have to work. It's very hard. I have been working there almost sixteen years. Well, at least I don't wash dishes; busboy is easier. We get $2.00 from each waiter. There are six, so I get $12 a shift. They make a lot, but they just give us $2.00.

When I came here, it was to see if I could find the opportunity to better myself. I think this is why many come. Some people maintain their customs from Mexico, and others try to better themselves. Since

I left drinking I have wanted to better myself. I never thought about that when I was drinking. I lived just the way I did in the pueblo.

In the pueblo I worked in the fields. I have some land, it's the land my son is working now. He's the only son; the others are daughters. The thing is, it's a lot of work, and at times when it doesn't rain it goes very badly. When it rains, it's fine, you can do okay. But when it doesn't, you have to borrow money. Then you can't pay it back. You waste your life like that.

Another thing is, you have to know how to live. I didn't know anything about how to live in San Juan. There are times you do well with your crop, but you don't take care, you spend the money foolishly. You drink lots of beer. You can't live in that joke. That's why one must think. I didn't know anything.

I'm going to tell you very clearly: people don't think about the future. They only think, well my crop was bad. So one spends money because they're sad, because things didn't go well. It's very difficult to live in a ranch there.

I have learned a little about how to live here. Principally you work more here than there. There you only work seasonally, during the planting time; after that, you don't work. This is one error there is in Mexico, in many areas, in many small pueblos: they work during the season, they plant their fields and harvest them, then they don't work. Here, no, it's different. You work every day. One has to think you can only better yourself by working more. We have worked more and bettered ourselves a little.

I was here for six years without my family. A friend was going back to bring his brother. He asked if I wanted him to bring my family. "Yes, of course." So my wife and daughter came, and working together, my daughter helped me, we did much better. I think it helped her too, because she is a young woman who thinks about how she wants to live. After a year or two she said, "Let me save the money I make for myself. Now I'm grown." And I saw that she had helped me a lot. I thought, she wants to better herself too. She likes to save her money. She doesn't spend it.

I have a friend here from San Juan. His wife is from Chicago and she likes *pozole*. So we invite them for *comida* and make *pozole*. The only thing is, they don't like to come over because he drinks, and then you know these *borachitos* [little drunks], they become very stubborn and then she can't get him home. But this is the family we visit with. We also have two of our daughters here. One is here with us and the other lives three blocks away.

We celebrate all the Mexican fiestas. Here the *fiesta de diez y seis* is very big. There is a big parade with floats, lots of flags, just beautiful. Then the *dia del grito de la independencia* they celebrate at the shell over on the lake. They bring groups and the dances from Mexico. You would think it was Mexico here. That's why we don't feel anything, we think we're in Guadalajara. No, even the blacks are there. They can't pronounce things very well, but they yell along with us, cheering; I think they like it too. The day of independence here is the Fourth of July. In Mexico, the Fourth of July is the day of the *Virgen del Refugio.*

Now we have all our permits. At first we didn't know if we wanted to put in the applications, because we didn't know if it was true or not, right? I gave $500 to an attorney. I thought if by chance this comes to pass I will have an attorney to help me. Well he did help a little, and ultimately it was easy to arrange, because by now we have been here for many years. We had good luck, most of the people did, but for some it was difficult.

This is the problem, to stay or return. We will have to resolve it eventually. We have to decide where we can live. We can't live here in Chicago. It is very cold, the climate is very difficult when someone is old. There is a lot of arthritis among the elderly, and it is dangerous to walk outside when it's icy. So we have to decide whether we should stay here or go to another state where it doesn't snow and isn't so cold. In the meantime it's better to stay here until we qualify for our social security.

We bought a house in Guadalajara. It's a good investment, because we bought it when the dollar was at 140 pesos. Now the dollar is 2,400 pesos. One of our daughters lives there. But I can't say what we are going to do. We are getting older now, and I am tired of working. I feel the years on top of me. I would like to work fewer hours. Now I work from six in the morning to three in the afternoon. I work five days, but I also go in on Saturday, because I get paid more for Saturday. I don't have insurance, or vacations. I take a vacation when I want, but they don't pay me for it. The Greeks don't know about paying, they're worse than us *mexicanos.*

You know, in Mexico we sit outside with our families for a little fresh air, and the children play in the street. I tell my kids, "Don't think things are so easy. It's very difficult. You have to take precautions to live here and keep yourself out of danger." There are areas that are peaceful, but other areas are very dangerous.

So yes, the biggest surprise to me was how difficult it was to live here in these capital cities. There are many gangs. You have to be careful. A friend who lives here went to a cantina and was drinking, and we went to pick him up. He had been robbed with guns for a quarter. This is something very rare. I never saw anything like it in Mexico.

I've been robbed twice, in the street coming home from the market. About ten of them came out. I had about $25 and a watch. And some of these kids were so young, maybe fourteen or fifteen. It almost made me smile, these kids taking a couple of dollars and having to split it with so many. How much are they going to make? Most people don't carry very much money. You have to take precautions. In some areas you can't go out at this time of night. I used to live over there on Chicago Avenue. That's why I moved. There are a lot of Puerto Ricans over there. They're really bad.

I just came here. I didn't think about anything. I left everything up to God. I didn't know if I could stay or not, or if I could better myself. In reality I had wanted to return; I had saved about $3,000. Then Julia came and I was so happy. Here, alone by yourself without your family, you are very lonely.

And we're still here. And I still haven't decided about whether I should stay or go back. The years are passing, and someday I won't be able to work like this. We will have to start thinking about what we will do. Maybe we'll stay here for part of the year and spend the other part in San Juan.

But when we were in Mexico this time it seemed so difficult there. It's very sad there. I think it's happier here. You go shopping there and everything is so expensive. I was trying to be very careful with the money, but no, it was impossible. Well, everything here seems happier, I don't know why. There are so many beautiful places here. Over there by the lake, it's just so pretty. And here you can go shopping and buy what you need and you spend less. There, no.

JUANA MARÍA CADENA TORRES
Maid
Austin, Texas

September 9, 1989, Juana's fourth anniversary of coming to Texas. It's a beautiful Saturday afternoon. Usually her Saturdays are booked, not at her regular job, but she is sought after to make steamers full of tamales or handmade tortillas for parties, or to care for someone sick, or to babysit so parents can have a weekend respite. But today is special. Juana is free—a day with friends in Zilker Park riding the little train, eating hot dogs, and watching the big soccer league playoffs.

After I was here one week I got a job, and in two days I earned $80. The *señora* told me, "If I see you are a good worker I will raise your salary, but if I see you are lazy then I won't give you a raise." Ayeeee. I began cleaning. Cleaning, cleaning, cleaning.

"Do you know how to run the washing machine?"

"Tell me and I will see if I can learn it." In the first day I learned everything! It's very different, because we don't have machines, all we have is a rock to wash in the river. I like it because you don't have to carry the clothes all the way down to the river. Everything is right there; you don't even have to go outside to hang up your clothes. You can wash even when it's cold and rainy. In Mexico we cook over wood, but I sent money with my sister to buy my mother a stove and a tank of gas. She still prefers to use wood, because she says the gas is dangerous. I want to build a house for her just like the ones here, with a bathroom, kitchen, and all. I sent 1,000,000 pesos with my sister the last time she was here to build a kitchen.

I was born in Rio Verde in San Luis Potosí. There are nine children in my family, and with my mama and papa there are eleven. I'm the seventh child. I was born June 24, 1962, the day of Saint John, that's why my name is Juana. It's also my mama's birthday.

Right now my family lives fairly well. I have a sister who is a primary school teacher. She's the oldest, she is single, and she is the one who helps my family. My parents are old now, in their seventies. Because of her my parents have security. When my sister got her teaching degree she worked and helped us so we could go to school. I am the only one who left.

The first week of September I went to the Normal [teachers' college] and the second week I came here. I told my parents, "I am going to leave. If God helps me I will cross over to the United States, and get work quickly." And thanks be to God I crossed and arrived with no problem. Since I was fifteen years old I had heard from people in Rio Verde who had returned, "The United States is very beautiful."

I told my mother, "I want to go. Before the day I die I want to see places outside of Mexico." So I came. I liked it a lot in Rio Verde working with my sisters. But I am very happy working here. I earn more in a week than my sister, the teacher, earns in two weeks.

My sister is fifty years old. She doesn't want to get married because she is very delicate and wants everything in perfect order. I don't want to get married either. I am very happy by myself. If I got married my husband would say, now you can't have any friends. Well, I'm the type of person who likes to have friends from all over the world. Right now I have over twenty friends that I correspond with in Mexico.

Every four months my sister comes to visit me. She has a passport. She brings all kinds of things: tamales, *picadillo* with chili, cheeses, chorizo. I said to her, "How did you pass with all these things? Didn't they check you?"

"They checked me but they didn't see these things." Most of the time it's luck.

"But how did you pass the chorizo?"

"*Callate!* I hid it here!" Can you believe it, she came with chorizo wrapped like a belt around her waist? She didn't want to get too close because they would see she smelled like chorizo. They always take chorizo away, but without the chorizo and Mexican cheese, the enchiladas will never taste the same.

How can I tell you? Someone here lives much better than in Mexico. There, if you don't have a career, they don't have work for you. If you haven't graduated from secondary school, there is no work. But here, none of that matters. We come and they hire us anyway.

I don't have a bank account here because they ask for so many things, social security and all. I have sent money back by telegraph, but sometimes it takes up to two or three months, so my sister says to wait until she comes up. Sometimes I have $2,000 or $3,000 hidden in the house for her to take back. She takes care of my bank account there. Between the two of us we are able to help my parents and the others to study.

Also many people here give me clothes. I give them to my sister to take to the people who don't have clothes. I sent $10 to a woman who didn't have the money to buy books for her children, and my sister and I are helping two other children there. One is a little girl. She is only nine years old, but she wants to be a teacher. I told her I would help her if she wants to study hard.

There are so many things I like here. You live better and have secure work. I live with the family. I don't pay rent and I eat with them. They always say, "Juana, do you want beans, tortillas, chili?" The beans and tortillas I don't need, but the chili, without chili I can't eat. I always like to eat what they eat. It's very good, all vegetables and herbs. The *señora* is always on a diet and she is so tiny, I want to be like her. I am very fat by comparison. I would love to be tiny like her, but I miss the food of Rio Verde.

Have you heard of the Mexican soccer player who is in Spain named Hugo Sanchez Marquez? This soccer player fought to find Mexican food in Spain. He couldn't find any—really. He was dying to come back to Mexico so he could eat. In a pueblo the people with money eat meat, but if you visit someone who is poor they will give you a fresh hot tortilla with chili. They will always apologize because they don't have meat, but the tortillas are so delicious.

When I have time off here, I make tortillas *de harina* or sometimes I buy *minsa*. Nevertheless, they aren't the same as the tortillas made with fresh corn, so big and beautiful. I learned to make tortillas when I was seven years old. At first my tortillas turned out ugly, but now they are real pretty, and left-handed. I write better with my left hand, and I make tortillas and work with my left too. They say people who are left-handed are intelligent. I don't know. In school my teacher tied my left hand to the chair. She said it was very bad to write with your left hand. There is a famous *mexicano*, Fernando Valenzuela, who plays baseball with his left hand. I doubt that anyone tells him it's bad to use his left hand.

I love sports, especially *fútbol*. Sometimes I pay for a taxi just to go look for a *fútbol* magazine called *El Balón*. I have been watching *fútbol* since I was five years old. Aye, if I could only be a man so I could play.

I collect the posters and postcards and all kinds of *fútbol* things. Two friends from Guadalajara sent me posters of *fútbol* players, and I have pinned them up on my wall. The *señora* told me I could put them up. My sister was telling me that there is going to be a new *fútbol* movie, on videocassette. I told her, "Buy it for me. It doesn't matter what it costs."

In Mexico I have a big poster of Hugo Sanchez that I paid 150 pesos for. I was supposed to buy a pair of shoes. My papa said, *"Hija,* and your shoes?"

I told him, "Look, Papa, the shoes wear out. I will always have my poster of Hugo." I would wear sandals so I could have that poster. When I was at home on Sunday, my day off, I would get up at four in the morning to finish making six kilos of tortillas before the *fútbol* game. That's what I really really miss.

I would even get married if I could marry a *fútbol* player. My sister says, "No, if he lost the game, he would beat you." But I really like *fútbol.* I told my family, if I die I want to have my poster of Hugo Sanchez with me.

This is the reason I would go back to Mexico, because we don't have Mexican *fútbol* here. I miss it. I would go for Hugo Sanchez. I want to go to Spain to see him. It's in Europe, but if I could get a passport I think I could go to visit. I have plans. The first plan I had was to come here to work. My next plan is to go to Rome to see the Pope, and then to Spain to see Hugo.

RAYMOND RAMIREZ
Retired
Bryan, Texas

In the shade of the wide front porch a ceiling fan stirs the heavy air ever so slightly, keeping the summer heat at bay. After supper Mr. Ramirez relaxes on the porch glider with the afternoon paper. Mrs. Ramirez takes up her knitting. She gets only two or three rows on her grandson's new school sweater before Ruby, their next-door neighbor, comes to visit. Their conversation always begins with the weather. Then they discuss the local news, and about the time that Mrs. Ramirez serves glasses of Pepsi over ice on TV trays, they are talking about old times.

When World War II came I volunteered. They didn't want to take me because I didn't have my papers. I was born the fourth of April, 1921, in Monterrey, Mexico, and migrated with my family around 1925 or '26. The army got in touch with the Mexican consul, who then called Mexico. The president, from Monterrey, told them if I had volunteered, to go ahead and take me. From then on, everyone who wanted to go voluntarily could, because now they had permission. About four months later I was on my way to England, and that's where I got my citizenship papers.

At the time we came north, immigration was just a tax. You paid *diez* centavos or something like that, came over here, and started working wherever you could. We settled in Calvert, Texas. I went to school there for four years, and my father started farming by the hour.

We were so poor that we slept on the floor. During the winter we would all bunch up on one mattress and cover ourselves as well as we could with old clothes and blankets. Sometimes we would even use this, what you wrap the bales of cotton with. We would get two or three of those from the farmers, you know, and put them on top of the old clothes so we wouldn't get cold.

But my father always had some money. He used to have one or two cars, Model Ts, Model As. He would buy this, exchange it for that, and he would wind up having one or two cars all the time. I don't know how he did it, but he was a good trader. Saturdays and Sundays when he wasn't working, that's what he did, and he always provided for us. He would trade corn. He would buy loads of corn, we would shuck it, and he would sell it for a higher price at the store. Or he would trade a sack of flour for a sack of sugar. Then with that sugar, a big hundred-pound sack, he would make his candies. He would make every kind, and he showed us how too. Peanut patties, milk candy, pumpkin candies, coconut candy, *pipitorias*—that's Mexican candy. Oh, a lot of candies.

When my dad was thirteen or fourteen he could play the bugle real good. So, he volunteered with Pancho Villa to be his bugler. My brother still has one of the bugles. My dad had some close calls. I think they all did. And my father . . . I wish he was alive. He used to sit and talk and tell us so much about what happened.

When my mother found out that I was going overseas, I wrote her a little paper, "Mother, I'm going over there, but I'm coming back. Don't worry. Now look, only you and I know about this. It's written in this paper." There's a song in Spanish that says, "It's almost time to go to the station." Something like that, but it rhymes so good in Spanish. So I wrote it down and I told her, "Remember this." I also said, "I don't know what time I'm getting back, but when I'm just a ways from the house I'm going to start singing this song." And I wrote it down.

Ya parece que en la estación
Da brinquitos mi corazón.

I got home about three o'clock in the morning and I started singing, and my mother was waiting. She was there sitting with my niece, who had been very ill. She was sitting rocking her in the cradle.

On September 16, 1945, I got out of the service. I was one of the first ones to come back on the *Queen Mary*. Well, in fact I was on recuperation leave. They were going to send me to the Pacific. I was lying in bed when the news came out. My mother was in the kitchen; I hollered to her, "Mother, did you hear that?" She came running. I was in a brace and she thought I hurt myself. "The Japs just surrendered!" We started crying. I said, "I don't have to go anymore." Well, I think God was on our side. We just were happy, you know. Yes, the radio was right close to me when they said, "We interrupt this program to give a special announcement."

I was in a crash landing over there. I still have trouble with my back. But I'm alive! It was a forced landing, and the plane went off the runway. There were a lot of holes, bomb craters, and that's how we all got banged up. It was nothing compared to other men who really got hurt.

Seven of my brothers went also. One of my brothers died in the service. It's just part of life.

When I was in the service I would send so much money home. God help me, I didn't know how to gamble, I didn't smoke or drink, but I started gambling: poker, blackjack. My first sergeant was a professional gambler. He and another sergeant by the name of Howard always tried to beat me out of my money, and I would always beat them. They wanted to make a deal with me to go to other camps to gamble and I said, "No. I'm not a gambler."

"Then how come we never can beat you?" They thought that I was a professional, but God knows I didn't even know how. But I would break the games and send my mother two, three, four, five hundred dollars at a time. God was helping me. It wasn't my doing. I think He was looking after me.

I've got a cigarette case. I got it from one of the prisoners we took. He didn't have any smokes and I gave him three packs of cigarettes. In turn, he said, "I want you to have this." It's a cigarette case. I've still got it. He was Italian. He made that by hand. I've been wanting to go to the Red Cross so they can get in touch with someone overseas to see if I can give that person back his case. It's something that would be nice for him to keep. It's made out of aluminum. If we ever meet again I'll have it handy.

One of my boys was wounded in Vietnam. He didn't want to tell us. We had to go to the Red Cross to find out why he didn't write. We didn't hear from him for about six weeks. The Red Cross told us, "Give us three days." Then they called us and said, "If you don't hear from him in the next five days let us know." They had already talked to him. He was in the hospital, but he told them not to tell us. And he refused the Purple Heart because he didn't want us to know. He sent us a letter right away saying that he was on maneuvers. Then he sent us a letter saying that he was coming home for my daughter's graduation. So he came home. We had a party, six or seven hundred people, for a supper that I made for her graduation and the homecoming of my son from Vietnam. He still didn't tell us anything. The only one who knew was my other boy, Willie, but he never told us until two days after the party. They were throwing grenades and a piece of the grenade hit his leg and he jumped into the dugout, but he was wounded and didn't know. They found him in a pool of blood.

My children are grown now, seven sons and one daughter. My wife and I always taught them to work hard, put a little money in the bank, and forget about it. Just keep puttin' it in. And if you need a little more money, do a little extra work. That's what I've been doing all my life. My wife has been a good banker. Ever since we got married, the first check, I signed it and gave it to her. I have given her my money all my life since we got married. I bought this house with cash. I have one in Corpus Christi. Then I bought another one on Highway 21. When her sister passed away, they sold her house, so I bought it. I bought another one, over farther down. And that pickup that I got, it's '88. I bought it cash. I don't like credit. Credit is just . . . they just take your money. You buy a truck on credit you gonna wind up paying, if it costs you $15,000, by the time you get through paying for it, you're gonna pay $20,000. If you pay cash, it's yours. You just bought your insurance.

I think if I hadn't volunteered in the service, I'd probably have been sent back to Mexico. And I would have had a hard time gettin' back to the United States and trying to establish myself the way I was before. Once they send you back to Mexico it's very, very hard.

MIGUEL RODRIGUEZ
Lumberyard Manager
Chicago, Illinois

When their first child was just a baby, Miguel and Elena rented this second-story flat. From there they both worked and saved to accomplish the American dream of owning their own home.

Time passed and another dream took precedence—a good education for their three children. With the prevalence of gangs and drugs in their Chicago neighborhood, that didn't seem possible. What's more, they wanted their children to speak Spanish and learn about their Mexican heritage. So they traded one dream for another and five years ago moved the family to Mexico. Miguel stayed behind, working in the United States to support them.

This year Michael and Lisa, the two oldest children, graduated from high school. They have returned to Chicago to live with their father and go to college.

Having maintained a friendship with their former landlady, Miguel, Michael, and Lisa have just moved back into the flat they left fifteen years ago. Except for three beds and three chairs it is still unfurnished. Sounds echo through the high-ceilinged rooms. The same maroon-and-gray linoleum Miguel put down many years ago still covers the kitchen floor.

Handsome, serious, and soft-spoken, Miguel sits in the window seat and describes his life in the United States.

For the poor person work is like medicine. If you are working your day passes quickly, and you feel you have done something. I like to work. I never like to arrive late and I don't like to miss. When they see this they know I am a hard worker. Then when I ask for time off to go to Mexico I don't feel bad. They know when I am there, they can count on me. I am dedicated to my work.

Other people aren't like this. I see many young people who come to work. They have graduated from high school, but they don't know how to add and subtract, they don't know how to work. I only went to third grade. In my case there were schools where I lived that went up to *secundaria*. But my father left us when my brothers and sisters and I were little. So I had to go to work.

Soon I will be here twenty-two years. I came as a tourist and went to work that same month. And since I arrived I have been working at the same place, with the company I began with.

Well, I left the company once, for a month. I asked for more money and they wouldn't pay me. So I asked for my vacation and went to work at a company across the street. Later they called and asked me, "What do you want?" Originally I had asked for fifteen cents an hour more. This was in 1979. So they said well, we'll pay you the fifteen cents. But I told them no, now it was seventy-five cents because the minimum had gone up. So they gave me the seventy-five cents. It must be that my work is good, because I've never had any problems.

I began cutting wood on the machines. I worked a year cutting lumber, then they gave me the opportunity to drive the forklift that carries the lumber. I learned how to drive it quickly, and I have been driving for twenty years. It was a little difficult at first because the owners don't speak Spanish. I had to learn to communicate, so I took classes at the library to learn English. I learned enough to speak and fill out applications. I drive the forklift, load lumber, and sometimes I help cut, or manage the people who are cutting. Because of the experience that I have, I know what they need cut. Most of the others have five or six years, and I have twenty-two.

I never have had any problem with other people. I don't know why, but I have never lived with this idea of having problems. There used to be several gangs in the area, "The Latin Kings." I would work on my car in the garage, and they never did anything to me. I don't do anything to anyone and they don't do anything to me. I think that's what it is. I never had any problems with Immigration either. I think if one knows how to live he can live wherever he wants. I never had any problems when I was alone, and now that my family is here I haven't had any problems. I've never had problems with the police or being robbed. I don't know if it's because I don't look for trouble or that I have good luck. But in truth, we are living in good areas. It's very tranquil here, but I know if we lived in another barrio we would have problems.

We always thought that there was another world on the other side of the border that we wanted our children to know. Many people here think that this is the whole world. There are children who speak only English and can't communicate with their grandparents, and then there are children who speak only Spanish and won't have opportunities here. We wanted them to study in Mexico when they finished grammar school so that they would speak both languages.

When we decided to go we had talked about it, but we never told anyone until the night before we were leaving. We packed the van with everything and left. We arrived at my mother's house. Everyone wondered why, but that is what we had planned. It was hard and it was sad, because Elena stayed there and I came back to work. But I think it worked out. It's been five years now.

When we took the children back to Mexico they began at the American school. It was very inexpensive then. I had planned to return to Mexico in two years, but after that the school became very expensive. There was nothing to do but continue working. Originally I had thought they would go to the university there, but they wanted to come back to go to school here. I am very happy because they are looking toward their future, and they can speak both languages. When they went to take the SAT exam, the others who were taking it didn't even finish or fill the page. So I feel good that they know both languages and they are educated. For them, once they graduate they can decide what they want to do. They will have opportunities on both sides. What's more, it makes me feel good because they say they're from Guadalajara.

We both sacrificed so that this would be possible. Elena has had to take care of the children alone, and I have been here also alone, working every day so that I could support them.

Elena worked too, we worked as a pair. It's different here. The husband and wife are like a partnership. There the man is the boss and that's it. There isn't any communication with the wife. I have never been jealous, so we have never had problems in that regard. We both have confidence in each other.

I think because the children started out in Catholic school they learned discipline and respect for their family. They have never forgotten that I am their father. They would come here for summers and then I would go there for a month or so each year. I don't know. My wife is a strong person, and I think she was able to control them. They never spent time in the streets, they always came home. Michael came to work the second summer he was there, and then the last two summers both he and Lisa have come here to work. And I go there two, sometimes three times a year; it depends on the money.

My idea is to return to Mexico as soon as possible. I want to see that Michael and Lisa are doing well in school and work a few years more. It would be fine if Elena came here too, but Dolly is still in school, and Elena can't live here easily because of her arthritis. I would like to work a while longer and then perhaps I can return to Mexico and start a business.

I know that this isn't my country, but I have made a living here. I have never been treated badly. Here you can have anything you want if you're willing to work for it. That's not true in Mexico. I've never regretted coming here.

ELENA RODRIGUEZ
Wife of Miguel Rodriguez
Hairstylist
Guadalajara, Mexico

It's nine o'clock in the morning and the day sounds begin: the "aaaagua" call of the water vendor, the garbage collectors' cowbell, the penny-whistle call of the knife sharpener, the bicycle bell of the mailman, the swish-swish-swish of the street sweeper's broom. From behind the heavy sliding metal doors that separate house from street comes the answering swish-swish-swish of a maid cleaning the salon and patio. There is no sign announcing her salón de belleza, but Elena already has customers waiting for haircuts. The routine is different here. Even in this upper-middle-class neighborhood only 20 percent of the households have telephones, so appointments, even in doctors' and dental offices, are very casual. The physical layout is different too. The salon is in the front room of her house and the patio doors are always open, so that the air, the bright morning light, and the jacaranda tree that umbrellas over all give an outdoor feeling. While Elena is cutting hair, the women arrange their chairs around her. They may not know one another but they carry on a lively discussion of styles, bargains, foods, and married life in Mexico.

For Elena, as gregarious as her husband, Miguel, is quiet, this is the perfect occupation. She completed the year of coursework to get her beautician's license when she returned to Mexico. In the minds of her customers, her skill and affinity for style are enhanced by being from the United States, where she learned the latest trends and technology.

I was fifteen years old when I went to Chicago with my papa. He was married to a colored woman and we lived in a colored neighborhood. When I entered the school there, I was the only white person. Everyone stared at me and I was frightened. I just didn't like it at all.

No, no, no! I was afraid of the Negroes, and the houses were so ugly. Here they were brightly painted, and there they were so dark. I kept telling my papa that I didn't like it. He didn't say anything, and after two months or so I became more accustomed to things and liked it better. After a year we returned. A *puertorriqueño* wanted to marry me and my father didn't like him. I wasn't interested in him either, but my father didn't want to take any chances, so he sent me back to Mexico.

My mother was in Mexico. She and my father were never married. When I was six they took me away from my mama's side. It was a tremendous shock. My grandmother, my father's mother, then raised me. She sent me to school, and from then on my father took responsibility for me. But they tricked me. They told me that when I was finished with the school year they were going to let me go back to my mama, but it was lies, because they never let me go back. They took me from Pachuca, where I was born, to Mexico City, where my grandmother lived. That's where I was raised.

So after a year in Chicago I returned to Mexico to finish my studies. Then, only a few months before I would graduate, we received a telephone call saying that my papa was gravely ill. That day was a fiesta and I had curlers in my hair and everything. My grandmother said we were going to leave on the one o'clock flight. It was already almost noon. So quickly, just as I was, we went to the airport and flew directly to Chicago. From this day on we never returned to Mexico.

My papa was in the hospital with a tumor in his brain. From then on he remained paralyzed. By then my papa had divorced his colored wife. His new wife was from Guadalajara. My grandmother wanted me to return to Mexico with her, but I didn't want to. I had a boyfriend in Mexico, and my grandmother wanted me to marry him. She wanted to force me to marry him. He's the cousin of Cuauhtémoc Cárdenas, who ran for president. My grandmother told me, "He's a good boy, a good worker." But I didn't love him.

My papa came to my rescue. He asked if I wanted to stay in Chicago or go to Mexico. I told my stepmother, "Tell him I want to stay." My grandmother returned to Mexico and I stayed. He was sick, so I had to stay. He died in 1966.

After, I lived with my stepmother. She loved me and was a very good person, but finally she came back to Mexico because my father had left her money and she wanted to buy some houses here. So I stayed in Chicago alone.

But I was lonely and would come for vacations to Mexico. This is when I met my husband. My half-sister told me, "You know, Miguel is going to the United States, to Chicago. Maybe you can help him get work." I found him work with a friend who worked with me. Then he asked me to be his girlfriend. This was in November and we were married in June.

Every year, after we were married, we would come to Mexico for our vacation and he would always say to me, "When we save some money, let's go live in Mexico." I always said yes, okay, we'll go to Guadalajara. I always liked Guadalajara.

I never have wanted to become an American citizen. It has its advantages and disadvantages. You have the advantage of all the opportunities there, but then you lose those here. You can't buy a house or have a business or anything like that if you are an American citizen. I also like the conveniences in the United States. You can get things easier. Things like dishwashers here are too expensive. There, everyone has one. I really don't know why, but everyone, even the poorest people who are earning the minimum, can buy the things they want. I have seen that people who don't earn much can still go out and buy a microwave oven.

Everyone has one; they may have two, a large and small. And here hardly anyone has one. There everyone has a telephone, you can't live without one. And here it's been more than two years since I put in the application and look, nothing. There are so many things I like about the United States. There you have your rights. You fight for them and the law supports you. If there is a law you obey it. Not here. These are the things I have always liked about the United States.

They say, "I am American and I have my rights."

If you hear this you say, "Well *caramba,* here everyone has rights." There, to have rights they don't ask if you have papers. If you buy something at the store and they don't deliver it the day they say they will, you can make a claim and they don't ask whether or not you have papers. You can make a claim. This is what I have always liked about the United States. The rich and poor all have the same rights. It's not like here in Mexico. Here only the rich person with money can make them listen. But the poor person, no. The poor person always has to be bent over doing whatever the rich man says. This is the one thing I have never liked about Mexico. In the United States everyone is equal, everyone. If you have work and you want a car you can buy one just as new as your boss's.

Anyone has these opportunities, whether you have papers or not. In the schools they never ask for your papers, your green card or anything. If you are intelligent and you arrive there and you study and work, when you have the English you can have everything.

I know two brothers. They worked in a restaurant at nights. They gave them dinner, so they only went home to sleep. Look, they went home with their hands swollen from so much sweeping, mopping, washing dishes, and they had to wash with hot, hot water because it was a pancake house, for the grease and syrup. If they broke something the owner would take money out of their pay. They had only one day of rest, and when someone else didn't show up they would call them. But these boys were earning only $1 an hour and they were working sixteen-hour shifts. They were being abused.

Then they found a job mopping in the airport, where they could earn the minimum, which was $3.35. But the restaurant owner was angry because he couldn't find anyone else to work for sixteen hours, no one. He told them he would pay $2 an hour. They said they would rather work where they earn $3.35. So the boss said, "Okay, you go and I will send out the Immigration." So they stayed at the restaurant, working for $2 an hour. Finally they realized they were being treated illegally. One went to the airport and the other to a steel foundry, where he began at $7.50 an hour.

For those who have recently arrived, it's their own ignorance. When they learn, when they open their eyes, when they can hear, hear that everyone has the right to progress, and that the rights in the United States are for everyone, then they say, "Even though I don't have papers, here there are laws."

The bad thing about Mexico, the only thing I don't like about Mexico, is you can't sue anyone. In the United States you sue someone if they don't complete something. And they pay attention to you. Here no, you have to go to the Department of Consumers. They send you here, and they send you there, and no one pays any attention.

I don't understand the Mexicans. I tell you I will never understand them. They have so much need. Yet how is it that there is a lot of work and they don't work? You call them, they say they will come, and they never come. Tell me, wouldn't it be better if they just told you no and that's that?

What I like here is the climate and the freedom. They burglarize houses here too, but there is more security. You can walk anywhere you want. The people are more tranquil. They live with less rush than in the United States. If you get on a bus in the United States you have to look around to see who is going to rob you. But here, it's more secure.

Now the kids know Mexico and they know the United States, the differences. They like it here, but not to live. It's good, they have the rights of both sides. They also know the culture of Mexico, the ideas of those from Mexico, because they are very different from those of the United States. I think it was good we came. Even so, they both want to return to study. I tell them good, go back and study and after, if you want, you can work here or there.

DOMITILA NAVAR CORRAL
Retired Partner of Family Dairy
El Paso, Texas

Miss Navar and her older sister still live together in the house where they grew up, next to the dairy. From the street a comfortable but modest single-story house conceals the large Mexican colonial style courtyard with rooms all around. Friends and relatives enter by the back gate and usually find the Navar sisters in the sitting room. The sisters are still very active, with visitors coming and going all day. Their calendar is filled with family and church obligations.

A very handsome woman wearing a royal blue dress and modest high heels, at eighty-one Miss Domitila Navar is still the unofficial secretary, taking phone calls, relaying messages, and planning their schedule. Her life has been dedicated to her family, first her parents, now her brothers, but also her nieces, who frequently call or visit. One summer when seven of her nieces were in high school, she took them to Europe for three months, specifically to Spain, so they might see where the Navars originally came from. She enforced two rules: they were to observe and understand, but they couldn't criticize; and they could speak only in Spanish.

Beyond the sitting room is the daily dining room, and beyond that the French doors are closed. Every Sunday when they were younger, Miss Navar and her sister cooked the family dinner for fifty. It was served in the enormous family dining room, where the long formal tables and buffet are still set for special occasions and fiestas.

Paulina, the maid, comes in with a woven reed basket of fruit covered with an embroidered cloth.

Today is grocery day. My brother takes my sister shopping on Tuesdays. Tomorrow is our wash day and Friday is the day we iron. We keep these days so that we always know what we have to do tomorrow.

There isn't really that much to tell. My sister and I grew up helping my mother with the large family we had. After we finished school my father didn't want us to work. It wasn't the custom for the daughters of Mexican families to work, so we stayed at home. My older sister was a bilingual secretary. At that time there were very few. And she learned telegraphy in English and Spanish. She was offered very good positions, but my father never wanted her to work. I studied for an accounting career, and I helped my brothers in the office.

I think our family was the same as others. When everyone was young they had religious obligations to complete. They were, as you would say, a must.

I am more than eighty-one years old. I came with my parents to El Paso, Texas, on July 23, 1915. I was seven years old. This was when the revolution began. My grandfather and my father were *comerciantes* in Corrales, Durango, and they didn't want anything to do with the *revolucionarios* who came to our town, so they sold everything they had and left. They established themselves in the city of Durango. But the revolution continued escalating, and the *revolucionarios* began coming to Durango too. It was very dangerous for Grandfather and Father because they were very well known. "Are you with this side or the other?" And they didn't want any part of it. That was when they decided to come to the United States.

There were my parents, an aunt, and my grandparents. The whole family came, and to this day we have continued to be united. When we arrived they said we didn't need papers or passports, we could just pass. But my father insisted that it be formal. He wanted to legalize our residence, and on July 23, 1915, we crossed into the United States.

When we arrived, my grandfather and father wanted to see what they could do for the family. My father began buying cattle, and we went to live on what was then called Lincoln Avenue. That was when he entered in the dairy business. It began growing little by little until the dairy was too big to be there. That's when we moved here. The North Loop wasn't here, and there were no streets or houses. Now they don't even have the cattle here. They still have the dairy, but they bring the milk from outside in refrigerated trucks; they process and distribute it here. But it is the same business that my father began.

In Mexico, my father and grandfather were known as *Don* Aldeberto and *Don* Macedonio. Here they were unknown. It was very different and difficult. But they knew how to live and how to accept it, and with the blessings of God they were able to get ahead. My grandfather was a very hard worker, as was my father, and they struggled. From the time my father bought the first cow, my oldest brother, when he was very young, began helping in the business. He helped bottle the milk and deliver it. From there he would go to school. Then when the business began to grow, there were more brothers and they worked with my father. After, when my other brothers grew up, they all worked together. And to this day the business is 100 percent family.

All my brothers have a lot of respect for their sisters, especially their oldest sister. They all visit us each afternoon. Their children also have respect for the family. We are what we are because of our parents. It's sad when children forget this.

My parents never spoke English but they wanted to maintain our traditions, and the ways they continued we still continue. We always celebrate Christmas with the whole family, the New Year, the Three Kings on the sixth of January, and all of the birthdays. We celebrate here because the house is big and everyone can come. We celebrate with all the Mexican traditions, all.

When we have the dinners we eat a little of everything, a little American and a little Mexican. We always have American-style Thanksgiving dinner for the whole family, with the turkey and stuffing. The Christmas celebration is Mexican style with *tamales*. So we've made a mix of the traditions. And we often have *pozole* just because it is the dish our family prefers.

We never became U.S. citizens. We are still citizens of Mexico. People ask us why. I tell them we work here and pay taxes on the money we make here, but we will always be Mexican.

YGNACIA LOPEZ
Obituary*
Bryan, Texas

Funeral services for Ygnacia Lopez, 83, of Bryan will be at noon today at Santa Teresa Catholic Church with the Rev. John McCaffrey of St. Joseph's Catholic Church officiating.

Mrs. Lopez died Thursday evening at a local hospital.

She was born in San Luis Potosi, Mexico, and had resided in Bryan since 1949.

Mrs. Lopez was a homemaker and a member of the Guadalupanas Society of Santa Teresa Catholic Church.

**Bryan–College Station Eagle,* September 2, 1989.

She was preceded in death by her husband, Jose Lopez, in 1978.

Survivors include five sons and daughters-in-law, Raymond and Virginia Lopez, Angel "Blacki" and Beatrice Lopez, and Doroteo and Dora Lopez, all of Bryan, and Cande and Lilly Lopez and Felix and Mary Louise Lopez, all of Los Angeles; six daughters and five sons-in-law, Helena and Louis Garcia, Lupe and Tony Garcia, Irene and Jimmy Arevalo, and Margarita and Herman Brooks, all of Bryan, Mary and Leno Quintero of Houston, and Hilda Deleoin of Dallas; 62 grandchildren; 81 great-grandchildren; 15 great-great-grandchildren; and several nieces and nephews.

ARRIBA, RAZA

Arriba, raza dormida,
ya no es hora de dormir,
a pelear la causa justa
para nuestro porvenir.

Ya basta que el pobre diga
que es la voluntad de Dios,
cuando le niegan justicia
los jurados y el patrón.

Nuestra cultura y origen
nos tienen que respetar.
La Raza nueva está en marcha
y nadie la va a parar.

UP WITH THE RAZA
(PEOPLE)

Get up, you sleeping people,
Now is not the time to sleep,
We must fight the just cause
For our future.

Enough of poor people saying
That it's God's will
When the jury and bosses
Deny us justice.

They have to respect
Our culture and origins.
The new Raza is marching
And no one will stop us.

9

Up with the Raza

THE BEST AND THE BRIGHTEST

"Our biggest export is poverty." All over Mexico, from the academic to the man in the street, that explains who los mojados are. In the United States the refrain goes, "They come here just to get on welfare." Old saws repeated so often are accepted as truth.

Rather than tell us anything about the immigrants, these slogans reveal two proud countries artfully avoiding any recognition of each other. As condescending as is the American view, the immigrant's presence flatters U.S. society's idea of itself. The Mexican slogan is a self-deprecating shrug of the shoulders by a nation unable to control her economic destiny but still capable of an ironic laugh at the gringos picking up after her.

Neither attitude is surprising. The United States does take Mexico for granted and seldom takes her seriously. Mexico, on the other hand, takes U.S. actions seriously but refuses to dignify those actions by giving them notice. Humiliated in two wars in which they lost half their territory to the colossus of the north, Mexicans are not about to attach much importance to the loss of their people to los estados. They have lost too much already.

Instead, Mexicans prefer to see the emigrants as the dregs of society—the poorest, the least prepared, the least able. The stigma sticks too. They look down on the emigrants as people who have sold their heritage for a dollar. Their children, the Chicanos, are viewed the same.

These attitudes mask what is actually occurring. This migration is a people's movement, spontaneous, without planning or sanction by either government. The emigrants are not wealthy or highly educated, but neither are they the poorest or least schooled. Survival consumes the poverty-stricken. They can't raise or risk the resources to send even one family member north. People who do emigrate are self-selected—the most ambitious, enterprising, energetic, enthusiastic, adaptable, and persevering of the working and middle classes.

Mexico is sending the United States her best and brightest, just that group of people she needs most to build a dynamic and productive economy.

DR. ALBERT BAEZ
Physicist, Environmentalist
Greenbrae, California

When he was a young man, Albert Baez's passion for science and the new field of physics led him to a fork in the road, a conflict with his basic belief in social responsibility and furthering world peace. That didn't stop him. He melded his career as an internationally renowned physicist and educator with his ethics into a quest to bring science education to four continents and the remote corners of the world.

At seventy-seven years of age, Dr. Baez is always busy, his mind working with new ideas. A Year in Bagdad, written with Joan Baez, Sr., was published in 1988, and notes for another book are underway. He devotes his energies to environmental education and science-based community development projects in Latin America under the auspices of Vivemos Mejor.

After receiving my Ph.D., I got a job with the Cornell Aeronautics Lab. I needed to make some money because I had been living in poverty as a graduate student. My interest in war and peace really began there. They sent me on a mission on this aircraft carrier. Planes taking off from aircraft carriers were a relatively new thing in 1949; I was sent as a civilian observer to see how the parameters evolving from these new techniques could be put into a system—what was then called operations research. You know, how could you plan this whole thing scientifically? And I began getting the feeling that this was not the ultimate road to peace, for a physicist to spend the rest of his life designing the operations of war.

My father was a Methodist minister. Now, coming from Mexico, that's strange. My grandfather had established a school in Puebla called Instituto Metodista Mexicano. Its main purpose was to train ministers. If you look back at the history of American universities you find that most started as church-related institutions whose main function was to train the ministry; it was in that tradition. Puebla is a very Catholic town, so it was rather extraordinary. He himself was extraordinary, a Spaniard who had come to Mexico and had been converted to Protestantism. Protestantism—I'm talking more than seventy-six years ago—was a liberating idea for some of the Mexicans, because Catholicism as it was then practiced was often a very narrow approach to religion. As a young man my father felt, this is not for me. It was quite a discovery for him to be invited to a social function at this school. People looked different, they spoke with an air of freedom that he hadn't experienced before.

So my father fell in love with the director's daughter, Talia Valderama. The director, my grandfather, Pedro Flores Valderama, was a very unusual man, because at that time it was extraordinary for anyone to want their daughters to learn a profession. He sent all his kids to the United States to learn English. "Well, I'm not a rich man, and I'm not going to be able to leave money to my children, so I want them to at least know how to fend for themselves." So my mother went to Texas, and among other things she learned stenography and telegraphy, which in those days would be like someone getting involved in computers today. She had been to the States and had returned when she and my father met.

In due course my father graduated from that school and then asked for the hand of the daughter, as we used to say. My grandfather was not pleased at all. I have a very interesting little book that was kept by my mother and father in which they communicated with one another by writing notes. The messenger was my mother's youngest sister. She was only about eleven at the time and she acted as a courier. My mother would give her this book and say, take it to Alberto, and then he would write and say, take it to Talia. It was very difficult; they couldn't talk to each other. They had to invent ways. My mother also taught telegraphy to my father. In those days you know it wasn't dots and dashes, it was clicks—clickety, click, click, click. They communicated that way on the water pipes of the college, and I have the little book that tells what they had been thinking. Now in this my father is asking my mother, "Do you think we should get married? Do you think we should go to the States?" with complete answers by my mother.

As a result of these early communications, they decided yes, they would go to the United States. They were members of a religious minority, and they thought that maybe things would be better in the United States. It was also the time of the revolution, and they were having difficulty even getting food. I've heard my parents speak about the lack of milk when we were babies. Then the economic motive—how am I going to make a living in Mexico as a Methodist pastor? Oh, and the other thing, my grandfather was somewhat of an autocrat, as you can imagine, and so I suppose my father wanted to get away from that. Eventually they did go to Texas, Alice, Texas, where my father set up a church among Mexican-Americans, a Methodist church. But it was stoned by the other Mexicans, who didn't want these Protestants in their midst.

The aunt of mine who had been the courier was now grown and married, and her husband was the buyer for the Mexican railways, with an office in New York in the Woolworth Building. At that time that was the most prestigious business address. He liked that life and he loved my parents, so he said, "Talia and Alberto, you've got to come here, there's no sense staying in Texas." He knew that my father also knew stenography so he said, "Why don't you come and be my private secretary?" Anyway, he made things very alluring: "I'm working for the railways; I can get free passes for all of you." So that's how they went. They went to Brooklyn on the free passes supplied by my *Tio* Fernando Carrera.

When they first came to Texas I must have been about two. By the time they moved to New York I was about four, maybe five—I was born in 1912.

They landed in Brooklyn. It was completely alien for my father. It turns out that an American woman heard about my parents. She started inviting Spanish-speaking people to her house on Sundays and then invited my father to act as minister. After a while my father went to the local Methodist church in Brooklyn, I remember it was on Clark Street at the corner of Henry, near what is now called Columbia Heights. My father went to the minister of the church and said, "Here's a group of Spanish-speaking people, they need a place to worship, would you let us use your church on Sunday afternoons?" In less than a year the Spanish congregation exceeded the American congregation, and that began a forty-year career for my father in Brooklyn.

When I was seven my mother was pregnant again, and she wanted to go back to Mexico to have her baby. I never did quiz her on why she wanted to do that. Perhaps she didn't want to be seen by the other parishioners during her pregnancy. In those days they were very modest about those things. She may have had some notion that she wanted all of us to be born in Mexico. So back she goes to Puebla, to the college. My sister and I went back with my mother and spent a whole year with my grandfather. This time we were all very welcome. He was very proud of having a grandson and granddaughter, and I remember I was very well received by the older students, almost like a pet, because I was the director's grandson. So I have good memories of that year.

Also, in retrospect, it gave me the feeling that I had grown up in Mexico, even though I had only spent the first two years of my life and then this year, but since it took place at that particular interval in my life, those formative years, I just felt somehow linked with Mexico. I still feel it. So several advantages accrued from all this. One was that I never forgot my Spanish.

Many years later, I think it might have been in California, someone asked me about my background and I said, "I'm Mexican." My kids began saying, "We're Mexican." But then someone said to one of my kids, "Oh, don't say you're Mexican, say you're Spanish." Now I didn't feel that stigma at all in Brooklyn. Brooklyn was a melting pot, everybody came from somewhere. But when we went to live in Redlands, Joanie felt it because she was the dark-skinned one in our family. She wanted to make friends with the Mexican kids and they didn't want her because she was the daughter of a professor at the university. Then she wanted to make friends with the American kids, but she looked too Mexican for them.

Of my three daughters, Pauline is the only one who has spent time with me in Mexico. I think there are reasons for that. Joan, of course, because she is world famous, the world is her oyster, so to speak, and Mexico has never been particularly attractive to her. At the bottom of it I believe is a fear, born in Bagdad, of having stomach upsets. And I think that has passed on to Mimi as well.

Well, I went to Manual Training High School. Now, my contact with the radio club there gave me the active interest in science. It wasn't that I was taking science courses but rather that I was involved in building something myself. That even led me to construct a television set in 1929. That was at least twenty years before real TV came along.

In those days the makings of a modern TV set didn't exist. The tube that lights the screen and so on was much more primitive. My uncle, Frank Lavara, was a custom painter of cars. For a while he and my Aunt Eve lived with us. He was very good with his hands, highly skilled as a painter and very meticulous. Once he said to me, "Do you think we could build one of these sets?"

I said, "Sure, but I need someone who has hand skills and tools."

So he said, "Let's do it." I was the scientist—how old was I?—1928; I was sixteen. So we put this thing together. In those days they had experimental broadcasts from the ordinary radio stations. At midnight they would broadcast television signals for an hour, for the people who were experimenting. You could take the ordinary audio signal that would make the music and the sound, and feed that to a tube, and the tube would light up in synchronism. When you put the rotating screen in front of it, you got a tiny little light show. The images danced around in a rhythm with the music. I felt, I've got to put this thing together so I can have access to those experimental broadcasts. The last stumbling block was a special tube that cost $7. Today you might as well say $7,000, as far as what it meant to me. But I scraped and saved; I was able to buy that tube, and now this thing was ready to go. Then they stopped the experimental broadcasts. That was a great disappointment, but we still had fun out of it. Soon thereafter I was going to graduate and go to college. That was the end of that.

That brings up a sacred word, education. Because my grandfather was an educator, my mother felt that all three of her children had to go to college. She hadn't gone to college, but she had other kinds of schooling. Since my father's salary was not enough, my mother started working. She became a social worker with the YWCA. So she became a professional woman and brought in a salary possibly higher than my father's. A little out of the ordinary, but my mother was a great believer in education and had made up her mind.

My mother wanted us to go to college, but since neither my mother or father had any experience with higher education in the United States, my father went to the bishop and said, "I have a son and he's about to graduate, he'd like to go to college, where should he go?" Naturally he suggested a Methodist college, Drew University. I was a member of the second graduating class.

The school was so new that they didn't yet have a physics department. The physics course was taught by the chemistry professor, Louis Jordy. Before he died Jordy said to me, "You know, when you were in my class you knew more about electricity than I did." But eventually they did get a physicist. They were just beginning to form the faculty and were careful to bring people from universities that were renowned in the field. The physics man that they brought in was Marshall Harrington from Princeton. There was no physics department and no math department, so he had to teach whatever math and physics that were going to be taught.

There was a curious incident about Harrington. At one point when he was teaching calculus he became ill. I was one of his students, but I was not his best student. Nevertheless, when he was sent to the hospital he got in touch with me and asked, "Would you teach my classes?" In retrospect I think he may have sensed that I might be good at it.

I said yes because I knew that all I had to do was keep one step ahead of the class. What opened the door for me was that invitation by Harrington. Suddenly I found myself in front of a class, and at the end of two weeks I felt, I can do this. The reaction of the students told me that they were enjoying it and I was enjoying it.

Now mind you, I'm graduated from college in 1933, the depths of the Depression. There aren't many jobs available, but there are some teaching openings. I heard of an opening at Syracuse in the math department. I immediately borrowed my father's car, and within twenty-four hours I was meeting Campbell, the head of the department. He was very surprised, also amused, that I should take it so seriously. Well, he says, "What math courses have you had?" I hadn't had many math courses at all. Nevertheless he said, "Okay, I think you can do it." So that's how I got this one-year fellowship at Syracuse, and I ended up with a master's degree.

After that I went back to Drew, again looking for jobs. Since I had been both a student and instructor there and their one-man math department was taking off for India, they needed a replacement. So they offered me his job and I went back to Drew for a while. Then came the offer to teach at Wagner College, a Lutheran College on Staten Island. These are all small colleges.

By that time I had married, and both Pauline and Joanie were just babies. This was in the forties. My wife's half-brother, Bob Bridge, came to visit us. He said, "What are you doing here? You should be in California, that's the wave of the future." He had been taking premedical physics at Stanford. They needed teachers to teach the army courses that were being taught at all the big universities at that time. So my brother-in-law goes back and says, "You know, my brother-in-law is the best physics teacher in the world and you should hire him."

Now mind you, I entered Wagner as an instructor with a master's degree, only because it was during the war. They kept promoting me because they knew you couldn't take time out to get a doctor's degree. On the strength of my teaching they kept promoting me, and in four years I was a full professor. So with this wonderful title of full professor, here I'm applying for a job at Stanford and they say, all we can offer you is a lab assistant's job. So I said, "I'll take it."

Without a Ph.D. in this game you were without your union card; and why not get it at a prestigious university? On top of that my whole family was crazy about the idea of living in the sun.

Initially I thought I might continue in mathematics. The professors were world renowned. But no, they weren't meeting because there weren't enough students. Szego, the head of the department, said, "But if you'd like to come to my house once a week I'll teach you." That was possible in 1944. I would cycle over to Los Altos and spend a whole afternoon with Gabor Szego. That's the kind of place Stanford was at that time. Initially I got a job in the math department teaching calculus. The mathematicians thought that because I was working at the physics department I knew some physics. The physicists thought that because I was teaching in the math department I knew some mathematics. Well that lasted only about one semester before they realized I didn't know very much about either, but in any case I was always well liked as a teacher. In other words, you don't have to have very extensive knowledge if you have a gift of communicating and imparting it. It stood me in good stead.

I went to Paul Kirkpatrick. He had been thinking about an X-ray microscope, something no one had ever built and that the literature said could not be done because you could not focus X rays. He's now in his nineties. He and his wife had befriended our whole family. "Would you like to be a graduate student under me to develop this idea?" I jumped at the chance.

My thesis was the design and construction of an X-ray microscope. That branched out into X-ray astronomy. There are heavenly bodies out there that generate X rays, which can't be seen using a light telescope, but can if you have a device that can pick up and focus X rays. So it turned out, quite fortuitously, that the thesis that I wrote has had wider reading than many.

It was lucky for me to have pulled out of Cornell Aeronautic Lab early, because once the perks get high and you're living better economically, it's hard to leave. But now it opened new vistas, mostly in education. A year in Bagdad came immediately after Cornell, and teaching at Redlands after that. Then came *Sputnik*.

I guess *Sputnik* was 1957. By 1958 there were important activities in this country to stimulate improvement in the teaching of physics. After teaching six years at Redlands, I was invited back to Stanford as a visiting professor. That was a great honor for me. It was a lovely experience.

I was there, wearing the hat of a visiting professor, when Professor Zacharias at MIT started this project to improve the teaching of physics in high schools in the United States. He sent an invitation to the heads of all physics departments throughout the United States. Zacharias wanted people in physics who were also interested in the media, in making films. Based on a slide and tape show I had made in Bagdad, I was chosen to go to the initial meeting at MIT, where they were going to discuss the making of films.

Among all these physicists there were very few who had any notion of media. The only notion I had was what I had picked up from making my slide and tape show. So when there was a question period, no one was responding. I felt very meek. I was really not a full-time member of the Stanford faculty. I didn't want to presume, but when I saw that no one was responding, I got up and spoke about the importance of the media and even gave an illustration of the kind of film I would like to see made. I returned to Stanford, and within twenty-four hours Zacharias was on the phone saying to me, "Baez, your suggestion for a film was great. I think you should come and work with us."

The project, called PSSC, Physical Science Study Committee, is now fairly well known, because over the years the materials produced were used in many high schools.

After two years in Boston came an invitation from UNESCO in Paris. I've taken several stabs at retirement. Some were sort of imposed upon me. At UNESCO you cannot work past sixty. I was getting close to that, and I had promised my family that I would come back at the end of four years. At the end of six years I just had to come back. We moved to Carmel Valley, but still in retirement I worked for another four or five years producing films with Britannica. They are all on physics.

With this accumulated experience I have been able to internationalize. If I can work in Bagdad I can work anywhere. So I started generating UNESCO projects all around the world. Things have changed a lot within UNESCO. The United States pulled out, Britain pulled out. The reasons were valid up to a point, but we should get back in there now. Anyway, the international experience has become the focus of my life.

When I came to live here on the Boardwalk on San Francisco Bay, a new consciousness, a new awareness, was beginning to hit me. Just before I left UNESCO we realized that when you're teaching science to children you don't break it up into physics, chemistry, and biology. You talk about science. So we developed a program called integrated science teaching. It was toward the end of my tenure there that the notion began to take shape. In formulating the ideas about an integrated science, this environmental awareness was beginning to hit me, and I began saying the ideal integrating theme ought to be environment.

It was 1972, and Earth Day had come along. Awareness was beginning to arise. I noticed on the edge of this marsh at the Boardwalk there are signs that say ECOLOGICAL RESERVE. So here I was dumped into an ecological setting. I thought at the time, maybe this is the next thing I'm going to get involved in. Suddenly I get a letter from IUCN, the International Union for the Conservation of Nature, saying, would you like to be a candidate for the position of chairman on the Commission on Education of the IUCN. I wrote back, "I'm not an environmentalist, I'm not a biologist. I don't think I'm prepared."

They responded, "Your experience in the international realm and in environmental education indicates that you can help." I thought, the finger is pointing again, I had better accept. I've spent five years as chairman of the Commission on Education of IUCN. After I became chairman I realized I had a very serious responsibility. Now I'm working on the articulation of the environment as an integration of all the sciences.

Recently I had a very nice experience when I went to Mexico to establish a child-care center, a project sponsored by Vivemos Mejor. There is a cooperative in Las Vigas, Mexico, of women who weave. They're all women, no men are working there. They're all young, you look at them and think they're girls, but most of them are mothers. So who takes care of their children? A child-care center seemed in order, but we in the United States didn't dream it up. The board there said this is what's needed, and it should be a model. "We hope what you bring to us is a model of the best that can be done." I thought, gee, that's exciting. They sense there are good things happening elsewhere in the world and that we, their American counterparts, might be a conduit to that knowledge. You know, Montessori and that are old stuff here, but in Las Vigas?

I've spent at least fifteen years of my life promoting the improvement of the teaching of science. Science is one of the things needed in these countries if you're going to have a base for a future economy. Otherwise they'll always be the servants of the United States. I've set up programs in Asia, Africa, Latin America, and the Arab states, always for the improvement of the teaching of basic sciences. So I feel, well, with all that experience I would love to do something in Mexico.

I feel that I could make an impact in Jalapa and Las Vigas way out of proportion to what I could do here. Here, after all, I am a retired person, I've had my day so to speak. I could become involved, but here the need is not so great. So I'm enthused about the possibility of going back there and sharing.

Going back to when I was seven, spending a year in Puebla with my grandfather left a deep impression on me and the feeling that somehow I was brought up in Mexico, when in fact I only spent three years there. All my early childhood, up to the point where I was going to high school, I feel my entire education was deeply affected by my Mexican upbringing. I realize now that I'm not a Mexican in the typical sense. First, most Mexicans have been brought up in the Catholic environment, and many who come to this country come under very different circumstances than I. My own background is preachers and teachers.

Now when I go back I don't really go back as a Mexican, but as an internationalist, someone who has been around the world, who realizes that he was born in Mexico, who feels that perhaps there is something special for me to do there. It's in that sense that I go back. I realize that I don't know enough about the political or economic life. There are whole ranges of Mexican activity that I don't know or comprehend, but I don't think it matters, because when I do go back I find people who are interested in what I can offer and who are saying, yes, come help us. That's a nice feeling.

DR. CELESTINO FERNÁNDEZ
Vice President
for
Undergraduate Academic Affairs
University of Arizona
Tucson, Arizona

At thirty-three years of age Dr. Fernández became one of the youngest college administrators in the United States when he was promoted to Associate Vice President at the University of Arizona. Not yet forty and bursting with wiry enthusiasm, he manages to combine teaching and research with his administrative responsibilities. His love is Mexican music, and he is an ardent fan and researcher of los corridos. *From the visitor's side of his desk, listening to his half of telephone conversations in perfect Spanish, one becomes absolutely certain that, although he came to the United States very young and has fully achieved the American dream, Dr. Fernández is still very much a* mexicano.

The change was so dramatic. It was complete culture shock. We went from a small town in Mexico with a population of about 700 to a community of about 48,000 in California. The traffic seemed like it never stopped in Santa Rosa, whereas in Santa Inez we'd see a bus or a truck go by only once in a while. There we had the cobblestone streets, here it was all pavement. Santa Rosa is almost rural, but coming from a community of 700 people, it looked like a megalopolis. I was eight and a half.

Yes, the size was different, but there was much more than that. Everything and anything, all the way from hot running water to electricity, at any time of the day. In Mexico we had electricity maybe a couple of hours a day, but we didn't know when, so one never depended on it. No refrigerators, no stoves, no washing machines, and we moved into a home with all those things. Beyond that, it was very enclosed. There were a lot of windows, but it was enclosed. In Mexico our bedrooms were enclosed, the kitchen was enclosed, but that was it. The rest of the time we were, in a sense, living outdoors.

The food of course was radically different. My mother continued to cook the same, but it tasted different because she cooked over a gas stove as opposed to an open fire. She still made her own tortillas, but they didn't taste the same either. There we used lard for cooking and here it was mostly oil. Nothing tasted the same.

The milk! Coming across the border here in Nogales between Arizona and Sonora took a long time, with all the shots and questions. Finally we came through customs. So my dad was going to treat us to a special lunch. He knew what American kids liked, so we went to an A&W Root Beer and he ordered hamburgers, fries, and milk. Now a hamburger, we'd never seen anything like that, and we weren't about to touch it. My sister and I were not about to eat it. Even my mother was very apprehensive. Then he explained to us that the French fries were potatoes. We knew what potatoes were, but we had never had them cooked that way, so we kind of nibbled on those. But the worst thing of all was the milk. It came in this mug that had been in the freezer, so it was cold—ice-cold milk. I was used to getting up in the morning, taking my glass to my grandfather, who would fill it directly from the cow. Of course milk from the cow has steam coming off it because it's so warm. Then during the day we would drink it as it sat on the counter, room temperature, but it was never refrigerator cold. It was never processed. Here milk is very thin, it doesn't have any taste. There, depending on the time of year and the type of grass the cows were eating, you could taste the difference. That was a big shock for me because I liked the cattle. I hung around with my grandfather and helped him milk the cows. It took me years to get adjusted to the milk here.

Today I drink milk here, it's fine. But my grandfather is still alive, he's ninety-two. When I go back, we go out in the morning and fill the glass; I drink a couple of glasses of that milk. I like it.

We knew everybody in Santa Inez and everybody knew us, not only in that little town, but in all the towns and ranches around. Everybody was family in that respect. In the evening we would go to my grandmother's and sit around the fire and chat. Even when I visit now, that's what we do; we sit around the kitchen and talk. We moved from that to Santa Rosa, California, where we didn't know anyone.

My dad knew his boss before our coming. He had worked several seasons with this particular gentleman and his family. He helped us obtain our documents when we all came up in 1957. My sister and I didn't know anyone, and we couldn't communicate. That fall my sister entered the fourth grade and I entered second. I mean we just sat there. There was no one else in the school who spoke Spanish. There was one black family and one American Indian family, and we were the foreigners. It was a lot of emotional stress. I remember telling my parents to send me back, that I would go back and live with my grandparents. I didn't want to live here. I didn't know what any of the kids were saying. They'd come around at recess and try to talk to me, and they were laughing and stuff. They weren't necessarily laughing at me, but I didn't know what they were saying, and I couldn't say anything to them at all.

School was different from in Mexico. There I had gone to kindergarten and Catholic school with the nuns, and I was one of their favorites. The teachers were friends of my family, it was all family. Here, I had a very nice second grade teacher, Mrs. Albright. She was very warm. We still communicate. We were close but it was very different. She made sure that I was taken care of. We would walk together and she would hold my hand. It was real important because I was scared.

There are good memories too. The principal would come around, take me out of class, and we'd walk around the schoolyard. He'd try to teach me English. Now I know that's what he was trying to do because I only learned one word and that was *coat*. I had this huge coat that had been given to me. My parents' boss had five boys, so they gave me a lot of clothes. There I was in this coat that was too big for me; the sleeves hung down below my hands, way down. He would tug on this and say, "Coat, coat, coat."

During that first year I never said a word. The teacher wouldn't have known if I was mute or not. I never said a word. It was after that summer, coming back, that I remember speaking. I could do mathematics. That was it. I was very well mannered, not one of the assertive middle-class kids of the United States, not at all.

I still remember all these people who were good to me, attempted to teach me to speak without an accent. In fifth grade, Mrs. Neff would have me take *WH* words like *when, where,* and *why* and have me hold my hand about six inches from my mouth and overcompensate for the *WH* sound 'til I could feel the breath on my hand. I would practice twenty minutes at a time almost every day—*wh–a–ere, wh–a–en, wh–a–y.* I can still feel that air on my palm.

Kindergarten in Mexico is almost like second grade here, particularly with the nuns. There was no nonsense, no playtime, you don't take your little mat and have naps or cookies and milk. We had to learn how to read and write and mathematics and so on. So that gave me a good start.

That first year I was actually a couple of years ahead of the kids here in mathematics. The teachers saw that. They knew that I wasn't a dumb kid—I just couldn't speak. So I think they gave me a good deal of attention. I also believe that being a foreigner in this country is different than being a minority student. We were clearly foreigners. We were like a novelty. Everybody was interested in us in the school. They had never had any other foreigners there. We were the center.

My parents always stressed the importance of education, but they themselves never really had that much opportunity. My dad had a sixth grade education and my mom a third grade education in the Catholic school in Santa Inez.

From elementary school on I worked after school and weekends. In the winter, picking up brush in the apple orchard after they prune, and in the summer picking apples off the ground, then later in the packing house. In high school I worked at a golf course and in a bakery. I always had a job, so I never had the opportunity for sports or anything like that. I'd just rush off from school to work.

So, it wasn't easy. My dad owed a good deal of money in simply bringing us here. He used to work in the apple orchards, but in the winter it rained and there was no work. So he would save up in the summers and we'd use it up in the winter, and it went around like that. But we all worked to help.

High school was tracked. There was remedial, intermediate, and advanced; advanced was college-bound. Well I was in the advanced in everything except somehow, for my junior year, I was assigned to Mr. Hanson. He taught remedial English. It was hard to get out of there, and it became easier to stay rather than hassle. All I got in there were Cs. An Anglo friend of mine in there got nothing but As. He and I were real close, so toward the end of the academic year I said, "You know, all you ever get are As and all I ever get are Cs. Next time we get an assignment, you do yours and I'll do mine and then we'll exchange. Then you copy mine in your own writing and I'll copy yours in my handwriting. So I'll have my name on yours." I kept telling myself Mr. Hanson doesn't care what I do. He really doesn't read what I do, he just gives me a C no matter what. Well, it turned out I was right. He got an A on my paper and I got a C on his. I said, "Well, tough."

I applied to several universities and colleges and was accepted at almost all of them, but my parents couldn't afford it. I was offered a scholarship at Santa Rosa Junior College, so I took that. I was still in community college when I married. My wife really put me through college. By the time I got to Stanford I had a number of fellowships and scholarships, but she always worked and maintained the household.

At Stanford I worked on a research project with five other graduate students and a faculty member who had received a very large grant. We worked on this project all the way from developing a survey instrument to collecting the data and analyzing it. About five dissertations and a book came out of that, a big, big project. In our first publication together the professor had assigned different chapters to each of us. We prepared them, and then another student and I wrote the introduction and conclusion. Finally we sent it out to preview readers before submitting it for publication. Well, it came back. They didn't know me, we didn't have names on the chapters, but mine was judged the best, the most clearly written. There were three different readers and they all had the same comments. Then I knew that Mr. Hanson was wrong.

I feel Mexican and I behave American. Inside, my feelings, my values, my attitudes, my beliefs are based in Mexican culture, but my behavior is very American. I feel very comfortable here. I understand the system and I can work it. My wife says when I'm in Mexico I'm Mexican. I know that system as well and can fit in and behave Mexican. I'm the only one in my family who is a naturalized American citizen.

I haven't left Mexico behind. I always carry a letter in my briefcase from my grandmother, written four years ago when I was promoted to Associate Vice President for Academic Affairs. She knows that I work at a university. She doesn't know exactly what I do, but she knows that I have an important position. She wrote me a letter of congratulations. She says, "We know that you've done a lot in terms of education and your career, but you never make us feel uncomfortable. When you come here you're Tino. You treat us as if we were equals." I know exactly what she was talking about because I have cousins who, after being in the United States for five or ten years, will go back to Santa Inez and dress in a tie and a suit—in this little town. It makes no sense whatsoever, right? It's presumptuous, it's irritating to people, and rightly so. When I go there I help milk the cows because I enjoy it. I enjoy riding horses in the country. There are different chances, different opportunities.

Mexican culture has a certain wisdom I appreciate. My grandfather is *Don* Chema. You don't just call yourself by the title of *Don*. I can't be *Don;* I'm not old enough, I'm not wise enough. Unlike American culture, Mexicans value age. There is respect for someone for simply being older. They don't feel bad if they are ninety, because they are still respected. Here, people are channeled out of the job market when they're too old and sent off to retirement communities. It's a different orientation. When they're old here, they want to be young instead.

In a faceless kind of society there are people who are bigots. My wife has experienced it in some strange kinds of ways. She's blond, blue-eyed, but people have said to her, "Oh, you don't look like a Fernández." People have a mind-set as to what they expect a Fernández to look like. There are other things, people asking if our kids are Mexican or half Mexican. Parents tell their kids stories about Mexicans that come back to our kids. For my wife it's real upsetting. We experience it all the time, even in an educational environment. There are people here in our lovely university who still have certain images about Mexicans, about Mexican-Americans, about non-Anglo-Saxons. You affect the people you can, you try to change them, and the rest, that's their problem. It really comes back to what my dad used to say to us, *"Así son los americanos."* We would come home from school and complain about something and he'd say, "That's the way they are." It's like, we're okay but that's just the way they are. Don't worry about it; you have to figure out how to work with them. We were *mexicano,* we were proud of that. We had an identity. We were just living in the United States and working here.

We came up here with almost the same idea all Mexicans come up with. We'd work for a couple of years and then go back and do something down there. That something changed over the years. At one time it was putting up a *granja,* a chicken farm, another time it was pigs, the next time a little store. It changed but we never really lost that emotion of going back.

One time we went back for about six months because my parents thought they were going to make it. Later we went back for another four months and tried again. It never worked out. Then one thing happened and another and years passed and my parents said, "Let's wait till the kids are out of school." Of course we're not all the same age, so we were never all out of school. My dad just retired last year and they still maintain a home in Santa Inez. They've been fixing it up over the years. They were saying they're going to go back and retire there. I think they'll go back for some months there and some months here, but they'll never go back to live there. What happens is you become binational and bicultural. You're comfortable in both countries but never fully integrated in either. You don't want to be, because you know the best world is in the margins, in between, where you can choose and take what is best from each culture.

GUADALUPE BUENDÍA MENDOZA
Restaurateur
Albany, California

You can reach the warmth of Mexico even on a gray northern California day just by crossing the threshold of Lupe's Monterey Café. Shiny orange Naugahyde booths line the walls, bright-colored plastic flowers sit on each table, and red, white, and green cinco de mayo *streamers float suspended overhead. There is color everywhere. Light from a dozen hanging chandeliers, each with six 100-watt bulbs, is reflected and refracted by thousands of translucent cut plastic beads curtaining the twenty-foot-wide floor-to-ceiling window. Add to this the promising spicy aromas from the kitchen and* ranchero *music emanating from the jukebox. The effect is gay, brilliant—a reflection of Lupe herself.*

"Hola, how are you?" she says to each customer who comes through the door. There are pretty young women who are the waitresses, but Lupe is the hostess. Seven days a week, morning to night, she goes from table to table tending her customers as if they were guests invited to a grand banquet.

Lupe's shining eyes and warm smile, and her bright orange dress with polka dots the size of silver dollars, all conceal her heroic journey. A fatherless child from a poor pueblo in the shadow of Aztec ruins, she has come to be the proud owner of a restaurant that is an institution in its community.

Well, I was born in a little pueblo in the state of Mexico named San Augustine Octipa, and this was in the year of 1938. I have one sister and two brothers. I never knew my papa; he left when I was a babe in arms. So really we were very poor. We were left as orphans, and my mother had to work to feed us.

When I was very young I always helped in the streets. I was always asked for in the houses to accompany the *señoras*. Really I was hardly ever with my mama. I was always with someone else until I grew up. If someone got married, they wanted me to accompany the young woman so that she wouldn't be alone.

I was about six or seven years old when a *señora* took me. She had a clothing store and her daughter had a hardware store. They would send me for change like an errand girl. I would leave money here and take money there. Well one time, I wasn't looking and a car ran over me. I had the money in my hand, and of course when the car hit me the money flew all over. The car ran over this leg, and the lady had to carry me to the Red Cross. I don't remember how much time I was in the hospital, but I stayed with her after getting out. I would help play with their children; I was still a child myself.

But then my mother came for me, because I had been in the accident. So I went back to the pueblo but I didn't like it, because now I was accustomed to the other village.

Then my *madrina* [godmother] said to my mama, "Let me have Lupe. She can accompany me." Her parents were in Mexico and she was in the pueblo alone, in San Augustine. So I went with her. She was just a young girl too, just a little older than I. So there I grew up. Well, I grew a little.

When I was maybe nine or ten my brother got married in Santa Clara. He said to my mama, "Why don't you let Lupe stay with my wife, because she doesn't want to be alone." So there I was with my sister-in-law, only she was a little ill tempered. When she wanted me to make tortillas I wanted to play, and my sister-in-law would get mad. She would say, "She didn't make the tortillas," and then my brother would hit me. I didn't like the character of my sister-in-law, so when my mama came I told her I didn't want to stay with them. My mother said fine, let's go home. I said, "No, I don't want to go home, I want to go to work."

I was about twelve years old, but I could only take care of children because I was still little. One girl told me she knew a woman who had a little child who was an invalid, and "If you want, you could take care of her." So I said yes. It was there that I grew, and with them that I became a woman, because I stayed a long time with this family.

The little girl was an invalid, and I would bathe her and take care of her. I was there a long time, eight years. They were good people, but then they went to Cuernavaca and I didn't want to go. The little girl was growing and growing, and she was very heavy for me. They wanted me to come because the little girl loved me. I thought about it—should I go or not? When I was a child I always thought about going to the other side. In the pueblo you always hear of the United States, the United States. I thought, one day I am going to go, I am going to go.

I began to save money in a bank account. I thought, someday I am going to go. Well, I began to ask; I began to read the newspapers. In the newspapers they put notices saying they need someone to come to the United States and take care of children. I had a friend from the Suarez family, the oil family in Mexico. They had a goddaughter in Fremont. They told me, "She wants you, if you want to go." I began writing to the *señora* and that's when I came.

I was about twenty-three. *Señora* Suarez helped me get a permit. So I went by plane. That way I didn't have any problems. I thought, good, I want to progress. It was always my dream to go.

I stayed a long time in that house, working, taking care of the children. They didn't pay me very much, $20 a week. Well, for me it was good money. I was very content because they were very nice people. I was there for three years. I began to think, well, here I am not going to progress. They didn't want me to go out anywhere. If I wanted to go to the movies, they took me. If I wanted to go somewhere, they took me, I think because they didn't want me to progress. I told them, "I want to go to school."

"Aye, why would you want to go to school?"

"I want to learn English." Finally they let me go to school one evening a week, and at once I agreed.

Then I made a friend, a Panamanian woman. I began to talk to her about my situation.

So she asked me, "Why don't you leave there?"

I told her, "Well, I don't have family here, I don't have anyone." I had come with a permit, but now I was illegal because my permit had expired, and the *señor* would always tell me that he was going to send for Immigration.

I told my friend about it and she said, "Leave, come to our house. Come to our house and we will find work for you."

So I said okay. When I left, *uffff*, the world fell! There was a huge fight, and *uffff*. They yelled at me and told me they were sending the Immigration, and who knows what.

Well I only stayed one day at my friend's house, because she told me, "You know, Lupe, we don't want to have problems." So I asked her to take me to another family that I knew in Oakland. She took me with all my things to a house where I could live in a little apartment. So that was how it was. I went to Castro Valley to clean houses.

That Christmas a friend had a party and she invited me. That is where I met my husband, Roy. Well we didn't see each other for a long time, but he kept thinking in his mind that he was going to call me. This was December. Well, time passed. In March, he began to ask my friend for my telephone number. My friend didn't want to give it to him. He said, "Give it to me, give it to me." In the end she gave it to him and he called. We were *novios* for six months and then in 1970 we got married.

My husband was a fine person. He worked at Mexicali Rose as a cook. After we got married he didn't want me to work cleaning houses, and he took me to gather dishes. I didn't like their manner there because—I don't know—a lot of the people would fight among themselves. I told my husband, "I don't want to work here because everyone here likes to talk about everybody else."

So he said, "But what are we going to do?"

"Well, I'm not going to work there. I want to have a restaurant." See, I had the idea of a restaurant.

He said, "Aye, but what would we do for money?"

I told him, "I don't know, I'm going to see." So every day I would buy this paper—we were still newlyweds.

I began reading the *Tribune,* in the announcements for small businesses. That's where it came out. This little place on Gilman was for sale. So I told my husband, "Look, there is this place for sale. It's little, just like we want. Let's go, let's go!" He wanted to go tomorrow, but I told him, "No, come on, let's go now."

We went, but right then, that day, just to see it. Then the next day we went again for a cup of coffee. They only sold hamburgers and sandwiches, it was real little, but I thought it was fine.

My husband said, "Aye, you're very demanding, but I will speak with the owner and find out how much he wants." But the owner owed so much. He was in debt for everything, he owed everyone—the milkman, the butcher, the Coca-Cola—but the little place was very nice. So we bought it and continued paying his bills. He gave it to us cheap, but we had to pay his bills because he was very behind. We bought it the seventh of September.

I went to work that day, but I didn't know English. No, I didn't speak English, this was in '71. I was forced to learn. My husband didn't want to leave The Mexicali, so he sent me and I didn't know any English. We had to have another woman. I would wash the dishes, and she was the cashier and waitress. Now I never wanted to tell her, but I'm telling the truth, when my husband would come for me he would say, "Let's see how much we sold." And we never had any money in the register.

I told him, "If I am here washing dishes all day and you are at The Mexicali, we aren't going to make any money, because I don't know what's happening with the money. Why don't you ask for permission for time off at The Mexicali?" They gave him his vacation and he never returned.

Well, all the other man's clientele left us. We didn't have any customers. We only made $70 a day. We began with the hamburgers and I would make some little casseroles of rice, I still have them, they are real little. The two of us worked, he and I. We opened at six in the morning and closed at four in the afternoon. Then once it got started we began closing later at eight, eight thirty, and then nine o'clock. Little by little. I began sweet rolls, we began having more clientele. The breakfasts; I didn't know how to say "sausage." I didn't know what they were telling me. I couldn't say "pancakes." But I spoke as well as I could. I would have to analyze it, because I had never studied or anything. I still don't speak very good English, but I would just mix the Spanish and English and I wasn't embarrassed.

We kept getting more and more clients and we began to hire employees little by little, and then my husband said, "You know what, I am going to get a place in Oakland on Seventh Street."

I really didn't want anything in this area. I wasn't in agreement. But in the end he opened it and I stayed in the Gilman. From there we continued, but really I didn't want the Seventh Street. I hardly ever went there because there were so many problems. At first he had good business, but they began to rob him and to take money from the cash register.

We still had a good business there on Gilman. In this tiny little place there wasn't room for all the people. That's why I told my husband we should apply for our beer license.

There had been three owners in the bar next door. They couldn't make it. So we talked to, his name was Bill, we called him Billy. We told him, "When you want to sell the bar, why don't you sell it to us?"

"Yes, I will sell it to you. Give me $6,000. I will leave everything." We didn't want anything, the bar or the furniture. We only wanted the location, we wanted the space. So the young man said, "That's fine, but I still want six thousand."

Okay, that's fine. I told Roy, let's do it so we can begin to work. *Bueno.* This was in '75. We enlarged it, oh, we had a lot of customers and we began to employ people. At times it would be filled. The people from the race track would come; everyone kept coming. So this passed, but the other place began to fall and fall, there in Oakland.

By '82 we no longer had business in Oakland and we were maintaining it with the Gilman restaurant. In '83 my husband owed a lot of taxes on the Seventh Street restaurant. The moment arrived when they seized the place in Oakland. They wanted to seize the Gilman too; this is a true history. But I wanted to save the place. I got money from wherever I could to give $10,000 to the *federales* so they wouldn't take the Gilman. It was very tight, very, very tight, but however we could we saved the Gilman place. The *federales* didn't take it.

We saved it, but we were left with no money. Then in June the landlord died and his sons took over. They told us everything would be the same, but then some customers who knew them told me, "Lupe, we can't guarantee it, but we have heard rumors that the owners are going to evict you." I didn't believe them. I never thought that they would evict me, because their father was a very good person, may he rest in peace.

But the sons were very ambitious and underhanded, and when I went to pay the June rent they told me, "You have to go!"

Bueno, I cried and cried, because we had been there twelve years. Mr. Walker, who always came to eat with us, told me, "Why don't you come over and look at this place on Solano Avenue."

We went to Solano. I told my husband, "Look, this space is empty. Aye, hopefully God wants it to go well for us." We called Mr. Mason, the owner, and the City of Albany, and they told us yes. So we moved.

And what do you think? We were robbed the twenty-fifth of August. In Oakland we were beaten up very badly and robbed of everything we had. The robbers had taken my purse with all my things and $3,000 I had to remodel the new restaurant. They opened the door and pulled us out, but because there was bread and ham and stuff on top they didn't notice that we had another $5,000 at the bottom of the grocery bag. So with this we paid our deposit for the building.

Mr. Sweeney from the bank came to see us, and I told him we needed a loan for $10,000. He said yes, but then we told him that we had been robbed of everything and we had nothing, nothing. But for my reputation, because people knew me, Mr. Sweeney said it didn't matter. Then friends loaned us $100 or $200 here and there, when we ran out. The construction was very expensive, I think about $100,000. But I always had faith that we were going to progress.

Everyone came to help us. Some young men who had come from Mexico helped us. I told them, we don't have the money to pay right now. When I have the money, I will pay you. They helped us day and night. We finally finished, and the day we opened it was filled, thanks be to God. And thanks be to God, to this date it has done well. I tell you this really is beautiful, because so many things can happen to someone. Truly, one suffers. That's why many times, when someone comes looking for work I know what it's like, because I have passed that way too. So why would I not give work to that person who truly needs it?

When we were fixing the restaurant, the house across the street was for sale. Mr. Mason told the owner we were good people. My husband told him that we didn't have any money because we were just beginning, but that we were going to progress and would he give us a chance and let us move into this house. He agreed to it.

So we gave the down payment on the house and moved in. This was in '84. By '85 we were fine. And by '86 we were doing a little better. But that is when my husband died. I don't know, for him I was like his first love. We were both in love, and we had a good time together. We got along very well. For me he was a very good man.

We never had children. He had his children, and we had hoped for a family too, but with the restaurant we were always very busy. Really, we didn't have the time to think very much about children. We dedicated ourselves to the business, we got older, and the time passed us by. He had his children, but I also want one of my own, even if it was only one.

So I have stayed and it has gone fine, thanks be to God. I work hard. It's hard, alone. Well, all of the muchachos help. And my nieces and nephews, I brought them up here and they also help me. We all work united. The cook now has six years with me. They all have their papers and we all help each other. My nieces and nephews have their papers now too. I am paying them like anyone legal. I take out their taxes and run everything just right with the government.

I still like to work, and all of us Mexicans come to work. We don't need the help of anyone, just that someone gives us work. It isn't important what people think, we come to work, whether it's washing dishes, whatever. No one comes to ask for help. Unh-huh!

If a Mexican comes in and you ask them what they can do, they tell you the truth. "I don't know how to make that, but if you teach me I will learn." Then we teach them and they learn. Someone who is Mexican who doesn't know, is better than someone sent from unemployment. If they're from unemployment they say they know, but they never do, and they want to start at $8.00 an hour.

This is what I tell the muchachos: "Get ahead!" I tell them, "Look, you have opportunities to be paid better. *¡Progresan muchachos!* Go to school, study, and progress. We are in a country where we can progress, where nothing is difficult because here, everyone tries to help you."

Everyone asks me, "Why don't you become a citizen?" When my

husband died everyone told me, "Now become a citizen, Lupe." But no, I can't. I feel bad, sometimes I think I should, but if I were a citizen I would have to ask for permission to go to Mexico. I can't do it. Well, this is for me. I don't know, I feel very Mexican.

Each year I go to see my family and the pueblo where I was born. And there are times that I give *cooperaciones* for the church and when they need money for the school. I love my pueblo. It's a tiny pueblo on one side of the pyramids. I bring clothes and little things for everyone. I bring flowers to my mama. You may think that when you come to the United States one would forget his pueblo, but you never do.

It was always my dream to progress. It didn't matter what the work was, all I wanted was to progress. We were very poor and I never knew a father. I was never able to have the pride to say "papa." So this was my idea, to work and to progress. And thanks be to God he helped me and until this day is helping me.

MARTIN DEL CAMPO
Architect
San Francisco, California

The office of Del Campo and Maru is in an old building just two blocks from the San Francisco–Oakland Bay Bridge. Once San Francisco's industrial area, built near bay shipping, it has recently been developed into upscaled offices, warehouses, and factory outlets. The exterior of the building retains its industrial origins under the fresh paint and high-tech style, but once inside it's hard to tell. Under the architectural look—the white walls, the furniture, the color, the potted plants, the drawings and models—its former identity is obscured except for one detail: a tall, old, weathered wooden T *with* AMERICAN LICORICE *in faded letters, mounted in stately honor just inside the front door.*

With a beaming smile and in a deep, warm, soft voice he enunciates each word as if it were to be savored. His quiet dignity contrasts with a shock of white hair and an emerald green shirt with a royal blue tie. You can't really tell that he's Mexican; his identity is obscured. But a word, a thought, a remembrance—the pride in his heritage is scattered like shiny pennies throughout his conversation. He is Martin del Campo.

I was born in Guadalajara a long, long time ago, in 1922. I had a younger sister who died in childhood at a year and a half of age. So I was the only child. Because of my sister's death, my father and mother decided to move. My father wanted to erase the past and leave the town where everything and everybody reminded him of his daughter. So he went to Mexico City to make a living, to start from scratch.

He found a job selling paints for Sherwin-Williams I remember, and since he was a very entrepreneurial guy he managed to start a contracting business. As a contractor he actually designed and built many large buildings. I really admired him. He was very, very entrepreneurial and courageous as well.

When it came time for me to go to college, he strongly encouraged me to be an architect. He gave me no choice really. He was very loving, but very forceful, and in those days kids didn't argue with their parents. I wanted to be a musician. I had studied the violin and would have liked to continue. But he pushed me to become an architect. I completed the architectural course at the University of Mexico.

In the fifth year of school I met a young man whose father was also an architect. His father had died. He had inherited some of his father's work and talked me into joining him in business.

By then I was married. I had married an American woman who came to study in the school where I was studying, in Belles Artes. It was the school of San Carlos. They call it San Carlos because it was the school of art founded in the early eighteenth century by the King of Spain, Carlos III. My wife-to-be was studying painting and sculpture.

So we got married. Almost immediately, not quite, but nine months later, we had our first daughter. Then about a year and a half later we had another one. So we had two daughters, and I was trying to make a living in this business with my partner and we were not succeeding. Being a student, a father and husband, a contractor, and a designer as well was just too much.

To make things worse, I was involved in politics. I had joined a party that was just beginning, called the *Partido Popular*. It was a left-wing party sponsored by a union leader. Through some friends I had joined and was in the youth section. I really believed I was doing the right thing and was very sincere, so I put a lot of time and effort into it. It was just too much. This was in 1948.

Esparza y Martin del Campo: that was the name of the firm. We had several good jobs, and we managed to break even or sometimes lose money. One day a young employee in our office told me, "You know, if I were you, I would go live in the United States for a while. I used to live there and I worked in Los Angeles for an architect. I don't remember him suffering the way you do. You know you don't know where the money for payroll will come on Saturday, and you're always really *angustiado*. You don't know where you're getting the next peso, really completely disorganized. When I was in the United States things were very orderly, and everybody really knew how to do business. If I were you, since you have a gringa wife, it should be easy for you to get a visa and move there for a year or two and learn how gringos do business, and then you come here with your newly acquired knowledge and you'll really do well."

So I thought, what a good idea. When I mentioned it to my wife she was delighted, because she was not very happy in Mexico. She relished coming back to her own country. Eventually she talked me into going to Michigan where she was from, instead of Los Angeles, which was my first idea. She was right, because her family was there. They helped us. We could live with them until we got established. So we ended up in Detroit, Michigan. This was 1949, with two little girls, for what I thought would be a year or two at the most. I thought the moment I learned the secret of how to succeed in business, I'd come back to Mexico. I never thought I would stay here. I'm sixty-six and I haven't learned it yet. I think the secret is not being an architect.

Well it was traumatic. I'm sure for my in-laws too, but for me it was very traumatic, because I felt like a poor relative inside their house. They were very nice but my in-laws, my wife, and I were there with the two children. We rented a bigger house to live all together. My wife immediately found a job teaching, and my mother-in-law took care of the two girls, and my father-in-law worked for General Motors. So it was a working family.

I was so unhappy with the situation I asked myself, "What am I doing here suffering? It's horrible; I'm going to go back to Mexico!" I knew that my wife wouldn't like the idea of going back to Mexico because, in a sense, she had reacquired her country. So I didn't chance asking her. I just made up plans. I'm going to cash my paycheck, take my two daughters, take a flight to the border, at the border we just cross walking with our Mexican passports, and I call her from the other side. Then she will join me back in Mexico. We'll go back to Mexico. I wanted to cut off this suffering.

I made only one mistake, and this fouled up my plans. My boss had been very decent to me so I didn't want to leave suddenly. I told him I wouldn't come back after this pay period. He said, "Why?"

I didn't want to tell him I was having in-law problems, so I said, "Well, I just think I should go back to Mexico. I realized that I wasn't quite ready to move away from there." He thought that it was because I wasn't paid enough. So he talked to his partner and they offered me a big increase in salary and reassured me that I was going to progress in their office and I should not feel bad about it. I thought, gee, maybe I am making a mistake. I better stick around longer. That saved my wife having to go back to Mexico.

Well, we had been in Detroit for about six months; I decided I would not go back. So one day I said, "The thing to do is just divorce. We have too many fights, too many arguments. Why suffer like this?" We decided, why don't we go see an attorney and get a divorce. Someone recommended an attorney who was an old Polish gentleman. I remember, his name was Grezensky—Mr. Green they called him, because they couldn't pronounce his name. So we took the streetcar; we didn't own a car. We took the streetcar way, way, way far into Detroit to visit the attorney. He was a very kind fellow who welcomed us into his office. When he asked why we wanted to see him, we said, "Well we would like to get a divorce."

"For goodness sake, why?"

"Well, because we don't get along."

"Do you have children?"

"Yes, we have two children, two daughters."

"That's a tragedy. How could you divorce having two lovely daughters? I can't understand you getting a divorce."

He had told us in Michigan there's not a law that allows divorce because you don't get along. You have to have real mistreating from one of the partners to the other. He said, "For instance if he would hit you, if he would have hurt you physically."

And my wife says, "Well, he has a very bad temper, you know. He hit the table so hard he almost broke his hand."

"He hit who?"

"The table."

"Oh, the table, not you?"

"No, not me."

"Oh well no, that doesn't count."

So he said you have to have cheated on each other sexually, or you have to have committed a horrible deed on each other, but just not getting along was not reason enough.

Well, he wouldn't let us divorce. He wasn't a very good businessman himself, because he didn't even charge us for a consultation.

When we lived in Mexico all my friends thought I was completely henpecked. My wife thought I was a horrible, domineering macho. I must have been in between, but to her it was too much. Well, it took me years to be sensitized to what women's liberation means. It was primarily my daughters who brainwashed me, and I am completely and truly brainwashed. I agree with all the concepts of women's liberation. But we had a hell of a time in our married life—many, many conflicts and problems. Now that we've been married forty-three years we get along real well. She's accepted my shortcomings. She doesn't mind being the one who washes the dishes, and I don't even come to the kitchen. She accepts that as part of our life and I accept her too, but it took us a long, long time.

We stayed three years in Detroit. Then someone I worked with had talked so much about California, especially San Francisco. He would say, "What are you doing here in Detroit when there is a place like San Francisco." That's all I heard for months, and I thought well, why shouldn't I go to San Francisco? So I acted on his wishes, and it was a revelation. Not only did I love the town, but I loved the atmosphere, the people.

San Francisco has great attraction to Mexicans. It has such perfect weather and such tolerant attitudes. One of my aunts came to visit us in 1978. She showed us the house where she and another aunt and my grandmother had lived in 1917, during the First World War. It's on Woolsey Street in Berkeley.

Well, I came to work with Wurster, Bernardi and Emmons, a very prominent office. They were very liberal in their views. It was when Eisenhower was running against Stevenson, and the office looked like the Stevenson headquarters in San Francisco. They had banners sticking out of the windows, and the bosses went around collecting money for Stevenson.

I felt very happy in San Francisco. I found a much more inviting atmosphere. Most of the architects in Detroit were very conservative.

I was very unique in my family because I was the only one that had taken these left-wing leanings.

Then in the school of San Carlos there were many leftists, people like Diego Rivera. He had just been kicked out of the Communist party and was looking for a place to put his efforts. He joined our party and became a very influential member. Eventually he left it. He never stayed very long in one thing. But he was the head of fund-raising, and I was the head of youth section fund-raising. So you see, I really believed in the cause.

At that time I sincerely believed the answer to Mexico's problems was socialism, so when I came to the United States I thought I was going to "enemy land." I'm going to go there because I want to learn their techniques of how to survive. But my idea was to come back to Mexico to live.

It took some years of living here to make me realize that people are not necessarily the government's policies, and there is very little difference between the boss and employee here. As a matter of fact the boss usually works harder and sometimes doesn't make as much as the employee. There is a form of socialism in that way in society here.

My father had read a book about the treatment of Mexicans in Texas. I don't remember the name of the book, but he really worried that I would be treated like that, as a truly second-class citizen. Humiliated. Of course that was not the case at all. Among the professional group that I move in, there is no personal discrimination. Still, sometimes people don't realize that it is happening. Discrimination is very subtle, and that is why I have remained involved with affirmative action laws.

I worked for Wurster, Bernardi and Emmons for about three years. Then I was let go because they had run out of work. Perhaps because I got let go, I realized that I wanted to have my own business as a form of independence. That way no one could let me go. I opened my own business but only with terrible struggles, really, years and years of starvation and frustration. The first time I opened my office was in 1955 in Santa Rosa with a partner that had already established himself. But we made some major mistakes and went completely out of business. I had to go back to work again. Since then I decided that I wanted to be in business no matter what the risk. To me it's not an optional thing, it's a need to be on my own.

During that time my family in Mexico still wanted me to come home. Especially my father, who was a very emotional man. My mother was more philosophical—as long as we were happy and surviving, it was okay that we weren't there. But to my father it was a tragedy. He loved to be near me and near the little girls that he had remembered. For him it was a struggle to get us back. When we left, his business wasn't doing so well, but he programmed himself to do well so he could attract me back. He started a new business, and after ten years or so he convinced me I should go back. He had started a hotel.

When I went back to Mexico I really thought that was a permanent move, that I would never come back. But the hotel wasn't that good a business. It looked better than it was. I didn't imagine that I wouldn't feel much at home there. Yes, I had my life here and I was very comfortable working in the United States. I liked the way people did business here. My daughters were established here. One was about to finish college. They were the ones that got me back.

I came back again to a town that I knew well. When I decided to come here I wasn't sure what I wanted to do. I wasn't sure whether I would try to open my own business again. I had done it before, I knew the ropes.

Then in 1970 I started what is now this office. I've had many, many partners in my life. Just this year I bought my former partner's shares, so I am now a sole owner. Over the years I've counted nine different partners. Yes, someone told me I was the Tommy Manville of architecture. Tommy Manville had nine wives.

Recently I began a new career, so to speak. It started when I realized that you have to be able to make presentations to clients in order to get jobs. I joined Toastmasters, which is a group for self-training in public speaking. My daughter Felicia, who has been a great influence in my life, told me about it. Besides making speeches, they have competitions. For the tall tales competition I made up a tale about being invited by President Reagan to help him solve the problem of the wetbacks. I won the club championship. Then the winners of several clubs compete, and I won the division. I managed to tell this story several times, and a friend asked me if I wanted to do it in a nightclub as a benefit for the ACLU.

My first solution to the wetback problem was to give the seven states that used to be part of Mexico back to Mexico and let them have the problem, not us. But Reagan didn't like the idea of having to go through the border to his ranch in Santa Barbara. So the next idea was, why don't we annex Mexico and let it be the fifty-first state? No, that didn't work because then every third person you see in the United States will be a Mexican, and that's the problem in the first place.

The third solution is what they are now doing: make the employer responsible for making sure they have a permit. That will completely cut off immigration because no one will give them a job, and that will create such a crisis in Mexico that the government will fall and become communist. Then the problem will finally be solved, because the first thing the communist government does is build a tall wall to prevent people from leaving the country.

I did another one about past lives, that I used to be a madam in San Francisco, a madam of a house of prostitution in my past life. Well if I could pursue it I would love to, it's really fun. Every time I appear they give me ten dollars cash, which I declared on my income tax. I really cherish those ten dollars, you know.

RAMÓN MORALES SANCHEZ
Foreign Language Consultant
Moorpark, California

When Ramón and his family stepped off the Greyhound bus in 1969, he didn't speak a word of English. Now, twenty years and four languages later (five including his native Spanish), Ramón flies around the world, one week Paris, the next Tokyo, and then to Mexico City, teaching teachers how to teach languages.

Tall and slim, he looks like an athlete and is so handsome he could be a movie star. He is poised, self-confident, and articulate, but it's with a fierce conviction that he still sees himself as the little Mexican boy from Zamora.

I need to be honest with you. I just need to say there are many, many stories like mine, if not even more successful. It reassures me that the people who come from Mexico are perhaps at an advantage over those who are unfortunate not to have had that cultural experience in the first years of their lives.

My father came from Zamora, Michoacán, to the United States for the first time around 1950. He worked at the largest egg farm in the world at the time, it was called "Egg City" in Moorpark. By 1968 my mother had told my father that the kids were growing up and she needed his help. There were nine of us, and my older brother was already starting to get into mischief. A visit to Mexico convinced my father.

On May 12, 1969, we crossed the border at San Ysidro. Then we took the bus, then a taxi to Moorpark, California, to live with my father's sister and her family. I was nine years old.

By July my father had found us a house, and we moved close by, to Camarillo. A little sister was born later that summer. She was our *gringa,* or *pocha.* But what I remember most about our move there was when the landlady came for the rent we had to hide. It was a low-income complex, not supported by the government or anything, just little cottages. Finally, we were turned in by one of the neighbors: too many kids living in the house. We had to move.

By the time my father found another house his sister had also immigrated. They lived with us for a short while, just the way we had moved in with my other aunt and uncle. We were all very close.

We went to Pleasant Valley Elementary, which was the oldest school in Camarillo. Most of the *mexicanos* and Mexican-Americans in my little part of town, the barrio, went there.

The interesting thing about Camarillo was that it was not a large, established Mexican-American community. The barrio was three or four streets and that was it. It had not been there very long and had not decayed socially. There was a nice transition from the white Anglo community to the Mexican barrio. I think that's why, as I was growing up, I did not feel at all discriminated against.

I did feel embarrassed about being Mexican, an immigrant, and a farmer's son, but my own background and what I felt about being Mexican helped me to overcome that.

I was excited to come to the United States, but Mexico was still home. Two years after we arrived the whole family went back, and we kept going back at different times. I took a personal interest in going back and getting to know my family there, my grandparents on both sides. I feel I was the transition between the Mexican part of the family and what became the Mexican-American part.

So anyway, in elementary school, here comes this little Mexican boy. It was fun and I did well. In seventh and eighth grade I was a "smack," one of the real smart kids who always does his homework.

In the middle of seventh grade we moved to a house in Camarillo that was outside of the barrio. There was only one other Mexican surname family, two at most, and the rest were Anglos. So most of the friends I made were Anglos. That was another influence, because at that age, between twelve and fifteen or sixteen where you're pressured by your peers, I was not with Mexicans or Chicanos.

A lot of the barrio kids did not have the sense of belonging to Mexican culture. They did not consider that to be their culture, yet they could clearly see that they were not Anglo. They needed some kind of middle ground, because the problem in that neighborhood was, these people felt prejudice from Mexicans who were fluent in Spanish, who were proud to have come from Mexico, and who were eating tortillas and frijoles and living as they would in their little ranch in Mexico. These kids didn't have that tie; they didn't have any kind of feeling of belonging to that culture. At the same time they were not Anglos. They had an accent, they did not speak English very well. They spoke some Spanish, but they were speaking more Spanglish. They did not fit in. They were in between someplace.

There's the tendency for the social breakdown to take place if there are no roots to hold it together. A lot of these kids rebelled against the ways of their parents, which were provincial. The parents were like my parents, they never had an education. Therefore the parents of these kids had a hard time keeping them in school. The kids wanted to go out and work. A lot of them got jobs right away, in tenth grade as soon as they were old enough, and they quit school. They did not want to listen, they were not the obedient sons and daughters, they had no respect for what the parents stood for. I remember kids saying to me that they were ashamed because their parents were ignorant peasants, they were docile and domestic. They were ashamed to come from that kind of background. They did not see themselves ever accepting the way of life that their parents had led and that their parents wanted for them.

Yet they could not integrate themselves fully into the all-American Anglo society because they were physically different, because they were economically different, and because they were linguistically limited. They were growing up without a whole lot of cultural base. As a consequence they didn't have the education to try to get better jobs and make a better living. So their salaries were already kept at a subpoverty level. They couldn't afford to buy nice things, and they could never hope to leave that neighborhood and move into a nice house. They're stuck, victims of a cycle, and then the cycle repeats itself. They in turn had nothing to offer their children.

The barrio began to grow because these people stayed. Their children grew up, and they stayed too. Some of the kids my age now have children that are ten, eleven, twelve years old. They dropped out of high school at fifteen or sixteen years old and got pregnant. They're now parents and they still live in that area.

A group called MEChA, Movimiento Estudiantil Chicano de Aztlán, part of the Chicano movement, was established by a group of university students in Arizona and New Mexico. It was an effort to find a place to belong, or to find your culture if you were not Mexican or Anglo, by birth. In junior high I was an officer in our MEChA chapter.

Kids involved in MEChA were at the borderline. Those who continued to stay involved and had support from their parents continued in school and did well. They became involved at MEChA at the high school level, then graduated from high school, went on to college, or got a good job after high school, or went to junior college. The kids who were in MEChA in seventh grade but didn't have that support at home, couldn't understand why their parents acted the way they did. They were the kids who dropped out after eighth grade. The dropout rate for Mexican-Americans specifically in the tenth grade is between 60 and 70 percent. So that means of all the returning tenth graders who are Mexican, maybe 70 percent of them will drop out before the end of the year. Fifteen percent of the entire group of kids that started high school might go on to college, but that doesn't mean they graduate.

Sports also helped shape my attitudes. I had gone out for cross-country and track in junior high and I did well. That put me together with a group of kids that had some objectives, some clear goals, even if it was just training every day.

What propelled me to want to succeed was my running. I did very well as a freshman. I was the third best runner on the team. Then the next year as a sophmore, then as a junior and senior, I had become the best runner in the county.

Maybe it was being a little "smacker," but I was the first kid in our family to assimilate the language. Anytime my mother or sister needed to fill out a job application, or any paperwork, I was the one that did it. I would go with my uncle to the doctor because the doctor didn't speak Spanish, and I was the one that went with my mother to the parent-teacher conferences.

In high school, languages, particularly French, became a special interest and continued into college. Then I took Russian. At that point I decided I wanted to go to Europe, to France, and study. So at the end of my sophomore year I went to France.

It synthesized me even more in my Mexicanness. I was not yet an American citizen. I still had my Mexican passport, so I went to France as a Mexican, not an American. While I was in France my interest for Russian faded only because there were conflicts in the scheduling of the courses, and instead I discovered the Chinese department.

Chinese-American relations were going to be very important for international relations, and I decided that I needed to go to China as well. There were still problems studying in Beijing or mainland China. Instead I chose to go to Taipei, the Republic of China. I lived in Taipei for a year with a Chinese family and attended courses at the university there.

Each time I studied abroad I was still Mexican. It was a direct comparison and contrast to being American. Even though I felt American, I was still Mexican. That was just the way I was seen. When I met Chinese people, they did not think of me as your average American. That made it easier; in some way I didn't represent the negatives they might have of Americans. The positives I had, because of the years I had lived in the United States. There's a romance about being Mexican where there are not too many Mexicans. It's true.

I came back from China after that one-year experience and continued my education at Humboldt State. I have a bachelor's degree in international relations and a bachelor's degree in French.

When I finished my teaching credential at Cal State Northridge, I taught French and Spanish at Camarillo High School. So I went back to work with some of the teachers I had had as a student.

After teaching at Camarillo High School I took the position with a large publishing company, and have been a foreign language consultant for three years.

Linguistically, we Spanish speakers in the United States live in a very static situation. In Mexico the language continues to develop. Influenced by events, American English, and technology, the kids that speak Spanish in Mexico today have a different vocabulary and language from those who left Mexico twenty years ago and never returned. Even those people that do go back to Mexico sometimes have a Spanish that is not current. So it's important to keep in touch, and keep going back, and be exposed to those changes, linguistically as well as culturally.

It is from this that I have come to totally disagree with the notion that Spanish at home in any way inhibits a Mexican from assimilating into American culture. At the least, it gives that individual a sense of identity. It is who they are, and that cannot be denied. That's very important to any individual but particularly to an immigrant, who is already at a disadvantage coming to this foreign culture. The idea that you should reject your own culture means you're rejecting all the positive experiences in your life. All the negative ones too, but the positive ones are the ones that will help you succeed.

That's certainly why we could not, as a society, outlaw the use of one particular language and at the same time make another language the only official, legal, accepted one. There is no need to legalize what is already obvious and what's already practical. It simply creates a negative environment for people who don't speak the legal language, instead of motivating them to learn it.

I reject the notion outright that Mexicans don't assimilate. I reject that altogether. As a total group of immigrants Mexicans don't appear to assimilate, perhaps because there's that open, revolving door. Those that did assimilate are being replaced by new arrivals.

Unfortunately, what happens too many times is those people who reach the point where they could transition into both cultures very easily lose the appreciation or the notion of how valuable it is to be able to do that. They have made a conscious decision that they're not interested in going back and forth, and they have chosen American culture as their main culture. That in turn changes that person's attitude toward those who are coming, the new arrivals. This person, who has made a complete, 100 percent transition to American culture, looks back upon those people and thinks, "I could do it, I did it, you should do it too. I didn't need any special favors. You don't need any special favors either." It should be, "How can I make your transition easier than mine was? Why should you have to go through all the struggles that I went through?" Unfortunately it's reinventing the wheel every time.

Too many people relate to "what I did," "what happened to me," what's obvious, as opposed to the other events that helped shape our conduct and attitudes. I see that with a lot of educators of Mexican descent, a lot of the people out there in academia, a lot of the people in business. "If I did it, you can do it too." They've lost touch with their own beginning. It's so important that people who are capable, who can transition into Mexican culture or American culture, consciously keep that, that they don't allow themselves to ever lose either the gift or the skill, to go into Mexican culture and be accepted. See, because the minute we leave Mexico, we are *inmigrados*.

Once you forget who you were because of your concern with who you've become, it keeps you from being understanding and supportive of the new arrival. Many of these people see Juan, who just arrived from *el rancho en Moreno de Valencia,* as who they were. They're embarrassed and ashamed that they could have been that and they reject it, consciously or unconsciously.

That's one reason why Mexicans are seen as not assimilating—not because of the person saying, "Yes I did, I assimilated; look at me," but the person saying, "That's not me. I had no problems. I don't know why they have problems."

I hope that I will think of myself as Ramón Morales Sanchez, the little Mexican boy that came from Zamora, Michoacán, until I die. I hope I will always think of that.

IV

THE FUTURE

RECORDANDO A MEXICO

No se fijen, amigos, si grito,
si a veces suspiro, si canto or si lloro,
es que estoy recordando a México
mi patria bendita, mi fe y mi tesoro.
No me culpen si hay llanto en mis ojos
o a veces el gusto me brinca en el pecho,
en mis venas siempre vive México,
mi tierra morena, mi cruz y mi lecho.

Es mi gusto gritar con orgullo
¡qué linda es mi patria,
costumbres y hermanos!
que un mariachi repita conmigo:
¡que viva la Reina de los mexicanos!

Que bonitos se ven los nopales
bañados de tunas allá en la ladera
los magueyes allá en la llanura
y el águila real sobre su bandera.

Es mi gusto gritar con orgullo
¿qué linda es mi patria,
costumbres y hermanos!
que un mariachi repita conmigo:
¡que viva la Reina de los mexicanos!
¡que viva la Reina de los mexicanos!

Rafael Buendía

REMEMBERING MEXICO

Pay no attention, friends, if I shout,
If at times I sigh, sing, or cry,
It's because I'm remembering Mexico,
My blessed homeland, my faith and my treasure.
Don't blame me if there are tears in my eyes
Or if at times there's joy my heart,
In my veins Mexico always lives,
My dark earth, my cross and my bed.

It's my joy to shout with pride
How beautiful is my homeland
Her customs and people!
May a mariachi repeat with me
"Long live the queen of the Mexicans."

How beautiful are the nopales
Covered with fruit on the hillside,
The magueys on the plains,
And the splendid eagle on the flag.

It's my joy to shout with pride
How beautiful is my homeland,
Her customs and people!
May a mariachi repeat with me,
"Long live the queen of the Mexicans.
Long live the queen of the Mexicans."

10

When You Sing There Are No Borders

THE ARTISTS

Mexico—Luis Barragan, Cantínflas, Baltasar de Echave the Elder, Carlos Fuentes, Sor Juana Inés de la Cruz, Frida Kahlo, Octavio Paz, Anthony Quinn, Lucha Reyes, Diego Rivera, David Alfaro Siqueiros, Rufino Tamayo—all born from the violent conception of the mestizo: half Indian, half Spaniard. "In the light of traditional moral systems—the Spanish, based on honor, and the Indian, based on the sacredness of family—the mestizo was the living image of illegitimacy," says Octavio Paz in Sor Juana. *"From this feeling of illegitimacy grew his insecurity, his perpetual instability, his tendency to swing between extremes." Joy to sorrow, valor to terror, acclamation to apathy, fidelity to betrayal, passivity to anarchy, patriotism to insurrection. These ferocious oppositions, caged in one soul, have often caused political, economic, and even religious chaos on the way to building modern Mexico. Yet the blast furnace of those same counterforces has forged one of the most aesthetic, profoundly creative people of the contemporary world.*

In murals, performance art, music, mariachi, punkarachi, *New Wave* norteño, corridos, *syncretic altars, theater, film, low riders,** la charreada, cuisine nuevo, *textiles, pottery, poetry, prose, architecture, artists have taken*

---

*Low rider: a popular Mexican-American subculture devoted to a unique style of customized cars.

291

up the standard, carrying north a people's special, unique notion of the world; changing it, changed by it, continuing it.

The United States—Rodolfo Añaya, Judith Baca, Patrocinio Barela, Graciela Carrillo, Ana Castillo, Rupert Garcia, Pedro Gonzales, Gilberto Guzman, Freddy Fender, Tish Hinojosa, Little Joe, The Low Riders, Santiago Jimenez, Flaco Jimenez, Santiago Jimenez Jr., Lidia Mendoza, Edward James Olmos, Linda Ronstadt, The Royal Chicano Air Force, "El Chunky" Sanchez, Carlos Santana, The Sir Douglas Quintet, "Spain," Gary Soto, Toltecas en Aztlán, Rudy Treviño, Luis Valdez, Raul Valdez, Ritchie Valens.

VICTOR OROZCO OCHOA
Muralist
San Diego, California

Set into a bosquet of tall trees stationed as sentinels, gigantic heroes, gods, coyotes, moons, and suns swirl and tumble in brilliant primary colors over a broad, round structure that began as a water reservoir for a world's fair. This is Centro Cultural de la Raza in San Diego's Balboa Park. Victor Orozco Ochoa works here.

A big man with long arms, large hands, and a visionary imagination that seems in perfect scale to his paintings, he fervently carries the muralist tradition of his culture. There is something familiar about Victor, hard to place. Then it comes: the remarkable resemblance to a young Diego Rivera.

My dad was a *pachuco,* a zoot-suiter in '43 in L.A. He was a big guy and he wanted to go in the army during World War II, but he was undocumented, so they wouldn't let him in. He hung around the barrios, working, and started dressing up like that, you know, the slick dressers of the forties, gabardines, wools, and stuff we don't even know about anymore. In the sixties he always used to criticize me for being such a sloppy dresser.

Faded clothes, jeans, I used to wear khaki shirts, sixties stuff, huaraches, corn necklaces. My dad was definitely against that. I think he wanted to be progressively more middle class. When he was a bachelor and still going with my mom, they were pretty zoot-suited down. I have some photographs of them. My mom had a big *copete* [pompadour], and he wore triple-soled blue suede shoes—I still preserve a pair—and a big-brimmed hat. He smoked marijuana.

But when he got married and I came along, he made a 180-degree turn and became a model family man. He wanted a bunch of kids, but we were so big, both my sister and I, we were born Cesarean. In those years the doctors said, "You're not going to make it if you have another Cesarean." They really scared my mom, you know, the spinal and all. My dad was really disappointed. They only had two children.

I think I've considered myself Chicano since the late sixties. I'm forty-one now. When I entered San Diego State I came in touch with people who were more political, that influenced me. Still, I brought an attitude that most people didn't have, the experience of being a Mexican and feeling like a Mexican, then coming to the United States and feeling neither Mexican nor as a U.S. person. I hate the word *American* because it's such a weird statement for me.

I've been working as a muralist for about twenty years. I have something like fifty murals around town, so it's pretty crazy.

My mom is from Colima, my dad is from Hermosillo, and I was born in L.A. in '48. My parents had been living in the United States for ten or twelve years. They were kind of afraid to speak Spanish to us because of the discrimination. Being light skinned, we passed as different kinds of people and lived in a part of L.A. where there were a lot of what we call Okies and gypsies, in trailer courts.

Then in 1955, as part of "Operation Wetback," they caught on to us and kicked us out. I was seven years old, American, and I didn't speak any Spanish at all.

I remember these guys came in. They had long trench coats and big-brimmed hats. They came in the nighttime. My mom has always been nervous, and when they came in she was very frightened. But they were friendly enough to see if we could work it out to legalize ourselves. But I think my dad was burned out, working like a dog. When they came for us he got a truck for all our stuff. I think they gave us three days to get out.

I was already in the second grade, but because I didn't speak any Spanish, I started first grade again. I went through elementary school and then another year to secondary or the *politecnica*. I liked school, but it disappointed me as I went on in Mexico. So on my own I came back and tried to go to junior high school in L.A., living with different relatives.

When I first came to junior high I was having a hell of a problem. My English was almost zero because I wasn't practicing it. My Spanish was better, but it was strange to come back and try to blend in.

I remember I was in East L.A., at Montebello Junior High School, and some freshly unpacked Mexicans showed up at school. At recess they were talking and they asked me something; I started speaking Spanish to them and showing them where the snack bar was and certain things that nobody had bothered to tell them. One of the teachers told me I wasn't to speak Spanish. I remember attacking him. I said, "You're full of shit. I can speak Spanish to these guys if I want. Why shouldn't I?"

I returned to Tijuana. Then I tried again in San Diego. It was real difficult, moneywise. My parents were making twenty bucks a week and it was just not enough. If they sent five bucks to me a week or every two weeks, that was nothing over here. So I started working right away.

I worked in a silk screen shop when I was sixteen. I worked there for seven years and put myself through the university. I got a B.A. at San Diego State.

I always worked; my dad had me selling eggs from the time I was three or four years old. He always had me peddling something. That's just the way it was. In the summer before crossing over, I worked as a photographer. I always liked to draw, so I got one of those correspondence cartoon courses from a comic book. One of the lessons was retouching a negative. My dad said, "Oh I know this guy who has a photo studio in Tijuana, why don't you go over there and see what you can learn?" I worked there for six months. They weren't paying me, but I learned to take photographs, how to retouch them, how to illuminate them. We'd color in these sepia-tone photos with Q-tips. Finally I said, I need to get paid if I want to continue my education. So I ran one of this man's photo shops on my own. This was from elementary school until I was sixteen.

One of the things, I don't know, it's difficult to mention certain things you get involved in that may not be as kosher as other things. I went to school with kids that were the sons and daughters of *traficantes*. It just happened that I went to school with them, and I spoke English because English was my first language. Their parents started asking me, "We'll give you some money if you'll make this phone call for me," which was for marijuana, not just kilos, but major amounts. When you live on the border these things are constantly going on. I also grew up in the sixties, where drugs were part of the culture. If you look at murals from different periods of time you can see where a hallucinogenic style of painting was very influential, in all types of art.

I'm one of the cofounders of Centro. Artists from all the disciplines came together there, so that the whole gamut—musicians, actors, poets, photographers, dancers—influenced me. It made school look like nothing. In painting the first murals, one day was worth more than the four years that I spent in school.

Painting and drawing; I was silk-screening, I was color mixing. Mixing colors to me was easy. I started printing colors and using different materials to silk-screen: vinyls, lacquers. One of the things I did was billboards. Because I was big I could silk-screen with this big squeegee. I used opaque projectors and lettering was easy, technical illustration is easy for me, small Rapidograph ink drawings of nuts and bolts. I did aircraft illustration for Boeing, a parts catalog. I think I was fortunate that throughout my career, even as a Revolution and Second Street, Tijuana, photographer, I could make money and do some kind of visual art that was important to me.

Then to make something big: the first time I did a large painting somebody at the university gave me this huge canvas. I was pretty poor and I said, "Great. Let me have it." This big canvas. I started doing this portrait and flashing the paint around. You know, 5′ × 7′. Everyone was having a problem going big. I don't know if it's because I have long arms or I'm big, big didn't seem big to me. I could use a big wide brush as easily as a Rapidograph. The teacher thought it was great. It gave me confidence.

When I'm painting a mural, it's usually in a barrio that has everything from transients to winos to *cholos* and street people, whatever kind of people, Ku Klux Klan too, the whole gamut.

I was painting this Geronimo out here in the front of the building and this jeep came up on the grass with four Ku Klux Klan guys. They were wearing these cowboy hats and these "White Power" T-shirts, with those little plastic vests that they wear, those kinds of western-looking things. I had a navy guy from the hospital and a couple of students that were helping me on a volunteer basis. The jeep ran up: "Hey, you Mexicans, get the hell out of here. Go back to Mexico where you belong." I was way up on the top of the scaffolding, twenty feet up, and I looked at them. Then they ran off, and one of the guys kind of followed a little ways to see where they went. I had a feeling; if they come back—I set a 2×4 close by and was ready to jump in case they had weapons. You have your back to the street all the time. I had already been painting three or four hours when that happened. I painted like twelve more hours without stopping. To me, it was like hey, something's happening with this mural. There's some kind of interaction here. I noticed the students were depressed, they were all run down.

I just did a mural with the Soviet muralists. It is very surrealistic, what I call therapy, because when I do small paintings I like to experiment and do certain textures that you have to do well. One thing I learned in school was the technical use of materials.

The spiritual part—I flunked art history; it was awful. They would show the slides and go, "Botticelli, Italy." So what? I remember waiting and waiting for "Guernica" to be discussed. The teacher just put through "Picasso" and the date. I wanted to know more, but to this teacher it was not important to say, "There was a bombing going on, there was this screaming of children, that's why there is a certain agony." That's where I began noticing that art meant different things to different people. Later, I took that class over again because I wanted to get my teaching credential. I developed perfect sight recognition the second time, but now I knew why I wanted to learn European art history. I had been battling and criticizing it for such a long time, I had a need to know the details and it became important.

The relevancy of *"los tres grandes,"* Diego Rivera, Siquieros, and Orozco, was always in the background. Yet I hadn't studied it very much. I had been surrounded with images of those murals and knew that the work had social voice. I felt an artist had more responsibility in Mexico, but I wasn't around artists that much, and in those years Tijuana was pretty raw. In the sixties I started looking at the books and pictures, but it wasn't until I could afford to give my dad the money for gas. I calculated how much gas it would take—we had this little Ford van—to go back and forth to Mexico City. I said, "Look, I'll pay for the gas and we can sleep in the van." I gave him $90. I was crazy to go see what was going on. My dad and I went to Mexico. We went to the "Poliforum Siquieros." Some of the other things impressed me, but the "Poliforum" was kind of muddy, a little too conglomerated, too much stuff. I liked Siquieros's other murals that were more clear-cut.

I'm particularly tied to two things that happened in the late sixties, the takeover of Chicano Park and this building. We were in a bigger building in Balboa Park. I was associated with other visual artists; we painted canvases and theater backgrounds. The city wanted to move us out of that building. We told them we weren't going to leave until we had a place of our own. Finally they gave us this building. With these sixteen-foot-high walls staring at us we started designing things large, working on big paper.

In 1970 the people of Barrio Logan took over Chicano Park. Some of them said, "We've got to paint these pillars." But they were pretty tall and it was like we were a little fearful. So we started working on the wall inside this building first, using a scaffolding. It became a kind of training ground. It wasn't until '73, after going through a year of red tape and mumbo-jumbo with the Department of Transportation— they didn't know how to handle us—that we finally said we were going to go ahead and do what we wanted. At that time I was the director of the Centro, so I allocated some monies for materials, and we put tables out there and brushes and rollers. We researched some of the base coats and bought gallons of paint. Those first days there were something like three hundred people painting out there. It was like beserkland, a lot of energy. It looked messy, but at the same time it was colorful energy. Ever since then, it has been one pillar, another wall, another wall. It's unstoppable.

I was caught in the middle of the billboard scene, where you throw a message to a passerby in six seconds. I didn't mind putting up big commercial colors and situations to get the message across. We didn't have a radio station, we didn't have a TV station, we didn't have our own newspapers. Our voice was oppressed and we, the muralists, were going to speak for our community. We had to say something.

I'm not sure that designwise the Mexican muralists were something that I wanted to replicate. Some of the images were impressive to me. Initially I wanted to return to my roots, and I had a conflict with some Chicano students: "Oh we're Chicanos and we've been here in the United States, so we need to paint what we've been doing in the United States." I was more of a—the Soviets have been calling us Mezicanskys all month long—I was more of a Mexicanist than the Chicanos, who had never been to Mexico, so I was doing pre-Columbian stuff, Indian stuff, gods, trying to describe philosophies and legends. I hung around other artists that were doing similar things. There's this "Plan Espiritual de Aztlán," it's kind of like a little Chicano bible. I was interested in the Indian part, but I knew I was a border phenomenon, I wasn't just Indian. It was a focus of a particular time.

Then the issues became important: bilingual education, police brutality, the farm workers was a big issue, education. I gravitated from the pre-Columbian to the issues. I thought a lot of Mexican people didn't accept the fact that we are part Indian. That was an issue, our own inner racism, battling within ourselves. I continued being a Chicano. One of the reasons that the spirit still continues is that I'm working in a place where I can see a mural that was painted twenty years ago. It's a constant reminder.

I got married this year and we just had a baby. I really hadn't planned to have a family, although I've always liked kids. I've been doing murals with elementary kids since about '73. I always like their creative energy, especially the third graders, that's where I'm at. Whenever I hang around too many intellectuals, it's the kids that give me that other perspective in life. It took a lot of effort for me to avoid the basic buy-a-house, get-a-job, make-a-family, and concentrate on what I've been doing. I would love to have a house of my own, but I'm not going to drop everything for payments. I've always liked money, I've always liked cars, those kinds of things, but my focus was not to be a failure like everybody around me.

One of my nicknames has been "the Chicano dinosaur." At first it caught me off guard, but in a certain way I don't mind. In fact in one of my last pieces I did a dinosaur with a head of a low rider. It looks like a Quetzalcoatl. The trunk lid is open and it has a bilingual computer tape coming out and the backbone is made of tamale leaves. It has like big huarache feet and the back legs are crunching Coors cans. This was exhibited in New York in January.

People really don't understand how art fits in society. We used to call ourselves Toltecas here. Our philosophy is that of the artist in pre-Columbian times, where he was an integral part of society. I would compare an artist with someone who makes tortillas. He is a part of the reality. It isn't the European perspective, that art is either for the rich, the church, or whoever is in power. In the United States, art goes into an official government gallery or the money-controlled commercial galleries.

When you are a public artist in this society, you literally break the rules. It's on a public wall, no one buys it to keep in their possession or put in their bedroom. We need to educate the society that art could be a way of solving some of the problems. People think we need more police officers in this town. I would say, we need more art. Juvenile delinquency, for instance, could possibly be because kids have no other means for expressing themselves. Artists could offer some of the answers.

The Border Art Workshop has been very important to me. At the Centro we've always thought of ourselves as being at the most transitive border in the world. I'm involved with a project that will deal with the out-of-control sewage situation at the border. We'll design a border art park with acreage in both countries that will be irrigated by reclaimed water. It will have public art, sculpture, murals, and art activities. To me that's very important because everybody knows it's a problem, but they don't realize that artists could be part of the solution.

My parents never reimmigrated. They always stayed in Tijuana. I hung around San Diego to be close to my parents. Then I realized that because I was from both sides, I knew how to transact on the border.

When my dad died five years ago, I thought, what am I going to do with my mom—am I going to bring her over here? I don't like living in the United States. I've never really felt the sense of community here. No matter how old the barrio there's something that wants to destroy the fact that we are a community, that we are growing. Chicano Park was the bellybutton of the barrios and they put Interstate 5 right through it! We don't have political influence in this town even though we're almost 30 percent of the population. I feel the contrast; when I go to my house in Tijuana neighbors will bring a *bocadito*. If they made a meal they'll send their kids over with a plate of tamales. I've never experienced that in the United States. So as a bachelor I thought, I'm going to build myself a place where I can work and have enough space.

I've been building the house for five years. I couldn't just move in with my mom, and I wanted to build something of my own. To me it's political, the fact that I don't want to get stuck buying property and owing forty years. In San Diego everything is over $1,000 a month. Then there was the reawareness of living in Tijuana. The region is growing by leaps and bounds. You can't maintain communication by phone or a weekly visit with the artists and events that are going on in Tijuana.

Then there's something I really like about raising a family in Tijuana. Later I might want to live in the United States, but for now I feel comfortable. My wife's family thought it was going backward, because they're first-generation Mexican. I'm sensitive to her feelings, but I'm so damn hardheaded that I don't care what her family says.

Ideally art, which should be an integral part of life, would be part of the solution. It transcends governments and borders, not to erase the border but to delineate its importance. I'm so egotistical that I feel proud of being a Chicano and I feel proud of being a border phenomenon. I'm a survivalist in that I think there are solutions, but I'm hooked up to the reality that it's not going to happen quickly.

I wanted to do a mural on the Berlin Wall. I always thought that was a good idea. Unfortunately the wall here is chain-link.

JOSÉ "EL COYOTE" DE LA TORRE
Rodeo Star
San Lucas Evangelista, Mexico

Don José returns to his small pueblo every three months. It has changed very little since he was a child seventy years ago. He and his sister still share this two-room adobe house that belonged to their parents; the detached kitchen is the only addition made in their lifetime. Just beyond the kitchen Don José's favorite Arabian stallion paces the corral.

For a man who has trained the horses of our childhood heroes and who continues to live, travel, and perform throughout the United States, these humble beginnings are a source of renewal.

First we went to Spain. The Señor Juan José Cortina, who was highly known and respected here in Guadalajara, took us. He was a *gran haciendado,* the owner of a great hacienda. What's more, he founded the Club Atlas de Guadalajara, and through his hacienda he maintained the Atlas soccer team. So we went. I was sixteen years old, and we were there in '33, '34, and '35.

We had been there three years when the Spanish Civil War with

Franco broke out. It began in the newspapers, and we went along very carefully. We continued working with the horses so they would be in perfect condition for the bullfighting season in Spain, France, and Portugal; then the boycott of the Mexican and Spanish bullfighters began. When they told us that we couldn't work in any arena *taurina* in Spain, France, or Portugal we returned to Mexico. I was the only one to bring back my horses. I left some, but those I kept were fine, fine horses.

Then in a fiesta in Mexico I met some Americans. We became friends. They asked me where I was going and I told them to a *Fiesta Charra*. They said, "Well here's a newspaper announcing where the fiesta is going to be."

So I took them and introduced them to the owner of the arena, a friend and, "No, you don't pay here." They were in Mexico for two weeks and we became good friends. One was the chief of police in Dallas, and he said he could arrange my entry in the upcoming fair. So I went to the feria in Dallas and Fort Worth and rode in the exhibitions and rodeos. This was in '38.

That's where I met a Canadian show promoter named Mel Hinkle and contracted with him to go to Canada, Toronto and Calgary. That's where they have the largest rodeo in the world. It's great.

Afterward I traveled with the rodeos all over the United States. Tim McCoy contracted with me and I was in his show for six months, but the money ran out. It was *cinco de mayo* for sure, when we ended in Washington. There were twelve of us from Mexico.

Through Tim McCoy I met my wife. We began to correspond and in the end we got married.

In this time I went everywhere. I've always had a permit, so I would return home for a month or two. In 1948, I was living in San Francisco, at 1373 Clay Street, and we had the horses in Sunnyvale next to the airport. We would go there every day, and every night I would return to sleep at the house in San Francisco. We also went to Palm Springs. We went everywhere, but I lived most of the time in California.

I worked with Monty Montana and his troupe. A white bread bakery sponsored Monty Montana.

I spent a lot of time in Cisco Kid's show. Oh yes, of course, Cisco Kid would do shows all over too. The Cisco Kid was a good man, very good. For me, the Cisco Kid was a great person. The Cisco Kid called himself Duncan Reynaldo, but he was Armenian. No, that's right. He didn't like us to call him Mr. Reynaldo. No, never. "José, no, no, José, Duncan."

No, when the Cisco Kid died I went to his funeral. I have even saved the telegram his wife sent me. She still lives in Santa Barbara. No, I spent a lot of time with him. I lived on a ranch that he bought near Coldwater Canyon. He bought it from another artist, Hopalong Cassidy. It was very pretty, over there near Malibu Canyon.

No, I have worked with all the cowboys. I knew them all. I worked in Oklahoma on Dale Robertson's ranch. He always wanted me to come back.

Then I worked at Hearst's Castle over there, San Simeon, on the coast of California. It's very beautiful. Yes, I trained Mr. Hearst's horses. He had his stables right there on the beach and he had some fine animals. I lived there for a year training his horses. I even went to his birthday party. Oh, it was a big fiesta with movie stars and famous people from Hollywood. It lasted for three days.

A couple of years ago the directors of the museum in Oakland were in a saddle shop in Pleasanton that belongs to a friend of mine. He told them he had never seen such fine work in rawhide as those of his friend José de la Torre. "Well who is José de la Torre?" they asked.

"He's here."

So they called me. "We hear you have some things in the buckaroo style and we would like to exhibit them." They wanted me to loan these bridles, reins, and crops, and to place a price on each piece. I didn't want to because I didn't want to sell them. But I loaned them and what do you think? They were stolen from the museum; they broke the glass cases to steal my things. They gave me $40,000 for them.

My sister, the one who died, was very good at making these things. I liked to make them too. A collectionist in Pasadena, a good friend of mine, has some of the things my father made in the American style, but I don't have many pieces left.

I still work with the horses; I go back and forth buying for clients. Just recently a friend and I returned from Costa Rica with twelve horses. It was very hard in Nogales. Aye my poor little friend. "José, you don't happen to have 100,000,000 pesos in your bag?"

"Why?"

"Well this is what the *aduana* is asking to pass the horses in Nogales."

"Just to cross?" It's a *sinvergüenzada* of the Mexican government, that's all. They saw that he had a trailer that cost $75,000 for the twelve horses.

My friend was mortified. I told him, "Come on, let's go." We went to have a coffee right there on the border. I asked the receptionist, "Is Rodolfo in?"

"Who?"

"Rodolfo!" He is the secretary. No, these are big men, even to their mouths.

"Listen Rodolfo, there is this. At the *aduana* there is this problem. They want to charge us 100,000,000 pesos to permit the horses to cross the country from Puerto Hidalgo, Chiapas."

"Oh no, I will arrange the permits."

No, the head of the *aduanas* arrived at the corrals where we were resting the horses. "Señor de la Torre, don't get nervous."

"Well it is going to make me nervous to pay that much money."

"No, no, here is the permit. I am very happy to have been able to help you." Not one cent did it cost me.

My father always told me, "Make friends that count, son. Why would you want a friend that wasn't worth anything?"

CESAR ROSAS
Lead Guitarist and Singer with Los Lobos
Los Angeles, California

An electric blue T-shirt and the signature sunglasses, that is about as fancy as he gets. Cesar's informal, genuine manner is no different when he's performing. When he talks about his life and growing up, his fingers hold a curve as if their memory is set by guitar. He tells his story to the accompanying punctuation of silent riffs and strums.

When I was a little kid in Mexico I remember the Saturday night dances in the ranch. People would come from different areas. I'll never forget that, my mom and dad dancing. There was no electricity, right, so they'd bring generators and hang strings of light bulbs, socket and extension cords, and all these bright light bulbs. That was the dance area and you'd have the Norteño groups. The Norteño guys, the *bajo sexto,* and the accordion doing all these great songs of the time. I've been collecting that kind of music maybe ten or fifteen years. I would buy records and play them, "Man, I remember this song." When I was a little kid this song was a hit. These guys were playing underneath those lights over there. You know it was incredible.

That was actually my first influence in music. When I came to the States as a kid I really loved music and rock and roll. This was before the Beatles, before all that stuff. This was right at that time that the fifties had gone over to the sixties: Ray Charles, Chubby Checker, the Rhythm Tens, absolutely! KRLA. I have such warm memories about that music. Those were my first influences with American rock and roll. It was a big, big influence on me. The songs were fresh.

My dad was a diesel mechanic. In Mexico he was very much involved with agriculture. So he was a farmer too, and we lived on this little ranch right outside Hermosillo. I grew up there. My first school was in Mexico.

It's kind of a strange story. My dad was born in a little town called La Purisima, Baja California, way down near La Paz. His family was Portuguese, and my great-grandfather, they tell me, was a pirate ... bootlegging, smuggling. Anyway, my dad was born down there but his mother migrated north.

During that time, there was an American, a rancher who owned a lot of land in Hermosillo. So he hired my dad to take care of his ranch. He took my mom there. When they got there, we started being born. There aren't many of us. The only ones living now are my older brother Pete, then it's me, then Rudy is younger, and Patti is the youngest. We lost a little brother between me and Pete. Back in the fifties, in Mexico, it could get really tough. A lot of poverty. Not only that, all the odds were against us because we were isolated, living in a little ranch with no electricity, no running water, no indoor plumbing. When you're a little kid you're just happy to be anywhere. I saw a lot of hardships, but I never connected it to anything. You sense that there's something wrong, but you just go on being a little kid, being happy with whatever you have. Oh, they struggled so much.

My grandmother, who has now passed away, lived in Chula Vista, right near the border. She also had a house in Tijuana and would commute. My cousins still go back and forth. Since we had family there, we lived in Tijuana for about six months, getting our papers, you know all that red tape. Although I hadn't yet come to the United States, all my cousins spoke English. So finally we crossed the border. When everything was all set, we went to East L.A. My dad knew some people and they let us stay at their house in Boyle Heights. That was the first time that I had been to the United States, and it was strange.

But coming to the United States—I'll never forget that! I was really afraid. The U.S., this big old monster. I was panicked. These people were speaking this other language, they dressed differently, acted differently. It's like going to another planet, you know. What intrigued me though was these other people who also spoke Spanish. All these emotions were running through me. It was scary.

I remember the first time seeing black people. Around my neighborhood in Boyle Heights there were a lot of black people coming from the south side, south L.A., areas like Watts. A lot of black people, right in a certain spot. The cultural thing was like a bomb. Yet as time goes on you start growing and you adapt.

Also rock-and-roll music. I'll never forget that as a little kid. That was 1962. The fifties were just over, but there was still a lot of great music out there.

My older brother, Pete, got started playing guitar. I didn't start till later. He used to play Mexican music and he was getting into flamenco music too. He played really well. I was just so fascinated with the guitar. It was amazing to me that you could get the sound out of this little box. That was my first love.

I remember the first guitar. It was my brother's first guitar too. He handed it down to me. My aunt, my dad's sister, who lives in San Ysidro, used to sing and play in a trio when we were kids. And this guitar! I still have it, it's a *requinto*. I think one of the famous trios from Mexico. It was either Los Panchos or Los Diamantes. She finally gave this guitar to my brother, Pete.

Being a left-handed musician is not easy. That was the first guitar that I could call my own and change the strings. I started plucking on it, learning chords. A few years later like 1967, '68, they used to have what they called "Teen Posts." Like neighborhood youth centers, where they offered programs in crafts and there was a gym for working out, for kids to get into boxing and all that. One day I was passing by on the way to a friend's and I noticed there was a big ol' sign, "Free Guitar Lessons—Come on Saturday." It knocked me out. God. So Saturday morning there I was with my guitar. I was only one of four kids that signed up, and I had my own guitar. I was ahead of myself, but I didn't know the theory. My teacher was sort of amazed because, "You know all those chords but try F." I said you know that's why I'm here. I want you to teach me what they're called. I started learning, and right then and there I knew that music was for me. When I got my first electric guitar and amplifier, "Man, that's it!"

My parents always encouraged me. They were never biased. Of course there was a period where music started getting loud, I mean really loud. I had my own band and we would be in the garage, you know garage bands. We would be rehearsing and it was like in the afternoon, and my dad would come home from work. He didn't want to hear that. The poor guy was tired from working all day. He'd come home full of grease and all burned out and we'd be like blowing away the neighborhood. My dad would get really upset. He tolerated it, but he'd get pissed off. But my mom would say, "Leave him alone, leave him alone." Yeh, my dad took a lot of beatings from all over. God bless him.

I write music but I don't consider myself Bob Dylan. I write rock-and-roll music. It's good enough for me. Within our group, Los Lobos, Dave writes the music and Louie's the lyricist. There's a certain formula we have, a balance. Louie and Dave write their songs, themes involving social issues, more humanistic. Then you have me who never gets involved with that. I mean, coming from where I came from, it seems like it should be the other way around. But for some reason I write the rock-and-roll songs that don't have a lot of social meaning to them. They're just real simple, real basic rock-and-roll form. You write the songs you know. Everybody has a God-given talent. It's given to us by somebody else and it's what you do with it.

Believe it or not we all went to Garfield High, except Steve who plays sax with us. Steve joined us much later, in the eighties. David and I were in exactly the same year, same class, and in fact went to the same junior high school together. We were all musicians, see. By the tenth grade, I was starting to get involved in rock and roll. That's when I started making my own band, getting my feet wet, playing with a drummer and bass player.

At Garfield, there were all these different types of people. There were the people in gangs over here, over there were the straights involved in academics, then people heavily involved into drugs, and then here were these musicians. A lot of musicians came out of Garfield.

While these big dances were being put on, the rock-and-roll guys were having garage dances. People actually would put on a rock-and-roll thing at their house. They'd open up their garage and the band would set up in there. There'd be like three or four hundred kids, jammed in a backyard. People would bring beer, and it would be like a whole happening. This stuff went on every weekend. You would just hear word of mouth, "Hey there's gonna be a party at Pason's on Pico Rivera." Little flyers, people would xerox little flyers and pass 'em out. You'd get there, sometimes they'd charge a dollar to get in, maybe fifty cents, and it'd be just a big ol' happening. It was so typical. Always the police would come in, bust it up, and helicoptors would come over. The neighbors would eventually complain because it was so incredibly loud. Loud, loud, I mean loud! You could hear it three blocks down the street. It was an East L.A. thing. Just like a party, but with a band, with a full-on, blown rock-and-roll band, blasting away. It was a lot of fun. I was all involved with that. I used to play like R&B stuff for those Art Lebow things and Eddie Torres and Huggie Boy too, with the Midnighters. Then, after, just to sort of unwind, I would go to one of these other parties.

I went to Garfield High. It was at a different time, but still like the movie—*Stand and Deliver.* I think the fact that that happened shows that there's a lot of remarkable kids there, a lot of geniuses. I got a pretty decent education. Whatever you want is there, and nobody can ever tell me any different. Kids there have gone off to become mayors and top people in many fields. It's what you make of it. At the same time, I feel we were deprived a little. We didn't have certain things that we should have had. Like the so-called better areas in L.A. would get more facilities and more funds to do more things. Still we basically had everything at Garfield. It's a lesson in life—I don't know how to explain it—it makes you struggle. It makes you aware of a lot that kids who have it all are never in touch. I have my own theories. There are a lot of wealthy people out there that have it all but never have had these experiences that humans need to give incentive in life, to make you feel that you've achieved something. We all need that.

Well you know, in East L.A., there are many generations. They're full-blown American folks. They just happened to be of Mexican descent. There was always drugs. But it was like any other neighborhood, that's the thing. A lot of folks don't understand East L.A. because it's gotten such a bad rap throughout the years. They don't understand because they never lived there or don't care to go there. They think that life in East L.A. is a big gang fight, drugs and gang fights. In fact, that's not true at all.

Of course back then the worst thing you could do was smoke marijuana. You had the complete extreme, heroin addicts, but there weren't manufactured drugs like now. I never got involved with any of that stuff. It wasn't my family; to this day I don't understand what it was. My brother, me, thank God, none of us ever had a problem with any of that. If you go to East L.A. right now you will see the standard neighborhood, right? Regular schools, then little areas that are bad off, and you just don't go there. That's like anywhere.

My parents were always renting. Back then we couldn't afford to buy. Then after living many years in East L.A., we finally bought a house. I already knew Dave for years and ended up moving to a neighborhood right near his house. There was this neighbor, two houses over, named Frank. Frank and Dave were heavy rock-and-rollers and good friends. So I was sitting there playing my guitar one day and this guy, Frank, walks right past my house. I was playing there and I looked at him and he looked at me. He went in his door. Then he came back out and said, "Hey aren't you a friend of Dave's?"

I said, "Yeh, aren't you Frank?"

"Yeh, wow, you live here now?"

"Yeh, we bought this house." So we became really good friends.

One summer when he was on vacation we started playing. He'd play this dobro and he'd play blues and I'd play a few songs. We'd sit around, buy a few beers, and just kick back. We'd play the rock stuff, but then we'd play a Mexican song. It was really weird to us. Songs that I remembered when I was a kid living on the ranch. You know, *huapangos* that Miguel Aceves Mejia used to sing. Frank would play a lick and say, "I'm learning this song." He's not from Mexico, but his mom was. I mean, he's hard-core Mexican descent, but he grew up in America, in a different reality. Now here we are. Two guys, two different worlds. I was more in contact with the Mexican roots. I was still heavily involved with that, yet part of me was being Americanized. I was like in that other culture, playing in rock bands.

Although I hadn't really, really been involved in playing the Mexican music, it was always in my blood and my ears and my heart. See rock-and-roll was, "Yeh, I want that, I wanna get on with that and absorb it. Everything." But yeh, this is the stuff I hear at my house, the stuff I grew up with. Mexican music, that was my other world; but I had never executed it, never played it. So when I started playing, it just all tied in. It was so familiar to me. I started playing, doing the riffs, and before we knew it we had played a couple of songs. Man, I remember that. 'Cause you gotta understand that after playing rock-and-roll for four or five years, to go and play something of your own culture there was something, I can't explain it, but there was something so rewarding, so easy, and so rich. I really got kicks out of it and so did he. I mean we'd finish a song and we'd laugh. Literally, we'd be laughing. We'd think, man, this is so silly, but it's such a cool song, you know?

We'd say, there's more to this music than a lot of people realize. We started learning that. We started getting hip to that. Man this music is difficult. It's really hard to play. It's much harder than playing rock-and-roll music. So we started saying, wouldn't it be cool if we could get another mandolin and we'd have two mandolins doing harmonies like the way they used to do it on the records, on the violin parts. 'Cause virtually the violin and the mandolin are the same instrument. They're tuned the same, but you bow the violin and it doesn't have frets, and the mandolin is the same scale but it's a fretted instrument. It's a whole different approach to playing, but in theory it's like the same notes and everything, the same tune. We said, "Man, we should call Dave."

We were just out of high school with nothing to do. We were sort of looking at our lives and, "Well we're still kids having a good time. We're not under any kind of pressure trying to have any kind of career right now. We're just sort of doing this." We had little jobs but we didn't earn any money.

Then we said, "Wouldn't it be cool if we had a bass player." We called in my bass player from my R&B band, Robert. I used to call him "Big Bob." See his parents are from Guadalajara too, so he grew up listening to mariachi music and all that. Frank had a *guitarrón* he loaned to Robert and Robert started learning. Not only was the music strange, but these instruments were foreign, especially the *guitarrón*. There's a whole different concept and theory put into that instrument. We were learning as we went along.

Well before we knew it, Louie came in. We got Louie to play rhythm guitar. I don't know, we just were getting kicks out of it. It was like we rediscovered this music that was always in our houses, but we had never personally executed it.

There was this guy in the community. He was already middle-aged. He's still around. His name is Fernie Mosqueda, and he was putting on programs for the kids, a youth center for getting kids that were in gangs off the streets. He'd coordinate programs and fund-raisers. So one day we were all there in Frank's living room playing this music and Fernie walked in. He was gonna see Frank. He says, "What are you guys doin', man? What happened to the rock-and-roll stuff?" So we said we still play around with it. He says, "Well how come you guys are playing Mexican music? It sounds great."

We said, "Get outta here."

He said, "Play a song for me." We played it and it just blew his mind completely away. He said, "Damn, what kind of music is that?" We had been researching it, we knew the history and all. We were trying to play it in true traditional form. The traditional stand-up bass, your mandolin. We were doing exactly the same thing. We were playing Mexican music the way you would play it in the ranch, the real raw way, you know.

And then another week or so passed and Fernie came back again. He said, "Guess what, guys? I'd like to propose something. I'd like to share something and see what you guys think. Next month I'm having a fund-raiser for my kids, and I want to put together a program in Compton at a VFW hall."

I said, "Yeh, and?"

So he says, "Can you guys play?"

And we just burst out laughing. We said, "Get outta here. We would never play in front of anybody. This stuff? We don't even know it."

He goes, "Man you guys are crazy, you guys play really good." I mean we were no dummies, we knew we could play. We felt embarrassed. We felt timid. No one's ever even heard of that. I mean, kids our age with long hair and everything playing this kind of music. It doesn't tie in. It doesn't make sense. He goes, "I'm serious man, you guys are good. I want you guys to play."

We said, "No way, Fernie."

He goes, "Look, how much you guys want? Well, within certain limits."

"Well, we don't want anything. We don't even want to play."

He says, "Come on guys, come on."

"All right, Fernie, maybe we'll think about it. Come next week."

Next week he comes and say, "Hey you guys gonna play?"

We had thought it over and had gotten up enough nerve, so we said, "All right, we'll play. We'll do it for you."

He says, "Look, I'll pay you whatever, like fifty bucks or something."

We said, "God, we're gonna get paid for this." What happened right there was something very interesting. It created not only panic, but now we were in a situation we couldn't get out of. There was the pressure to learn a few more songs and get this whole thing together, this whole little set, our presentation—and a month to do it.

Later on he comes back and says, "Look guys, this is my own paperwork. I gotta do it. There's this contract that I gotta do 'cause I don't want these people to think down the line that I'm taking the money. This all has to be legit." So, this is to hereby, that on such and such a date, this band, and it had a little line to fill in the name. Signed by. We had to fill in that line. But see, there was no name.

So it was the day before Fernie came back for the contract, and we were outside going, "We gotta come up with a name." I had been buying records and surveying this music, and I knew a lot of the bands, bands from Mexico in the fifties and sixties. I remembered this band called "Los Lobos del Norte." They're still around. To hear those names, some of those Norteño bands, "Los Rancheritos de Topochico." It was so funny. I told the guys, "Los Lobos," and everybody was laughing. Then they started saying, "Los Lobos, that sounds sort of cool." "Los Lobos, yeh, but we're Los Lobos from East L.A." You know we couldn't call ourselves, "The Shoes," or a typical Americanized rock band name. It had to be appropriate. "Los Lobos de East L.A." We just got a kick out of it. We wrote it in "Los Lobos del Oeste de Los Angeles."

The day of the gig, I remember there was a little kitchen area where the *mamacitas,* the ladies that were there making the tortillas, and the *menudo* and food for people that were gonna come. We had just driven up in my little car, and Fernie greets us at the door. "All right, you guys made it." Then a few of the *mamacitas* walked out and oh, I remember one saying to the other ladies, "Van llegando los músicos." Oh they're here. Then she did a double take. Wait a minute, these aren't the musicians. I could see that expression on her face. I remember thinking, oh man, I told you, Fernie.

We walked in. Here were all these people and everything and we walked in with our instruments. Everybody did a double take like, "Where in the hell did these guys come from? Mars? They're supposed to play Mexican music?" But we started tuning up, and when we brought out the upright bass and the *guitarrón* the people figured well, these guys don't have drums. Then we started playing all these *huapangos* and boleros and man, people just went nuts.

Later Dave got an accordion and learned to play it. We started learning how to play *Norteño, conjunto* music. We treated these songs like rock-and-roll. They weren't. They didn't sound like Flaco Jimenez. It was faster, louder. That's how we got fired.

By that time we already had full-blown electric guitar amplifiers. We were all rock-and-roll, playing Ritchie Valens's songs and everything. Just for the fun of it. Anyway we got fired from this restaurant, Los Lomos. We went on to another place, Tlaquepaque in Placentia, and a lot of the clientele from Los Lomos went over to Tlaquepaque to see us. So we had a little following. After about a year and a half we quit. We ended up back at the garage, back where we started. We looked at each other and said, "Now what?"

I remember saying, "Hey guys, I really think we have to start writing." We had tried folk music and we had a lot of great memories, but we didn't succeed as far as record labels and all that. It wasn't like we were jumping on the next stand. It's just that rock-and-roll was in our blood too and we wanted to work that out. So we started writing music that would have all those influences, songs that had a little bit of everything.

One night after that a couple of the guys went to see The Blasters, a local rockabilly band. At the end of the show one of the Allman brothers ran into Dave in the parking lot and Dave says, "Hey, we're big fans of yours."

He kind of looked at Dave and says, "Hey, don't I know you from somewhere?"

Dave says, "I don't know. I have a band called Los Lobos."

"Really? Didn't I see you guys on TV?" This was five years after public television had made a documentary about us. Believe it or not they still show it.

"Yeh, your band is cool. I like that Mexican stuff."

Dave said, "We don't play that anymore."

"Oh really? Man you gotta come over to my house." So he invited us over and these guys had 78s of Flaco Jimenez and Lidia Mendoza! Los Alegres de Teran! They knew all this stuff. These kids were hip cats, man.

"You guys play rock now, huh? We'd like to hear your band one of these days." So we went into the garage and made a little demo with some of our own songs and gave it to them. They went on the road, and somewhere back east put it on. They flipped out and called us. "Hey, we're doing a gig next month at The Whiskey. Can you guys play it?"

"Yeh, sure we'll play." That was a turning point.

We played that night and it was just amazing. We were just the opening band, but I remember comments from the other bands saying, "How the hell are we going to follow these guys?" And we were just the opening band. There were all these people with spiked hair and purple mohawks and straight guys and guys from the media. We got reviews in the local papers, in Hollywood, the whole L.A. area. From there on we started playing the L.A. circuit. Now was like a whole new different clip of us, of the L.A. scene, the L.A. sound.

From there on we sort of left East L.A. We lived there, but we really didn't play East L.A. anymore. We played these clubs where you could play your original music. We got to know all these bands, the alley music scene that a lot of people were afraid of. They were making a big noise in the world. We were all friends, and they weren't really as bad as some people make them out to be. The Germs, The Blasters, Black Flag; and here we were playing rock-and-roll and Tex Mex.

Before we knew it we got signed to Slash Records, then touring all over the United States, everywhere, it snowballed. We started writing more of our own material, one album after another. Now we have five albums. Then the La Bamba thing became a big hit. It's really strange to us. We felt, in a weird way, who else could have played it? Not to be boasting about it, but we had already recorded one of Ritchie Valens's songs. Great music. We have a great respect and love for that kid, you know. Rancheros. That stuff. It makes you cry, man.

When we came together we were just out of high school, but as we got older it got a little more complicated. We adapted, our wives adapted us. Then we had children and here we are. We're all family guys. I have my three girls. Amber, she's the oldest, she just graduated from high school. Then there's Ruby, she's six, and little Vicki is a year and a half.

Music is what we do all the time, but when we're off the road I like to just take it easy and get into my photography. Basically I lead a very normal life with my family. We have our ups and downs, you know you got to pay the bills. Other than that I deal with everyday life like anyone else. I collect guitars, I write my songs. A lot of my time is spent at home, but I go down to Rosarito; I have a house over there out by the beach, a little shack that I go to and forget all my problems. Once you cross the border it's like *phewuuuuuu*. I've been going down there a lot, every couple of weeks. Get some fishing in, you know.

Right now we're kind of happy slobs because we've been off the road for a long time. But when we're working, boy I'm praying to get home because it's so hard. This is the longest time in our careers that we've had off, it's been about five months. We're usually on the road ten months out of the year. Once in a while we'll invite the families. For some reason they always like to go to New York. It's that shopping.

It's been a struggle, but it's been more fun than anything else. I used to think that this must be a crime, there must be a law against having so much fun and being successful. But then I think that no, I was destined to do this, so here I am and I give it my best.

I'm a little shy, yes, but I didn't have major problems with it. I'm not afraid to get out in crowds. There are times when you get panicked, man. Not so much anymore, but when we were getting out there. The intensity and magnitude of the crowds, from playing in a little club, a small place and you're just having fun, it's great, then all of a sudden you're out there. And now it's not intimate. It's bigger than you. It's just too big. That's when you kind of get panicked. I'm very self-conscious like a lot of us, but not so much I can't take it. It doesn't show. We fake it really well. That's showbiz. You can't let 'em see you sweat, as they say, but we sweat a lot.

RICARDO AGUILAR MELANTZÓN
Writer
Ciudad Juárez, Mexico

He speaks in time-intense, rapid-fire bursts, yet his conversations go on without constraint, flowing freely from one topic to another as if time doesn't matter. Ricardo Aguilar not only manifests the deepest cultural traits of both sides of the border, he finds physical and psychic balance between working in the demanding, fast-paced university on this side and living in the relaxed, leisurely style of Mexico. As an associate professor of languages at the University of Texas at El Paso and living with his wife and daughters in Ciudad Juárez, he crosses the line between these two worlds every day.

There are words here on the border that can't be translated into either language. It's a very, very interesting culture, especially if you constantly go back and forth.

Images, sensory images, tend to stick in my mind and they stick for a very long time. It's just that way; photographic visual images, olfactory images, taste images. They just stick and don't go away until I write them down.

I'm pretty observant, and two years in the navy, on a ship, really streamlined those innate skills. *¿Cómo?* It made me take a direction, and I started writing and writing and writing. I began with letters because I didn't know where to start. I wrote 735 letters to my family and friends and myself. I wanted to keep a record, kind of like a diary.

Anyway, the border has been part of my life and my wife Rosita's life, our daughters' too. My father-in-law was kind enough to give us this house as a wedding gift. So if we would leave Juárez to live in El Paso we would have to leave this house. It's nice and I'm very comfortable here. It's right downtown. For example, I can just walk downtown and buy reviews that some people have to wait months to get in the library. I just go there and grab them. Chago, my barber—I have to go there today—and I have been having a running conversation for thirty years. I'm writing about Bero, the guy that shines my shoes; shining shoes is an art form in itself, and I'm writing about it. But these people, it's the conversations you have, the history of Ciudad Juárez in their heads. I love to talk to them, because while they're shining shoes they remind me of so many things I've forgotten. I take a whole bunch of shoes and stay for hours listening to them.

I was born in El Paso, September 16, 1947, so my birthday is tomorrow, the *diez y seis de septiembre*. When I was little I always thought that they made the parade for me. My mom is Cajun, from New Iberia, Louisiana. My dad's family immigrated from Zacatecas at the end of the last century.

My dad worked for the electric company in Juárez; he's an electrical engineer. And my mom has always been a homemaker, but she's also dabbled in trying to get some businesses off the ground. She has some apartment houses. We lived here in Juárez. My mother's mother and father lived across in El Paso. So I used to spend a lot of time over there also. You could say that ever since I was a child I have been going back and forth.

I completed my primary school here in Juárez at a private school, La Escuela Maria Martinez, which is still here and which my daughters attended. I did my high school in El Paso at a Jesuit school. Then I went to what is now the University of Texas at El Paso. I did a couple of years there. I flunked out, got five Fs one semester. I wasn't interested in studying. That was the Vietnam era. I was just waking up to things. I was eighteen, nineteen. But then I got greetings from the U.S. government.

I am one of those people, weird people around the world that live on a border and have dual nationality. I don't have a Mexican passport, but according to Mexican law I am a national of Mexico because my dad is Mexican. However, I did serve in the U.S. armed forces, the Naval Reserve, for six years; I joined in 1966. I then came back and completed my B.A. in French at U.T. El Paso.

I was trying to support a family and stay in school. We were really poor. It was hard to get fellowships, and I was unable to go anyplace else. So I continued at U.T. El Paso, getting an M.A. in Spanish literature. I was fortunate to be accepted into the University of New Mexico doctoral program in Latin American literature. This is in Albuquerque. I completed the doctorate in three years and then went to work. Well I worked for a year at U.T. El Paso, came back for a year and completed my dissertation. Then I went to work in Seattle, Washington, in '75, '76. Then back to U.T. El Paso as director of the Chicano

Studies Center in 1977, and teaching. I'm now an associate professor, tenured in the Department of Languages.

Since then I've written on academic subjects. My dissertation, later published as a book, has to do with a left-wing poet in Mexico whose name is Efraín Huerta. He is one of the four most important poets in Mexico after *Contemporáneos,* which is a very big, important school. Also a dictionary of Juárez Caló I did is now being published—the second edition. I've got a couple of books of poetry, and I've got a series of stories that are published in Mexico by the Universidad Veracruzana that deal with the border and growing up. The other thing, five years ago my friend Sergio Elizondo and I started a publishing house, Dos Pasos Editores, here on the border. We publish Chicano literature in Spanish exclusively. We have five books now and we're waiting to see if more books sell so that we can bring out another one.

Right now I'm writing a book of short personal essays. I find I have very little time to write because my life is so structured around the academic world. So I write during the hours that I give exams. I know that the students will copy anyway, so I don't watch over them. I take those hours and do something for myself. I have about 160 pages of essays and I'm trying to work through them, put them in categories, revise them. I write for an hour, whatever the test takes, and that's the way they are, whatever is going through my mind at the moment. I've written from death, to love, to cold, to the water pipes breaking, to trips, to my motorcycle, which I love. There's a lot of stuff on the motorcycle just because it seems I barely get off the bike and something else has happened. That'll get me going.

I've always been very, very interested in poetry as an art form. A class on contemporary Mexican poetry got me going because it introduced some very interesting, very exciting young poets of that time. I started reading a lot. I thought, well these people are saying the same things, things very close to me. It wasn't until 1970, '71 that I was able to have a little time for myself, when I really started developing into a writer. Before that it was mostly academic.

When I was in Albuquerque during 1972 I wrote a chapbook of poetry. I wrote the whole thing in that year during my off time. And from then I continued to write poetry, because I thought that that was the thing that I did best, that I was most comfortable with. Then I found out that I wasn't very good at all. I was learning a lot of things about how to construct poetry, a lot about criticism of poetry, but I didn't have the innate ability to write a poem.

But I do have a penchant for telling stories. I've always been able to observe, remember, then tell. My narrative is very visual. It's also very violent in the sense that it is very fast. It's fast paced. Fast-paced novels have always intrigued me. I love reading Poe, things that grab me and take me away with their pace. Somebody told me that I wasn't a short-story writer because I didn't have the pause necessary for narrative. Bullshit! In a short story you have to grab them and run.

I've been writing a lot on young Mexican poets. There's a boom of contemporary Mexican poetry coming down the line. There are five hundred poets writing and publishing in Mexico right now. You know for a country of eighty million, that's a lot of poets, and they're doing great work. I would say that twenty-five of them are going to be of the stature of Octavio Paz or better in a few years. I have been bringing them up here and presenting them, trying to establish a relationship—a real relationship with Mexico and people in the United States, so there will be a communication between writers. These intellectuals affect the lives of people. And when you write there is no border.

Every once in a while some bureaucrat in Washington or Mexico City gets heartburn and all of a sudden you have border problems. During the elections in 1985 PRI [Partido Revolucionario Institucional] got to the point that they couldn't control what was happening anymore. So when the PAN [Partido Accion Nacional] realized they were being subverted and manipulated, they started closing the bridges, just blocking them. As one of the people who goes back and forth every day, I got caught in the middle. For a month it was touch and go. I started writing personal essays about what will happen if the border is cut, if there is no communication, with half my family here and half my family in El Paso.

I guess we all have problems crossing. They know me. All they have to do is punch the number of my plate in the computer and they know who I am: my name, my work, what I've done. They know I've been in protests all over the place. Probably in the computer they have my CIA file and my FBI file. I've had people on the bridge say, "Good morning, Dr. Aguilar," but I know where it comes from. Every once in a while there's someone there, usually a Chicano, that's what's weird about it, it's usually somebody just like me, who stops me and makes my life difficult. One day they wanted to take the tires off my bike. I said, "Why don't you bring in the dogs and have them sniff first?" So they did and it was okay. You know, what can I carry on a bike? Sometimes they just want to make it difficult. In the winter I wear a beard, a Greek fisherman's hat, and glasses—there is an anarchistic quality, so they stop me.

I also teach at the University at Juárez and we're developing a review called *Entorno*. It's in Number 24 now. I love that work, I really do, because it has to do with presenting new people who are writing well. It's *fabuloso*.

Something else about my family, something that people don't ever want to consider. I've been doing some research that got going with a novel by José Emilio Pacheco. It had to do with the concentration camps and the whole question of the Jewish diaspora coming from Israel to Spain to the Synagogue in Toledo to the Synagogue in Thessalonica in Greece and then to America. Many of us who are descendants of people coming north during the *colonia*, especially the early *colonia*, with names like Aguilar, most probably are the descendants of Jewish *conversos*. Nobody wants to accept it, but I think it's a very important realization. There may be alternative streams in our culture that we don't recognize and that are very, very important for the development of the New World. We always talk about Spain throwing out the best of its people, the *comerciantes*, the artisans, and nobody ever talks about where they went. I'm convinced that a large group of them came over here.

One of the reasons for the development of the *colonia* of the New World into a very—*¿cómo te dijera?*—a very efficient society apart from the *mestizaje* was that they brought knowledge; know how that has been forgotten of course because of the Inquisition, *¿no? Pero eso también*, that's one part that nobody wants to consider about immigration, long-term immigration. Not all Mexicans are Catholic. The culture comes from millions of roots; that's just one. It's just wonderful. If you're going to talk about immigration you have to talk about those influences also, and this border we share. When I say *we*, I mean both sides, *¿no?*

Instead of motivating and fomenting integration into this area we export it. Our university, for example, the community itself, is the greatest exporter of Chicano talent to the nation. *Es cierto*. You leave to get a job. But when you want to come back to El Paso it's impossible, because the infrastructure for coming back is not created. My case was just—*¿cómo?—fuera de serie:* I wasn't supposed to come back. I was supposed to stay in Seattle like everybody else. No, you go to Stanford, you go to UCLA, everywhere. El Paso, El Paso, where are you from, El Paso? *¡Ching!*

My daughters go to school here in Juárez. The school system is excellent. There are no drugs in the school. It's strict. They give them a lot of homework. They make them dress up in a certain way. I know that this is not fashionable in the United States anymore, but I think it builds character, *un poquito.* They're also very nationalistic, which is another thing we've lost. They march in parades, dance in the ballet folklórico, they clean up their school, they paint it, they fix the gardens as *trabajo social,* social work. I like it. It breeds respect, and I think respect is one of those things we need to bring back into society. I don't mean to exaggerate. It's unfortunate though, because respect breeds good family ties and societal relationships. *No sé.* I don't say it's free, you have to earn respect. But for example, respect for the flag. Tomorrow at *la fiesta del diez y seis,* when I stand at the *desfile* and the flag goes by, I feel goose bumps. I feel something very, very important when the flag goes by. And I feel the same about the American flag, because I was in close-to-death situations under it. It's *algo importante.* I don't mean flag waving. And I don't think Bush is right about amending the Constitution. But you don't mess with family values or with the respect you have for your own country, because if you don't have respect for those kinds of things you don't have respect for yourself.

I've read a lot of shit. But that, I might add, has influenced me in a positive way. I've read science fiction, detective and spy novels, ever since I was a kid, because my dad was an avid reader of that material.

Of course I've read the Latin Americans: Fuentes, Paz. I've read Borges, Alejo Carpentier. Efraín Huerta and the poetry of Pablo Neruda have also influenced me. I love Rosario Castellanos, Elena Poniatowska, she's great. The classics, the American classics, and the *Alexandria Quartet*—it's a wonderful novel, fundamental for anyone who is going to write. I've gone through the spectrum, but I always come back to Tolkien. He is my steady. I've read him ten times, and every time I read him I love him.

Still I think I have been most highly influenced by the contemporary Mexican writers. That is to say, what I'm writing now has a lot to do with that style, or that break in style. It stems from the " '68 generation," which I am in many ways a part of. The break took place because of the young people in Mexico. That watershed established totally new categories.

I consider myself a Chicano. I was born over there, I received the adult part of my education in the United States as a Mexican. But I can't separate myself from what I feel for Mexico. It just happens; I think it's a question of geography. If I would have been born and raised in Las Cruces I would have been a totally different person. To be honest with myself, politically honest with myself, and culturally honest with myself, I have to be a Chicano. I can't be a Mexican and not be an American. And I can't be an American without being Mexican. I have very distinct ideological visions, which have been developing through the years, ¿no? I think I fit within the tradition of Chicanismo. I feel my voice has, both in Mexico and the United States, some influence in what is going on. I say things, then I hear them resonate and come back to me. They tell me that right or wrong, good or bad, at least I'm awake.

AL CHICANO

Ahí va un corrido, señores,
señores, ahí va un corrido
quiero que cruce el Río Bravo
y llegue hasta los oidos
de aquel que llaman chicano,
de ese que tanto ha sufrido.

Ese que tanto ha sufrido
de sangre y raza es mi hermano,
su padecer me ha dolido,
por eso en mi triste canto
que se le brinde yo pido
un trato justo y humano.

Que acaben ya sus penares,
que acaben sus sentimientos,
que brille un sol de justicia,
que sea la razón su aliento
que vea la luz de la aurora,
que vea que está amaneciendo.

Un grito sordo se escapa
de este mi pecho angustiado
y en el a Dios le pregunto
por que sufre así este hermano,
que nace sin ser culpable
sobre suelo americano.

Sobre suelo americano
ha de seguir mi corrido
y hasta en lejanos poblados
habran de escuchar seguido
este mensaje al hermano
que tanto, tanto ha sufrido.

Desde este México mío
te tiendo humilde mi mano,
no tuerzas nunca el comino,
no temas a los fracasos,
que un día mi hermano querido
tendrás el triunfo en tus manos.

Juan Záizar

TO THE CHICANO

Here goes a corrido, ladies and gentlemen,
Ladies and gentlemen, here goes a corrido,
I want it to cross the Rio Grande
And get to your ears
About those who are called Chicanos,
Those who have suffered so much.

Those who have suffered so much
Of blood and race are my brothers,
Their suffering hurts me,
For this in my sad song,
I salute them and ask
For just and humane treatment.

May there be an end to their sorrows
May there be an end to their painful feelings,
May the sun of justice shine,
May there be reason to live
May they see the light of daybreak,
May they see that it is dawning.

A silent scream escapes
From this my anguished heart.
And of God I ask
Why does my brother suffer so,
Without his fault he was born
On American soil.

On American soil
My corrido will travel
To the distant peoples
Who will frequently hear
This message of my brothers
Who have suffered so, so much.

From this Mexico of mine
I extend my humble hand,
Don't waver on your journey,
Don't fear the failures,
One day my dear brothers
Triumph will be in your hands.

11

Those They Call Chicano

THE CHILDREN—PART I

Their parents, grandparents, or great-grandparents came north years ago. When and why, even who came has faded with each generation. But now the children, or more likely the grandchildren or even the grandchildren's children take up the search for the vital signs in their heritage. On the surface the cycle is typical for almost any immigrant group. A deeper look, however, reveals a special poignancy to the search. Theirs isn't just one European culture that has melded into another. It is unique among cultures.

The entire New World was conquered by European powers. In every case but Mexico the native peoples were exterminated or colonized by pure-blooded Europeans who retain power to the present day. From the intermixing of conquered and conqueror at every level, Mexico evolved into the only mestizo society in the hemisphere. The "cosmic race" of Mexico's leading philosopher of the early twentieth century, José Vasconcelos. La raza *of* los Chicanos. *This is not a matter of casual consequence for a person of mestizo ancestry. Within one body and soul each person struggles to reconcile the conqueror and the conquered, the racial, familial, personal, and spiritual traits of their pre-Hispanic forebears with a deep commitment to Catholicism, the Spanish language, and the formal culture that attends it.*

The result is a people of enormous vigor within whom, as Alan Riding describes in Distant Neighbors, *coexists a strange contrast of both ritual and* disorder that *"illustrates the predominance of the spiritual over the material."* To them, *"the mechanical efficiency, punctuality and organization of an Anglo-Saxon society, in contrast, seem purposeless."*

The irony is in that very thing that lured them north in the first place, the job. The job was, and is, the vehicle that forces them to adapt to mechanical efficiency. That the job could have so great a consequence was not on the immigrants' minds as they stole across the border thinking of the better life they would build in Mexico with their gringo earnings.

But the job demands fundamental change. It demands that immigrants exchange their fatalism for optimism, the optimism that they can control events around them. And that optimism demands they accept the curse of isolation: no one else, not even God, is responsible for that control. The job deepens that isolation because in America your job is the basis for your very identity. What you do is who you are. In Mexico you may have worked to survive, but a job didn't define your life. People there work to live, not live to work. Who you were there was seen in your time to be: Sunday with family in the country, grilling carne asada, corridos sung with compadres and enough tequila, el cerro on horseback.

The job also takes their children. In America the job demands success and success requires, if need be, breaking with parents. It expects the children to earn more, spend more, have more than the mother and father have. The children still love their parents but are just a little ashamed of the mestizo they see in them. They reject it to move ahead in a society not of their parents' making.

And this is the final irony: the reconciliation of the mechanistic society, as exemplified by the job, with their own mestizo heritage. This irony is what the children face in forging a new alloy of themselves that fully integrates all that they are.

RAMIRO QUINTERO
Bail Bondsman
Bryan, Texas

Outside Ramiro Quintero's bail bond office, just across from the county courthouse, double-parked cars and a constant coming and going seem almost frenzied in comparison to the inertia gripping the rest of downtown Bryan. Inside, people line the edges of his tiny waiting room. He's on call twenty-four *hours a day, but he takes his time and gives everyone their due. Adjacent bail bond offices aren't jumping like Mr. Quintero's. Maybe their public relations or advertising aren't as good, but then they charge a percentage. Ramiro has his own formula, a kind of sliding scale gauged on sincerity, necessity, geniality, and motherhood.*

I been residin' here in Brazos County since 1950, when we moved from Burleson County. So I've been here, oh, close to thirty years. But we live a comfortable life here in Brazos County.

My mother's mother was born in Tampico. My grandfather was born and buried in Guadalajara, Jalisco, in the big cemetery over there. My mother was born in Guadalajara. My father was born in the *estado* of Michoacán, in a small community called La Piedad. They used to have a big hog farm in La Piedad. I was there about four years ago, the first time in my life. We're all ancestors from Mexico. All my people live here in Texas, all my brothers and sisters. We have two brothers buried here in Texas.

Well, I was born in a small community by the name of Somerville. The population's about 2,000. It's approximately thirty miles from here.

What happened was right after the Mexican revolution, on my mother's side, they were very prominent people. They were very, very wealthy back in there. But with the turn of the revolution, my grandmother ended up a broke lady, my grandfather also. Very, very broke and discontent. Discouraged, being affluent with plenty a money, with plenty cattle, with plenty land, and overnight to have nothing. They were kind of a shame to society, so they had to get away. So they migrated through the pastures and what-have-you, what little roads there was back then, little villages. They ended up in the small town of Somerville, Texas.

My father came looking for work, to turn a buck. Years earlier he'd heard about the gold rush. So he decided to come to California and he ended up in Texas. There's where he met my mother. It all started from there.

It just so happens that they met there in Somerville, and being young they fell in love. My dad didn't have a dime and my mother didn't have a quarter either, but they fell in love and their first house was a little henhouse. Real small, down poor henhouse, but they were in love, and that little henhouse kept a little roof overhead, and that's all they had.

From there they started working together buildin' a family and started to raise up theirselves. A year or so later they had their first son, Francisco. Francisco happened to be named for my grandfather, which was Francisco Villa Real on my mother's side. We Hispanics always try to name one of our first offspring to the nearest godfather, grandmother, deceased grandmother, or whatever to keep the name in the family. From there they just kept on going.

My father had no formal education whatsoever. He didn't know how to read or write, didn't know about the four seasons of the year, and my mother was his teacher. Through the years she taught him to read and write, add, subtract, general basic information, necessities of life. It was amazing, before too long my father picked up how to read and write, speak and write English fluently, and Spanish also. He was a very sharp man, very sharp. He kept a lesson of everything that he touched, he sure did.

In Somerville there's always been a railroad track. It was the dividin' line between the east side and the west side. And it just so happens the minorities back in there lived on the west side of town, which was always the poor. The browns and the blacks generally had their side of town and that was it. It was segregated, definitely! Segregation was a way of life and was well accepted. So my father seen either you were one side of the track if you were poor, and if you were well-to-do or white you lived on the other. When my brothers were being born and comin' up in life he seen this thing of segregation come up pretty strong. He couldn't fight the system because he didn't have any ammunition as far as money or influence, but he was always bothered with it.

His main goal was to educate his kids, to send 'em to college. They would do without, literally do without. If Christmas came around there was plenty to eat but not no new clothes or nothing. He wanted his kids to get educated. He didn't want his kids to have the problems he had with communication, the problems he had with culture, education, and workin' so hard for a livin'.

He worked manual. He worked the Santa Fe Railroad ties, and his job was to haul lumber all day long on his shoulders. Real hard work, in Texas heat, and then that liquid they put on these railroad ties, they call it creosote. This stuff was bad. It penetrated your clothes and took all the skin off your shoulders.

He worked real hard at the Santa Fe Railroad. We used to talk back about one time he broke an ankle and the way they worked. You had so many ties that you had to do. You had a quota, so many before you made just a few dollars per day. Whether he worked or not his family had to eat. 'Course there was no food stamps, no commodities, no handouts. So with his ankle broke he had to drag his ankle and keep haulin' and keep haulin'. He'd say, "Look here, see the way my foot is? Y'all go to school. Y'all go to school. Don't care if they throw rocks at you." Well they did from time to time, "duck your head, pretend you don't see, you go to school, get your education." These other things in life, you can always get them, but the education they can't take away from you. A hard-workin' old man. Just determination and hard work.

There was eleven in the family, nine boys and two girls. Lucky my mom had those two girls. Back then no Speed Queens an' Norges an' Maytags or nothin' like that. Just a board and hangin' clothes. Life was real hard in them days raisin' eleven kids and sendin' em out, let's see, about seven through college. For a man who didn't have a day of formal education that's something.

In 1950 is when we came to Bryan. Bryan was just a different climate. Bigger city, bigger town, there was more movement. People were different because there was a whole lot more families, more automobiles, more little old jobs, more churches, more different schools. Had about six elementary schools back there, two high schools, two junior highs.

See, over in Somerville there was just one. I take that back; there was two. There was a black school and a white school, and the browns went to the white school. But they were on one side of the classroom and the other side was white. Segregation still existed. But not in Bryan. It did not exist. That was one big change that we seen when we got here, you know.

There was one school in Bryan called La Escuela Ibarra. Actually the name of the school was San Jacinto Elementary, but everybody was Mexican so they called it Escuela Ibarra. A lot of the Hispanics went there by preference, they just wanted to go because the other Hispanics were there. People kinda resented it because we went to Bowie School here. It was about the same distance as La Escuela Ibarra but my father said, "No! You're gonna go to Bowie." There was always talk in town, well why did Mr. Quintero's kids end up in Bowie? Does he think he's too good for Escuela Ibarra? He said, "No, I think Escuela Ibarra is good, but I think this school is a little bit better and I want the better school for my son. If I have to pay a little bit, I'll pay it. That's fine." So he always wanted the best schools, the best education for his kids.

When we got to Bowie School it was a different story. We were accepted. If segregation existed you couldn't notice it. I didn't notice it. There was all the same bathrooms, same cafeteria, same auditorium, the same teachers. You set in class accordin' to alphabetical order, in other words you were not segregated. That was back in the fifties.

What was more of a shock than anything was startin' school. Goin' from a large family, being the last child, and my brothers playin' football and basketball in high school, being on the honor roll, and here I am the last one, the youngest in the family, and here I go to Somerville School District. My first day and Mrs. Welch is over there, and she's s'pose to be real mean and strict and discipline with a big stick. And here I am a six-year-old child that can't defend myself, because I'm too small and I can't even communicate. So, it was something, you can imagine. If you go to a foreign country at our age you can communicate with hands or make signs, you go voluntarily. So I felt in a state of shock that first day and I've never been able to forget it.

I knew little if any words in English before I went to first grade. I didn't know what the word *bathroom* was. So I can feel, I can feel like these youngsters that come here from Mexico. What they went through is what I went through back in 1950, my first day of school. I can see these youngsters taken to school. Their mothers want to participate in the PTA, they can't. They want to participate in organizations, they kind of feel neglected or left out. If it pertains to work they can do it, but when it's a language barrier it's hard. Even if their heart's as big as a watermelon they can't do it. They can't communicate, they can't converse. Then they begin to feel they're inferior. It's real sad.

By the second week of school I had to converse. The other students, they'd make fun and giggle at me.

Our family's always been close. Comin' up, the biggest thing was discipline. The worst thing you could do was bring the folks *una queja* from a neighbor. A *queja* is basically a gripe or a complaint. "Your son broke a limb off my tree," or broke my window, or kicked the chicken. That would tear it. You'd get a whuppin' or a scoldin' or something. The way my dad would punish us is work. Every day he went to work he had chores for brothers or sisters to do. Needless to say, he would keep up with them. He would just tell us once and that was all. You do this, you feed the hogs, you see about the chickens, you take care of the little cows, you milk the cow. Everybody had chores. Every afternoon he'd come by, "What happened?"

"Well, I had to go help the other brother."

"No, no, your job was this. Go finish it up, because it's not done." If it's ten o'clock at night you'd finish it. There was always discipline and control over the family. That was the main thing, discipline and control. They were not whoopers or hollerers or screamers. They just spoke one time and that was it. The father was the breadwinner, the father was in charge of the whole house, what he said went, and the mother went along with him. There was no room for discussion. He was the boss and he never was wrong. No matter how wrong he could be, he still was right and that was the way of life. He kept real control of the family. He knew where everybody was at, and the later you came in at night the earlier you would get up the next day to go to work. You sure would, yes sir. Kept up on everyone, stayed on top of everything.

Nowadays mother works late, father works late, nobody takes charge. That was just a different environment entirely. Now there's nobody home. Summertime no tellin' what kids do around the house. Not then; there was too much to do. Children kinda grew up faster. They learned a little bit more about responsibility. You know, if you had to cut two or three cords a wood to make four or five dollars, well you weren't gonna explode with that four or five dollars. And if your sister had to be on a board to wash your clothes, she was gonna make pretty damn sure you didn't get 'em all tore up and bent out of shape. It was too hard.

We didn't always have new clothes, but we had plenty to eat. How my father did it, I don't know. He was a horse trader. He'd trade chickens into the hogs. There might have been three or four hogs today an' he might have thirty or forty tomorrow. He learned the value of the dollar quick, and he understood the value of things. If he saw a cow worth three or four dollars, he'd take that cow and buy it and convert that to four or five, in a day or two. He would take a cow and trade it for three or four pigs. Then he might slaughter the pigs and buy some corn and take that corn and change it for somethin' else and he kept on.

He'd leave the house on Saturdays early in the mornin' with two or three pigs and when he come back he'd have three or four dozens of chickens and maybe a horse or mule or something. If he could prosper a little bit, he would. He would never come home empty-handed. He brought somethin' home every time. Saturday was just a big day. Other people took all day off to go get a haircut. He took off Saturday to try to prosper and try to make a dollar or two. That's how he managed to survive and send all those kids to school.

When I graduated from high school, I had a real hard decision to make. I'd been thinkin' about it, and I had seen my other brothers go to college an' my mother an' father workin' so hard. They were up in the age range where they had sent so many to school, and I could not see them burdened for another four or five years. So I decided to take a trade. I became a master plumber by the age of nineteen and a half. In one year and a half I gained my masters in the plumbing industry. I did.

Then through many sacrifices my dad had prospered and you know he was well liked in the community. Over the years he was able to acquire some property, lots and houses, this type of thing. You have a big family, you always gonna have a lot of friends. And my daddy's friends' sons and daughters would get into trouble, and knowin' he had a little monetary value, they were always comin' to him and, "Hey, my brother-in-law's in jail." "My son-in-law's in jail, could you post a bond for me?"

Back in the good old days there wasn't so many requirements like we have right now. If the sheriff knew you were in good standing, he knew you, he knew the people, the main thing was just to make sure they went back to court to take care of their business.

I kinda got interested in it. About 1978 I decided to venture into it. There's two things in this that you have to learn quick. One, you can't be too greedy. Being greedy can cost you money. Makin' quick decisions can cost you money. You have to be cautious and try to judge people. You know, what kinda character they are. So you have to have a certain judgment of character. If you're goin' to be tryin' to help these people, which we do from time to time, you have to understand their position, you have to understand what brought this thing about. I can't just take their money and put them on the streets. I have a moral obligation to all my clients.

And I ask them to come by. You got problems or somethin' like that, well come by. Come by and let's talk about it. Over the years, people have gotten a lot of trust in me. We've made a lot of citizens out of a lot of bad people. It's just judgment.

I'm more satisfied in my day's work if a mother comes to me crying over here and tells me she's got a problem and she ain't got $35 in her pocket. I'll be glad to help her because I'm a father and I come from a poor family. I'll bend over backward to help her if she's trying to help herself. I'd rather help her than a man comin' in with a bunch of money tryin' to impress me.

We meet a lot of wonderful people, wonderful mothers that rejoice when things are not as bad as they expected. They go see these attorneys who blow it outta proportion. They want so much money, to keep em outta the pen, knowin' they're not gonna go to the pen. My clients say, "You know what, you make more sense than my attorney."

I say, "Well you know what, first of all, I don't have to lie to you. Second of all, I deal with every particular court every day." I know how much time is involved. When they start to plea bargain I know the maximum, I know the minimum because I have more people comin' through. An attorney can only represent one particular client at a time. What's their sign say? "Practicing Attorney." They're practicing with your money. Oh boy. It's terrible.

We make bad decisions from time to time. Some people will fool you. Some people are cons and you fall for it. I think, hey, you learn from the lessons in life. It's not gonna kill you to take a lickin' every now and then. But as long as there's a poor man or a poor woman out there comes into my office and they're sincere, I'll work out something with them. I don't care if it's $5 a month or $5 a year. I'll do it.

We have three sons and one daughter. My daughter works here in the afternoons, she goes to college. So it's kinda family-owned business. Who knows, it might prosper one of these days. If it would I could go over to Mexico more often.

I love Mexico. I purchased a small ranch over there, I go every six months to get away from that almighty dollar and the hustle, bustle. We constantly kill ourself. We say I've got to do this, I've got to do that, I've got to be to the bank by nine o'clock. We're just pressured and keepin' our body tense. That's one of the reasons I don't have a watch. I could care less about the time. I don't have to be watching that watch all the time. So when I get off, I just get off. If it takes five hours, if it takes six, fine and dandy. It's very complex here and everything's got a deadline. Over there they take life easy. They enjoy their families more. They converse with their families. In the afternoons they sit on the porch or patio. Even the poorest man has an old mesquite tree. He'll sit under there with his wife and family. They'll sit out there.

It's about two hundred miles from the border. But we enjoy it. We've got a lot of work to do, but hopefully I'll retire out there one of these days. I love it. I just relax.

MARY MARGARET NAVAR
Niece of Domitila Navar*
Communications and Marketing Consultant
Austin, Texas

You can almost guess Mary Margaret's story upon meeting her. In 105 degrees of humid Texas heat she is completely cool. Not even a glisten graces her upper lip. Personality traits of determination, defiance, perfection, confidence, sympathy, and warmth are impeccably described in her dress: a lovely bright rose silk blouse with mauve linen pants, stockings that match perfectly, and suede shoes just a shade deeper. A discourse on color and texture refined from her Mexican heritage.

My older brothers are named José Aldaberto, Rafael Francisco, and Luis Seferino, Spanish names about as ancient as you can come up with. But I was born in the assimilation years so they named me Mary Margaret, or as my aunts, the matriarchs, call me, Maria Margarita. They never call me Mary Margaret.

Growing up in the assimilation years was very different. Because of the heavy, heavy racism they decided I would learn only English. But the maid taught me Spanish reading comic books. I would go to her room at night and we'd hang out. She'd smoke and I'd read Mexican comic books and we'd watch Mexican soap operas. On Mondays and Tuesdays when she was washing and ironing she would sit me up on top of the washer, and while she ironed I would read. She would make me read aloud and in Spanish to her. So I learned it anyway, and now my verbal structures are more Spanish than English.

*See chapter 8.

I was born January 22, 1951, in El Paso, Texas, and grew up in a very conservative Catholic family. I went to Catholic kindergarten, grade school, high school, and then two years at U.T. El Paso. As a junior I transferred to University of Texas at Austin. Basically I did that to get out of El Paso and expand my horizons. I felt Austin could provide that and it did. I've been living in Austin for eighteen years.

My father and his family came from Durango, Mexico, from Parral and Corrales. My great-grandfather owned land in that area. I think they had crops or grazed cattle, I'm not sure which. During the revolution years, 1910 or so, Pancho Villa was going around collecting resources. Somehow my great-grandfather did not see eye to eye with Pancho Villa. They exchanged threats on many occasions. The story is that Pancho Villa would ride into the family compound looking for children to take as hostages so he could force my great-grandfather into giving him what he wanted. It was getting pretty heated. Pancho Villa was becoming very popular, so my great-grandfather decided to head north with all his family.

They wanted to get back to Spain. That was their dream. A priest in the state of Durango agreed to take them, but they weren't able to bring anything, just a single chest filled with everything they had. They grabbed the children, and with that one chest got on the train heading north. The story is that theirs was the last train to cross a particular bridge before Pancho Villa had it blown up.

They finally made it to El Paso and the priest gets sick and dies. There they are, penniless.

My grandfather, a young man at the time, and already married to my grandmother, decided to buy a cow. One cow, a milking cow to feed the family. Well after feeding the family he found there was milk left over. So he started to put it in bottles and sell it. When they got a little more money coming in they bought a second cow and eventually built up a whole herd and a little dairy.

My grandfather built this all from one cow, named La Paloma. It's an immigrant survival story, but it was her, that cow, who helped them survive. My aunt says that there were days that they went without eating anything because here they are strangers in a land that they didn't know. They struggled for many years.

My grandmother and grandfather had seven sons and three daughters, and all of them, except my two aunts who never married, had an average of four to six children. So on my father's side of the family, including cousins and second cousins, there are at least a hundred people related to me. My generation has already had children, and those children have had children.

The family, my father's side of the family, has always been very Catholic and very devout. In the early sixties they got special Papal permission, in what we call the big house, to build a private chapel. At that time it was the only private chapel in the state of Texas. They have been big supporters of the local Franciscan and nun orders. Every time a cow or some kind of steer is slaughtered they distribute the meat amongst the family, the seminary, and convents.

On my mother's side, my grandparents are from New Mexico. My grandmother on my maternal side comes from Luna County. Luna County was named for her grandfather. They also moved to El Paso and started a dairy farm. As a matter of fact the families worked together. My maternal grandfather would supply my paternal grandfather with raw milk to process and sell. One was the producer and the other was the distributor.

Back in those horse-and-buggy days they would bring the big tanks—ten-gallon drums—to my paternal grandfather's house. That's when my father met my mother. My father totally checks out this gorgeous woman and says, "Who is that? I want to meet her."

My mother's side really didn't immigrate. They were already in New Mexico, the precursors to what became that part of the United States. There was always this perspective that they were not Mexican. They considered themselves Hispanic.

When my grandmother and grandfather were alive, my two aunts would cook for the entire family every single Sunday. It was my grandfather's dictum that all the family had to come together. If you weren't there, and he always knew if you didn't show up, boy, were you in trouble! You got raked over the coals. Your parents got raked over the coals. Everybody had to be present and accounted for. Sundays we would have this massive dinner where they would lay out this long table with huge pots of mole or enchiladas, *arroz, frijoles, ensalada. No, todas las semanas, cada semana. No te imaginas! Entonces* they had a dining room table that stretched out forty feet long. Every Sunday I'd say fifty people came together. It was fun for the kids, totally. We got to hook up and play. We were right there in the dairy, so we'd take off into the haystacks, a whole other world. You can imagine. I would say they probably did that for twenty years. Then my grandpa died in the early sixties, the aunts got older, and it kind of waned. Lucky I'm not married. I would have been the one to come up with all of those dinners.

Well, I had to escape to Austin. Otherwise I would have been married to some lawyer from Juárez. In fact, that's the point at which I decided I had to get out of town. When I was at UTEP there was a lawyer from Juárez. He proposed to me and, you know, I almost accepted. Except, and I can remember so clearly, I was sitting at the student union one afternoon thinking to myself, "I can't do this. I can't go through with it. I have to get out of town." That's when I decided to transfer to Austin and pursue my education instead. I denied his proposal. That's okay, six months later he was married anyway. So sincere!

It turned out that my best friend from high school wanted to go to Austin to do architecture school. So I said, "Well I'm coming with you. I'm going to study languages and culture." That's what I did.

It was tight. I almost didn't get away. They let me go because of my father. Now, what happened was, as a young man he had a beautiful tenor voice. Well it turns out that he auditioned for Arthur Godfrey in Chicago. Arthur Godfrey wanted to be his agent and took him to New York City to audition for the Metropolitan Opera. They adored him. They totally begged him to please come to New York. Well this was a very difficult decision for him because it meant leaving the family business, traveling nine months of the year; basically leaving his family. He decided not to accept their offer. I think he regretted that decision the rest of his life. So when I come up with this bright idea to fanny off to Austin to pursue my education, he did not hesitate more than two seconds.

"You want to go to Austin to pursue your education? Fine. I'm 100 percent behind you."

I can thank Arthur Godfrey.

My father ended up giving private family concerts the rest of his life. His good friend who was a pianist would come over on Friday nights, sit there and play songs, and he would sing for hours. Or we would have a dinner. My mother and father were very social when they were younger. They liked to entertain their friends. After dinner they would sit, you know like in the old salon days, and my father would sing. He loved, loved, loved music. He had, he has, somewhere in the angelic choruses, a beautiful, beautiful voice.

My mother did not want me to leave El Paso. She fought hard. I was her baby.

Austin opened up a lot of options for me that I never knew existed. Here, the university is centripetal, pulling in. In El Paso the university is centrifugal, where people come for their classes and then leave.

People want to stay here. That's what happened to me. So for many years my mother would insist, "Okay, I'm going to let you go to school, but as soon as you finish you're going to come back." Naturally I enrolled in every possible class that would keep me here. Year after year after year. So I ended up with an undergraduate, then a master's. One year I worked at the French/Italian department, and then I got into graduate school in comparative literature. Later I transferred into anthropology and folklore, which was just—I loved it—a *métier* that I had been looking for.

As a part of my folklore program, I took a course in Museology, and one of the projects was to put together a—pretend—proposal for a museum exhibit. The best project was actually going to be sent to the National Endowment for the Humanities for funding. I had hooked up with a colleague, and ours turned out to be the best project and was submitted. We got money; it was a show on religious home altars that ended up both an in-house and traveling exhibit. From there I went to Washington as a fellow for the National Endowment for the Arts, the folk art program. That's how I learned the pragmatics of proposals.

Back in Austin I was able to give technical assistance to groups who needed to know what Washington wanted to see. I went into business, into membership development and public relations for the Hispanic Chamber of Commerce. This meant implementing my anthropological skills and getting to know the community and what programs would establish the appropriate visibility and organizational development.

My great-grandfather and my grandfather were both very, very strong entrepreneurs; having left all their resources in Durango, they built a comfortable status in the community. I never experienced discrimination. My family has always been well respected in both the

The Future

Anglo and the Hispanic communities, though they probably were discriminated against early on when they didn't have a lot of assets. The original dairy name was San Antonio Dairies, but in 1938 or 1939, they changed the name to Farmers' Dairies, which obviously is an Anglo name. They wanted to fit in.

I grew up aware of economic class, of different status, because of all the people who worked for the family and who I developed friendships with. Ranching of course is a male arena. Except here comes my dad with his little sweetheart. The ranch hands would saddle my horse and help me with grooming. They and my father taught me a lot of horse and ranching skills. So even though I personally grew up in comfortable surroundings and had the best of all possible resources, I knew that other worlds existed not as fortunate as mine. Also my father always instilled in us a sense of humility. You were never to flash assets. You always were to be a humble person. He would refer to himself, and I'm talking about a partner in a multi-million-dollar operation, as a cowpoke.

The early fifties were heavy assimilation years. Children were punished for speaking Spanish in school. You were sent home, or you were sent to the principal. It was like cultural obliteration.

So here I am, this West Texas desert podunk girl. I'm thrown in the middle of this forty-thousand-student campus. At that time there were very few Chicanos at this campus, probably like 3 percent. So I didn't have a lot of people to relate to who were Chicano. But I hooked up with some people and just kind of made friends across the spectrum. I acclimated very well.

I also became aware of another reality. The activists in the Chicano community were very pro Pancho Villa and pro agrarian reform. But I came from a family of land bearers who were the enemy of Pancho Villa. So I pulled back. I rarely confessed that I came from a landholding family because that was a target of criticism back in the Chicano activist days of the early seventies. I was very private about that information, always. I learned a lot from the Chicano movement and I agreed with the struggle because I myself had seen it in the lives of my family's workers. In many ways I agreed with the struggle, yet my family had struggled too, and I held to that. Later, in my anthropologist's training I realized that there are as many Hispanic, Mexican, Chicano experiences as there are realities, and mine was just one example of millions that

exist. There was nothing to be ashamed of. I was able to retrieve that part of my heritage.

My mother, interestingly enough, even though she fought my departure, was a very independent woman. She's the one who ran all the house finances. She trained herself through correspondence courses to be an interior designer and architect and has built several churches in the El Paso area: the Franciscan Monastery, the Nun's Church, and another church down in the valley. She built them. She's a brilliant woman and she's had only an eighth-grade education. It wasn't a career for her, because she never put it before my father. My father always came first. And here was an opportunity for me to take her as a role model and carry it one step further, which was to put my career first.

There are certain traditional behaviors that I don't accept for myself. I don't have to get married. I don't have to stay home. I don't have to have children. The rules no longer are applicable. The immigrants physically cross the border into the United States, then their descendants cross mental borders from worldview to worldview: from worldviews that are more conservative, patriarchal, to worldviews that are more liberal and egalitarian.

I had very few examples other than my mother. My aunts dedicated their lives to my grandparents, and then after my grandparents died they dedicated their lives to their brothers, my uncles. My uncles are there every afternoon. They drop by at four o'clock for beer, peanuts, a snack, to say hello, see what's going on, and then leave. It's a tradition. Their lives are totally for their brothers. It's a study of collectivism versus individuation. They started as a collective, a very conservative clan, unit. Now certain shoots have started to individuate. Crossing that border for myself was a consequence of following my instincts. Back then there was something that told me that I had to get out. If I didn't, I knew the road was right there. I was already looking at my future, and it choked me. I couldn't do it. In crossing that border the first step was taking any opportunity that was there, telling my friend on her way to Austin, "I'm hooking a ride with you." Getting here, then realizing that I could make it by myself, creating a new circle of friends, new circles of influence, new circles of resources, and new realities.

I followed a mystical thread and I count my blessings every day.

MARIO DEL CAMPO
Son of Martin del Campo*
Director of Marketing
San Francisco, California

He is head of marketing for his father's successful architectural practice. At first glance Mario is indistinguishable from other good-looking young San Francisco professionals. Tall, with dark, wavy hair and fair skin, he's hard to classify. His dress is professional but not Montgomery Street. His classic white shirt is tailored with a fullness brought in at the waist. The traditional charcoal tweed wool pants are also full. There's a style to them, almost hip. But these details become the background, the setting. Mario's deep voice is the focus. He speaks in measured cadence, almost as at a poetry reading.

Very conveniently, my earliest memories are of right before we left for Mexico. At the time we lived in Mill Valley. It was the only time we lived in one of my father's designed homes. It was a nice redwood house overlooking the Bay. So right around 1962 or 1963 we were getting ready. "You know," my father told me, "we will be going to Mexico. We are going to help your grandfather." His business was just getting underway. It was the Hotel Victoria in Oaxaca.

I remember hearing this news and thinking, "Oh my God!" I knew of my Mexican heritage in a very vague way, but I certainly didn't think of myself as bicultural. At that point in my life I was just a normal Mill Valley kid, a Marin kid from the early sixties. I did remember my grandfather visiting and being aware of the difference, of the Spanish. But it was a great shock to me. I guess I was about five and you know, I was not pleased.

It was just like waking up. Mexico was so much more a country of smells and sounds; the United States was very clean and sterile. I remember arriving in Oaxaca and the school made of stone, the arches, the big Mexican flags, the displays of patriotism, and how old the culture was. Really, it was impressive to me.

*See chapter 9.

Before I knew it, I was speaking Spanish. I was able to relate to kids my own age, to find out what kids in Mexico were thinking about. Yet because I lived in my parents' hotel, I was also constantly exposed to American and European kids. Mostly I would hang out with American kids, and they would bring bits of news about what was going on back home, the latest fad.

Like I remember one kid telling all about *The Man from U.N.C.L.E.* This was really the thing. You weren't cool if you didn't know about *The Man from U.N.C.L.E.* My sisters even brought me a little attaché case with guns and spy stuff so I could be sort of a James Bondian.

It was weird. They released some *Man from U.N.C.L.E.* episodes as movies in Mexico. Since there was no TV at that time in Oaxaca, they brought TV shows with subtitles dubbed in Spanish. It's so different to see these shows on a big screen. Very strange. Like I remember seeing an episode of *I Dream of Jeannie,* down there in one of those big old-fashioned movie theaters.

I felt so much like a gringo, even after I learned Spanish. But at some point or another I started to make friends, and pretty soon everybody wanted to come up and play at the hotel. The swimming pool, that was my big feature. I had these little boats we would sail in the pool. It was fun—electric boats.

Oaxaca was just something. It was a striking place. Life moved slower; you couldn't be more immersed in Mexico. In Oaxaca it was raw milk; you had to boil it. The food was very different. Mole, for instance—what an incredible substance. Now it's very much the thing in Southwestern cooking, but at the time I remember thinking, "Oh my God, chocolate chicken?" I've heard the secret ingredient is Pepsi.

But mostly Mexico is associated in my thinking, in my mind, with the strongest things of life, the realities: life, death, changes. I think this grew out of two very personal experiences.

I developed a special friendship with a hotel employee. He was our chauffeur and would also shop for the kitchen. He'd also pick me up from school, and we'd drive around in a blue '57 Chevy station wagon. My friends and I were trying to amass our airplane collections, and he used to save little airplanes out of Jell-O containers for me. So I could just trade for anything. Then in the midst of our friendship he developed a brain tumor and died. Almost simultaneously my grandfather died.

That period encoded my brain with those strong things that affect you, the realities: life, death, changes. And I was six, just the age to be very impressionable.

It's easier now for me to talk about the culture of Oaxaca and how interesting I found it, but I really missed the United States. At the time my feeling was more like, "Oh yeh, it's okay, you know, but I like Safeway." The media especially. No TV was a shocker. Before we left for Mexico my father had been down on TV, and for a while we had no TV in the house. I watched it at other people's houses, but that made it forbidden fruit. By the time I got back from Mexico that was like all I wanted, a TV. I just became immersed in what I had missed. I became a real media fiend, and that persists to this day.

When my sisters visited my father in '67 or '68, they found Mexican boyfriends, musicians. Later after we returned to the United States they came up to visit. Their single records were out, and they were flush with their first success. They were Beatles-type groups, Beatles clothes and Beatles hair. As the little brother, I just thought these guys were really cool.

There was really a nice feel from them. They were making a little money and starting to discover themselves and to be creative. Then, all of a sudden they were gone. We just didn't hear about them anymore. It was when the Plaza de Tlateloco massacre happened, in '68. I'm sure they were grabbed and at the very least had their hair cut off in the streets.

The last time I was in Mexico was October 1988. It was the twentieth anniversary of that massacre. There was a big rally, with Cárdenas as spiritual leader, to remember what happened to those students. I think a lot of people were radicalized by those events. I elicited all kinds of stories from my grandmother. It helps you realize the effect that something like Tiananmen Square can have twenty years down the line. It's shocking. My grandmother and all of her friends had stories about medical students and wonderful young people they knew who had been killed. Their bodies were never found. Nobody knows what happened or how many died.*

*In 1968, just before the Olympics in Mexico City, a demonstration by students and workers was brutally suppressed by the Mexican Army. The similarity of that event

One friend of mine, a Hispanic Sephardic Jew, thought it was amazing that I would come out and announce myself as part Mexican. "Oh, you're not really Hispanic. You're not really Chicano. Your ancestors were Europeans." Friends have said that to me. "Oh Mexico, greasy country!" Another time my sister went to Texas with a boyfriend and she was shocked. She never realized that there was prejudice against Mexican-Americans. They said, "Wow, why do you call yourself Margarita? You look so nice and white, you could just call yourself Margie or something. No one would know." That experience made my family a little more cognizant of not wanting to abandon our Mexicanness.

A lot of these people didn't know about Mexico. Chicanos here don't know. Sometimes I think about Chicano art and low riders and I feel they're culturally impoverished. If only they had more of a clue of what's going on there. It reminds me of someone who's trying to reconstruct a lost civilization from fragments. Like they have a *Virgen de Guadalupe*, a picture of a *pachuco* from the forties, a "zoot suiter," and a picture of the Mexican eagle. But sometimes I feel if only they could go to Mexico they'd somehow understand the totality of it.

I also know other Mexican-Americans who are very intimidated by the whole thing, scared. All they know is that some people may be prejudiced against them. So the only cultural heritage they have is a sense of something dark hanging over their heads.

After returning from Mexico I had sort of an ugly duckling period, but by the time I was a senior in Lick-Wilmerding High School I was really enjoying myself. I guess you could say that I had really hit my stride. I was starting to do art and graphic design, and I was beginning to have some clients. But it was in college, the California College of Arts and Crafts, that I started to dig back in my culture. I began to realize that you don't just pull these things out of thin air. I used to have the worst time coming up with ideas. I was always a refinement kind of person. You could bring me the smallest grain of an idea or a rough sketch and I'd love to take it and work it over and turn it into something. But to come up with something original, that

---

to the massacre of students by the Chinese Army in 1989 in Beijing is especially evident in the way both were denied and rewritten, outright and unequivocally, by their respective governments.

was what first drove me back into my Mexican culture. I needed some kind of universe of images, and I discovered how rich that culture had been.

There was great admiration at CCAC for Diego Rivera, Orozco, and Siqueiros, muralism in general. Also there was interesting Chicano art being done here, street art, the guys who manage to channel their graffiti impulses into doing stuff on the walls. There was one kid at CCAC who was asking me, "What is that Chicano lettering font they always use?" It's just so funny. There is a certain way of lettering everything on the walls, even the price tags in the Mission. I used to try to copy it down, to make an alphabet of it. It's very difficult.

My last stay of any length in Mexico came as the result of a job offer to sell real estate in Cabo San Lucas. That's a totally different world. In Baja California the people don't seem to realize that they're part of Mexico. They'd just as soon think of themselves as part of the United States or somewhere in between.

I met my girlfriend, Valerie, in Cabo. We've lived together ten years now. She loves Mexico and she's trying to learn Spanish. My family loves her. It's a real toughie though, because Valerie's Jewish. I don't really feel Catholic, but right from the get-go this is what has held up getting married. I imagine we'll find some really reformed rabbi who isn't closeminded and make our own ceremony. It will have to be a multicultural ceremony.

Before I went to Cabo I had started my first musical group playing a sixties rhythm and blues, like the early Rolling Stones or Beatles. But by the time I got to Cabo we had moved into punk. They couldn't figure out where I was coming from down there. Everyone there was into country-western and margaritaville. Disco was also a big thing and that, I was sure, was going to be the death of all culture.

Now, I'm starting a band again. We've started exploring soul music, all kinds of indigenous music: Mexican, Tex-Mex, border. I've had real trouble incorporating Mexican themes and musical styles. It might be because I'm playing with *gringos*. They like the idea of Mexican-tinged music, but I think they find it difficult to get that kind of groove. It's not that dissimilar from soul. Part of the problem is that these guys are not Californian. To them, I'm Italian. It barely enters their mind that I'm Mexican. They call me Mary-o. But if we can get to the point where we reanimate all the little fragments of these different cultures it will be great. That's my goal in all my art, no, in my life.

ANA DE HARO
Disk Jockey
El Paso, Texas

Copper-colored curls, milky-white skin, petite but rounded; yes, she does resemble Goya's famous Maya. But Maya doesn't look anything like the hip, dynamic DJ belting out jokes, news briefs, and updates on the latest trends, forecasts, fads, movies, and music—the wake-up jolt more effective than a strong cup of coffee for thousands of El Pasoans.

I really don't have time for acting anymore. It was really a fluke that I got into radio; I never even considered it. In high school I used to pay someone to do my radio shift. And here I am, seven years in radio.

I have to be at work so early in the morning, and we put in so many hours. On the air it's just four hours, but off it's doing commercials, planning for the next day's show, public appearances, live broadcasts. I really don't have time. Plus, I think I've developed, by being behind the microphone where nobody sees you, a mask. Right now theater would probably be very, very difficult for me, because you have to become a child when you get onstage and not have any inhibitions whatsoever. I miss it a lot. I miss the happiness I used to get from it, and the strength.

I never knew. When I first got in front of a microphone it was so intimidating not to know who I was talking to. When you're on a stage, even if you can't even see the audience, you can feel them and you can feel which way they're leaning. They give you an energy. You know that you're performing well by their laughter or their silence. In radio there's nothing like that.

When I first started on the radio I didn't know who I was talking to. It was so strange. But because the Rio Grande Valley is 90 to 95 percent Hispanic, I got a picture of my mother, someone very, very typical Rio Grande Valley, and when I talked on the radio it was like talking to my mom. It was right on target. If I had gone to Idaho or to Nebraska and put a picture of my mother in front of the microphone,

I don't think they would have connected with me. But she is Mexican and I had a sense of what was important in her life; I could select my stories. I mean you have a two-minute newscast. You have to be selective and you have to decide what's important to your listeners. I was able to decide by virtue of knowing my audience, even though it was my mother.

My father was a big storyteller, and I grew up at the dinner table just listening to his family history. He always described the story of how his family left on an ocean liner from the Port of Veracruz to New Orleans, where his father had gotten a job. His mother's father was there at the port to say good-bye to them. They wouldn't leave the deck and go downstairs until they had waved good-bye to their grandfather. It was the last time they saw him, because he passed away shortly afterward. But they moved to New Orleans. So he grew up in the United States, but like his father he was born in Mexico City. His mother was from Veracruz.

My grandfather's family came from Spain, and my grandfather's mother and father were the *chambelán* and lady-in-waiting to Maximilian and Carlotta. He was brought up and tutored in that aristocratic environment. My grandfather knew eight languages, and he taught my father six.

My mother didn't come to the United States until she married my father. She is from Monterrey. There were eight kids in the family, and she was brought up in a very strict environment. She was a Garza, Garza Delgado. Her father was a Garza Nieto and a big businessman, very involved in politics. He was governor of the state of Nuevo León when my mother was growing up. I only met my grandmothers. My grandfathers had died, but they had a big impact on both of my parents' lives.

My father was the one who took a lot of pride in his background, I guess because his family had come from the town of Haro in Spain. When I went to Spain four years ago, I made a point of going to Haro. It's in the wine-growing area near Burgos. According to the family history, my great-great-great-grandfather was the count. He was Conde de Haro, and his daughter married the Duke of Alba. Have you ever seen the Venus de Milo painting hanging in the London National Art Gallery? Venus is looking in a mirror at Cupid. According to the family history, that painting was part of the de Haro's dowry when she married the Duke of Alba. She became the Duchess of Alba, who had the illustrious affair with Goya. She was the *Maya Desnuda;* I think we have the same body, because she's kind of chunky on the bottom too. That's in my father's family papers. So he always liked to tell us these stories, and to me growing up and listening at the dinner table, it was like a land so far away with princesses and counts.

A lot of times I run across people that say, "Well, you're not Mexican." But I'm probably more Mexican than a lot of people, because both my parents were born in Mexico. I'm a first-generation American, but I've retained their pride.

I knew early in life that being Mexican was different. I was proud of it, but there were many times in my life that people wanted me to be ashamed. When I was growing up in San Antonio I remember kids telling me, "Well don't tell my parents that you're Mexican, otherwise you can't come over," or "Don't speak Spanish at our house because we're not allowed to hang out with Mexicans." We lived in a white middle-class neighborhood in San Antonio. San Antonio now is one of the most Hispanic cities in the country. But when I was growing up there in the early sixties there was a lot of prejudice.

South Texas, the Rio Grande Valley, is even more Hispanic than San Antonio. Even so, when I first moved there, in fifth grade, the same story. They had upper, middle, and lower levels. I was in upper level, and I noticed right off the bat that that's where all the white people were, and the lower level was where all the Mexicans were.

But you see changes. The Rio Grande Valley city government has made progress in incorporating Hispanics into power. And from what I understand, even El Paso has changed quite a bit. For the longest time, white people were in power.

I had a very politically involved father. He was a personal secretary to Henry Wallace when he was vice president under Franklin D. Roosevelt. Then he was in the OSS during World War II, before it became the CIA. I remember growing up, my education, more than the twelve years that I spent in formal schooling, was at the dinner table. History, as far as learning about World War II, as far as learning about economics, the way political systems work, it was all at the dinner table. Even though my father had grown up in the United States, he retained many Hispanic values. But there were lots of differences between my parents, because my mother didn't move here until after she married.

The Rio Grande Valley was nice for my mother because she's like most Hispanics: very, very close to her family. There, they were only four hours away. When my father first brought her over from Monterrey to San Antonio, he was a college professor. At that time it was a good profession, but he wasn't making *beaucoup dinero*. My mother was so accustomed to having maids and cooks that she was just lost. Really lost and homesick, because she didn't speak any English.

According to my dad, it was love at first sight. They were both older when they got married; my mother was thirty-seven and he was forty-two.

Now my grandmother, you would think that she would be happy about letting her daughter, who was thirty-seven years old, get married. Quite the contrary: "Why do you have to get married? You have everything you need here. You have a house, you have food, you don't need to get married. Don't worry about it." She really wanted to hold on to her, but I think my grandmother knew that my mother was going to have to move far away, and in Mexico you try to keep the family all close together.

My mother was used to parties and teas and traveling and charity work with the church. She was used to that type of lifestyle. It was quite different. Even though they're both from Mexico, I don't consider them to be traditional Mexicans whatsoever.

My father was not macho at all. He understood. He had my mother on a pedestal, and he understood the changes she had to go through to adjust to the type of lifestyle she had never lived before. So he would allow her to go home and see her family whenever she would start getting depressed. From what I have seen, a lot of Mexican men will not allow that. You're their woman and you don't travel by yourself. You travel with them.

Still, I kind of envy my mother, because she has three brothers and four sisters and they are one tight family, even after my grandmother passed away. Her best friend is her first cousin, who is like one month older. She grew up with all her family right there, whereas I grew up with my family either being in Monterrey, Dallas, California, or New Orleans.

When I moved out of the house I thought my mother was going to have a heart attack. It just simply is not done, especially for a woman.

My aunts are like, "Oh God, I just can't believe that she did that!" and, "You know what they say about women who live alone." I must have an exciting life as far as they're concerned. Here I am, waking up at 3:30 A.M. to be on the radio at 6:00 in the morning. They think that I'm out until all hours, but I'm in bed by 9:00.

It's interesting how my parents' attitudes meshed. My father was such a liberal, liberal Democrat. I suppose because he was brought up in Dallas for most of his life, and because he had gone to Southern Methodist University and Georgetown University and had worked in Washington, D.C., and all over the world, his attitudes were very, very liberal. And my mother, very, very strict, very, very Catholic. I kind of ended up in the middle. I have a lot of my father's social attitudes and a lot of my mother's moral views.

I really never thought I could live up to my mother's expectations as to what a girl should be like. I think that what she wanted was a dainty little girl who wanted to stay home, play with dolls, and cook. And I liked playing with dolls, but I also liked playing football with my brothers and playing catch with my dad. I used to go to the basketball games with my father, and I was always very, very independent and outspoken. If I had an opinion on something I would say it. I'm the youngest and the only girl.

I was a cheerleader in junior high, but my mother didn't understand. She didn't think football games and cheerleading were very important, because when she was growing up in Mexico they didn't have anything like that. I'll never forget when she told me I couldn't do the splits because no man would ever marry me. My father would go to my football games faithfully when I was a cheerleader, but my mother never went. And when I would tell her, "Mother, I need a dress for homecoming," she didn't understand the concept of homecoming or proms. It hurt. Instead of a *quinzeañera,* I had a big "sweet sixteen" party.

My father had cancer when I was in high school, and I was sent to spend a summer with relatives in Monterrey. It was strange to spend three months with a bunch of Mexican teenage girls. I know how to act and I know the culture very well after dealing with it. They all worried about their appearance, perfect nails, and all that. They didn't like blue jeans or shorts. Shorts! I might as well have been a streetwalker. But I was their cousin, and they would take me to their *cenas,* but they would like find the weirdest guy to introduce me to. And it was like an insult. *"Ah es mi prima, la gringa."* You know, when I'm in the

United States I'm a Mexican and when I go over there I'm a *gringa.* If I wanted to talk to a guy in the United States, no problem. But over there it's like you're loose. No, it was very different, and I didn't know how to find the happy medium. I started acting like them, and when I came back to school in the fall I would go up to people and try to give them an *abrazo,* a hug. I think they thought I was queer or something, but that's what I had done all summer long.

I had to really use my acting ability. I act very different when I speak each language. When I speak in English I'm loud, playful. In Spanish I speak more quietly and proper.

I liked drama, which wasn't too pleasing to my mother. My mother told me that it was okay in high school, just as a hobby. She understood that I liked to be a ham because she was the same way. But as a career, well you know only loose women became actresses.

There was a play I did my senior year in which I had to kiss the boy onstage. It was just a little kiss. Just smack! My mother went to the show and I was a nervous wreck. I thought my mother was going to faint. "Oh, what is everybody going to say?"

Then in college, I didn't even tell my mother, it was a Harold Pinter drama called *The Birthday Party.* I just knew she would hate it. I played a little floozy, this little eighteen-year-old girl who wanted to play around. She gets drunk, the play never actually says, but supposedly she was violated on the dinner table. I didn't tell my mother that I was in this play, but opening night for some strange reason, I guess mothers have that sixth sense, she was there.

She locked me out of the house! I was a disgrace to the family and God forbid that anybody find out. My father had already passed away, but all my father's friends were at that show, and what were they going to think of me? She thought I was actually drunk!

We had little battles like that all along. I didn't start dating until the end of my junior year in high school. My mother was like, "There is no way a boy can come and pick you up at the house." When she was growing up that was just simply not done. And to be in a car with a boy? No, you have to meet them somewhere.

She told me one time, I was already in college and we were watching that TV show *Family.* Buddy, Kristy McNichol, got her first kiss on this episode. Just my mother and I watching TV, and Buddy gets her first kiss in the kitchen. It's just something innocent, stupid actually, and my mother goes, *"Tu nunca vayas hacer eso!"* I thought, oh my God, you're two years too late.

I'm surprised that I didn't think you could get pregnant from toilet seats, because these are the ideas that she had. Can you imagine discussing sex with someone who tells you not to kiss and you're already nineteen years old? She just always told me never to trust men. She never really talked about it, she just alluded to it. "Don't let them get you in trouble." If the car pulled up after a date my mother would open the door and be there waiting so that nothing could happen.

When my father passed away, because he was a college professor, it was written up in all the local newspapers. All my friends knew it. So whenever I would have a guy over, remember, this is when I'm already in college, we'd just be sitting in the living room having an iced tea and my mother would be in the back room. But because she felt that if there was not a man present in the house the guy, as they say in Spanish, *"te falta respecto,"* wouldn't respect you, you know, he would try something. My mother would yell out, "Ana, your father wants to talk to you." This was after my father had already died. The guy would look at me kind of strange. I kind of laugh at it, because I knew where she was coming from. She just didn't want the guy to pounce on me on the couch.

Well, my mother and I were having a lot of conflicts. So I decided to just go off to school. I told her the day before I was moving to San Marcos to Southwest Texas State University. It was four hours by car, but you would have thought I was going to the moon. I was just a terrible daughter. She was going to die, and someone was going to find her alone in the house. She just painted this really awful, really lonesome picture. But I just had to think about me, so I went.

She just tore up the telephone lines between South Texas and San Marcos. You know, heart condition, come home, I'll buy you a car. I ended up going back. When you feel that your mother is the only immediate family you really have. . . .

After I graduated and had worked in radio for five years I went to Austin to work at a radio station. I didn't like the job and I was miserable from day one. I called my mother. It was like who do you talk to, who do you turn to. Instead of saying, "Come home," it was, "No, you're going to be just fine. It's going to work out." I was really surprised.

All of a sudden she was telling me I could do it. She's been like that ever since.

I came to El Paso a year and a half ago after leaving Austin. El Paso was the last place I would have considered moving to. When I arrived here, it was three o'clock in the morning and it looked like a large city at night, all these beautiful lights. I thought, well this won't be so bad. But when I woke up the next morning and opened the sliding glass door, this is not what I expected at all! There were no trees. I was out in the desert and these mountains looked like dirt piles. I thought, what have I done?

Being so far away from home—I think that's the one thing that I don't like. But the thing that makes El Paso so wonderful are the people. I think that no matter where I go I'll feel close to my family as long as there's a Mexican-American community there. I can get homesick, but then I see a woman who just because she's Mexican-American reminds me of my mother, you know, the way she carries herself or the way she talks or the way she screams at her daughter, and I feel at home.

One thing: because I'm twenty-eight and single it still just kinda gets my goat every time I see my aunts. It's like, "Do you have a boyfriend yet? Are you getting married anytime soon?" They're like really worried.

My mother has already said that if I ever do get engaged, of course my uncle would hire a private investigator to check him out, make sure that he was okay, that he didn't have any really outstanding debts. Oh joy! The joys of being Mexican! When my mother was growing up everybody knew each other, and they knew the families for generations. My mother, even to this day, "Well, so are you dating anybody interesting?" and the first thing out of her mouth, *"¿Es de buena familia?"*

I don't have any prospect of marriage yet, so I hope they can hold out. I know they're worried. The thing is, I'm torn. I have that independent side of me, but then I have the side that wants to please my family. They measure success by if you are married and how many children you have.

Most Hispanic men are real macho. There are very few like my dad. But when I find a prospective boyfriend, I want him to be Mexican-American, Catholic, and from a good family. I consider myself to be pretty open-minded about it. But that's what I want, maybe because it would make my mom extremely happy.

MARÍA JIMÉNEZ
Army Officer, Fort Sam Houston
San Antonio, Texas

Spunky, tough, liberated, she has no nonsense about her. In her mid-twenties, and the mother of two children, María is headed for Officer's Candidate School at Fort Benning, Georgia.

I'm number six child. There's nine living. My mother had twelve children. There were six girls and six boys, if everybody had lived, which would have been a lot of fun.

Oh heck, it was fun growing up. I always had fun. We would, oh God, my sister was a good schemer. We used to do all sorts of stuff. My mother would go grocery shopping once a week. And when my sister was old enough Mom left her in charge of all of us. The grocery store was an all-day event. It probably took my folks about an hour or an hour and fifteen minutes to get over there and then another hour and fifteen minutes back. To say nothing of the time they spent at the store. And I'm sure they wanted to sneak a moment to themselves also. I remember they'd be gone the better part of the day. So my sister—we would do all sorts of things to the house—but she had us all so under control.

One time we cleared out all the furniture in the living room, moved it up against one wall. And the house was set up so that it was kind of like a rectangle. The living room had three doors: the front door coming to it, a door that led into one of the bedrooms, and a door that led into the kitchen. Then there was a bedroom, another bedroom, and the kitchen. They all had connecting doors. No hallway, just all connecting doors. So we moved all the furniture to one side of the living room, pulled the mattresses off the beds, put them in the living room, had all the pillows, all the blankets, the whole living room was just padded. And we'd get up and run around the house, get to the beginning of the mattresses, do flips, get up and run around the house again, do flips, and we did this for hours. We did different flips, and by the time everybody got to do two or three turns, you had a good half hour there.

Then my sister had it timed, I mean, almost exactly. She said, "Okay, that's it." Everybody cooperated and put everything back away and folded everything back up, put the furniture back, cleaned it all off, and when my mom would show up we'd all just be, you know, sitting around waiting. We'd all run out and help bring the groceries in.

I don't know how it was for my sisters, the older ones, but I remember this distinctly. I received a comprehensive English lesson the summer before I started school. We were all in the driveway, it wasn't paved and my sister had a stick, and she kept writing words out for me and telling me what they were. She was teaching me everything I knew in Spanish in English, in one summer, trying to get me to the point where I knew most of my vocabulary in English. I don't know why they did such a comprehensive lesson on me. They probably said, "She's not going through what we went through." So, anything my sisters did for me, I did for my brother, and then my brother would do for my other brother, and it just kind of went all the way down the line.

Okay, the school that I went to nobody ever talked about college. I didn't know what a college was. See, I didn't go to high school in the same town I went to elementary school, because they didn't have a high school in my home town. I had to go ten miles to go to high school. That's when I started hearing about college and college and college. So you go from an environment like that to a university in a class of 400 or 500 people in the auditorium and you look around and you're the only nonwhite in the whole room. You're the only nonwhite. My God!

We were migrant workers. When we went up north we were minorities, but for some reason we never even saw blacks. We always ended up in these little rural areas where it was all white.

Everybody went. That was fun, except you work your butt off. You think about it now and say, "Jesus Christ, how did we get eleven people in the station wagon with clothes for everybody?" Blankets, work clothes, church clothes, one set for church and three sets to go to work, and then you could take a couple of pair of shorts, and then you had to take plates and spoons and silverware and glasses and pots and pans and everything that you needed.

When we stayed in Michigan it was what you call *un campo*, which is all migrant workers. They assign you a little house. It's kind of like a little wood-frame, one-room thing. You have the kitchen/living room area, then a half wall like a T with one sleeping area and another one behind it. And it's Army bunk beds. We had four bunks, and my dad and brother slept in the car. I think they did that just to get away from everybody.

You had to take everything that you needed, all of that in a station wagon. I don't know how we did it, I really don't. I try and picture what it looked like to somebody else, seeing this car, fully loaded with Mexicans, rack on the top, riding low. That's where all the jokes come from.

My dad was the kind of man who was rarely around. As a matter of fact, I have very few memories of him before the eighth grade. Then it was only because we used to get into arguments. But when I was a kid I could name on one hand the memories I have of him. He was always working. I don't blame him, he had a lot of pressure. He had a lot of kids.

But since I started noticing it, my mom and dad's relationship has always seemed rather rocky. Consequently, he stayed out a lot. He's your typical Mexican male, I'm going out with the boys and you stay home with the kids. She dresses him so he can go out. I guess if you grew up with the mentality to put up with something like that, you can. He got past that, but it took a few years.

My mother used to come in our room; the girls slept in one room and the boys in another. She would come in right before lights out and talk to us. "Don't let what's happening to me happen to you all." Her talks got really intense once my sisters started dating. "Don't let him go out and you don't know where he is, and you don't know how to drive, and one of your kids is sick and you don't know how to get them to the hospital." Let's see, I must have been about ten or eleven when I started hearing this. Like nightly.

Well like I said, I didn't know what college was. And it was really weird because you don't want to say, "What's that?" People are going to say, "Where did she come from, the moon?" You don't want to ask questions but you want to find out. So you pull your ear when people are talking about it. But then my sister graduated from Pan Am [Pan American College]. So okay, that's what college is. Then when my sister Virginia went to UT, we went to drop her off and I said, "Wow!" You know, her dorm and Texas stadium. We walked around a little bit and everybody was like, "This is all right!" I thought, "I could get used to this sort of thing."

When I finished high school I got a full-time job. That was when I decided I didn't want to be a secretary. This was the pits, data entry. There were ladies there, like our supervisor, a woman in her fifties, making like maybe $200 more than we were. She had been there forever. Extremely boring.

After doing that for almost a year, my sister called me. "What are you doing with your life? You want to move to Austin?"

I said, "Sure."

So I went up there in September, got a job, night shift, five o'clock to one, computer, CIT data entry work.

So my sister says, "Well, as long as you're here, do you want to go to school?"

"I don't know." I didn't know what the hell I was doing, so I decided to talk to an admissions counselor.

The guy was from El Paso. I walked in and he said, "Where you from?"

"The Valley."

"All right!" and we started talking in Spanish. We had a good time just talking. He said, "Well, you want to come to school?"

"I don't know. I don't know if I'd fit in here."

He says, "Ah, don't worry about it. After a while you'll feel like this is home. Listen, give it a chance." He was really good. "Have you taken the SAT? Why don't you take it, there's one coming up in November; you can have your results by December. If you make it you can start in January. Take the test. What have you got to lose?"

"OK, I'll take the test."

He told me to call him as soon as I got the results and we'd see. When I called him he says, "That's great! You really scored that high? That's a great score, you're in."

This is someone that came from a town of 1,250 people. It was like, my God! Here I am, a little speck of dust in the middle of this whole thing. So I started, I was learning something for a change, and I just kept on going. I went straight through, every summer, every fall, every spring. I worked like crazy to make it through. Working fifty-seven hours a week plus taking twelve hours of college, I remember thinking, "When the hell am I going to sleep?"

I majored in accounting. I had wanted to go into dental, but after my first biology class I said, "This isn't going to work." I didn't have the science background to compete. The projected job market said accountants were going to be in need for the next ten to fifteen years. It was a logical major.

Anyway, everybody was graduating but I didn't want to do what everybody was doing. Friends that had graduated with my sister would come back into town and you could tell they were miserable. They hated it, nine to five, fight the traffic in the morning, fight the traffic in the afternoon. It didn't appeal.

The military was something I wanted to do when I was in high school, since my junior year when I got an offer from the air force academy. But my parents didn't let me accept. The reason I've stayed in is because I liked it. The money is not that great. People that graduated with me are doing a lot better in the private sector. There's pros and cons to everything. It's longer hours. It's not a nine to five job. That's what I like about it.

You can be a minority twice over in the military and you can be a minority twice over in the private sector; you're still a minority. I mean what are females going through in the private sector? They do the same job as a male and they get paid less. Here, in the military, I'm a female, I do this job, I have a counterpart, same rate, same time and service as I am, he's a male. We get paid the same. He has the same benefits as I do.

I have always been rather realistic, I guess. If you can tell me what you expect out of me I will do it. As long as the goals you're setting for me are within reach, even if I have to work my butt off to do it, I will do it. But if you tell me I have to do something that I know there is no way I can do it, then that's where my motivation just completely goes down the drain. Rarely do you ever get that kind of request in the military. You might think you can't do it, but you can. Like if somebody had told me I would be rappeling off of a twenty-foot tower, I'd say, "Ha!" But once I got in there and saw how it was I said, "Hey, this actually looks like fun." You start feeling more confident and the next thing you know you're coming down that thing and, "Can I go again?" Which I did. It builds a lot of confidence. If you had told me six years ago that I was going to run four miles: "In your dreams, I can hardly run one."

My problem was expressing myself, not on paper, not one-to-one, but in front of twenty, thirty, or more people. And now, hey, that's no biggie. I'll get up in front of an auditorium. I teach army stuff. The latest class that I've taught was the M18 A1 claymore mine. It's an antipersonnel mine. There are certain things that every soldier needs to know how to do. Once a year you get tested on the stuff. And the one thing that everybody messes up on is the claymore mine. There are so many little steps, and if you do one step before you do the other step you could blow yourself up. That's why it's graded so strictly. I did the grading. I taught the class.

A lot of the other classes were much faster. They called me in on it. I told them, "You want me to do it? You want me to do it right? It's going to take time. I can be out here two days, I don't care if that's what it's going to take." You'd be amazed at how many people didn't know the claymore and had been in the service for six or seven years. They were supposed to learn this way back in basic. I felt great because the people that I taught did really well. People actually noticed. The head guy said, "Hey, you know what y'all doing, givin' your own guys the grades or something." It was like, oh no, you got a female teaching something that has to do with infantry.

Being in the army made a difference when I had my children. I was working at the club when I had my first child, so I wore civilian clothes. When I got to the point where I couldn't deal with sixteen-hour days anymore, my boss changed my schedule. I'd come in at ten o'clock and leave at five. Then I'd get my time off to go to the doctor, and if I really felt bad I'd call in. That was accepted. But it wasn't until the last month that I got so huge. It was waddle, waddle, waddle. But up until then I was working days, nights, everything. In the kitchen I always had my snacks, and they made sure I got my vegetables.

I liked my doctor too. Same doctor for both kids. I liked her, we talked all hours. But I've always been fighting not to be typical and what do I come up with? A boy and a girl. That's it. That's all I want.

I'm going to be in Georgia for nine months! Nine months! The whole reason for me getting out of the enlisted side of the house is that I don't feel I'm being fully utilized. I want something more challenging and believe me, Officer's Candidate School is going to be a challenge.

I keep telling myself it's worth it. It was a hard decision. Oh my God, we went back and forth about it for six months, before I finally decided. My husband is supportive though. He's not your typical Mexican.

My husband is taking care of the kids. They are moving to Austin to stay with our family. He will take care of them for this next nine months, and when we find out where we will be stationed it will be his turn. He wants to go back to school. My little boy needs to be in preschool because of what he's going to be up against as far as what the other kids know once he does get to school. See, he's never been in an environment where there's been more than two other kids. He doesn't know how to socialize. He knows about sharing with his sister, but now this will give him a chance.

I just don't want them to be spoiled. I saw a lot of kids that just wasted their parents' money. Spoiled rotten. Parents paying another semester's tuition and they're spending their time at the lake, drinking. I want to make sure I can help them, but I don't want them to end up taking everything for granted. I don't have a plan yet to achieve that goal, but that's what I want.

MICHAEL RODRIGUEZ
Son of Elena and Miguel Rodriguez*
College Freshman
Guadalajara, Mexico

Through their parents' foresight Michael and his sisters, Lisa and Dolly, have had the best of what Mexico and the United States have to offer. Still growing, they don't have a long history to reflect on but they know what it is like now for young Americans. Theirs is a magnified, personal vision of the future.

I was born in the city of Chicago in 1969, March 28, at 2:50 P.M. I went to public school from pre-kinder up to third grade. When we changed houses I went to Catholic school through the eighth grade. Then when I graduated from eighth grade we came to Guadalajara. My parents didn't want me to study high school in the States, with the pressure of drugs and the gang violence. The problems did exist. My friends pressured me to be involved in gangs and all that. I really didn't pay that much attention, but my parents were aware that maybe when I went to high school—they had heard stories from other parents and families.

*See chapter 8.

So they brought us here. I really didn't mind. I wanted to know how it was, because I had only come for a month's vacation every year.

My sisters were the ones; they didn't want to come here. The first month they would say, "I want to go back. Take me back. Everything is so awful."

At first it was hard. Most of the Mexicans say you are a *pocho* or Chicano or whatever. They think you're different because you try to speak more English. I guess you try to speak English so you won't forget it.

I spoke some Spanish, but I didn't know how to express myself or write well. I started eighth grade over at the American School so that I could take two years of Spanish before I got to what you call *preparatoria* here. When I got to the tenth grade, I started to study more about business administration in Spanish, plus the civil rights and laws of Mexico, the culture, and history. I am graduating as a *technic* in business administration.

I know people are different here, but not like they think in the United States, that they only ride burros and wear huaraches. There are cars here. It's normal, but it is a different culture and they have different ideas.

Even though our family is separated I think we're united. My dad calls every month, and I write every two weeks and he writes back to me. He comes here three or four times a year. He spends time with us, and when he comes he tells me that he expects a lot from me, because he's over there working so that we can get a good education. If not, we wouldn't be able to get it there.

Since I was fifteen I have worked summers in Chicago with my dad. It's a plywood company; they treat wood so that it doesn't burn, and they have thirteen stores where they sell lumber. My dad is a supervisor where they make the certain sizes that different companies order. I worked outside fixing lumber, sorting it into sizes. It's hard work, especially this past summer, when the temperature at twelve noon was 110 to 112 degrees—well, you can imagine. I made $4.50 an hour. Two years ago I worked in a factory where they made juice and made $7.00 an hour plus a lot of overtime. That year I saved all my money so I could fix my car. Last year, I don't know, I knew I was coming back this year to live, so I spent all my money with my girlfriend.

She has been waiting for two years. I told her, Okay, that's cool. I'm going to come back and we are going to start college this September. We are going to work and study, and once we have a career we will get married. That's the plans we have.

In high school over there, you know you can do whatever you want. You can go to one class and not to another. Maybe after that I wouldn't want to go to school anymore. But here I have to go. If you miss one day they call your house.

If I had stayed there I probably wouldn't have studied. I would just be going out with my friends, not working, knowing that my dad was working. I learned to be responsible here because my parents let me show them I could be responsible.

Here, I see people that study have careers, live comfortably, and have a lot of the things I want to have. I want to work so I can give my family the best.

Even though I wasn't born here in Mexico, I consider myself Mexican. My children would have to know both cultures so they won't be thinking like the people over there, that everything in Mexico is just dirt, no cars, just like it was a ranch. I would bring them every year or two so they could see their relatives. If I see that things are going bad while they're going through school, I would bring them down here because I know they would get a good education. If I could get a good job, I would come here to stay. I would definitely come back. There are a lot of problems in the States.

I like the way people live here. Even so, there is a lot of corruption. I have had to pay bribes. Like when I went the wrong way on a one-way street. You just give them money. Here you can do whatever you want if you have money. But if you don't, it's really hard. I don't actually know how people live here on the minimum wage. If you live in the good society here you have more advantages, better education, and everything. But the poor, I don't know how they live. I guess that's why they want to go to the States.

I will be graduating June 16, and we will leave a few days later because I want to work before I go to college. I haven't picked the college. I'll wait until I get there. There are a lot of business schools. I've already studied business administration for three years. My big advantage is that I could come back here to study because I am graduating with Mexican and American diplomas. I speak good Spanish and

English and I know how things operate here. When I get there I will learn how things operate in the States.

LISA RODRIGUEZ
Daughter of Elena and Miguel Rodriguez*
College Freshman
Guadalajara, Mexico

I was born July 17, 1970, in Chicago, Illinois, and raised there until I was thirteen years old. I was brought up in a Catholic school, so it's like I really didn't know much about the outside, the rough city. Supposedly it was a rough city.

When my parents decided to come down to Guadalajara I was very angry. I had come on vacation, but didn't like it. I would get sick. I hated the food. I looked at everyone as, "Oh jeez, these poor people, they live in bad conditions." Before, I would say "these people." It was totally different. I started to cry and my parents said, "No, it's going to be much better down there. I want you to know your culture." It's like, my culture? I really didn't understand what they meant by that.

So when I came down here and to school I didn't have many friends. Everyone spoke Spanish, and the people that spoke English, well they were from Los Angeles. I didn't know anyone from Chicago.

The first two years I hung around with the kids that spoke English. "The American System," they call it at school. That's when I met my boyfriend. I didn't want to go out with him because he's Mexican. I had heard that they're really macho and they're so strict. Oh, I just didn't like it; I didn't like the idea. But I went out with him. He didn't speak much English, so he said, "If you teach me English, I'll teach you Spanish."

Because of my boyfriend I started hanging around with the Spanish-speaking kids. At school they call them the *fresas*, strawberries: those are the girls that really think they're it. The boys are the *cremosos*, the creamies.

At first they really didn't want to talk to me because they don't want to hang around the kids in the American System. I wasn't in the

*See chapter 8.

American System but since I spoke English they considered me from the American System. They would say they didn't want to socialize with the American kids because they have different ideas. They have no morals. They told me, "But you guys, why do you want to live over there?" Two years, and I still had the idea that I wanted to live in the United States.

But as I started learning more Spanish I also learned more about their ideas. I think I was influenced a lot, because my mentality changed.

At the beginning they told me, "Oh, girls in the States are really easy."

I told them, "No they're not, where do you have this idea?"

"Oh, we've seen it in all the movies." See they're influenced by the TV and the movies. They think that all the girls in the States sleep around with all the guys and no American guy takes any girl seriously. I mean they have these weird ideas.

See I didn't know how to socialize with the upper class, because I'm middle class, I mean maybe lower middle class because of where I was raised. Socializing with these people, my way of acting in front of people has changed. I knew, well wait a minute, I can't act this way in front of these people. Before, I thought, it doesn't matter where I am, I'm going to act the way I want to. But then I started meeting different kinds of people and I realized it can't be like that.

I realized that education is very important. Before, I thought, forget it! I just want to get high school over with. Conversing with these people, I began to realize that it's important to go to college. They all talk about college. If the Mexican young people here have a good standard of living, they really strive for a good education and they want to be someone in life. They don't want to be just anyone.

When I go back in the summers and speak to my friends in Chicago, I see, like they're dropouts. Some of them are moms already, and they're only fifteen or sixteen years old. I say, "Well, man, why don't you finish school?"

"How can you think of school when I have to raise a kid? I have to go to work."

The mentality totally changes from Chicago to Guadalajara. And I changed a lot hanging around with these Mexican kids.

Another thing here is the age. People here are more socially mature than they are in the United States, although the kids are not emotionally mature. Kids in the States have gone through a lot. They can take a divorce in their family, they can take an argument, a crisis, or something like separation. Here a kid can't handle that because they're used to the family being together.

I'm graduating in June. In September I want to start Northeastern University, or Circle. I want to study psychology, specializing in special education for the retarded. Here they lack a lot of facilities for those kids. They don't pay any attention to them. There isn't any money. The government doesn't have enough money to support these institutions like they do in the United States.

I don't want to study psychology here. One of my psychology teachers told me I should study here at the Universidad Autónoma. I went to see their program, "Psicologia para Mexico." I'm not interested in that. I can specialize over there and at the same time maybe graduate with a double major. I need to work in the afternoons because it's going to be two of us going to college. Also I want to work because the American School here is so expensive and my little sister still has to go through high school. So, I want to help my dad with that too.

After I graduate we'll see what I want to do. I really don't know yet. I think I will want to work in the United States, because here the professions are very devalued. Like I have a job tutoring kids and I really like it, but they don't pay anything, 4,000 pesos an hour [$1.60]. Still, it's really rewarding working with kids. And all my kids love me. Every time they come to class they give me a kiss. And now that I'm leaving they say, "Oh Miss, *no se vaya, no se vaya.*" They're nice kids.

I now have stronger friendships here. I lost a lot of my Chicago friends because they got married. I don't think we knew that much about true friendship; we were still young. But I have a lot of good friends here. They already gave me a going-away party, and they are coming to visit me in December.

I always thought, before I came down here, if I ever had kids I would stay in the United States. But I was really narrow-minded. Now my horizons are wider. I think I would bring my kids down here. I would like them to be raised here but I would speak to them in English. I don't want the same thing that happened to me when I came here and didn't know Spanish. Of course it all depends on who I marry, but I do want to show my children the culture of Mexico.

Many people ask me if I consider myself American or Mexican.

Usually I like to say I'm Mexican. Like when I go back to the States I like to go to the Mexican neighborhood. It's called 26th Street. One time I went to this Mexican restaurant with a friend. The waiter asks me, "Where are you from?"

"Guadalajara."

"Oh, Mexican girls are so beautiful."

So, I like to say I'm Mexican. I feel Mexican.

One thing I know, right now I'm really scared to go back. I haven't lived there for a long time. I'm scared. I don't know how I'm supposed to socialize. But my teachers tell me that in college you meet people from all different parts of the world. It's going to be a change. It's more responsibility, I know that. But I have had good discipline.

DOLLY RODRIGUEZ
Daughter of Elena and Miguel Rodriguez *
Sixth Grader
Guadalajara, Mexico

I was born in Chicago, Illinois, December 11, 1975. When I was little we came to Guadalajara. I remember when my parents decided to come, like I thought this was Chicago until I was twelve years old. Then I knew I was in Guadalajara. I knew I was in a different culture with different people.

Well, I knew Spanish but not so well, and everyone made fun of us. Not really made fun, but they would laugh. It was in fun, because every time you'd talk they would correct you. My teachers were kind of strict. In English I knew adverbs and everything, but you had to learn them in Spanish and the words were kind of long. They were much stricter here.

I made friends easily. I like to have friends. I like school, too. The teachers here make it interesting. We have activities. In the States we had activities, but not as fun as here. There are sports. I am in after-school activities too. Right now I'm in basketball. Sometimes I stay for volleyball, sometimes for swimming and basketball.

When I was in fourth grade there was a race for all the schools in

*See chapter 8.

Guadalajara. They gave us trophies. I raced 100 meters and 200 meters. I liked it. My sister and brother are in my school too, because it goes up to twelfth grade. They help me a lot.

Most of the friends I have are here because I haven't been to Chicago in four years. I might be going back this summer. I don't know if I want to go, it depends, because my sister tells me that in the States the laws are different from Mexico. See, over there the laws are better but then people smoke or do drugs. Children my age and everything. And the schools are not that good over there. Right here everything is more relaxed, everything is more calm. It's better here. I'm a little nervous, because over there my mom says you can't go to the corner to walk, to a park, nothing.

I am going to get a double diploma here, but I want to go to college there because what I want to study is over there. It's more advanced over there. I want to be an astronaut.

When I'm eighteen I can decide whether to be Mexican or American. I don't know what to decide. I would like to get married with an American. I would live there a little while, then come to Guadalajara or somewhere in Mexico. I would want my children to speak both languages, but I consider myself American because I was born there and I lived there eight years. I barely have five years here, so I don't know. Maybe I'm American. I still like the United States.

THE CHILDREN'S
CHILDREN—PART II

Some of the children's children are second- and third-generation Americans. Others are descendants of families who lived on Mexican land before it was acquired by the United States. Today there are children whose forebears were here before the Pilgrims landed at Plymouth Rock.

AMBROSE CRUZ SAENZ
Tamale Restaurant Owner
Bryan, Texas

Mr. Saenz is in his seventies and retired. He has turned his tamale parlor over to his youngest son, but every day finds him at the restaurant, overseeing business and greeting customers.

During the Depression my father brought me here to A&M College to go to work in the mess halls. I remember those days. They used to pay me $45 a month and that was a lot of money. We had the suits tailor-made, so I was dressed like a king. On top of that I played violin and we used to have a little band. We were called the "Bolero Kings." We had beautiful shirts with big sleeves like boleros and black pants with a stripe up the leg. Had pretty good music too. We were one of the first to play orchestration. There were nine of us. We played all the popular music of those days, Glen Miller, swing. We'd earn $3.00 or $4.00 a night. And sometimes, the doctors had the right to have liquor, so they would give us a whisper, "Hey boys, come here." And they would give us a drink.

I still play the violin. At night I go to the other house by myself so I can play. I like good music, Mozart and Rachmaninoff, Bach, Liszt, Franz Schubert, that kind of music. Every time they have a symphony on television I love to watch it.

There were two things I wanted to teach my children: To be honest, that's the only way to live, be honest with everybody. Secondly, I wanted my children to have the knowledge, the inspiration, of music. Music is my life, and I wanted them to have the same feeling. They say music is the language of your soul, of your spirit. And I wanted them to have that inspiration because they say this: A man inclined to beautiful music will never commit a horrendous crime.

ROSE REYES PITTS
Program Consultant, Hispanic Chamber of Commerce
Austin, Texas

Her persona embodies many of the characteristics with which she describes her mother. Physically this petite young woman has been gifted with classic Mexican beauty: skin a creamy café au lait, delicately full lips, dramatic dark eyes, all in a softly rounded face set off by luxuriantly thick black hair.

Edinburg, Texas, in the Rio Grande Valley—I was born there, my father before me, and his father before him. His mother came from Mexico when she a young girl. Their families lived in the same neighborhood, and I grew up knowing them all. I have fine memories of them because they just loved all the children. Both sides of my family were pretty much like that. The children are very important, and everything is for the children.

And my mother, she grew up on the Rio Grande River in a mud and rock house with no floors. Her parents were born in Star County, right on the border. My grandmother still lives there, in a ranch they call La Puerta. I remember it as a happy and wonderful house in a farming and ranching community. To me it was like cowboys and Indians, because it's dusty and everybody wears boots and cowboy hats.

My grandmother's mother was also born in that area. The whole family has a lot of Indian features, not necessarily dark skin, just the facial characteristics. Supposedly my grandfather's family didn't accept my grandmother's family because they had so much Indian blood. That was never a problem for my mother of course, because she is a saint.

My father's family still lives in Edinburg. They've stayed close. My father talks about the great opportunities he had to live in Chicago or here and there, but he's funny, he visits me and he is restless. Almost immediately he's ready to go back.

My parents have a nice life in the Valley. They're happy there, and they just don't understand why I don't want to raise my family there. They really feel sorry for me.

They met at the university through a mutual friend. My father sent his cousin to go ask for her hand in marriage, and they had this wonderful, traditional wedding. They are teachers. My father teaches high school, government and social studies, and my mother taught first grade for twenty years. After she received her master's degree ten years ago, she became a diagnostician. She tests children that excel and children with disabilities, to get them in special programs. They've both been with the Edinburg School District all their working lives. It's hard for me to believe that my mother will retire next year. To me she's just young and healthy, absolutely the most wonderful person I've ever met, a really smart woman too.

My mom is very traditional. She really doesn't have a lot of friends that she spends time with. Her friends are my dad's friends' wives. She just does everything for him, a very traditional Mexican wife, but she amazes my friends and she amazes me. Considering the kind of upbringing she had, she is so smart and so modern. I remember when I was going away to college she told me that she was going to take me to the doctor's so I could get a pill prescription. I was horrified because I didn't need to be on the pill. "Mother!" But she said, "In case you need them, you'll have them." Things like that, she was very smart about those kinds of things, but very traditional.

My dad is very *mexicano,* very macho. In fact, even though I have a good relationship with him now, we never really communicated when

I was growing up. It never bothered me, because I was so close to my mom. She always smoothed things out. I never realized it then, but now it sort of hurts my feelings. My father never really talked to me. If he wanted me to do something, he would tell my mother and my mother would tell me. When I married things got better; he had a little more respect for me. He talked to me. And since I've been a mother we get along great.

My dad does all the men things. He barbecues, he keeps the yard perfect, keeps the cars. Of course he never changed a diaper. I can't even imagine that—I mean, I can't imagine being married to a man who would not help feed your child or change her diaper.

He always gives my mother a lot of credit though. He says she's the leader in the family, the one who's kept us all together, the smart one. And she is. She handles the household, pays all the bills, knows about the insurance and finances. He doesn't want to know about it. Even though he's real macho, she controls what happens, the important things. She really is in control of my father. But sometimes I'm sort of embarrassed by the way he treats her. We'll be sitting there and he'll say, "Marcie, get me a glass of water. Marcie, this food doesn't have enough salt." And she just waits on him, but really she's in control.

I've never been able to see things that way. I was never attracted to men that would ask that of me. My husband and I have an equal partnership. He helps me a lot. It's funny, I really appreciate those things about him because I would never, I couldn't be happy having somebody tell me to get up and get them something. But there are things that I really wish my husband was better at. Like my father was a man who did all the man things, the yard and the cars. And he would barbecue at least once a week. All the men love him. My husband's not like that. He has probably never ever washed my car in the five years we've been married. I always think, one of these days he's going to, like, start washing my car. Of course I appreciate the fact that he's not macho, but sometimes I wish he would be a little more like my dad.

What really amazes me is to go home and see some of the women I went to high school with. One girl—I always thought she was really beautiful, you know, so popular—was telling me about her life. She married this man who won't let her go anywhere because he just thinks she'll cheat on him. Of course she said she wouldn't even dream of cheating on him. If she's sitting at a stoplight and she glances over, he thinks she's trying to attract attention from some man in the other car.

But growing up in the Valley, especially with all my family there, was really nice. I hear my husband and other friends tell stories about their unhappy childhoods. But I just can't think of any. Really, in my family, everything was for the children, all of our vacations, the weekends, and holidays. My parents gave the absolute best they could not even afford, you know in clothing and everything we had to have.

Of course the holidays were traditional. Christmas was always so much fun. All the women, and there were a lot of women in the family, would get together at my grandmother's house and make tamales. They would make fifty dozen, just a ton. It was just the women. They would gossip, tell stories, and it was really funny, because that was the only time that you could really, like talk about the men. It was a lot of fun. At all the family gatherings the women were in a different room than the men. The men were usually outside barbecuing or drinking beer, and the women would be inside. To me, that's ridiculous.

Our birthdays were big events, we had piñatas, always, yes absolutely. Had to have a piñata. In most cases because we were so close to the border we'd get to go to Mexico and pick our piñata and the candy and things that went in it.

Once a month we went to Mexico so my dad could get a haircut. I remember being afraid though, and I felt so sorry for the beggars on the street. My father always made me believe that when we went over there we had to stay together and hold hands. But we always ended up doing fun things.

Every time I go home I make at least one trip to bring back tequila, a piñata, or some kind of trinket. Now we have hangouts. We always have to go to Trevino's in Reynosa and have a margarita. Somebody asked if I was afraid that they wouldn't let me back in. They just ask, "Are you a U.S. citizen?" They've never asked us for papers, because they're just accustomed to the people in the Valley coming back and forth. It's never been a problem for us, and we're all dark-haired and dark-skinned.

Until I went to college it never occurred to me, because I never ever felt like I was a minority. Even in school when you study about civil rights, it never really occurred to me that I was the one we were talking about.

My wedding was in the Valley. I did a lot of the traditional things.

I really didn't want to, but I decided it would make my parents happy. I knew that's what they wanted, and to me that was part of getting married. So we had the *lasso,* and *aras, rosario,* and the *cojines.* The *padrinos* were all close friends of my parents. It was a combination wedding though, so I also had six bridesmaids. At the reception we had a big Mexican orchestra, *conjunto.* It was a December wedding and I decided to have my bridesmaids wear black and white. I thought it would be very elegant.

My aunts and my grandmother were just horrified! They thought it was a funeral. About a month before the wedding, my aunts called and asked me to lunch. They took me to a very nice restaurant. You know, they were sort of acting weird and finally one of my father's sisters said, "We just wanted to tell you that we just don't want you to ruin your wedding by having black. We have these fabric samples that would be lovely. This beautiful green for Christmas, or even this red would be okay." They just couldn't accept that I was going to have black bridesmaid's gowns.

This was just a month before the wedding and the gowns were already made. They were beautiful and it was a lovely wedding, but they just couldn't see it. They thought that was a crazy thing for me to do. But I did it just the same.

I always thought I would end up marrying somebody that was from the Valley. I think the reason I fell in love with my husband, and was able to marry him even though he's not part of my culture, is because he's Catholic and he's really close to his family. So we had similar values. To my family, that's what saved Vance, he was Catholic.

I want my daughter to have a close family. I don't know how I'm going to create the feeling I had when I was growing up, that I had lots of family, lots of people that I could depend on, that cared for me. My brother and many of my friends from the Valley have moved here. My parents come often. They try to take a long weekend so that they stay an extra day. And we try to visit as often as possible.

Right now I'm teaching my daughter the Spanish songs I learned as a child. She loves to sing along. Every opportunity I take her to the celebrations: *cinco de mayo* and the *diez y seis.* It's important to me that she is exposed to that culture.

Also, even though there were a lot of strong women in my family, I didn't have a lot of role models outside of my mother. Her pediatrician is a *mexicana*. I'm trying to find a dentist for her, for sure a woman and then hopefully a *mexicana*. I want her to see the possibilities. I want her to experience so many things. I want her to see it all.

JUAN CADENA
Director, Muscatine Migrant Committee
Muscatine, Iowa

Juan describes himself as an activist, and he is. He doesn't accept any idea without scrutinizing it from all sides. A voracious reader and passionate conversationalist, he has opinions, and humorous stories to illustrate them, on almost any topic.

I work for the Muscatine Migrant Committee. We're a government-funded organization that's been in existence for over twenty years. We provide medical help for migrants and seasonal farm workers. I've been the director of the program since 1971.

"Migrant" and "immigrant" are not synonymous. Our definition of a migrant is someone who has earned half of their income within a twelve-consecutive-month period in the past twenty-four months. And the fact that they're from Mexico or any other country or are white or speak Spanish or don't speak Spanish is really not relevant. On the other hand, 99 percent of the migrants are Mexican-Americans and *mexicanos*. With seasonal farm workers it's just the opposite, 90 percent are white, European-Americans from Iowa. I don't know what percentage of the migrants are Mexican citizens. Fifteen years ago, a great percentage of our migrants were from Texas and were American citizens by birth. In the last three or four years we have had a higher proportion of Mexican citizens than before.

I grew up in the Midwest. I was born in Texas, but we moved to Saginaw, Michigan, when I was ten years old. When we first moved to Carleton, just across the Saginaw River, there was a little—what we call *colonia*. It didn't amount to much, there were only eight migrant houses, and we lived right down the tracks in another little house near the sugar beet company. We made friends with everybody in the *colonia*. We all went to the same school. Well, a couple of years later my father bought a house about three or four miles from there, in the Buena Vista neighborhood. We were only half a block from Saginaw, but I kept in contact with the people from the *colonia*.

We used to have Mexican dances. First in a real small hall, then we graduated to the auditorium, then to the armory. By the 1960s, "Los Relámpagos del Norte" came and there were two thousand people at the dance. It just grew and grew. After I left Saginaw in the seventies, Vincente Fernández came to the Civic Center and they had a real turnout.

So there is a substantial number of Hispanics in Saginaw. The community college, when we left, had over 200 Mexicans enrolled. A few years ago, I went back and they had 400 in the community college.

When I was a community organizer we had clubs in each of the high schools for Mexican kids, to encourage them to go to college. One school had over 250 kids. The Graduation Club was started back in the forties for all the Mexicans who are going to graduate from high school. They have their own prom and bring speakers such as Senator Chavez and Senator Montoya, to give a special commencement. The kids still go to graduation with their respective schools, but they also have a separate one just for Mexicans.

I don't know if they still do, but in Saginaw they used to celebrate the *diez y seis de septiembre* and *cinco de mayo*. I don't think half of them know what the heck's being celebrated. That's the truth. I was in San Antonio and these Mexicans, my wife, Martha's cousins, live in an affluent, nice neighborhood on the north side. They were all excited because they were going to this Festival San Jacinto and Martha says, "Well what is the celebration about?" And they didn't know. *¿Verdad, Martha?* They didn't know. I knew, but I didn't say nothing. They said, *"No sabemos lo que es,* but we have a lot of fun." But this whole holiday is about when the *mexicanos* got whipped by the whites here in San Jacinto and they don't even know. They're going out there to celebrate. So you know they don't even care. Even the whites don't know what the San Jacinto's about anymore, and nobody gives a hoot.

In Saginaw I had no real close friends that were not Mexicans. I wasn't unfriendly with anyone, but I really never got associated with whites very much until I went in the army. Actually in those years I never paid any attention to who was from Mexico and who was from Texas, who was from Saginaw, who was from out of town, no attention whatsoever. I never even thought about it until I came here.

And here, when we first came to Muscatine it was like I was wearing a sign on my forehead, "I'm Mexican." It wasn't just my perception, because when my relations would come down from Saginaw to visit, they would say, "What's wrong with the people in Muscatine? They stare at you." Well, that's not true anymore, but that was the situation when we first came here in '71. It was like a little cultural shock for me too, because I was confronted with this, "You're a Mexican." I knew I was a Mexican, but I didn't want people to be looking at me like, "Hey, Mexican!" They didn't say it, but that's the feeling you got. In Saginaw it wasn't that way at all—the relationship between whites and Mexicans is real good. There's really not that obvious discrimination. There was a little bit in the forties but not after that. Now there's even a lot of intermarriage.

See here, it was pretty bad. I was standing in line at the bank one day—this is one example—and this guy says, "This is the way Mexicans line up for food stamps," and everybody was ha-ha-ha. Well I didn't laugh. I felt like grabbing the guy and throwing him through the window. But I was going to a church council meeting, I was president. Now how would I be getting into a fight? I was getting a little more religious, so I started thinking and acting different. A few years before I probably would have tried to throw him through the window.

Another time I called this number for a house to rent. I guess he was busy and didn't notice that I had an accent. So when we got there he said, "Stop right there, I'm not renting to no Mexicans!" You know it was kind of comical.

I said, "Did I hear what you said?"

He said, "That's right, I don't rent to Mexicans."

I said, "Oh Christ!" So I called the civil rights commission, I was going to do something, but I never followed up on it.

A couple, Anglo friends, did a consumers' report here. We would send a Mexican couple, or pretend-to-be couple, to rent an apartment, and the landlord would say there wasn't any place to rent. Then our Anglo friends would come right behind them an hour later and, like magic, they would have a vacancy. After about twenty cases, they wrote a report. Those landlords were mad! But see we started exposing all that foolishness. Then in the schools there was also a lot of discrimination. I'm sure there still is, to some extent, but it has changed a lot. ¿Verdad, Martha? There's a lot of good Anglos in this community.

I was considered real militant in Saginaw, and when I came here I was in the mood that I could do anything. That's the way I was. I sort of enjoyed it, you know. I was thirty-four, so I was no young kid. But nothing scared me, nothing.

I don't know. We had this old Mexican guy that was being ripped off in West Liberty. This was a long time ago, but this justice of the peace had rented a place to the Mexican. In the first place it was small, a real shack. But beyond that there's no way that any thinking person could have expected the old guy to pay this kind of rent for the amount of money he was earning. So a friend and I, he was a law student, we went over there. Out comes this justice of the peace, and this guy looks like he's from *Petticoat Junction,* had his striped coveralls with this little hat and the whole bit. He said, "We don't want all those Mexicans coming into town. They park their cars and half of the time they're leaking oil and they leave all those oil spots all over and all that." My friend was saying, "Write that down, Juan." And I was writing notes, writing notes.

The justice of the peace would tell his lawyer, "They're gonna get me. They're gonna get us, Ernie."

"Ah, don't worry about it." But you could see he was all worried. So finally the lawyer said, "Juan, I'll talk to you, I don't want to talk to your friend. I'll talk to you, just you and I."

See, we were playing the good cop, bad cop. I went in but told my friend, "You stay out of here." Then I told the justice's lawyer, "Well, I'll keep this lawyer away from here if you cut the rent in half and . . ." And this is exactly what the man had wanted. He agreed to everything.

"You're not going to take it any further than this?"

I said, "No, we'll forget the whole thing."

So we went back for the old goat to sign the papers and he said, "Well, I'm sorry what I said about Mexicans, it's not only Mexicans that do that, niggers and Puerto Ricans do the same."

Can you believe that? He was serious. God, I'll never forget that. How can you get angry with somebody like that? You can't, these people are crazy. He was apologizing and insulting us at the same time. I've noticed that people are like that. If you really look at them, they're hilarious. The only time I'm really worried about a racist person is if they're in a position to determine someone's economic or social future.

Before I came here I was a coordinator for the grape boycott, for Cesar Chavez in the Saginaw area. We confronted a lot of people, people who would spit on us and say, "Go back to Mexico, you wetbacks!" And we were all from the United States. A lot of Anglos were helping us out, but in a way I was a racist. I wanted Mexicans to be doing something for Mexicans, but we were all American citizens. When I joined the grape boycott movement it was being led by some seventeen-year-old Anglo girl, and 99 percent of the people doing the marching were Anglos, nuns, and priests. I took it over and chased them all out. I didn't tell them directly to leave, but in a month or so they were all gone except the real hard-nosed. I would have 100 or 150 and they were all Mexicans. *¿Verdad, Martha?* The Anglos didn't want me because I was coming across too hard. They wanted to make waves but not BIG waves, and I was making REAL BIG waves.

But here in Muscatine it was a different ballgame than Saginaw. If you're really trying to do something useful and to really help or change conditions, you have to adapt to the conditions that you're dealing with. You can't just sing the same songs.

In Saginaw there really wasn't that many poor people. Now I'm used to it, but when we came here, we went riding around to the southside. We saw Anglos, blue-eyed, blond kids with stringy hair and dirty faces, scroungy looking, and I said, "Well wait a minute, I thought I would have to go to the Ozarks to see this. Not Iowa, the breadbasket of America." I thought everybody would be like you know, *Ozzie and Harriet.* But you see a lot of poor people, and really I don't know how you would say it, riff-raff maybe.

We don't have that in Saginaw. There's a large middle class, and everybody works in the plants, and they all make a lot of money. There I could say, "Look at the way the poor Mexicans live here." Because there were a few poor Mexicans. But here, I can't say that because we have as many poor whites.

Another difference, in Saginaw everybody works side by side there at the plants, and it doesn't matter whether you're white, yellow, or blue. You earn the same kind of money, the same kind of education and everything else.

People wanted me to get involved with the union here too, like the grape boycott. But I said, "It isn't going to work. In Saginaw we used to go to a supermarket. I would take six people and we would turn away

50 percent of the people. Here you can take 200 people and you aren't going to turn 5 percent of the people away. They don't identify with the union. In Saginaw everybody was union." I don't care if they were Polish or Mexican or black, they were all union people. So it was real easy to close down a store. Here it wouldn't work. People are not union oriented. Cesar Chavez came and people said, "Let's get him down to organize." It isn't going to work. The whole thing was a different world, and I found that out real quick.

I've read a lot of books. The bible has influenced me. I've read Espinoza, Jung, Marx, Ché Guevara, Fidel Castro, Mao Tse-tung, Gandhi, and Franz Fanon. Spicer, an anthropologist, influenced me too.

In school when I was growing up in Texas, the history books were always lying. My dad would correct the history like Pancho Villa and the Alamo, and say, "This is a bunch of lies. These *gringos* are telling you a bunch of lies." So I started thinking for myself. I remember once the nuns wanted us to sign some papers they were going to drop over China and I didn't sign them. My sister Lupe didn't sign it either. She was the only one in her class and I was the only one in mine. I said, "How do I know communism is wrong? How do I know that they're not right and I'm wrong?" White people have been lying to us all these years, and they have discriminated against us in Texas, so how come they're supposed to be so good? They broke all those treaties with the Indians and treated them like dogs, and now they're going to tell me that they're good and the Chinese are bad. I said, "No. I hope the Chinese come and take this country over." That's what I told them.

And the nuns would say, "We're going to have Father come and talk to you because you're a communist." I said, "How can I be a communist? You don't even know what a communist is." I didn't completely buy that little trick of the land of the free and the home of the brave. The United States, I do agree, is probably the best country in the world. And I'm glad I'm an American citizen and was born in this country. But the point is, you can't just swallow everything that they try to tell us, especially when it comes to minorities. I always saw the United States was an extension of Europe, and if you were not of European ancestry somehow you weren't American. What the heck, I was born here, but if I said anything against the United States they would say, "Why don't you go back to Mexico." Well, why don't you go back to Europe. Why should you be trying to send me to Mexico. What's the difference?

Like one guy—we were at a school board hearing where I was pushing for bilingual education—he told the superintendent of schools, "You mean to tell me this man"—talking about me, I was sitting right in front of him—"expects us to teach his kids Spanish in school?"

And then I told the superintendent, "You mean to tell me that this man here expects me to teach his kid English in school?"

He said, "What do you mean, you speak Spanish at home, don't you?"

I said, "Well what do you speak at home, Chinese? If you expect me to teach my kid Spanish at home, then you teach your kid English at home."

He said, "Well I don't mind, maybe you people already living here have the right to speak Spanish, but I'm talking about the other people coming in."

"Fine, I'm okay if you speak English, but all new people coming in should speak Spanish. What makes you right and me wrong?"

He said, "Well because we're the majority."

I said, "No, no, no, what about Zimbabwe? You white Europeans want to push your culture and your language everywhere. In Zimbabwe you're the minority." I wanted to make the same argument. If he would say my argument wasn't right, it would be because he thought I was a second-class citizen, but why should he be more of a citizen than me? I'm a taxpayer. It's my money too. It's my country too. It's my school system too. It's a matter of perceiving what we're all about here in the United States.

Mexicanos are always trying to test how *mexicano* I am. They're always trying to correct how you speak. It's a nuisance. *Mexicanos* think that we here in the United States are trying to be *mexicano*. We're not. I'm not trying to be *mexicano*. You know I'm not American to a lot of people in the United States, but in the same vein I guess I fall short of being a *mexicano* according to somebody's criteria as to what a *mexicano* should be.

That's one reason why our kids speak Spanish. Martha and I have never, even once, told them we want them to speak Spanish or pushed them or corrected them. We just speak Spanish to them and to that extent they have learned Spanish. If one of my kids told me they don't want to speak it, I'd say fine, don't speak it. I'm not going to push them.

I think the church plays a role here, and I think the church should play a big part in all of our lives. I'm an ordained minister in the Catholic church. I'm a deacon, and Martha took the same training. Of course, a deacon cannot be a deacon unless his wife consents. So we're of the same vein here. We have a Spanish-speaking church. In our community we had a debate a few years back. Some of the parishioners, namely Hispanics, were trying to integrate English into our church life. One lady was from Argentina, a man was from Colombia. Interestingly enough, the people that were following in their footsteps were the *mexicanos* that had been in the United States only ten or eleven years. All of us that didn't want English in the church were born in the United States. We were the ones that said no. The reason that we had these different points of view was the *mexicanos* and the Hispanics didn't really realize what they doing. They were trying to be nice, but they didn't realize that we were not in a position to be nice. Our culture in this community is hanging by a thread, and the only institution in the community that's exclusively Spanish-speaking is the church. If we start sticking English in our church here in Muscatine, I guarantee that in five or ten years there won't be a word of Spanish spoken in here. We'd be overwhelmed. I said, "Now if you people want to vote, if you want to do away with Spanish, and that's what you vote, I'll respect it. But I tell you, if you want Spanish here don't put in any English." Consequently we didn't do it.

Now we have this *mexicano* priest. About a month ago he came up with an idea from the pulpit. "I'm noticing that a lot of kids here don't speak Spanish. I'm thinking of integrating one reading and part of the consecration in English."

I said, "Oh no, here we go again." So after the mass Martha and I went to McDonald's for coffee by ourselves.

When we got home the kids already had a big argument going on. They were discussing what Father had said. Now Father had said it in Spanish, but they understood. And this one, Pancho, says, "I'm telling you right now Dad, if they stick English into that church I'm leaving. I'm going to Saint Mathias. If I wanted English I'd be going to Saint Mathias. Why should I go listen to broken English when I can go over there and listen to genuine English?" And Manuel said, "Yeh, let's kick that priest right out of that community." So see, they think the same way I do. This is fifth-generation Mexican, and their friends are all Anglos.

See, that's what I told Father. I said, "Look Father, we have all these Mexican people coming into this community and they need this church. My kids and my wife and I, we can go to any church. I did my first communion in English, so that wouldn't be any problem. But once we start in English, where are all these people coming into the community going to go? The recent arrivals? They don't fit into an English-speaking mass."

I joke about my nieces marrying *gringos*. I was over at my mother-in-law's at Christmas, and my sister-in-law walked in with her Anglo boyfriend. She was in front of him and I could see him coming. In Spanish I said, "Quick give me the Raid, there's an Anglo in the house!" She told him. So they came to visit us when Martha broke her leg, and they brought me a can of Raid. But that Anglo guy went with me to the bowling alley, and we're friends. They're not married yet, but he's sort of my de facto in-law. It was more of a put-on. I think we should all make a joke of racism, not to put people down, but to show how stupid it is.

Realistically, here in the Midwest especially, how could you avoid mixing? You're limited completely. How can a Mexican guy go to the University of Iowa, where there's what, 40,000 people, and expect him to find a Mexican girl? In my own immediate family, my nephews and nieces, out of twenty-eight, twenty-five have married non-Hispanics. Of those twenty-five, none of them speak Spanish.

Even my nephews and nieces do not speak Spanish, and they're only third-generation. You don't have to be too far removed from Mexico to not speak Spanish, especially in the Midwest. I know some kids that are first-generation here in Muscatine that at least claim that they can't speak Spanish. So I don't give any credibility to some recent claims that by the year 2,000, one half of the people in the United States will be speaking Spanish. The United States will have close to 260 million people. Hispanics probably would be about thirty million, and out of those thirty million, maybe only twenty million will be speaking Spanish and the other ten won't. Where do we get the idea that the rest of the 200 and some million people are going to be speaking Spanish?

San Antonio, a city with one of the highest populations of Hispanics and Spanish speakers, has only 6 percent who can read Spanish, according to an article that I was reading about a week ago. Whereas in Los Angeles and Brownsville it's in the 30 percentile. They just have more recent immigrants from Mexico into those particular areas.

I don't use the word *chicano*. I'm not comfortable with it because that's not the way I learned to use *chicano*. We asked this old man from Davenport, his name is Castillo, I don't even know if he's still alive, when was the first time in his life he heard the word *chicano?* He said he had heard the word for the first time in Muscatine, in 1916. The first time I used *chicano* was in the forties. To us, *chicano* was like the kids now use *dude*. Well, I don't know how they talk right now, but a year or so ago they were using *stud* or *dude* and all that.

Whether you're Chicano or Mexican you're no different than the rest of the kids, you have your peer group, the *palomilla* or whatever you want to call it. We had our own way of speaking. At those times in the forties for example, instead of saying *zapatos* or *chinelas,* we used to say *calcos.* For pants we used to say *tramaos* and for shirt, *lisa.* And *cabeza* we used to say *chabeta,* and for women we used to say *chavala* or *chavalo* for men. And for blacks, we used to call them *tiracho.* For whites, we called them *gabo* and for Mexican, we used to say *chicano.* If I was talking to a peer I would say *chicano;* if I was talking to my father I would say *mexicano.*

It was a slang word, and I didn't use slang with my dad; I wouldn't say *tramaos* either. I wouldn't ask my mother, "Where's my *tramaos?*" I would say, *"¿Onta mis pantalones?"* But at a certain age, you're not going to be speaking like that. You don't expect to hear a white guy at the bank saying, "Hey, stud!" It would look kind of dumb, right? Well, it's the same as a thirty-year-old man with a family and all saying, *"¿Hey onta los chicanos?"* That's something you'd say when you were fourteen, fifteen, sixteen. For me to use *chicano,* I might revert back to it when I'm talking to my brothers. I don't have any problem using the word *chicano,* but in the right context. You can't stay a foolish kid all your life.

NELDA BRAVO
Rural Technology Assistance Consultant
College Station, Texas

Nelda wears a colorfully embroidered Mexican blouse, and her hair is in a dark, thick braid. Sometimes bitterness seeps into the words of this gracious young woman, but her voice, a soft rounded Texas drawl, speaks of pride in her heritage and a spirit of determination.

Before my parents married my father had been in World War II. He was one of the "Flying Tigers"; he served on the Burma–China Trail. After he got back from the war he traveled through Mexico with the *federales* on mules vaccinating cattle for hoof-and-mouth disease.

He had had his wedding tuxedo made there on the border. He went for the fitting and returned to the interior. He went to pick up his tux, practically on his way to the church, and it turned out to be a "zoot suit." It was the time of the "zoot suit" riots in California. At the last minute he had to borrow a suit to get married in.

So they married and returned to Puebla. My mother immediately got pregnant. She had her first baby in Mexico, and her mother came down on the train to be with her.

Then my father came here to College Station to go to school on the GI Bill. When he graduated he took a job in the State Department with AID, the Agency for International Development. They were then pregnant with me, and as soon as I was born they left for Paraguay. I was about a month old.

There are five kids, two girls and three boys, and we were raised almost entirely in the foreign service environment of Central America.

We were in Honduras until 1963, when a revolution broke out. I had just turned nine, and one day at school we were playing in a big field of rushes. We had a game of tying knots in these tall grasses, then going to the end of the field, and running back to get caught in the snares. We had been playing, and all of a sudden these airplanes were coming. They strafed the playground! Strafe, stop, strafe, stop, like they were playing with us. We tried to run to the schoolhouse, but there were all these booby traps we had made as part of our game. It was really terrifying. It was the American school, so this was a warning, "American families, get out."

But they didn't allow American airlines to come in, and Central American airlines wouldn't transport American families out, so we had to drive. My parents had a gray-and-white '57 Impala. The older boys were teenagers by now, big hulks. Here we were, this long trip with everybody and whatever we could carry. So I had to go with another family. I knew other families that had been separated. Many of the kids I knew were children of government officials and their fathers had been assassinated. The Pan American highway had been cut through by then but it wasn't paved yet. Once we were on the road there was a caravan of families, and it was kind of an adventure. Geographically it was an incredible trip through the mountains of El Salvador, Guatemala, and Mexico.

From Honduras we went to Uruguay. We stayed there until guerrilla warfare began. When we came back I entered the sixth grade. It was my first experience living in the United States.

My mother had always told me that each of these countries we had lived in had different cultural protocol, and if you didn't understand the custom it was acceptable to sit quietly until it was over. So everybody gets up to say the pledge of allegiance. I didn't know it, and I had never seen this done before, so I just sat there very quietly. The teacher then gave a stirring talk about our communist neighbors in the south and pointed out the fact that I had breached etiquette by sitting through the pledge of allegiance. After that I always stood up for the pledge of allegiance, but I was so terrified I never really learned it. I would just kind of move my mouth so they wouldn't think I was a communist.

Since I had gone to private schools and spoke Spanish, I had never experienced any kind of prejudice or difference in the way I was treated in the classroom. But here I noticed that the teacher treated the Mexican kids differently. Then sixth grade is where kids start maturing sexually and getting ready for junior high and dating. They were more mature than I was, much more worldly. I didn't have too many friends, and when I discovered that people lived in the same place they were born, it was a shock. I had never known anybody who had lived in one place and had all their cousins and grandparents in the same town. It was a shocking year for me, a horrible year. I didn't understand anything that was happening. I had always considered myself American, from the

United States. At the end of that year we moved to the Dominican Republic.

My mother had raised us to be good little Mexican girls. Apart from the regular household chores that kids have, we would always have to do things for the males. Even though we had maids and ironing ladies, we still had chores. Mine was cleaning the bathrooms. The girls always had inside chores, while my brothers did outside things: mowing the grass, helping my dad build shelves in the basement, something infinitely more interesting than toilets or cleaning. I was always jealous because they got to do men's work, and girls don't do things like that. I can remember listening to the mowers and thinking how wonderful it would be to be out in the sun and air. We did a lot of mending: underwear and socks, fixing rips and buttons. In a household with boys there was a lot of that. I learned to embroider and hook rugs in school, and I learned to crochet and knit from the maids. We always had to straighten drawers and closets and polish shoes. Inside on a Saturday morning, ironing handkerchiefs and straightening closets for your brothers and father. Folding underwear and putting them in nice tidy little stacks, it was infuriating. I hated it. At a very early age I began arguing with my mother about this stuff. I'd say, "I can't do this, I can't!"

She'd say, "No, you have to learn how to do this because someday you'll have to do it for your husband."

"I don't care. I won't do it. I won't marry a man who wants me to do this."

It was awful. If we had chicken, my brothers got the bigger pieces, they got the breast. We could have the thighs and the legs. It was okay for us to get up and down during dinner; my mother would never sit through a meal. She was always heating tortillas or waiting on them. It infuriated me to be expected to do that stuff and it still does.

Two weeks ago I was in Austin for a business meeting, and I stayed at my father's house. My mother passed away about a year ago. My brother, Marshall, who lives with my father, says, "Will you wake us up tomorrow?"

I said, "No."

So he says, "But how are we going to get up?"

"The way you always do when I'm not here, I guess." And I went off and went to bed.

The next morning before my alarm goes off there's this little knock at the door and my sister comes in and says, "It's time to get up."

I said, "What are you doing here?"

She says, "Well, Marshall called me last night and asked me to come over this morning and wake y'all up." She lives just a few minutes away, but she's married and has her own house. She came over to wake everyone up and put the garbage out.

The relationship with my mother had already changed dramatically by the time I was preadolescent, about nine. There was nothing that I could do right. It's a paradox to me. She came from a family that emphasized education, yet my mother hated the fact that I was a bookworm. I had hiding places where I would go to read instead of learning how to iron handkerchiefs or mend. I would risk getting in trouble in order to read.

I didn't fit in, not only with my mother but with everybody else. It was natural, in a way. I was in the middle, and I was the oldest daughter. I was supposed to take care of the rest and do things for them, like a second mom. My mother would always say, "But you are the oldest daughter." By the time I hit adolescence I was alienated from my mother and my youngest brother and sister. I looked up to my older brothers. They were in college, and they would come with new books and records, they were my link to what was going on in the United States.

But I was also very, very jealous of them. I remember one time in El Paso, we were visiting an uncle and they were all going to the dog races. All along I thought I was going too, but then my mother said no, young ladies didn't go to the dog races. I was crushed. They got BB guns and got to go target practicing. They didn't have the curfews, or have to be interrogated.

At that point, because of my curfews, I no longer fit in with the Latin Americans. I couldn't do the same things they did. Mother wouldn't let me go out after nine o'clock, and in Latin America they don't eat dinner until ten. The dance afterward would go until two or three in the morning, and sometimes they would stay up until five and then go to mass. So the hours I could keep and things I could do pushed me more and more into a fringe crowd of Americans.

By that time it was pretty open hostility. I was hanging out with the kids who were smoking dope, drinking, and skipping school. That was when nobody shaved their legs, no makeup, no bras, and I was doing all that stuff. I couldn't stand being the little decorator item. By that time I didn't fit in. I didn't fit in with the Latin Americans, and to the Americans I was too Latin American. There was no place for me. There were things I liked in each culture, but they weren't the things those cultures treasured.

My parents had moved to Guatemala, and I stayed in the Dominican Republic to finish my senior year. At that point I was given an option: they would arrange a marriage for me, or I could go to college. I had taken my SATs because everybody else took them, but it was really expected that I would marry. I was eighteen. I had friends who had been traded for sugar mills; their families had merged business interests. All the girls I knew had been married at fifteen or sixteen to thirty-five-year-old men. To me it was an ungodly punishment—an old man. And they had been locked away. They could no longer receive friends, they couldn't go out of the house. It was the end of their life. One friend had to wave from her bedroom window because she wasn't allowed out. I knew that would be me, and I knew that my family didn't have any sugar mills. I didn't know what the trade would be. I thought of it as a life of slavery, waxing floors and folding underwear. So for graduation I got a set of luggage and I went off to college.

I didn't know what a college advisor was, or that you're supposed to go talk to these people. I was a very mediocre student. It was just awful. I was never so lonely. Nobody spoke Spanish. I was completely out of the social element, I didn't know what the customs were or anything. I had been very sheltered growing up, and here I was on my own; I went completely wild. I was going barefoot in public, smoking cigarettes in public. My parents would have died if they had known.

I was raised to marry an ambassador or somebody like that. I knew all that Emily Post stuff. My mother had groomed us for diplomatic life. They did a lot of entertaining, and I always helped hostess for big parties. She would give us lists of diplomatic etiquette. I can remember she would ask me to grill her from these sheets of paper listing the diplomats, their wives, what their kids were named, and what countries they were from. She wanted me to be able to make small talk. I learned all that, but it wasn't good training for the United States.

When I first came back to the United States, I was sitting in the library waiting for my brother. I was wearing a dress I made myself. It was all embroidered, the greatest embroidered work of art that I had ever made and probably ever will make. I started talking with this student from a Middle Eastern country. He asked me if I made my dress. I was very proud of it and I said, "Yes, I made it myself."

He said, "That's very beautiful, American girls don't usually do this."

"Well, I'm not really American. I mean I haven't lived here all my life." I was really proud of my accomplishment.

Two days later there's a knock at the door. This guy is standing there. He tells my brother he wants to buy me for his wife. Not only was I American, but I could do all this sewing.

I'll be thirty-five next month. I have a bachelor's in Spanish and I've completed all the coursework for a master's in English. I have to write my thesis this year. It will be a comparison of the Plan de Aztlán,* the Chicano Manifesto, and the Southern agrarians.

I work with the Rural Technology Assistance Program. Texas funds research on highways, transportation, and traffic safety, and they want to make this available to smaller areas, smaller towns that can't afford to hire consultants. I work with very technical material, and although I'm not an engineer I now know a lot about engineering, roads, and traffic, and can facilitate putting people together with the information they need. The United States is moving to get back their edge in the world of science and technology. They want to set up the Rural Technology Centers in Latin America. So I'm setting up training courses for export to these countries. It's a very satisfying job.

Now, I think I have a pretty good grasp on my culture. It bothers me a little that I won't ever be considered a nice, sweet addition to the family. I'll always be kind of an outsider, but I can't be the person they're looking for.

JUAN VALENZUELA
Disc Jockey
Muscatine, Iowa

Juan has never been to Mexico, but he brings Mexico to the Midwest. His Spanish language radio program featuring Mexican music airs every Sunday,

*A plan adopted in March 1969 at the Chicano Youth Conference in Denver, Colorado; sometimes called the "Chicano Manifesto."

and once a month he brings groups from Chicago, Texas, and Mexico. They play for the dances Juan sponsors, drawing Hispanics from the Quad City area of Iowa and Illinois.

The thing that I really liked about growing up in this little town of Carrizo Springs, Texas, was that we were 100 percent Mexican-Americans. By that I mean there were no Anglos and no Mexicans. For the most part, our fathers were second generation. I really liked that, because there's a richness in growing up bicultural and bilingual. We had what I call "the flavor" in our life, being American, growing up American but with that Mexican flavor. I noticed something missing as I grew older. Like salt missing from your food. That's what I noticed as I moved out from this little town.

I was the second of twelve children, three of whom died. Even though I was born in a poor family, I remember a lot of happy moments.

I was bicultural and bilingual. English came into play real early in my life. Our schools were required by law to not let anybody speak Spanish. So at school we had to speak English, strict. But once we were away from school we spoke Spanish, 100 percent.

Our grandfathers and great-grandfathers still celebrated the *cinco de mayo* and *diez y seis de septiembre* and *bodas* or weddings and *quinzeañeras,* so we grew up with all that flavor. We also celebrated the Fourth of July, Independence Day for the United States. I enjoyed celebrating the Fourth of July. It made me feel, just like when you hear the National Anthem, the hair from the back of your neck raises up. You know it's just kind of strong. I felt real proud of being American.

I was very interested in history, and I really enjoyed reading about what went on before me. We got that at school. What went on before me on the Mexican side, I learned from the old folks. We would gather together in the pueblo, listening to them tell their stories from the past. That was part of my inside growth. It seemed like the more I knew from before me, life before me, the more I knew about myself, why I was the way I was.

It was a real shock when I went in the army and found that everything wasn't just like the books said. The books would say America is great, Americans are good people, we're always helping somebody. You know, every time we went to war it was because we were helping somebody. Those things made me feel like whites were good samaritans, and I enjoyed playing the white role in that aspect of my life. But in the army I found out otherwise.

When I started mingling and having friends of Anglo origin, I found that there were some real nice people there. But it wasn't just like what the books said. I believe there's good and bad in every race. I decided to take the good from each part of what I was. But I needed that Mexican flavor, so I didn't Americanize that much even though I live in America.

At that time I was drafted into the army, we were still migrating back and forth. I served in Korea. That's when I really felt that shock of discrimination. There were some instances growing up; in a little town in Minnesota, for instance, I didn't know how to skate, but it seemed like skating was the "in" thing in that little town. I wanted to go skating, but I just couldn't fit in. If we hung out together, my cousins and brothers, we got a lot of stares and whispers. I knew these people were talking about us. It wasn't hurting me. Maybe it made me stronger.

In 1966, while I was in Korea, my dad decided the family should stay in Iowa, in Muscatine. It's funny because I remember, when we used to migrate, sitting together at the table and talking about if we were ever to leave the hometown, where would we go? Where would we stay? We could never agree on one place, but Muscatine never came up.

My grandmother on my mother's side died in 1965, and my mother did not want to go back to Carrizo Springs. Even though my mother had her own family and my uncles had their own families, they were still close to my grandfather. They always traveled together, migrating back and forth, my grandfather and grandmother too. I think my mother's grieving was very strong, and she didn't want to face living there without her mother. When they were in Muscatine they were approached by the migrant program directors. They could stay and study English, and study for their GED, and get paid for it. So my mother and father stayed here. Two uncles and their families also decided to stay.

It was a shocker to see the discrimination here in Muscatine. Active discrimination, something you can see. There was also a silent discrimination that you could feel. Something that does not allow you to participate, and that's the one that I felt more. Also seeing discrimination against people from Mexico who did not speak English. Discrimination can take the form of being too nice, too. That's a way of not letting a person grow. I saw a lot of that. If I'm going to grow, I have to grow within myself and not by what others feel.

There were Mexicans who settled here before 1900. But those people were few, and I think the pressure must have been real heavy. Some of those people were hit so hard. I know some of them; they are Mexicans, and they deny it. We did not let that happen in the new Hispanic community. We had more support, more people, more media, things like that. I didn't want to lose my Mexican culture. It's part of me. And a lot of people didn't either. So they tended to stay together, unite among themselves. What grew here in Muscatine seems like two worlds, the Anglo world and the Mexican community. It's like a community within a community.

The Mexican community doesn't want to get involved with the Anglo community. But at the same time, there is discrimination within the Mexicans. If I struggle to be more American, I'm going to be discriminated against in my own community. In that sense I've had a lot more discrimination from my own people than from the Anglo community here in Muscatine. Myself, I tend to go both ways. I would say that most of my daily life is directed toward the English-speaking community, because that's where I have more contact in my job.

When I came to Muscatine the stereotype of us Mexicans was, they don't know how to do anything but physical labor or factory work. Bendac Tire Company, Heinz, Hon Industries; Muscatine has a good industrial base. You could feel the attitude, but it was not out in the open. The soliciting for labor was done in the Mexican community, but there weren't any Mexicans who owned their own businesses. There are now. It didn't take very long for this new community to start forming their own stores.

I had an alcoholic problem when I got out of the army, which did not help me grow up. In 1975 I decided to go through treatment. I started looking at being successful. That's when I hit the business world of Muscatine. It was a shocker, because I saw a lot of faces that were surprised to see a Mexican directing himself toward the business sector, where, in their minds, he didn't belong. I was approached by Carl Reichert, who owned a real estate company. He wanted to capture the Mexican market and asked me to work for him selling real estate. I took the opportunity right away. I enjoy working with people. I don't have a hard time meeting a stranger, and I can make small talk seem big. You might say I can be what Anglos call a "bullshitter." He gave me the opportunity and I took it.

In the last six months of that year I sold twenty-seven houses, and people were going, "Hey!" Here was a Mexican selling real estate. But I stood my ground. To me it wasn't something I was out to prove. Not just because they're Mexican, but give them an opportunity and those Mexicans will be successful too. That's the way I look at it. I am successful in the business world, but I'm still a Mexican.

I've met a lot of successful Mexican-Americans here in Iowa. Here in Muscatine there is a director, and we have teachers, but it really works both ways. There's discrimination in the Mexican community against those people. It's socioeconomic, rather than discrimination for being Mexican or Mexican-American. I feel that very strongly, and it hurts because it's my own race that doesn't want people to grow.

In my dealings I see a difference between Mexican-Americans and Mexicans, a difference in attitudes. All the aspects of their lives are different than ours. I'm real strong in my heritage and culture. But newly arrived Mexicans are also strong. They come and say, "This is the way it is, and who are you to tell me?" They tend to shy away from me. It's okay to get taken by a white person, but not from your own race. With that attitude it is harder for me to work with my own people. With Mexican people the more courteous you are, the more wary they are. They also say "half-breed." We're not half-breeds. That's the way they look at us, but they don't stop to think that Mexico was conquered by armies of single men. The mestizo, a new race, was born of the Spanish and Indian blood. In that, we're all half-breeds. I can feel that mestizo within me, and I'm proud of it.

A lot of Mexican males who come to the United States come alone. Socializing is a little different. It's like when I was in the army or a young guy out in Korea, I didn't socialize at church. I went to where the fun was. If I wasn't married, or didn't have a girlfriend, I'd be out looking for girls. The Mexican-Americans tend to look out for the Mexican that comes alone because the jealousy in the Mexican culture is there. If you have a wife or a daughter, you don't go to the same dances that Mexicans go to, because they'll ask her to dance right there in front of you. That doesn't cut it with the Mexican blood. And a lot of them are married back in Mexico. I guess it's just the animal in us.

Speaking about respect, the stereotype of machismo in the United

States is, I'm the man, I'm the boss. I'm not going to speak for Mexicans or Mexican-Americans, but I see a gentlemanly respect toward women. I open the door for women, I wouldn't let her carry the grocery bag. It's a matter of respect, your language in front of the opposite sex or even in front of your elders. People see that as being macho. To me it isn't macho, it's being a gentleman. The *caballero,* gentleman, comes from Mexican culture.

Family unity is important, but you also have to have a sense of community. You need to branch out. I encourage my children to go outside our family. Eighty percent of my life is English. For my kids, it's even more. Their growing up is based more in the Anglo community.

My daughter-in-law is the first Anglo in our family in all of the generations. It was hard for me to accept. I've apologized to her for that. I don't know who my new granddaughter will be like. With my son I tried to instill the heritage of being a gentleman, especially in the language. I say if you're going to speak English, at least speak it clean. I think, even though he's speaking English more than Spanish, he's taken that to heart.

I love music. It's kept me in touch with my culture. I always wanted to be a part of music. But I'm not a singer, and I can't play an instrument. I wasn't going to inspire any music that way. So I became a disc jockey and I fought for Mexican music.

I grew up with Elvis Presley, I had an Elvis Presley hairdo, and the kids called me Elvis. I knew all the songs word for word. When I was fifteen or sixteen years old I started listening to Mexican music, and it seemed to go deeper into my heart than the English songs. And I started learning the Spanish songs. When Ritchie Valens came along it uplifted a spirit within me. I loved what he did, and although a lot of Mexican-American bands were doing it before Ritchie, it was not known. When *La Bamba* came out I took the whole family to see it, my wife, son, and daughter. Raymond, my son, sat with some friends about three rows in front of us, and when the movie was over Raymond jumped up among his friends and yelled, "Yeah, Chicano!" It was a good movie. I especially liked it because I grew up in the Ritchie Valens era. I cried. My son was proud of that movie. I was even prouder because that was my era, and for another Valenzuela.

Twenty years ago I had no intention of becoming a disc jockey. I went to see why our local radio station didn't play Mexican music. "Well, we don't have a DJ that can do that." "How about me doing it?" I had the courage to stand up and say, "I'll do it, I'll learn." I explained what I would do. He liked it and today I'm still doing that show. It grew to six hours every Sunday, and has become part of the Mexican flavor of Muscatine.

MARÍA AGUIRRE
Pediatrician
Redlands, California

Four in the morning and María's day has already begun. She works out at the gym before 6:00 A.M. hospital rounds. Afterward, there are the young patients to see. In the late afternoon she picks up her own two children. Then there is shopping, dinner to cook, baths, and bedtime stories. Often the day doesn't end there—babies are born, children get sick, and María is on call.

These aren't her only responsibilities. As the oldest of ten children, she is on call to her parents and siblings, who are spread about the country. Tall, slim, and elegant, she manages this exhausting schedule with organization and humor.

First of all, I was brought up with the notion that it was much better to be white. It was much better. Just, you're a better person if you're white. I didn't feel sorry for myself, but I longed to be white. I just felt that they were better people, they couldn't possibly do anything wrong. This was from education, but also from my family. I remember saying something to my uncle about applying to Berkeley, because I had gotten in on a minority status. He said, "When they asked you what you were, what did you say? You didn't say you were Mexican, did you? Oh, my God! How could you be so stupid?" He knew that's what we were, but it would have been much better to have been able to pass for white.

The other thing is, I always thought that speaking Spanish was like a mortal sin. We couldn't speak Spanish in school. In the convent you were fined. It was a dollar every time you got caught speaking Spanish. It was like a bad language, something vile. Even your thoughts were in English. All I could assume was, shit, I must be making up for a lot of sins. Yes. And that's just an accepted way of life. That's the way it was; I don't think our family is very different than others.

Like my grandmother. Oh, my grandmother would have nothing to do with anyone who was dark. My father told me, "Don't drink coffee because you're going to get dark." Don't drink coffee? Yes. And black coffee! Why would you want to do that to your body? Get it darker? No, no, my father was always so proud of me because I drank milk.

What's interesting is my father's favorites are the two lightest in my family, and the one that he picks on the most is the darkest. I think there is some significance. And he is not very light, my father. That's the amazing part. My grandmother is the one that was really racist in that. It has something to do with the soul, you know, the light soul or the dark soul.

When I was six my mother put me in the public school down the street. That was so I would be eligible to go into first grade at a Catholic school when I was seven. I remember the nun thought I could go into second grade, but my mother wanted me to get the full education. It didn't matter how old I was.

I remember, one thing—our lunches. First grade. Having this sack lunch. Oh my God, this was the most embarrassing thing during that time. To have your mother give you a tortilla. Oh, my God, how awful. It was terrible. We would have given anything to have Wonder Bread, just to be normal. But no, a tortilla—with chorizo. Of course the red grease would seep through, right? And you'd have this terrible mark on your bag. Oh my God, I hated that. I hated it because you knew you were slime. It's so interesting, because my kids would kill to have a tortilla in their lunch, and nobody pays attention. I remember, the kids were lining up. We put our lunches down row by row. First of all I didn't have a lunch box. God, I would have given anything for a lunch box, but no, a bag, okay. I remember my heart going really fast thinking, Oh my God, are they going to see my lunch bag? I need to go get that thing out of there and turn it around so they won't see the big greasy stain. I remember screaming out at the nun. She let me do it, thank God. It's so vivid in my mind.

There was this one girl, Aurora. She lived with her grandmother and her brother. She always wore a braid. That hairstyle didn't change the entire time I was with her, from first to the eighth grade. One day I had to work with her on a project. I had this sheet of paper to write down our address and phone number. She wrote it down and she gave it to me. She was a very studious person, very quiet. She handed me the piece of paper and I'm looking at it and I'm thinking, "What is this?" It's just chit-chit-chit, little lines. I was really annoyed. I said, "Write that down, I need to have your address." So she wrote it bigger. But what I realized later, she was so ashamed of where she lived, you see, that she wrote her address really tiny, so that nobody could see it. To her I lived in a much better neighborhood.

My father wanted me to be a nun. And my mother, in retrospect, I don't think she really wanted me to go. But she didn't have the chutzpah to say, it's okay, you don't have to go. So after eighth grade I went to Catholic high school, a convent, for about three years.

I remember crying because I was homesick; I wanted to come home. It was boarding school, in Mississippi. In Mississippi, yes! I only came back in the summer. I was home for three months and then I'd go back again.

After my third year I decided I needed a summer job. I wanted money to buy clothes to go back, you know underwear and stuff. I went to this Catholic hospital thinking they owed me a job, because I was going to be a nun. It was run by the nuns. They had to give me a job even if it was as a maid. They decided to give me a nurse's aide job. After that I had an acute awareness of other things going on in this world. In the convent we never saw a newspaper or TV. You just studied, did your homework, you read your mail, and then went to bed. That was it. There was no contact for three years.

When I left at the end of my junior year in high school I didn't leave on such good terms. It was a school for young women studying to be nuns, but it was also a boarding school. And if you were an aspirant you couldn't be caught speaking to those who were boarders. The boarders were from Latin America: Nicaragua, Honduras, from very wealthy families. Their parents were from big corporations like United Fruit Company. The thinking was that you had no business speaking to them, they were girls of worldly ways, and you would forget why you were there. So you never spoke to them, never. If you were caught it was like a mortal sin; I really thought it was a mortal sin.

So okay, before the end of my junior year I was sitting on the steps talking to this girl who was a boarder. Somebody snitched on me.

Mother Superior called me into her office and let me know that I was basically scum. That's when I decided not to go back, which tore my father, especially my father, apart. I was his ticket to heaven and I wasn't going to go back. Mother Superior wrote to me, she just couldn't believe I wasn't going to go back. I had already made up my mind. My father took it very bad.

After that I went to Saint Mary's University in premed. I had decided to go into biology, so I went in and talked to the chairman of the department. He told me to give up. I was a female and Mexican and I was not going to get into medical school, so I should apply to nursing. He told me to forget it. So I did. I transferred to nursing. Still, I don't know why, but I kept taking the requisite premed courses.

I ended up getting my degree. Oh it's so stupid, I had enough credits to have a bachelor's in biology and nursing. But when I went to apply, you know you have to fill out the papers for your degree. That nun didn't think . . . what did I need with two majors? I didn't need two majors; just apply for one. Like I was being ridiculous, even though I had the credits for both. So I said okay. She would know best, I mean she was a nun, right? Oh. So I got it in nursing. The other one just went by the wayside.

I kept on working at the hospital that had initially hired me part-time, the county hospital attached to the University of Texas Medical School. It was the end of my senior year and they wouldn't give me the hours I wanted. I went to see what I could do about it. The woman there rearranged my schedule and asked if I had seen the notice on recruitment for medical schools. "Why don't you take an hour off and go down there?"

That's when I met Fred Lopez. We started talking about something and he said, "You know we're having breakfast tomorrow at Mario's. Why don't you come?" I thought, "What the hell, I'm not working anyway in the morning." So I went and it turns out that they needed a token minority for medical school in Berkeley. I wrote my application letter on a piece of stationery! Oh, what typewriter? I didn't have a typewriter! All I could do is write it as best as I could, you know, and hope to God. Oh! Pure luck, by the grace of God did I get in.

See, my father was so pissed off at me because when I finished my nursing I said I was going to move out of the house. It was not like my sister. My sister just threatened to move out. Oh she would go to my grandmother's, and stay one night, and get too homesick, and come back. She was always pulling that. I didn't say anything, I just said, "You know, Mother, I'm going to leave on such and such a day." I had already made arrangements. I was going to move in with three other girls. My father stopped speaking to me!

I was already a woman, with a profession; I had my R.N. It was unheard of, unheard of! I must be up to no good. I was twenty-four. Uh-huh, twenty-four!

But when my father found out that I had been accepted to Berkeley it was like the most marvelous thing in the world. He told my mother, it didn't matter where I was going to go, or where I was going to be living, it didn't matter how far away I was, the fact that I was in school was good enough for him. So actually, as much of a *cabrón* as my father could be, if it weren't for him I wouldn't have half this, because it was always to please my father.

Things were never good enough for him. If I came home with an A— why didn't I get an A. If I came home with an A, why didn't I get an A+. Oh! Actually, he was the great impetus in my life. I always thought my father was very bright. He would help me with college math problems, even though he never finished high school. He went to the ninth grade, that was it. The man knew what he was talking about, but oh, he was a terrible teacher. Terrible. My God, you didn't dare come home with a bad grade. I mean we got hit, with a belt. There was no such thing as banishing, or punishment. Forget it! We just got beat, and good and hard.

Well, you know we also went on the *pizca,* picking cherries. My sister was telling me, "You've got to go see this movie, *La Bamba.* It brought back so many memories, and for God's sake, don't go with your Anglo husband, because he will not appreciate this."

I said, "Well like what?"

"Well did you know that they took communal baths?" We didn't know that because my father would never let us associate with anybody else in the *pizca.* I don't know how he always finagled it for our family to be separate from the rest of the camp. We would take a bath only on Saturdays. The water was too cold to take a bath every day, and on Saturdays we had enough time to heat the water. We always took a bath inside, that is inside the little complex where we were.

Tita said to me, "Girl, was that a stable we were at?" Yes! A stable once and a barn another time. Yes, it was like our vacation. Have you any idea how protected? Listen, he did all right by us. Those people looking into the different shower stalls and peeking through, I thought, "Oh, thank God. I would have been devastated." Oh my God.

Oh yes, the mere thought of ever getting pregnant. There was no doubt in my mind we would have been dragged through the streets. I had this vision of being grabbed by my hair and being dragged through the streets—before the crime. My father always took things really seriously. Very very emotional, yes.

I think my father is really proud of me. If it hadn't been for him I wouldn't have had any kind of impetus. Every grade that I had before college was certainly for him or for fear. I was never too old to get hit, never. He was behind it. Yes he is proud of me, and he does do what I say once in a while. The last time I was there I had him put a heating pad on. I told him, "Just leave it there, it will be okay." I burned him. He left it there and never said a word. He is a difficult man. I don't know, I would have never stayed with a person like that.

But my mother's not a saint either. When we were fighting and she couldn't control us, she would call Daddy at work. At work! He's an auto body man, for God's sake! Get him on the phone, "Talk to your children." I can't imagine calling up David, "Stop whatever you're doing and talk to Zack." He would divorce me! He would ask to talk to one of us, and God help you because if he was going to talk to you, you were going to get it.

But you know I used to think that my mother was just perfect. I'll never forget, once when she made chicken. Every piece had been taken and somebody wanted another. They were still hungry. She gave them her piece. That was really impressive; I wouldn't have given up my piece. I thought she was a saint. I mean, how could you give away a piece of chicken?

Boys could never come to the house. No. I remember my father slapping my sister several times because a boy called and asked for her and he happened to answer the phone. He would hang up on the kid. She was a senior in high school, and he would proceed to slap her, really, a lot. Yes, I remember that. It's a miracle we got married at all. And have boys over? My God. God forbid!

I didn't start dating until very late, my second year in college. And it was bad enough that everyone had to give him the third degree. My father used to give them the third degree with his eye. Oh, I hated that. And of course you had your brothers and sisters looking out, looking out of the blinds, pointing, laughing.

This one guy that I went out with was a physician from Mexico. He thought it was ridiculous that I would want to go to medical school. Couldn't I take up the piano instead? I hated the piano. I knew how to play, but I wasn't going to do that for a living. After that, we dated very infrequently. He was very nice, a gentleman, one that would take me out and put a napkin over the prices on the menu. How nice—no one had ever done that to me. But mostly men weren't really interested in what I had to do or wanted to do. It didn't matter. Sort of egotistical. Actually, David was the only one who would ever tolerate me. We're so opposite in temperament. If I had married a man from my culture he would have had to suppress a lot of things. Not only with me but with my family.

So David had one up on us because he was white. If he were Mexican he would have had to be a super, super achiever, maybe the mayor, Henry Cisneros. Even then there would have been some criticism. Oh, David, he cannot do anything wrong. He is *el Santo*. And God forbid that I say anything to him in a short tone of voice in front of my father. He just cannot deal with it and will later on take me aside and tell me how terrible I am.

Oh well, I always get called up about some illness. "I have this pain here" or whatever there, you know. If I don't know what it is over the phone, "Why did you go to medical school?"

"Mother, please. I don't know because you're big." Thank God I'm a pediatrician.

There are things I do differently with my own children. One, I was never shown any respect as a child. My father really thought that children should be seen and not heard. They couldn't have anything to contribute, to a conversation, to anything. God forbid that you would say something if they were having an argument.

Still, I do remember laughing a lot, having a good time. In the *pizca* I remember laughing and laughing. I remember laughing more than crying or being sad. I do. But no one ever listened or carried on a conversation with me like I do with Marisol or Zack. I don't think my mother did it out of meanness, I think she thought I had nothing important to say.

I do see myself reverting back, telling them stories of what could happen if they don't mind me. "Let me tell you the story of the little boy . . ." Or "The Face": If you make a face at your mother, God forbid, your face will stay that way. People who look at themselves in the mirror go loco; they go crazy. Gross things. And everybody knew these stories, all my neighbors, it was like a phenomenon. But I swear to God everybody accepted them.

When I was growing up, from first grade even into college, you tried to forget where you're from. It certainly was not something I was very proud of. No, you wanted to be accepted. No, in fact, the more Anglo you became, the more Anglo a name you had, the better. I remember my mother registering me in eighth grade. My name was María Guadalupe Aguirre. All this time, my friends, "Hi, Mary. Hi, Mary." But what does my mother do? She goes and registers me, Gua–da–lupe! Oh, I thought, no, I just can't bear it.

No, I called the school! Pretended I was my mother; "Yes, I made a mistake on the registration form. My daughter's name, yes." I was beside myself. What if they found out that I wasn't Mary? Uh-huh, what if they thought I was Mexican? I mean, my God, a dead giveaway. Incorporate your culture? No! You tried to blend in and lay low.

I didn't really come to an awareness as to who or what I was until I came to Berkeley. Then it was okay. Oh, I was an oddity, but it was okay. I remember one of the first friends I had. She was Jewish and very generous with me. She was great. She would say, "Teach me to say something in Spanish." She just thought it was so marvelous. "What is the word for *to pee?*"

"*Mey–ar.*"

"*Mey–ar?*"

"*Si, mear.*"

"*Voy mear!*" Really loud. Everyone could hear, but then it was all right. It was okay.

SUPERMAN ES ILEGAL

Es un pájaro
Es un avión
No hombre, es un mojado.

Llegó del cielo y no en avión
venia en su nave, desde Criptón
y por lo visto no es un americano
sino otro igual como yo, indocumentado.

Así es que "Migra" el no debe de trabajar
porque aunque duela Superman es ilegal.
Es periodista, también yo soy
y no fué al Army, a que camión.

Y aquel es güero, ojos azules, bien formado
y yo prietito, gordiflón y muy chaparro,
pero yo al menos en mi patria ya marché
con el coyote que pagué cuando cruzé.

No cumplió con el servicio militar,
no paga impuestos y le hace al judicial.
No tiene "mica" ni permiso pa' volar.
Y les apuesto que ni seguro social.

Hay que echar a Superman de esta región
y si se puede regresarlo pa' Criptón.
¿Donde está esa autoridad de emigración?
¿Que hay de nuevo, Don Racismo, en la nación?

De que yo sepa no lo multan por volar
sino al contrario lo declaran Superman.

Jorge Lerma

SUPERMAN IS AN ILLEGAL

It's a bird.
It's a plane.
No, man, it's a wetback.

He arrived by air but not in an airplane
he came in his ship all the way from Krypton
it appears that he is not an American;
he is just like me, undocumented.

So you see Border Patrol, he shouldn't work
because even though it hurts, Superman is an illegal;
he's a journalist, well so am I
and he didn't go to the Army, oh what a deal.

And he is blond, blue-eyed, and well-built
and I'm dark, chubby, and very short
but at least I have already marched
with the smuggler I had to pay when I crossed the border.

He didn't comply with military service,
he doesn't pay taxes and he acts like a judge.
He doesn't have a green card nor a license to fly
and I bet he doesn't even have a social security card.

We have to deport Superman from this region
and if possible return him to Krypton.
Where is that immigration authority when you need it?
What's new, Mr. Racism, in the nation?

That I know of, he hasn't been fined for flying
on the contrary he has been named "Superman."

12

El Corrido Nuevo

A NEW VERSE

The future for the illegal immigration business is definitely bullish.
The Mexican economy doesn't look as if it's going to improve soon enough to generate the jobs needed for the country's population. Then, because Mexico is investing in industrial growth at the expense of agriculture, the rural infrastructure and amenities have continued to deteriorate, intensifying the exodus from the countryside. While most flock to the big cities, many campesinos *just keep on going until they reach* los Estados Unidos.
In the short term, immigration takes pressure off the Mexican economy. And money sent home from el norte, *a very effective, informal, grassroots foreign aid, keeps intact what remains of the rural standard of living. Immigration also keeps some population pressure off highly stressed cities like the capital and Guadalajara.*
North of the border, immigrants still meet the need for a low-paid, energetic, and disciplined work force. Pressure on U.S. industry and agriculture from low-cost foreign producers will keep demand high. Couple this with the scarcity of entry-level workers at the end of the baby boom generation, and there seems to be no lack of jobs for any Mexican who comes north.
Ironically, as baby boomers age, they will increasingly outnumber the active work force needed to keep their social security benefits coming. Mexico is a likely source of young replacement workers.

Ambivalence really sets in when the U.S. public, however guardedly, acknowledges that "These Mexicans aren't really causing that many problems," that they are productive, mostly taking jobs that would remain undone if left to Americans. They have always been pretty self-sufficient, since families, compadres, *and friends look after one another and use relatively little in the way of public services.*

So, immigration from the south will continue, waxing and waning with economic and political conditions in each country. Beneath all the rhetoric neither side can afford to stop it, even if they knew how. In the states along either side of the border, Mexicans and Americans continue to make their own arrangements. As independent in nature as the southwest Americans and northern Mexicans are, if it's not in their own interest they don't much care what is said three thousand miles away in Washington, D.C., or Mexico D.F.

Towering above all arguments, reasonable or prejudiced, the United States views its ability to control its borders as the privilege of a sovereign state. With increased pressure from people attempting to cross outside the law, it will escalate expenditures of manpower and material to demonstrate that commitment.

Yet, rising above even that, this migration, like any major movement growing naturally from the conditions of life, has always had a purpose and momentum of its own. Conditions change from time to time and person to person, but invariably the underlying reason is to provide sustenance and stability for the migrants and their families. If they cannot find it on their own side, they will seek it on the other.

They begin the process of creating, building, achieving that stability, that provision. In doing so, they pass something, a stake in what they have built, on to the next generation. That is what this great trek has always been about.

Indelibly etched in the very earth they travel, after more than one hundred years, this greatest movement of a people in human times rolls on. Like a river responding to the land, it gains momentum with gravity's pull, is nearly brought to a halt by some massive blockage, but it moves again, if only at a trickle, until a break is found. Only when it finds parity with its surroundings will it halt.

JESÚS (CHUEY) HINOJOSA
City Planner
College Station, Texas

As head of the Department of Urban and Regional Planning at Texas A&M University's College of Architecture, Jesús looks as distinguished as his title. He has thick salt-and-pepper hair and dark, sincere eyes; he wears a long-sleeved white shirt and tie even in the summer swelter of Texas.

There is irony here. Jesús, who has helped develop plans for the future of major cities throughout the western hemisphere, hails from a little southwestern Texas town of a couple of thousand people. Threading through the awards, diplomas, photos, and maps there is a path from a pinpoint on the map of Texas, where a child who couldn't speak English began, to where a man planning cities and teaching the next generation has his fingers on the pulse of the future.

Edcouch is a small town, about two or three thousand people, just fifteen miles north of the Mexican border, in the middle of the Rio Grande Valley ranching and agricultural region. I was born there December 25, 1935. Christmas baby, that's why my name is Jesús.

Now the Rio Grande is the border, a big barrier. But when my father was a kid it was just another river. They lived and worked on the Texas side because this used to all be part of Mexico. The river wasn't a border to them; they crossed to work in the fields of south Texas.

By the time I was a kid, to visit my grandparents and relatives, we had to cross the border and clear customs on the American side and the Mexican side. You were very much crossing a border—gates—you had to clear with your visas, permits, and everything.

I very seldom go back to Mexico. Though our grandparents have passed away, we still have relatives in Reynosa and Monterrey. My brothers are still in the valley, farming, and they keep more in touch. They go back and forth regularly. I guess I'm more like my father. I'm an American Mexican.

There's so much hassle to go to Mexico that it's discouraging to me. All this clearance with customs. I feel unsure of security. I'm not sure I can depend on the system to take care of things. We have friends, we have family in Mexico. They're great. I love them, and they're all very hospitable. But you always have this great unknown or uncertainty. You don't know whether you are going to be turned back. If something goes wrong, then what?

I had a very bad experience coming in from a conference in Canada. A very obnoxious lady at the U.S. Immigration Service questioned me, no, grilled me. I almost missed my flight. I never experienced anything like it, because every other time U.S. Immigration was very proper. Courteous, but firm. Serious, but never like this gal. She thought I was a Mexican citizen. I almost came to the point of blowing up. I had never been treated like that in my life, but most of the time they think I am not an American. I'm always an outsider. I have to justify myself, prove myself. It's a never-ending struggle.

Once when we were doing some research I went to the Texas land office in Austin. I found this old map of south Texas, probably one of the oldest maps available. Big sections of land were owned by the Hinojosas—Spanish Land Grant—from the 1700s and 1800s. Large parts of south Texas belonged to the Hinojosa family. I knew then that we came from people who were important, before Texas was a state, before the northeast was settled.

The segregationist attitudes seem to magnify racism. You know, we're all human beings on this earth. We just happen to have some slightly different backgrounds. Ultimately we have to look at a person for the values they represent regardless of skin color or cultural heritage. We're all immigrants or from immigrant stock. We're a microcosm of the world, the most heterogeneous country in the world, and that's what gives us our strength. And it's something we need to protect. Oh, I love the United States. With all its problems, it's the country with the greatest potential for human freedom in the world.

CARLOS SALINAS DE GORTARI
Presidente de Mexico
Radio Interview, February 16, 1988
Guadalajara, Mexico

For our side, the Mexican side, we must treat our people with dignity. In the visit I made to the northern border zone of our country I found they were ill-treated by their own compatriots on our Mexican side, unacceptably treated. Many of them are victims of extortion, abused. We must act with energy in the Mexican Republic so that our compatriots by right have their liberty of transit in our territory, because this is what our Constitution says. We must recognize that we have to have respect for ourselves.

I have asked that for the American side also, in what they do, they treat our Mexican people in a humane manner, with respect for their rights. We must remember that with the instability that we have, these *mexicanos* take many risks to find better employment, better salaries. Would that they be able to stay in our country, would that we could generate in the Mexican fields, in the fields Jaliciense, the opportunities for employment. But there is a reality, and this reality is that those southern states of the United States require and demand workers of the quality, the type of work, and the salary levels that pay our compatriots to migrate. It is fundamental that they recognize this, that the North American economy requires these workers, and before everything they must guarantee their rights as humans, not only on the American side where they know they are not documented, that they pay taxes, contributions to the social security, and they don't receive any services in exchange. It is like a net contribution to the North American economy.

And on the Mexican side as well, we must treat them with respect and castigate the extortionists. A Mexican migrant told me in the bus station in Tijuana that some of the public security forces there in the frontera know one by the manner that they are looking for orientation, and immediately they try to extort money from them. This is unacceptable.

There must be dignity on both sides of the border. With all the strength we can summon, we will recover the dynamic growth of our country, so there will exist employment for the majority of our people within the country of Mexico.

CUAUHTÉMOC MENENDEZ
Construction Worker
Guadalajara, Mexico
From Chapter 7

After working ten years in the United States, Cuauhtémoc returned to Mexico for good. His perspective on illegal immigration is based in his personal experience of life, work, and unemployment on both sides.

In the United States, to get rid of all the illegals, you don't need a border or the Immigration. Simply, if there is no work, what would the illegals do there? Really, I don't see the reason to form groups and lines at the border like in the thirties. The United States is an advanced industrial society, the same in the city as it is in the agricultural areas. It's logical that there is the need for workers. For the United States it is a great advantage, because Mexican labor is very cheap. The illegal produces his product much cheaper, and they can sell it cheaper to the American people. In this sense the illegal helps the United States.

He also helps Mexico. All of the *mojados* bring money back. We don't take money out of Mexico. Those of us who work in the United States help our country more than the rich who send their Mexican money out. We support our country.

Normally the Mexican who goes to the United States goes to work in jobs that many Americans don't want. In the first place, it's hard work. I'm not going to say that they can't do the work, but they don't want to work for the same price as the Mexican. It's clear that there is this contradiction, this antipathy toward the Mexican who is there illegally. They look at the *mojados* as scabs. The Chicanos and Mexican-Americans look at us from this perspective because they think we are the reason they don't have jobs. But it's not true. We are there at the convenience of the owners and bosses who want cheap labor, cheaper than they can get there. It isn't our fault. We have the necessity to work. I don't think it's a sin to subsist in another country that offers the opportunity to live a little better than is possible for us in Mexico.

Some Americans think they are going to take away our work, but it isn't certain, because it's an important factor to the economy of the United States. What I want to say is that I didn't take work away from any North American. What happened was, there was a competition for the work. I'm not saying I was better, but I worked harder, and they paid for the work. My boss always accepted me because my work was good; he knew it was good. I worked faster and harder. For this my work was accepted. You know, an American boss doesn't pay someone for his good looks, no matter where you're from, nor for friendships or *compadrazgo*. It's for the skill. If a Mexican can demonstrate that he's a good worker, they will pay him.

I think the Mexican works harder there than here. There isn't any reason here. What they pay you doesn't correspond. They don't pay you for what you spend in energy. With what you are paid there, you can eat in comfort. And a worker who is fed well has the energy to produce more, to be stronger. Here in Mexico you don't earn enough to replenish the energy you spend working.

Another of the positive things in the United States is you don't need so much bureaucratic paperwork to enter a company. Here they don't accept you unless you have a police clearance, and certificates from grammar school; now in some factories they require a certificate from the preparatory school. They have so many requisites. There it's much different. They give you a short form with a few questions, and instead of a recommendation, they give you a two-week trial. What recommends you is your work. This is a big difference.

MARTIN DEL CAMPO
Architect
San Francisco, California
From Chapter 9

Mexican immigrants are reluctant to give up their citizenship. Only 2.4 to 5.0 percent of those eligible choose to become U.S. citizens, as compared with 23 to 33 percent of immigrants from other countries. This explains why, in view of their numbers, they are severely underrepresented. Martin's personal experience describes the dilemma and a unique solution for many of those seeking a life in the United States.

God, the problem of immigration is a terrible problem, but it benefits both countries. Mexico has so many pressures of overpopulation and lack of work. To them it's great to send people out to a prosperous country to work. If they would make it easier, officially accept that this is a solution, it could be like the *bracero* program, structured and on a temporary basis. This is what the Mexican workers would like anyhow. Many don't return to Mexico because they are afraid that if they go they won't be able to come back here. In other words, open up the border.

It's both governments' fault that this is not done. The United States is afraid an invasion of low-paid labor would compete against American labor, and the Mexicans are afraid of an invasion of business investment. I think the fears are obsolete now. They are afraid of the United States taking control of their economy and eventually annexing the country.

It's a super, super difficult problem, and I don't even pretend to know how to solve it. But I think it is a matter of good faith, and a commitment not to kid ourselves about what is and what is not. There's no question that it benefits both countries.

Well the United States government has this terrible complex, a tendency to humiliate smaller countries, especially Latin American countries, by treating them as dependents or poor relatives.

Yes I saw once, President Duarte of El Salvador. He came to a ceremony, walked about twenty paces, and kissed the flag of the United States. He thought it was a show of friendship, but for any Latin American: "What? You're the president of your country, kissing another country's flag? What's more, a country who in a sense is your oppressor." The kiss was for the $530 billion spent there.

On the other hand I truly feel that I am of the two sides, of the two countries. I've lived long enough here to realize how Americans feel. Yet I still feel like a Mexican. There's no way out of it. You can't give up. It's not renounceable, your allegiance to a country, you just can't if you grew up there.

Well, what happens? I became a citizen of the United States in 1960. When I wanted to go back to Mexico to work, the consul of Mexico told me it would be best to go back and ask for reparation of my Mexican citizenship. I tried to do that and it took the four years I was living there, *en trámite* as they call it, trying to get it. And I didn't get it. When I finally received the letter from one of the ministries saying they were ready to review my case, I was ready to come back here. So

I said, "Why do I want it? I need to be an American to work there." So I came back here as an American.

The same consul that gave me this bad advice told me, "You know I gave you very bad advice. I found out later on that even though there is a law on the books that allows you to recover your citizenship, no one has ever recovered it. I also found out"—he was a very decent fellow and a good friend—"that I had the power to give you this paper that says you're a Mexican. So I am going to give it to you."

I said, "No, I don't want it anymore."

"Well, whether you like it or not, I'm going to give it to you." So he gave me a certificate that I am a Mexican, that I have never lost my citizenship. So I have a strange status.

It's impossible to have two citizenships, but that's an idea that I would like to advise the government in Mexico to take seriously. If they were to do like some countries—I'm thinking of Argentina, Turkey, and several others—once you are of that citizenship you cannot renounce it. In other words, once you're a Mexican, you are always a Mexican. If Mexico were to pass a law that says that, it would allow untold numbers of Mexicans who live here to become citizens, vote, and exercise power without losing the right to be Mexicans, which is what they don't want. That means that the government of Mexico would acquire a lot more influence through these people in the United States. I don't know why they haven't done it. If I could get close to people in the government I would advise them of that.

It's very traumatic, you know. I finally acquired my U.S. citizenship after eleven years of living here. I did it on my partner's advice. My lack of citizenship was hurting us, getting in the way of getting jobs. I don't think it was really, but at that time I thought so. And it's very traumatic to appear, if you're serious, if you're an honest person, to say, "I give up all allegiance to Mexico." You can't give up allegiance to Mexico. How can you? If you had to give up allegiance to the United States, you couldn't do it. How could you do it?

And what allegiance means is concern. That I worry when something happens to the country. That I feel good when good things happen, and I feel bad when bad things happen. That's what allegiance is. It doesn't mean that you take a rifle to shoot someone. But it's impossible to give up allegiance to a country. For instance I know that Willy Brandt, the former mayor of Berlin and later the prime minister, had become a citizen of Norway during the war. No one ever held it against him when he was running for prime minister: You gave up your citizenship! You became a citizen of another country!

You know it's just a practical thing. This whole thing of citizenship and allegiance is very primitive. It's like saying you love only one parent. One shouldn't be pitted against another that way.

ALBERT BAEZ
Environmentalist and Physicist
Greenbrae, California
From Chapter 9

Through his work with UNICEF, Dr. Baez organized science education projects in numerous countries of the world. He brings an intimate view of the benefits of science to an emerging country.

We have this image of the lazy Mexican, but I can't imagine a group of Americans doing the stoop labor that the Mexicans do in our fields. That image is obviously wrong. The Mexican is capable of doing hard, hard labor. And when you get the head of Coca-Cola, a Mexican, running a company like that, you know that Mexicans are capable of high-powered business too.

I would like to see more Mexicans involved in science, because the advances that countries such as Japan have made are due in great part to the fact that they are very, very science oriented. They've pushed science and technology.

Without that basic knowledge, Mexico will always be subservient to other countries. They will only be *maquiladoras,* never the innovators and the entrepreneurs. There will never be the hope of creating an economy that will sustain Mexicans at home, that they will not be drawn to the United States for their opportunities.

DR. JORGE BUSTAMANTE
Presidente, Colegio de la Frontera Norte
Tijuana, Mexico

Educated in the United States at the University of Notre Dame, Dr. Bustamante participated in one of the early documentations of Mexican immigration to the United States. He has become a foremost authority on border issues.

We have been photographically documenting those crossing the border. But we haven't seen that much change since the [1986] immigration reform law was passed. It coincides with the agricultural seasons: from September we see fewer people, and after January they return. For a period of three weeks in May 1987 there were fewer people, and the U.S. Immigration reported that the new law had been effective. Now when there are the usual numbers returning after the first of the year, they won't say the new law isn't working, they will say it's because of the peso devaluation.

The main problem is that it was a unilateral solution for a bilateral problem. Therefore, it has not been resolved. Until this is recognized, illegal immigration won't be resolved.

The law will make it somewhat more difficult for the immigrants, but there is a great fallacy built into it. It is supposed to penalize the employers, but a large loophole was left for them. According to the law, they just have to say they saw the employee's documentation. The employer doesn't have to make copies of it or verify it. There is nothing he needs. When he goes to court he just has to say that he saw what he thought was legitimate documentation. So as far as an employee sanction, it effectively doesn't exist.

And it can't exist. Anyone who knows Los Angeles or California knows that immigrant labor is a vital need.

And yes, the government of Mexico needs to recognize what they are losing.

A solution can only be worked out through a group consisting of representatives of both governments, the employers, and the immigrants themselves. But I'm not really optimistic that this will transpire in the near future.

JUAN CADENA
Director, Muscatine Migrant Committee
Muscatine, Iowa
From Chapter 11

In the short term we'll continue to see a lot of *mexicanos* coming across the border. And we will receive them; we need them because they're doing the work. As long as we need them they'll be coming in.

I've always said that eventually Mexico and the United States will be one country. There won't be a Mexico or United States and probably not a Canada either. You know we just broke some of the barriers with Canada, and I think that's going to be true with Mexico. As more countries move to support Mexico, as Japan and Switzerland have, I honestly believe that we will wipe out the border. Probably not in my lifetime, but in the foreseeable future. That's my hope; I think it's just a natural process, just like in Europe. Out of necessity they are becoming one nation in a sense. Even England, that doesn't want to; they're bringing her in kicking and screaming, but she is still coming in. Even with the war in Ireland, even with Poland and the Communist bloc, they are all going to become one Europe.

For our own economic survival that's going to happen here too. And as we Mexicans get more political power . . . it is changing; we have a black army chief of staff and Mexicans in positions on the national level. We are going to see more and more of that. As we have more power and more say, the attitude toward Mexico will change. We will make it change.

RICARDO AGUILAR MELANTZÓN
Writer
El Paso, Texas
From Chapter 10

Immigration. It is a historical movement. It is not a social movement; it is not an economic movement; it is not a political movement. It's a historical movement. People are coming up. They're diligent people.

They need to, they want to be paid for their services. This is a place where there's food and work and possibilities for a future.

Since the Republicans came in, they have done away with the possibility of a future for many Latin American countries. I blame Ronald Reagan and his *camarilla* of really very, very malignant people. There were solutions possible then, that there are no longer.

The present president of Mexico is right wing. He's trying to fix things by making public endeavors private. And I agree that the Mexican economy should be mixed, because that's the way it started out. Yes, little by little it began to be state-ized, became part of the state. That's wrong. But just selling it to the private sector isn't going to solve the problem. That's like selling it from here to tomorrow. The private sector is going to take advantage, as it always has. It's going to continue to treat workers badly, pay them slave wages. People are still not going to be able to save, their children are not going to have a future. Unfortunately, this historical movement is going to continue.

In Mexico there is no possibility of establishing an infrastructure in the small towns and cities from which the people are immigrating. Without this, there will be no reason for them to stay. Mexico has created this in its strategy to become a twentieth-century urbanized nation. It is still, whether they want it, whether we want it or not, an agrarian country. It is not a developed country. It is not going to develop into a developed country soon. The fields are left barren and everybody is moving to the cities or to *el norte. Por abajo.* Now we're the importers of beans and corn, the staples. *¿Qué hacemos?* I don't think there's any way of stopping it.

Then there is the church. It has done really terrible things to the Mexican families. *¡Cómo se dice la canción?* How does the song go? It's too little, too late, to last, or *algo así,* to try to stop the family from growing so much. One of the big reasons for immigration is the population explosion. *¡Imagínate!* Twenty kids in a family. I've seen them. And then you have single parents like hell. *Por todas partes* everywhere, because men are allowed to leave women with families. Juárez, the whole population of Juárez is single female parents with six kids. It's total irresponsibility. It's *todo* Mexico. The whole question of double standards and the church saying it's okay, go ahead and have *quién sabe cuántos hijos* [who knows how many children]. Bad! And just making the situation worse and worse.

But see, what's going to happen is that the United States is going to have to pay. If anybody in this hemisphere had the obligation to think about what's going to happen to the Americas, it was the United States, the big brother, *tú sabes*. Instead of creating the possibility for these people to work their own land or develop their own businesses, what happens? The U.S. backs North American corporate interests to go after any and all of Mexico's natural and economic resources. They're trying to get all the copper in Mexico into the United States. *Todas las cosas,* the petroleum *también, ¿no?* It's kind of like the little rabbit in the Quik commercials, *ssssssip,* takes it all in and then there's nothing. Nothing for them and nothing for us.

¿Qué va a pasar? [What's going to happen?] They can't stop immigration. There is no way to stop it unless a wall like the iron curtain is set up, the Berlin wall, or *algo así*—some *Star Wars* wall or something. I don't know. Even then, they'll find a way to go under it.

What eventually will happen if problems don't get solved is that the United States will have to reduce its southern border. The only way to do that is geographically. Invade and go all the way down to Guatemala. Probably so. It's going to have to happen, because otherwise institutions within the country will not be able to stand this great mass of people coming in, no possibility of creating enough new jobs, and economic insecurity on all sides. Mexico too will feel it very, very badly because it's losing its skilled labor. *Entonces* what's going to happen?

Either that or the United States has to try to create a magnet there. Would a Marshall plan work? *No sé.* I don't know. Look, if it's not in the form of money and it cannot be sold, then it might work.

PADRE LUIS OLIVARES, C.M.F.
Pastor, La Placita
Church of Nuestra Señora Reyna de Los Angeles
Los Angeles, California

In his study, alongside the plaza where, in 1777, eleven families recruited by Governor Felipe de Neve founded the City of Angels, Padre Olivares talks of a just and amenable future for those who seek the opportunity of el norte.

It's a war zone! This antidrug campaign that is being carried out is an attempt to control the border as the solution. There's no question that drugs are crossing, and there's no question that Mexico represents the funnel or channel with which other Latin American countries bring drugs into the United States. But let's face it. As long as there is demand, as long as there is a market, and unless people address the issue, not only on the basis of the people who are bringing it in and selling it, but on who is buying it, we don't have a solution. The scapegoat is the immigrant.

And likewise, you talk about unemployment; yes, unemployment is a problem for our country. There is no question that there is a scarcity of jobs. We are witnesses to that in our community, because the people who are affected most are people who worship here at the Old Plaza Church. We know there's a problem, but again, the immigrant is the scapegoat. They claim there are no jobs because of the entrance of the undocumented people into our area.

And the homeless. We have a critical problem of homelessness in this country—a wealthy country. They go around picking up the poor people living under freeway bridges here in Los Angeles. Again the attempt is to make the immigrant the scapegoat. Some try to blame the undocumented for almost any problem we are facing.

I was informed rather innocently by two police officers that the immigration and police departments are planning a sweep through the streets of illegal vendors in this area. Because this area is a park, it's illegal to have sidewalk vendors. But they make the assumption that the majority of those illegal vendors are undocumented people. So, they are going to come in with INS buses, and start picking these people up, and shipping them out on the spot.

That's one thing our own law enforcement agencies have to recognize. These people are operating from a mind-set that makes them distrustful of the political system: law enforcement, the courts, the judicial system, the press, the media. They are totally distrustful of that whole segment of society and consequently, when they come in here to the church, it's almost the last vestige of any institution that they can trust.

Parenthetically I might add, because of the church's historical failures in Latin America, were it not for the people's faith, fundamental faith, they would also be greatly disillusioned by some of the decisions the church has taken, relative to the injustices being perpetuated in Central America. Nevertheless, one of the last remnants of any institution in which they can put their trust is the church.

Last week, two police officers pursued two fellows into the courtyard here to ticket them for jaywalking. Oh, I saw them writing the ticket, so I came up. They didn't know who I was and were somewhat aggressive with me. Not realizing that I was the pastor here, they didn't like the idea that I stood there to witness exactly the treatment they were going to lay on these people. When they finished, they said, "How can we help you?"

I said, "Will you please come into my office?"

And they said, "Well, who are you?"

"I'm the pastor here." I brought them in here and said, "Look, I know you're doing your job. It's your job to enforce the law. It's against the law to jaywalk, but I want you to use prudential judgment about the kinds of illegal activities you pursue. There has to be some proportionate importance that you give to certain violations. These people make no distinction between the immigration service, the city police, the fire department, and the traffic regulation agencies. To them, you're all the same. I strongly resent you coming into private property. Let's face it, jaywalking as against the atmosphere that you create within this courtyard, where you know darn well that a lot of the people that come to seek help here are undocumented. I know it's your job, but at the same time I think you can exercise some judgment about the kinds of things you are pursuing."

Unfortunately the undocumented have become the victims of exploitation even by those who are supposed to protect them. A lot of people walk across the street here indiscriminately, tourists, every Saturday and Sunday I see them. They never bother ticketing anybody. And these two defenseless people, you know darn well they're not going to be able to pay any fine. They don't even have enough to eat. Where are they going to get $18 or $20, whatever the fine is for jaywalking.

I just came in from San Antonio, where a city policeman had been arrested on a complaint from an undocumented person who was the victim of a sexual assault. The cop felt that because the young man was undocumented he wasn't going to say anything. But the kid had enough sense and enough trust left in him to speak out, which is very unusual. He had enough trust to speak out, and they caught the policeman. Seemingly, this policeman had been doing it with other people. Police officers are supposed to be protecting whoever is within our territory, whether they are documented or undocumented. The police force is supposed to protect everybody. Well, that's the situation they encounter when they come here.

Putting all this in perspective, what we have here is two conflicting basic rights. One, the sovereignty of a country is the basis for any nation to protect its borders. Nobody questions that. But there is a conflicting right, the right every human being has, to seek a better life. That's the position of the Catholic Church. Every human being has the fundamental human right to improve his lot.

How do you reconcile those two evidently conflicting rights of a nation and an individual? This is where I think this so-called immigration reform has to seek guidance, from that kind of a principle, rather than strictly and exclusively economic factors.

Working with Cesar Chavez was really my first opportunity to work with exploited members of our society. They were the farm workers. I was pastor at Our Lady of Solitude Church at the time, and one of our seminarians wanted to volunteer to work on the grape boycott of the late sixties. So when I was asked by the order to supervise his summer work, I got involved in some of the boycott campaigns in East Los Angeles. I went to the farm worker boycott committee training sessions. As a result of that I got to know Cesar and became an integral part of the farm worker cause, not only in political campaigns, but to get just legislation as well.

During that time the Agricultural Labor Relations Act was passed by the California legislature. It's a model legislative piece for farm workers. I think it's an improvement on the Labor Relations Act of the country.

There's a bishop in Chiapas, Bishop Samuel Ruiz, a very, very prominent Mexican churchman, a social issues bishop. He gave a presentation here once and said, "You know I've been to the Lateran in Rome and I have my degree in canon law, and I have my degrees from various universities in Mexico and Europe, but where I have learned the most is the *universidad del pueblo,* the people's university."

That is the key to any attempt at defense of the rights of undocumented people. I say that because whatever I am doing, or whatever Congressman Roybal does, or Assemblywoman Molino, all of us, whatever we do is no more than an altruistic plan. We're doing something for someone and therefore there's a weakness. There is a weakness in that I'm not really addressing my own self-interest.

Now, I'm sure there's a lot of good in defending the rights of others, and good in speaking out for those who have no voice. I consider that a very important role of the church, and any church person. And I am gratified to know we have allies such as Congressman Roybal, a highly, highly moral and dedicated politician. We are gifted in California with such individuals. But again, their self-interest is to get elected. My self-interest is that for which I was ordained, to preach the gospel. Involvement in those causes does not directly affect my self-interests, so therefore it's on an altruistic plane.

We need to look at some type of organizing tool or medium that is going to empower the undocumented person to do something for himself. The one possibility I see for them in this country, because they can't vote, is through the labor movement, if the labor movement gets back to the intents of its mission.

I think labor's in trouble because it can be so easily undermined by management. If all labor is fighting for is higher wages and better benefits, management can give that to people without them even belonging to the union. But if labor organizes for the purpose of empowerment, whatever they get as the result of their negotiations, whatever they're able to accomplish, then that has empowered the worker. That's why the approach of labor to organize the undocumented has to be on the fundamental motivational factor of collective bargaining. The issue for labor ought not to be benefits or wages, the issue for labor ought to be collective bargaining.

I say that in view of the fact that benefits and wages do not ultimately address the self-interest of the undocumented person, because the undocumented can be easily bought. They need very little offered to them to break them off from any organizing process. It's done all the time; bribes, outright bribes by management to key people who have a voice in the machine shop or whatever.

Establishing more U.S. industry inside the Mexican border in the present form is not providing a solution either. The *maquiladoras* are hiring almost all women. It's undermining the social fiber of the family structure. The men are jobless and becoming more and more irresponsible. Then, they're able to pay women to those standards of fifty cents an hour. Potentially it could be a good solution. But how do you keep them from becoming another tool of exploitation in a foreign country? There are no jobs. It's tough times, I tell you. Really tough times.

The United States has the idea that Latin America belongs to the United States, and that we can do with it whatever we want. For example, agricultural policy: Latin America has been subservient to the interests of the United States in providing what they call these fast crops, coffee, sugar, those kinds of things that do not feed a nation but simply serve as the luxuries of the country to which they are subservient. That's a fundamental problem which this country is unwilling to look at from a different perspective.

I don't know, but I can imagine for example that the United States looks at Mexico's oil deposits as a reserve for its own needs. Therefore the less oil Mexico sells, or develops, or exports, the better it is for us, because it is a ready supply. I can imagine that. Obviously, that's not stated policy. They would never say something like that, but it's certainly within the realm of the way we think about Latin America. It's right in line.

We'll always have people coming in, and it's good for the country. Everybody says it's good for the United States, that we get this influx of people for the work force and for the country. I think it has been demonstrated time and again; the immigrant does a lot more for the country than what we've done for them. But, it is at such massive proportions at the present time that the influx is creating a social problem.

We had such a tremendous success in rebuilding Japan and all of Europe. You would think that people would recognize, not for wanting to be nice to Mexico or to Latin America, but for the good of our country. You would think we'd see it in our own best interest. Let's look for a solution that is not based on keeping people away, but in providing them with a situation in which they would not want to come. Let's develop an answer to their quest for survival right within the boundaries of their own country, their own culture, their own family situation.

Well, we want the economic advantage without the social problem. Okay, then let's provide for a solution to the social problem by being part of a development program in those countries where they come from. If it can happen in Japan and it can happen in Europe, why can't it happen in Latin America?

In the end, the policy of the United States, the reactions of Mexico, the absurdity and danger of the border are all irrelevant. If the past 100 years says anything it says that. Men or women—people—will do what they have to do, not just to survive, that is too mean a view, but to flourish, to make a world where they and their family can have dignity. That is what this great saga says to us. For dignity, people will undergo even greater hardships than this. And the question is, what kind of man, what kind of woman, what kind of mother or father, is it that will deny them? This is the only vantage from which this great migration can be understood, the only one that conveys its heroic nature.

GLOSSARY

adelante otra vez: "we'll move forward again"
adobe: handmade clay brick used in construction
aduana: Mexican customs office or officer
aficionado: fond of
agua de arroz: a refreshing sweet drink made from milled rice
alambrista: one who goes "over the fence" in crossing the border
    illegally
alegre: happy, joyful
algo así: "something like that"
angustiado: anguished
arras: good luck coins given to the bride at a wedding
arroz: rice
asi son los americanos: "That's just how Americans are"
[un] aventon de puro bueno: a great ride
aye Dios: "oh my God!"
bajo sexto: bass guitar used as rhythmic and harmonic accompaniment.
    Not as large as a guitarrón, it has 12 strings rather than the 6 its name
    would suggest.
balón: ball

bandito: bandit
barrio: neighborhood; in the United States, a Hispanic neighborhood
bocadito: literally "a little mouthful," a taste
borrachitos: "little drunk ones," inebriated
braceros: literally "arms," refers to contract Mexican laborers working in the United States
bravo: brave
bueno: good
cabrón: literally "goat," extremely insulting epithet
cada semana: every week
café de la olla: traditional Mexican boiled coffee with cinnamon
¡Cállate!: "Quiet!"
Calle Ocho: Eighth Street
camarilla: power group influencing affairs of state
campesinos: farmers
campo santo: cemetery
canejo: expression of emphasis
canela: cinnamon, refers to cinnamon tea
Canis latrans: zoological term for coyote
cantina: bar
carajo: expression of emphasis
caramba: expression of emphasis
centavo: a denomination of Mexican money, no longer in use; in conversation indicates a small amount of money
cerro: hill
chambelán: chamberlain
champurrado: hot chocolate drink made with corn flour
charros: traditional Mexican cowboys, skilled horsemen
chicharrones: fried pork skins
ching: from the verb "to hit," used as an exclamation
chinga: from the verb "to hit," used as an expletive
cholos: term used in the 1940s for undesirable young men, juvenile delinquents
chorizo: Mexican sausage
cigüeña: stork
cinco de mayo: national holiday celebrating the defeat of the French forces at the Battle of Puebla in 1862

cojínes: pillows, refers to kneeling pillows used in a wedding

colonia: colony, refers to the period when Mexico was a colony of Spain

comadre: relationship between the mother and godparents of a child, also what they call each other, feminine

comal: clay griddle for cooking tortillas and chilies

comandancia: command station

comerciantes: business owners

comida: dinner, the heaviest meal of the day, eaten in the afternoon

¿cómo?: literally "how?"; used almost as punctuation in conversation

¿cómo se dice?: "how do you say ———?" "how do you say it?"

¿cómo se dice la cancion?: "how does the song go?"

¿cómo te dijera?: "how can I explain it?"

compadrazgo: the system of godparent relationships

compadre: relationship between the father and godparents of a child, also what they call each other, masculine

compañeros: companions

conjunto: musical band

conquistadores: conquerors, usually refers to the Spanish conquerors of Mexico

conversos: converts

cooperaciónes: donation toward a public project such as the church or school

copete: bangs worn in a pompadour

corrida: bullfight

corrido: an epic poem or story set to music

cositas: little things

coyota: woman who guides the undocumented across the border

coyote: person who guides the undocumented immigrant across the border

Cristeros: a religious movement, 1926 to 1929, in response to the persecution of the church during the Mexican revolution. In the name of Christ, fanatic peasants stormed the western states of Mexico, leaving fear, death, and destruction in their wake.

cucaracha: "insect"; refers to the cooperation paid for food and rent

desfile: procession, parade

día de la raza: national holiday celebrating the Mexican people

día del grito: the cheer of "Viva Mexico" at midnight on the sixteenth of September

diez centavos: ten cents

diez y seis de septiembre: Mexico's celebration of independence

Dios: literally "my God," used in expressions of emphasis

domingo: "Sunday," refers to the allowance children and servants receive on Sunday

Don: term of honor for an elderly or distinguished person

drug adictos: drug addicts

enchiladas: traditional dish of meat or cheese rolled in a tortilla with a chili sauce

encuentro: meeting, convention

ensalada: salad

entonces: then

"Entorno": a Mexican journal, *In Turn*

en trámite: in process

es cierto: it's true, it's certain

¿es de buena familia?: "is he from a good family?"

escuela superior: high school

eso también: this also

fabuloso: fabulous

federales: the federal government

feria: fair

fiesta charra: traditional Mexican rodeo

frijoles: beans, traditional staple of the Mexican diet

frontera: the border

fuera de seria: outside the norm

fútbol: soccer

gabacho: a man from the United States

ganas: desire

gangas: gangs

gran haciendado: owner of a large hacienda

granja: farm

gringa: a woman from the United States

gringo: a man from the United States

gritando: yelling

grito: a traditional yell, somewhat like a yodel, used in songs and expressions of celebration

güera: a light-skinned woman, often refers to a woman from the United States

guitarrón: large bass guitar

hija: daughter

hijo: son, used in expressions of emphasis

hijo de la chingada: literally "son of a bitch," used in expressions of emphasis or profanity

hijole: derivative of "son of a ———," used in expressions of emphasis

hombres: men

huapango: one of the most popular folkloric dances, music, and rhythms of Mexico

huaraches: traditional leather sandals

ilegales: illegal immigrants

jamaica: a drink made from the hibiscus flower

la Coca: the Coca-Cola Company

lasso: satin cord used to "tie" the wedding couple together

lienzo charro: Mexican rodeo ring

machismo: a Hispanic cultural form of masculinity and male superiority

macho: masculine, refers to machismo

madre: mother

madre mia: "mother of mine," refers to the Virgin Mary

madrina: godmother

mamacitas: literally "little mothers," refers to a group of women

mamá, no corra, por favor: "mama, please don't run"

mañana: tomorrow

manito: literally "little hand," refers to someone from New Mexico

maquiladora: foreign assembly factory, usually located inside the Mexican border, employing Mexican workers

mariachi: musical group, typical to the state of Jalisco

marketa: anglicized word for "market"

más o menos: more or less

mensa: stupid

menudo: traditional tripe soup

mercado de abastos: large farmers' market that supplies smaller markets

mesita: area of outdoor tables

mestizaje: people of mestizo origin, Aztec and Spanish

mexicana: Mexican woman

migra: U.S. Immigration officer

milpa: cornfield

minsa: packaged corn flour for tortilla dough

mojados: literally "wet," formerly referred to those who get wet crossing the border at the Rio Grande. Now refers to anyone crossing the border illegally.

mole: traditional casserole dish with meat or poultry in chili gravy

mordida: literally "bite," a paid bribe

[el] mosca: "the fly," refers to the Immigration Service helicopters

muchachos: boys, young men

muchisimo tiempo: a long time

muy caballero: very polite, in the manner of knights

narcotraficantes: drug dealers

negrito: diminutive of *negro,* a term of affection

ni modo: it doesn't matter, no matter

[el] niño Dios: the Christ Child; Baby Jesus

no'mbre: literally means "no, man," expression of emphasis

[el] norte: "the north," refers to the United States

no sabemos lo que es: "we don't know what it is"

no sé: I don't know

no se vaya: don't go

no te imaginas: "you can't imagine"

"No Vale Nada la Vida": a song, "Life Isn't Worth Anything"

novela: soap opera

novia: a woman engaged to be married, the bride

novillero: bullfighter

novio: a man engaged to be married, the groom

novios: a couple engaged to be married

olla: pot

pachuco: 1940s term for a group of young men; synonymous with *cholos*

[el] padre: priest

padrinos: godparents

padrinos de matrimonio: godparents of the wedding

palomilla: group, clique that hangs out together

PAN: political party, Partido Acción Nacional (National Action Party)

partido popular: political party: popular party or party of the people

pasadores: guides who pass people across the Rio Grande
pases: bullfighter's movements
pendejo: foolish
pero eso también: but this also
peso: denomination of Mexican money
petates: woven reed mats traditionally used for sleeping
picadillo: a Mexican beef stew
piñata: a clay pot filled with sweets and decorated with colored paper, traditionally broken at birthday celebrations
pipitorias: a traditional Mexican peanut candy
pistola: pistol
pizca: picking, refers to the harvesting of crops
Plaza de Tlateloco: plaza in Mexico City
plaza de toros: bull ring
pobre Dios: literally "poor God," expression of emphasis
pocha: literally "discolored," refers to someone of Mexican and U.S. parentage
policía: police
"Poliforum Siqueiros": a mural by David Alfaro Siqueiros
politécnica: polytechnical school
pollitos: literally "chicks," refers to the Mexicans crossing the border illegally
pollo: literally "chicken," refers to the Mexican crossing the border illegally
ponche: a punch usually made of stewed fruit
[un] poquito: a little
por abajo: going down
pozole: traditional soup of field corn and pork or chicken
prepa: *preparatoria,* high school
presidente: president
PRI: political party, Partido Revolucionario Institucional, Institutional Revolutionary Party
Psicologia para Mexico: psychology for Mexico
puertorriqueño: a man from Puerto Rico
puesto: stand in a market
Purísima: the Virgin Mary
¿qué hacemos?: "what can we do?"
¿qué hule?: "what's happening?"

[una] queja: complaint

quinzeañera: celebration for a young woman on her coming of age on her fifteenth birthday

ranchero: country style, from the ranch

ranchito: small ranch

ratera: female robber who exploits the illegal immigrant

ratero: robber, one who robs or exploits the illegal immigrant

raza: race, often refers to the Mexican people

reconquista: reconquest, refers to the reconquest of the area lost by Mexico to the United States in the Mexican-American war

refrescos: refreshments, sodas

requinto: small guitar

revolucionarios: revolutionaries

ricos: rich people

rosario: rosary

ruta de independencia: route of independence, the route taken by Dolores Hidalgo in the fight for independence from Spain

sacas: sacks

salón de belleza: beauty salon

salsa: a spicy condiment of tomato and chili served with beans and tortillas

[el] santo: saint

secundaria: secondary school; seventh, eighth, and ninth grades

[una] semana taurina: a week celebrating the tradition of bullfights

señora: a married woman

sinvergüenza: scoundrel, without shame

sombrero: large-brimmed hat

son muy complicados: "they are very complicated"

sopa: literally soup, in Mexico, dry soup, rice, or pasta

sorteo: the sorting of the bulls

tacos: traditional serving of meat, potato, or cheese wrapped in a tortilla

tamale: steamed corn dough filled with meat or vegetable

taurino: referring to tradition of bullfights

temblor: earthquake

[el] templo: church

tianguis: people's market, traditional street market

tienda: store

tierra: earth, land, refers to homeland

todas las partes: everywhere
todas las semanas: every week
todo: all
tortas: sandwiches
tortilla: traditional Mexican flat bread made with corn dough
tortilla de harina: wheat flour tortilla
trabajo social: social work
traficantes: refers to drug dealers
tú sabes: you know
vagos: vagrants
vámonos: "let's go"
vámonos muchachos: "let's go, boys!"
van llegando los músicos: "the musicians are arriving"
verdad: right, true
Virgen de Guadalupe: patron saint of Mexico
Virgen del Refugio: Virgin of Refuge, saint's day, July 4
Viva Mexico: "Long live Mexico!"

Index

Adelanto, California, 201
Agency for International Development (AID), 384
Agricultural Labor Relations Act, 421
Agricultural policy, U.S., 423
Agricultural workers, 3, 12, 18, 20, 21, 23, 25, 30–31, 67, 70–72, 173–75, 176, 213, 230, 261, 355, 374, 399–400, 415
    family farms employing migrants, 77–93
    housing for, 71, 81–87, 91, 92, 355–56
    Immigration and Naturalization Service's policy, 68
    in Mexico, 28, 32, 213, 223
Airplane, travel by, 110, 115–16, 129–30, 163, 193, 219, 222, 266
    people who accompany immigrants, 129–30
Alamogordo, New Mexico, 58
Albany, California, 264–65, 267–72
Albuquerque, New Mexico, 18
Alcoholism, 42, 392. See also Drinking

Alexandria Quartet, The, 320
Alice, Texas, 250
Allman Brothers, 312–13
Alta California, 2
American Civil Liberties Union (ACLU), 278
American Consulate, Guadalajara, 165
Anaya, Rudolfo, 292
Architects, 272–79, 340, 341
Arizona, 2
Army, service in the, 358–59, 391
Artists, 291–321
    muralist, 292–300
    musician, 303–14
    rodeo star, 300–303
    writer, 315–21
Assimilation of Mexican immigrants, 199, 284, 396–98
    easing the, 284–85
    forced, 339
Austin, Duke, 68
Austin, Texas, 226, 335, 337–38, 340, 352, 359

Austin-American Statesman, 68
Auto parts factory worker, 211
Auto repair work, 53, 54
Aztecs, 2, 200

Baby, delivering a, 210–11
Babysitters, 201–2, 219
Baca, Judith, 292
Baez, Joan, Sr., 248, 251
Bail bondsman, 326–27, 332–34
Barela, Patrocinio, 292
Barragan, Luis, 291
Bendac Tire Company, 392
Benicia, California, 21
Best and brightest, emigrants as Mexico's, 247–85
  architect, 272–79
  college administrator, 258–64
  foreign language consultant, 279–85
  physicist/environmentalist, 248–58
  restaurateur, 264–72
Bicultural lifestyle, 390
Bigamy, 144
Bigotry, 263, 334, 344, 348, 377, 382, 408. *See also* Discrimination; Segregation
  reenforced by minority group members, 395–97, 402
Bilingual culture, 390
Bilingual education, 380
Billings, Montana, 18
Blacks, 237, 305, 329, 355
Boat, travel by, 173
Bolero Kings, 368–71
Border Art Workshop, 299
Border Patrol. *See* Immigration officials, U.S., Border Patrol
Border police, Mexican. *See* Mexican border police
Borges, José Luis, 320
Braceros, 3, 16, 22, 23, 27, 30, 213, 412
Britannica, 256
Brooklyn, New York, 250–51

Brownsville, Texas, 9, 174, 213, 383
Bryan, Texas, 243, 326, 329
Buena Vista, Mexico, 157–58
Burbank, California, 124
Bureaucracy in Mexico, 411
Bus, travel by
  to cross the border, 23, 27, 114, 186–87, 219
  by new immigrants, 202, 204
Busboys, 222, 224

Cabo San Lucas, Mexico, 345
California
  gold rush, 2
  under Spain, 2
California College of Arts and Crafts, 344, 345
Calles, Plutarco Elias, 10
Calo, Juarez, 317
Cal State Northridge, 283
Calvert, Texas, 230
Camarillo, California, 280, 281
Cantinflas, 291
Carpentier, Alejo, 320
Carrillo, Graciella, 292
Carrizo Springs, Texas, 390, 391
Cars
  hiding in, 58, 60, 162, 184, 207
  payment for driver, 136
  travel by, 99–100, 108, 208
Cassidy, Hopalong, 302
Castellanos, Rosario, 320
Catarina, Mexico, 11
Catholic Church, 10, 249, 319, 381, 419, 421
  Cristeros, 10, 11
  population growth and, 417
  services in Spanish, 381–82
Catholicism, 335, 336, 350, 373, 397–98
Centro Cultural de la Raza, 292, 295, 297, 299
Charles, Ray, 304
Chavez, Cesar, 378, 379, 421
Checker, Chubby, 304

Chicago, Illinois, 176, 219–20, 221, 222, 237, 238, 361, 363, 366
  crime and gangs in, 225, 233, 234, 360
  weather in, 224
Chicanos, 111, 247, 297–98, 321, 339, 344, 383
  street art, 345
Child care, provider of, 266–67
Children of immigrants, 325–402
  appreciation of Mexican culture, 344–45, 365–66, 367, 372–74, 380–83, 389, 390
  ashamed of their parents, 281, 326
  break with traditional behaviors, 320, 373–74, 386–87
  cultural differences from parents, 349–50, 351–52, 353
  daycare for, 88, 91
  delivering a baby, 210–11
  difficulty fitting in, 281–82, 330, 363–64, 387–88, 391
  discipline of, 330–31
  education of, see Education
  left behind in Mexico, 149, 153, 157–66
  moving back to Mexico, 341–43, 360–67
  quitting school to work, 281
  second families in the United States, 151, 152, 153
  second-or-later generations, 368–402
  social life of, 336–37, 365, 366, 372, 373, 375, 376, 390
Chula Vista, California, 129, 208, 304
Cisco Kid, 301–2
Citizenship, 238, 243, 271–72, 367, 411, 412–14
  allegiance and, 413–14
City planner, 407
Ciudad Guzmán, Mexico, 41
Ciudad Juárez, Mexico, 17, 132, 133, 315–16, 320, 417
  border crossing to El Paso, 130–33

Clothing, 52, 162, 221
  donated, 228, 260, 272
Coaching position, 62–63
Coca-Cola Company, 180, 414
Colegio de la Frontera Norte, 199
Colimo, Mexico, 293
Colorado, 2
Communications and marketing consultant, 334
Compostela, Mexico, 110
Compton, California, 104
Concord, California, 21
Concrete workers, 179
Construction workers, 59, 69, 124, 177, 191–92
Contract labor. See Braceros
Convent, 397–98
Cornelius, Wayne A., 68–69
Cornell Aeronautics Lab, 248, 255
Coronado, Francisco Vasquez de, 2
Corruption, 111, 133, 136, 362
Coyotes, 18, 19, 20, 118, 127–40, 159. See also Ratero
  account of a, 134–36
  charges of, 108, 116, 128, 129, 132–33, 135–36, 152, 173–74, 177, 184, 208
  informal networks for finding, 128, 134–35, 136
  leading the crossing, 99–103, 105–6, 107–8, 114–16, 161–62, 177, 184, 207, 222
  mistreatment by, 139
  mythic past of, 127
Crime, 225, 240, 269, 270
Cristeros, 10, 11
Crossing the border, 25, 27, 28, 58, 60, 99–140, 173, 207–8, 219, 372, 407. See also Illegal immigration; Immigration officials
  caught while, 18–19, 102, 105, 106, 109, 111, 112, 118–19, 135, 222
  daily, 132, 315, 318–19
  eventual success, 103

Crossing the border *(cont'd)*
  as huge service industry, 128
  length of stay after, 104
  safe houses, *see* Safe houses
  with a *coyote, see* Coyotes
  without a *coyote,* 110
Cultural differences, 62, 200–201, 238–
    39, 240, 258, 339, 341, 350–51,
    361, 364–65, 372
  clothing, 52, 221
  educating women for a profession,
    249
  electricity, 259
  food, 259
  household roles, 371, 386–87
  identity with one's job, 326
  informality, 52
  machismo, 55, 56, 57, 276, 349, 353,
    356, 370–71, 393–94
  male-female roles, 235–36
  between Mexicans and Mexican-
    Americans, 393
  between parents and children, 349–50,
    351–52, 353
  pregnant women, 62, 251
  respect for parents, 56
  stereotypes, 361, 362, 364, 414
  strictness about dating, 400–401
  treatment of older people, 263
  concerning work, 223

Dairy business, 242–43, 335, 339
Dances, 307, 375
Daycare, 88, 91
Delivering a baby, 210–11
Del Mar, Mexico, 19
Denver, Colorado, 18
Department of Commerce, U.S., 240
Department of Health, U.S., 81
Department of Labor, U.S., 80, 81
Deportation, 3, 22, 23–24, 24n, 67,
    78–79
Deportation Act of 1929, 22
Depression. *See* Great Depression

Detroit, Michigan, 274–275, 276
Discrimination, 277, 338–39, 385, 391–
    93. *See also* Bigotry; Segrega-
    tion
  in housing, 376, 377
Dishwashers, 222
Disk jockeys, 346, 350, 389–90, 394–95
Distant Neighbors (Riding), 143, 325
Documents, 153, 189, 208, 209, 239, 267,
    279, 415
  attempt to buy, 185–86
  false, 68, 80, 120, 207
    obtaining, 72–73
    passports, 44, 60
  receiving legal, 212, 213, 216, 224,
    242, 260, 304
Dominican Republic, 386, 388
Dos Pasos Editores, 317
Drew University, 253–54
Drinking, 222, 223–24
  alcoholism, 42, 392
Drugs, 164, 294–95, 307–8, 360, 367,
    418–19
  sale of, 136
Duarte, President, 42
Durango, Mexico, 335

Earthquake in Mexico, 41–42
Echave the Elder, Baltasar de, 291
Economy of Mexico, 68, 70, 124, 188–
    89, 193–94, 207, 225, 409, 417
  outlook for, 405
Edcouch, Mexico, 407
Edinburg, Texas, 369, 370
Education
  bilingual, 380
  convent, 397–98
  dropouts, 281, 282, 364
  first day of school, 330
  under GI Bill, 384
  in Mexico, 47, 55, 155–56, 175, 180,
    206, 214–15, 226, 235, 273, 316,
    320, 360–66
  second generation, 217–18

in United States, 47, 52, 60–61, 92–
     93, 110, 179, 205–6, 209, 216,
     230, 233, 251–53, 260–62, 280,
     281, 293–94, 316, 328
Educators, 248–59, 283, 315–21, 370
Eisenhower, Dwight D., 24
Elderly, attitude toward the, 263
Electricity, 259
Electronics workers, 191
El Paso, Texas, 57, 242, 316, 335, 346,
     348, 353
  migration to, 9, 10, 131–33
El Salvador, 136
Employees, 69–93
  family farm, 77–93
  fines for hiring illegals, 72–73
  restaurant manager, 73–76
  seed grower, 69–73
Employment. *See specific forms of employ-
     ment*
English, learning, 121, 188, 190, 191,
     192, 201, 204–5, 206, 216, 249,
     260, 261, 262, 267, 268, 269
  first day in school, 330
  foreign language consultant, 282–83
  from sibling, 355
Entorno, 319
Environmentalist, 256–57, 414
Expectations of the United States, 171,
     188, 199, 212, 227, 266
  disappointment, 171, 187, 212
  first impressions, 189, 305
  myths perpetuated, 171–72, 209
Ezell, Harold, 36

Factory workers, 39, 92, 152, 180–83,
     211, 219–20, 392
Families left behind in Mexico, 22, 23,
     26, 31–32, 143–66, 209, 220
  bringing them to the United States,
     208, 209–10
  children, *see* Children of immigrants
  grandparents, 109
  mothers, 164–65, 172

wives, *see* Wives, left behind in Mex-
     ico
Farm workers. *See* Agricultural workers
Fender, Freddy, 292
Fernandez, Vincente, 375
Fiestas, Mexican, celebration of, 224,
     243, 372, 373, 375, 390
Food, 228, 243, 259, 331, 336, 342
  lack of, 250
Foreign language consultant, 279–85
Foundry workers, 191
Franco, Francisco, 301
Frankfurter, Felix, 67
Fuentes, Carlos, 200, 291, 320
Fútbol, 228–29

Gambling, 231–32
Gangs, 225, 233, 234, 306, 360
Garcia, Rupert, 292
Garfield High School, 306, 307
Garst, 81
GI Bill, 384
Glossary, 425–33
Godfrey, Arthur, 337
Gold mines, 15
Gonzales, Pedro, 292
Gortari, Carlos Salinas de, 408–9
Government of Mexico, 42, 111, 133,
     417
  Catholic Church and, 10
  working for change, 194
Grape boycott movement, 378
Great Depression, 3, 12, 57
Guadalajara, Mexico, 11, 12, 16, 18, 39,
     43–44, 116–17, 154, 156, 180,
     188, 219, 220, 238, 272–73, 327,
     360–67, 405
  housing in, 224
Guatemala, 136, 388
Guitarist, 303–14
Guzman, Gilberto, 292

Hairstylist, 236–37
Haro, Spain, 347

Harrington, Marshall, 253
Hatfield, Mark, 165, 166
Head tax, 3, 22, 230
Heinz Corporation, 217, 392
Hermosillo, Mexico, 293, 304
Hinojosa, Tish, 292
Hinojosa family, 408
Hispanic Chamber of Commerce, 338
Holiday celebrations, 224, 243, 372, 373, 375
Hollywood, California, 20
Homelessness, 419
Honduras, 384–85
Hon Industries, 392
Hoover, Herbert, 67
Housework, 44, 186, 226–29, 267
Housing, 28–29, 36, 113, 151, 179–80, 182–83, 190, 193, 201, 212, 233, 241, 259, 271, 299, 308, 327, 369–70, 374
  discrimination in, 376, 377
  extended family living together, 206, 210, 211, 274, 280
  as investment, 217, 232–33, 332
  in Mexico, 43–44, 149, 154, 158, 179, 221, 224, 236–37, 259, 299, 315, 333–34
  for migrant agricultural workers, 71, 81–87, 88, 91, 92, 355–56
  zoning problems, 81–87, 93
Houston, Texas, 216
Huerta, Efraín, 320
Huggie Boy, 307
Humboldt State, 283

Illegal immigration, 3, 4, 27–32, 35, 58–59, 60, 405–24. See also Deportation; Return of immigrants to Mexico
  benefits to both countries of, 405–6, 409, 410, 412, 415, 423
  crossing the border, see Crossing the border
  elimination of the border, 416
  emigrants sent back to Mexico, 21, 27–28, 109, 174–75, 177, 184, 213–14
  caught while crossing the border, 18–19, 102, 105, 106, 111, 112, 118–19, 135, 222
  number of illegal laborers, 68–69
  number of illegals in the United States, 103, 199
  papers for agricultural workers, see Documentation
  passports, see Documentation
Illiteracy, 72, 328
Immigration and Control Act of 1986, 1, 3–4
Immigration and Naturalization Act of 1965, 22
Immigration and Naturalization Service, 24, 35, 109, 199. See also Immigration officials, U.S.
  letter to, seeking help in returning family member to Mexico, 165–66
  policy toward seasonal agricultural workers, 68
Immigration legislation, 2, 3, 24n, 67, 279
  bracero program, 3
  Immigration and Naturalization Act of 1965, 22
  Immigration Reform and Control Act of 1986, 1, 3–4, 68, 144, 153, 415
  McCarran-Walter Act, 24n
  quota laws, 3, 24n
Immigration officials, U.S., 17–20, 23, 24, 29–30, 178, 192–93, 409. See also Illegal immigration; Immigration and Naturalization Service
  Border Patrol, 3, 24–25, 101, 102, 118, 120, 123, 127, 133, 162, 184, 222
  headquarters, 110
  statistics of the, 103

immigrants' feelings about, 37
mistreatment by, 408
raid by, 72, 76, 185
Immigration Reform and Control Act
of 1986, 1, 3–4, 68, 415
families of immigrants and, 144
legal resident status open to illegals
by, 143, 153
Independence, Oregon, 178
Ines de la Cruz, Sor Juana, 291
Infidelity, 144, 148, 150, 151, 152,
161–63
Instituto Metodista Mexicano, 249, 251
Insurance, 72
Integration of Mexican immigrants. See
Assimilation of Mexican immi-
grants
International Union for the Conserva-
tion of Nature (IUCN), 256–57
Irapuato, Mexico, 17
Islam, 200

Jail, 174
for hitting a policeman, 177
for illegal crossing, 18, 19, 112, 118,
222
Japanese, 231, 414
farm owners, 30
Jimenez, Flaco, 292, 312, 313
Jimenez, Santiago, 292
Jimenez, Santiago, Jr., 292
Jordy, Louis, 253
Juárez, Mexico. See Ciudad Juárez,
Mexico

Kahlo, Frieda, 291
Kirkpatrick, Paul, 254–55
Korean War, 391

La Bamba (film), 399
"La Bamba" (song), 313, 394
Labor movement, 422
La Opinión, 41
La Piedad, Mexico, 327

La Purisma, California, 304
Las Barrancas de Los Laureles, 11, 15, 16
Las Vigas, Mexico, 257
Laundromat work, 219
Law enforcement, U.S., 239, 419–21
ability to sue, 240
Lawsuits, 240
"League of the Twenty-third of September," 122
Lebow, Art, 307
Legislation affecting immigration. See
Immigration legislation
Life of Mexican immigrants in the
United States, 199–44. See also
Children of immigrants
of auto parts factory worker, 209–12
of busboy, 221–25
of factory worker, 218–21
of hairstylist, 236–40
of housewife, 212–18
of junior high school student, 205–6
of lumberyard manager, 233–36
of maid, 226–29
of retirees, 229–33, 241–43
of truck driver, 206–9
of women supporting themselves,
201–5, 226–29
Linguist, 279–85
Little Joe, 292
Lone Tree, Iowa, 77–93
Los Angeles, California, 2, 12, 20, 31,
114, 180, 219, 222, 293, 294, 383
as destination of illegal immigrants,
108, 111, 129, 130, 131, 136,
208
East L.A., 305–8
music scene, 313
Los Angeles Times, The, 4
Los Lobos, 303, 306, 309–14
Low Riders, The, 292
Lumberyards, work in the, 12–14, 27,
28, 61, 62, 361
manager of lumberyard, 233–36
Lynwood, California, 113

McCarthy, Joseph, 24
McCormick, 219
Machismo, 55, 56, 57, 276, 349, 353, 356,
    370–71, 393–94
Mafia, Mexican, 122
Maids, 44, 186, 226–29, 269
Maintenance work, 239
Manteca, California, 31
Manual Training High School, 251–52
Manufacturing sector, work in the, 69
Marquez, Hugo Sanchez, 228
Marriage, 51, 122, 182, 207, 215, 238,
    262, 267, 362, 370, 371, 384
  arranged, 388–89
  courting in Mexico, 49–51
  meeting through a catalog, 13–14
  of Mexican to an American, 51–53,
    61–62, 102, 110, 176, 178, 273
  traditional wedding, 372–73
Mason, Colonel R. B., 2
Matamoros, Mexico, 213
MEChA (Movimiento Estudiantil
    Chicano de Aztlán), 282
Medical care, 87–88
Medical examination, 17, 22
Mejia, Miguel Aceves, 308
Mendoza, Lidia, 292, 313
Mestizos, 200–201, 291–92, 325, 326,
    393
Methodists, 249–51
Metropolitan Opera, 337
Mexicali, Mexico, 23, 27, 114, 119
Mexican-American War, 2
Mexican army, 194
Mexican border police, 110, 408–9
  corruption of, 111, 133, 136, 187
Mexican Revolution, 3, 9, 10, 242, 250
  soldiers in the, 11
Mexico City, Mexico, 215, 216, 237,
    273, 347, 405
Mexico-U.S. relations, 247
Michoacán, Mexico, 19
Military career, 358–59
Milpitas, California, 21

Mine workers, 3, 15
MIT, 255
Monterrey, Mexico, 349, 350–51, 407
Moorpark, California, 279, 280
Mosqueda, Fred, 310–12
Muralist, 292–300
Muscatine, Iowa, 216–18, 376, 378–79,
    389, 391–93
Muscatine Migrant Committee, 374
Musicians, 303–14, 337–38, 345, 368–69

Nathautl language, 2, 188
National Endowment for the Arts, 338
Neruda, Pablo, 320
Nevada, 2
Neve, Felipe de, 2
New Mexico, 2, 336
New Orleans, Louisiana, 347
Nogales, Mexico, 12
Northeastern University, 365
Northrup King, 77, 78
Nuevo Laredo, Mexico, 173
Nursery workers, 60
Nurses, 398, 399

Oakland, California, 183, 184, 269, 270
Oaxaca, Mexico, 341–43
Obituary, 243–44
Oceanside, California, 201
Oil resources of Mexico, 423
Olmos, Edward James, 292
Operation Wetback, 24–25, 293
Orozco, José Clemente, 296, 345
OSS, 348
Overpopulation in Mexico, 405, 412,
    417
Oxnard, California, 176

Pacheco, José Emilio, 319
Pachuca, Mexico, 237
Palo Alto, California, 31
Pan American College, 356
Paraguay, 384
Parking cars, 36

Partido Popular, 273
Pasadena, California, 12
Passports, 189
  false, 44, 60
Paz, Octavio, 143, 200, 291, 320
Pediatrician, 395, 401
Peru, 136
Physical Science Study Committee
  (PSSC), 256
Physicist, 248–58, 414
Piñatas, 372
Plaza de Tlateloco massacre, 343, 343n–
  344n
Plumber, 332
Poetry, 317–18
Police
  Mexican, 110
    corruption of, 111, 133, 136, 362
  in the United States, 420–21
Politicians
  in Mexico, 42
  in the United States, 348
    activists, 377–82
Poniatowska, Elena, 320
Pregnancy, 359
  cultural differences, 62, 251
  delivering the baby, 210–11
  wives left behind, 145–51, 153
Prejudice. See Bigotry; Discrimination;
  Segregation
Presley, Elvis, 394
Price-Fisher, 191
PROTEUS, 88
Puebla, Mexico, 249, 251, 257, 384

Quinn, Anthony, 291

Racism. See Bigotry; Discrimination;
  Segregation
Rafts, crossing the border on, 132
Railroads, Mexicans working on the, 2,
  328–29. See also Train, travel by
Rand Corporation, 69
Ratero (robber), 108–9, 128, 132, 207

Reagan, Ronald, 417
Real estate salesman, 392–93
Reasons for going to the United States,
  68, 119
  for adventure, 36–37, 38, 117
  for education, 110
  to escape unhappy family life, 46–47,
    57
  financial, 36–40, 44, 45, 68, 71, 110,
    121, 133, 172, 175, 180, 188, 207,
    213, 222, 238, 250, 406
  to join spouse, 208, 209–10, 218–19,
    223
  political, 242
  religious, 250
  as rite of passage, 38
  romantic, 37, 38
Restaurant workers, 69, 73–76, 121, 164,
  171, 184–85, 239–40
  busboy, 222, 224
  in Mexico, 203
Restaurateurs, 264–72, 368
Retirees, 229–33, 241–43, 264
Return of immigrants to Mexico
  intention to return, 199, 274
  involuntary, see Deportation; Illegal
    immigration, emigrants sent
    back to Mexico
  voluntary, 21, 29, 122, 124, 171, 235,
    236, 238, 264, 278, 299–300,
    341–43, 360–61
  difficulty of, 25
  periodic or seasonal, 23, 25, 26, 30,
    35, 45, 71, 104, 111, 156–57,
    173, 213, 280, 300, 333, 361, 407,
    415
  to retire, 224
  to see family, 15, 36, 44, 59–60,
    111, 146, 153–54, 186, 191, 192,
    207, 212, 220–21, 272, 280, 349
  to work in Mexico, 21
Reyes, Lucha, 291
Reynosa, Mexico, 407
Rhythm Tens, 304

Riding, Alan, 143, 325–26
Rights
    equal political, 239, 240
    human, 421, 422
    of nations, 421
Rio Grande River, 407
Rio Grande Valley, Texas, 348–49, 369–73, 407
Rivera, Diego, 277, 291, 296, 345
Robbery, 225, 269, 270
Robertson, Dale, 302
Rodeo star, 300–303
Ronstadt, Linda, 292
Royal Chicano Air Force, The, 292
Rural Technology Assistance Program, 389

Sacramento, California, 12, 15, 69–73
Safe houses, 136, 184, 207, 208
    account of woman running a, 137–40
    rates at, 139
Saginaw, Michigan, 374–75, 376–79
Salaries
    of American citizens, 190
    of Mexican immigrants, 28, 39, 44, 59, 61, 74, 75–76, 81, 84–85, 121, 124, 164, 171, 173, 174, 177, 180–81, 191–92, 213, 222, 239–40, 266, 361, 368, 369, 410
    cashing of paychecks, 89
    lack of benefits, 224
    in Mexico, 28, 39, 148, 171, 213, 365, 422
Sales, work in, 14–15
Salinas, California, 31
Salsipuedes, Mexico, 11
Salvation Army, 42, 88, 91
San Antonio, Texas, 173, 348, 349, 375, 382–83
San Augustine Octipa, Mexico, 265, 272
San Carlos, school at, 273, 277
Sanchez, "El Chunky," 292
Sanchez, Hugo, 229
San Clemente, California, 19, 184, 222

San Diego, California, 9, 115, 116, 129, 184, 294, 299
San Diego State, 293, 294
San Francisco, California, 21, 201, 276
San Jose, California, 2, 21, 201
San Juan, Mexico, 38, 43, 45–46, 183, 220–21, 223
San Luis Potosi, Mexico, 226
Santa Ana, California, 20, 151
Santa Catarina, Mexico, 19
Santa Clara, Mexico, 265–66
Santa Cruz, California, 21, 31
Santa Fe, New Mexico, founding of, 2
Santa Fe Railroad, 328–29
Santa Inez, Mexico, 258, 259–60, 263, 264
Santana, Carlos, 292
Santa Rosa, California, 258–62, 277
Santa Rosa Junior College, 262
San Ysidro, California, 111, 114, 134, 135
    as destination of illegal immigrants, 101, 102, 103, 106, 123–24, 129, 136, 184
Scientists, 248–58, 414
Seed growers, 69–72
Segregation, 328, 329, 330, 408
Sherwin-Williams, 273
Shoeshining, 59, 60
Silas, California, 28
Simpson-Rodino bill. See Immigration Reform and Control Act of 1986
Singer, 337–38
Single-parent families, 417
Siquieros, David Alfaro, 291, 296–97, 345
Sir Douglas Quintet, 292
Slash Records, 313
Snakes, 174
Socialism, 277
Social life, 90, 191, 223–24, 226, 243, 337–38
    dances, 307, 375

family gatherings, 336–37
fiestas, celebration of, 224, 243, 372, 373, 375, 390
sports, 228–29, 282, 366
Social standing of emigrants, 247–48, 347
Somerville, Texas, 327, 328, 329, 330
Sonora, California, 2, 13
Soto, Gary, 292
South Carolina, 173, 175
Southwest Texas State University, 352
Soviet Union, 144
"Spain," 292
Spanish Civil War, 300–301
Spanish Empire, 2
Spanish language, 382–83
  assimilation of immigrants and use of, 284, 395–96
  bilingual education, 380
  church services, 381–82
  as constantly changing, 283–84
Sports, 228–29, 282, 366
Sputnik, 255
Stand and Deliver, 307
Stanford University, 254, 255, 262
Stanton, California, 20
Steel foundry, work at, 240
Stender, California, 12
Stockton, California, 12, 21, 31
Storeowners, 217, 218
Supreme Court, U.S., 24
Swing, Joseph, 24
Syracuse University, 253
Szego, Gabor, 254

Tamayo, Rufino, 291
Tampico, Mexico, 327
Taxes, 72, 174, 271
Teachers. See Educators
Telephones, 237, 239
Television, 252, 342, 343
Teocuitatlán, 16, 17
Texas, 1, 2
  under Spain, 2

Texas A&M University, 407
Tianquis (open-air markets), 2
Tijuana, Mexico, 19, 122, 135, 208, 299–300, 304
  border crossings at, 99–100, 103, 105–6, 114, 118, 120, 123, 129
Toastmasters, 278
Tolkien, John, 320
Toltecas en Aztlán, 292
Torrance, California, 135
Torres, Eddie, 307
Train, travel by, 9, 11–12, 15–18, 132
Trevino, Rudy, 292
Truck drivers, 36
Tucson, Arizona, 9, 176, 178

Unemployment
  in Mexico, 194
  in United States, 271, 419
Unemployment insurance, 193
  illegal collection of, 71
UNESCO, 256
Unions, 379
United Fruit Company, 397
Universidad Autonoma, 365
Universidad Veracruzana, 317
University of Arizona, 258, 263
University of California at Berkeley, 398, 399
University of Juárez, 319
University of Mexico, 273
University of New Mexico, 52, 316
University of Texas, 356, 357
  at Austin, 335, 337, 338, 339
  El Paso, 315, 316, 317, 319, 335
  Medical School, 398
Uruguay, 385
Utah, 2

Vaccination, 12
Valdez, Luis, 292
Valdez, Raul, 292
Valens, Ritchie, 292, 312, 314, 394
Valenzuela, Fernando, 228

Vasconcelos, Jose, 325
Veracruz, Mexico, 347
Veterans, 229–33
Vietnam War, 232
Villa, Pancho, 230, 335, 339, 379
Villa de Reyes, Mexico, 38
Visas, 22, 189, 274
Vivemos Mejor, 257

Wages. See Salaries
Wagner College, 254
Wallace, Henry, 348
Water purification company, dishonest,
    183
Watsonville, California, 31
Weddings, 372–373. See also Marriage
Western and Second, 181
West Los Angeles, California, 73–76
Wives. See also Infidelity; Marriage
    left behind in Mexico, 21–22, 23, 26,
        31–32, 144–66, 202–3
    pregnant, 145–51, 153

    sending for, 208, 209–10, 218–19,
        223
    tracking down husband, 161–63,
        165
Workers, Mexican. See also specific occu-
    pations
    corrupt, 71
    as hard working and loyal, 69, 70,
        74, 80, 233–34, 271, 410, 411,
        414
World Cup games, 40, 63
World War I, 3
World War II, 3, 230–31, 384
Writer, 315–21

Year in Bagdad, A (Baez and Baez),
    248

Zacatecas, Mexico, 9, 114, 156, 316
Zacharias, Professor, 255
Zacoalco, Mexico, 19
Zamora, Mexico, 279